Lawyers in Society

AN OVERVIEW

Lawyers in Society

AN OVERVIEW

Edited by
RICHARD L. ABEL
and PHILIP S. C. LEWIS

UNIVERSITY OF CALIFORNIA PRESS
Berkeley / Los Angeles / London

University of California Press
Berkeley and Los Angeles, California

University of California Press
London, England

Copyright © 1995 by The Regents of the University of California

Library of Congress Cataloging-in-Publication Data

Lawyers in society: an overview / edited by Richard L. Abel, Philip
S. C. Lewis.
    p.   cm.
   "This book contains seven essays from the three volumes published
in 1988–89 under the general title Lawyers in society"—Pref.
   Includes bibliographical references and index.
   ISBN 0–520–20332–1 (pbk.: alk. paper)
   1. Lawyers.   I. Abel, Richard L.   II. Lewis, Philip Simon
Coleman.
K117.L372   1995
340'.023—dc20   95–36935
                                          CIP

Printed in the United States of America

1 2 3 4 5 6 7 8 9

The paper used in this publication meets the minimum
requirements of American National Standard for Information Sciences—
Permanence of Paper for Printed Library Materials, ANSI Z39.48–1984 ⊗

Contents

Preface

PHILIP S. C. LEWIS

This book contains seven essays from the three volumes published in 1988–89 under the general title *Lawyers in Society*, as well as a new introduction in which Richard Abel surveys recent theoretical developments and responds to criticisms of the market control theory, which informed many of the national studies.

The first two volumes, each with an introductory overview, comprise reports on seven common law and eleven civil law professions; the third volume contains eleven comparative and theoretical essays based on the national reports. Selection of the essays that appear here was hard, not just because of the high quality of all the chapters but also because they were intended to illuminate one another rather than be read in isolation. We have attempted to provide a cross section wide enough to be of value in itself (for instance, as the core material of a course) and also sufficient to suggest to readers the breadth of our original project and to encourage them to consult it. Chapter 3, on the German legal profession, has been updated by its authors, Erhard Blankenburg and Ulrike Schultz, to describe significant recent events, especially those accompanying unification; the other essays are reprinted unchanged. Had we been able to revise all the chapters there are omissions we would have filled and subsequent changes we would have described; we invite others to do so.

There are obvious gaps in our original coverage. We had no accounts for Africa or the Middle East and few for Asia or Latin America. We also omitted entire systems, both political (socialist, in all its forms) and religious (Moslem). There were substantive lacunae as well. The first two volumes described national professions in order to permit cross-national comparison, but transnational practice is growing rapidly, especially within the European Union. Some national studies discussed the expansion of productive units, but almost none described the cost of legal services. We skirted the redistribution of legal services by the state or philanthropy because the Florence Access to Justice Project had just concluded (Cappelletti, 1978–79).

Readers should be aware of these limitations and also of recent social changes and their consequences for the legal profession. The most obviously important political and ideological change has been the collapse of the official socialist regimes, the disintegration of the Soviet Union and the unification of Germany. Whatever the nature of the emerging polities, all embrace the market and tend to respect the independence of legal occupations, thereby offering increased opportunities for new forms of legal work (Sajó, 1993). China, which had virtually eliminated university-trained personnel from its legal system, now offers citizens some legal protections, and the rapidly proliferating capitalist transactions are expected to require the assistance of 80,000 Chinese lawyers.

In England, the implementation of Thatcherite ideologies that favor markets and competition and are hostile to occupationally based power structures has begun to blur traditional divisions within the legal profession and to shift the loci of power over legal aid and legal education. The evolution of the European Union's Single Market program has had a greater impact on the way lawyers work (encouraging previously individualist professionals to collaborate) than it has had in creating new opportunities for lawyers to operate across national boundaries (Ehlermann, 1992: 249 ff.). But judgments by both the European Court and the German Constitutional Court (the decisions of the latter reminiscent of those of the U.S. Supreme Court in the 1970s) have also relaxed some of the strict limitations on German practitioners and forced a reexamination of the statutory framework. Chapter 3 touches on these issues, as well as the reconstruction of legal education and practice in the former East Germany.

Blankenburg and Schultz make clear, however, that the German profession also has been affected by the increasing number who qualify for the bar: For the first time, a majority are entering private practice rather than public or private employment. State action may influence supply, since the German government finances the final stage of legal education. Japan and Korea have slightly eased the notoriously difficult examinations for entrance to their small government-run training schools (Rokumoto, 1993; Song, 1994). The continued growth of the profession in most OECD countries reflects the failure of educational and training systems to respond quickly to economic fluctuations, as demand slackens while supply remains high. This growth is transforming the demographics of the profession (most strikingly the increasing proportion of women) and affecting traditional structures of legal practice.

It seems safer to generalize about changes within the legal profession than about its relationship to the economy (Law & Social Inquiry, 1992).

What can we deduce from the fact that Iceland has more lawyers per capita than the United States, or that Japan has eighteen times as many lawyers per capita as Indonesia (International Financial Law Review, 1994)? The division of legal professions into two hemispheres—one serving individual clients, the other corporate clients—has been noted with concern not only in the United States and England but also in settings as different as France and Japan (Rokumoto, 1993). This may be related to the continuing expansion of some law firms, a phenomenon no longer confined to the United States and England or even the common-law world. Indeed, five of the forty largest firms world-wide are now Australian, as a result of interstate mergers and the opening to foreign lawyers of the rapidly expanding Pacific Rim economies. Although the Netherlands is small and has a low lawyer to population ratio, five Dutch firms are among the thirty largest in Europe. National differences remain marked (cf. Olgiati, 1994): Although firms are expanding in Brazil and Germany, cultural factors keep them small in Italy (International Financial Law Review, 1994). Only a handful of multinational partnerships currently exist, but transnational practice takes many other forms, including dealing with foreign legal matters from a home office, referrals (both one-shot and mutually exclusive relationships), cooperative arrangements, European Economic Interest Groups, and overseas offices.

The Working Group on the Comparative Study of Legal Professions (whose role in the genesis of *Lawyers in Society* is described in the prefaces to the original volumes) has continued to facilitate exchange across disciplines and nations, and it also supports subgroups pursuing more specific topics: cause lawyering, cultural history of legal professions, lawyers and political liberalism, women in legal professions, legal aid, the judiciary in regime transitions, legal education, and professionals in divorce. Further volumes are under way.

We wish to reiterate our gratitude to all those thanked in the prefaces to the original volumes, who are too numerous to be named here.

REFERENCES

Cappelletti, Mauro. (gen. ed.) 1978–79. *Access to Justice* (4 vols.). Milan: Dott. A. Giuffrè; Alphen aan den Rijn: Sijthoff and Noordhoff.

Ehlermann, C.-D. 1992. "The European Community: Its Law and Its Lawyers," 58 *Arbitration* 242.

International Financial Law Review. 1994. *The International Financial Law Review 1000: A Guide to the World's International Business Law Firms*. London: Euromoney.

Law & Society Inquiry. 1992. "Debate: Do Lawyers Impair Economic Growth?" [1992] *Law & Social Inquiry* 585–711.

Olgiati, Vittorio. 1994. "Process and Policy of Legal Professionalization in Europe: The De-Construction of a Normative Order." In Yves Dezalay and David Sugarman, eds., *Professional Competition and the Social Construction of Markets*. London: Routledge.

Rokumoto, Kahei. 1993. "The Transformation of the Japanese Bar? Observing its Processes and Mechanisms." Paper presented at the Annual Meeting of the Research Committee on the Sociology of Law, Oñati, July 5–9.

Sajó, Andrès. 1993. "The Role of Legal Profession in Social Change in Hungary." In Kahei Rokumoto, ed., *The Social Role of the Legal Profession*. Tokyo: International Center for Comparative Law and Politics.

Song, S. H. 1994. "Challenges to Legal Education in Korea." In P. S. C. Lewis, ed., *Law and Technology in the Pacific Community*. Boulder, Colo.: Westview.

1

Revisioning Lawyers

RICHARD L. ABEL*

In the fifteen years since we initiated this comparative sociology of legal professions a great deal of scholarship has appeared. Some writers have engaged, tested, qualified, criticized, or rejected the theoretical framework I developed in my contributions. Others have advanced and applied very different explanations for professional structures and lawyer behavior. Many have sought to comprehend the dramatic changes sweeping through the legal profession. This chapter reviews four major theoretical orientations: market control, competition between professions over knowledge-based jurisdictions, the ideal of professional independence, and economic interpretations.

THE CENTRALITY OF THE MARKET

In 1980, six years after I began teaching about American lawyers, I was drawn into comparative sociology by an invitation to a conference on the Final Report of the Royal Commission on Legal Services. During the following decade, I continued to address the issues implicated in the title of my contribution to that conference, "The Politics of the Market for Legal Services," a paper that was strongly influenced by Magali Sarfatti Larson's historical sociology of a wide range of professions in England and the United States.[1] I began with the view that markets, like sex, were simultaneously sites of pleasure and danger. Markets permit and encourage the emergence of professions.[2] They offer scope for self-expression and technical refinement and foster dreams of wealth, power, and status. Yet only a few reap these rewards, although all participants confront perpetual risk and many suffer ruin (as those "liberated" from communism are discovering).

One of the many paradoxes of market economies is that they drive actors to seek to neutralize competition, even though this is their essential

1

energizing force. Only the most desperate—recent immigrants to a city or nation (often racial or ethnic minorities) and new entrants to the market (youths and women)—remain exposed to unrestrained competition. They must accept employment without the support of a union or protective legislation or embark on entrepreneurship that requires neither formally certified skills nor capital investment: peddling, prostitution, gardening, housekeeping, baby-sitting, window washing, house painting, taxi driving.[3] Refuge from the buffeting force of competition can take many forms: controlling a market (sought by OPEC and other producers of primary goods), becoming a salaried worker for a large employer (civil service or the lifetime employment once offered by Japanese companies), securing a patent (and other monopolies over intellectual property), making large capital investments (a barrier to market entry by potential challengers). In rare instances the sanctuary is almost perfect: the De Beers diamond cartel, or the numerus clausus of some European notaries.

Those who sell services may find these strategies less effective than do those who manufacture products. There are no raw materials to corner, capital investment tends to be low, and, until recently, their intellectual products have been unprotected by law. Instead they have resorted to guilds, trade unions, and professional associations, which in turn invoke state assistance. As Larson explains, aspiring professionals must construct their commodity and then control the production *of* and *by* producers. The first step is to persuade potential consumers that the service is both valuable and too difficult for them to perform. Lawyers have several advantages in this regard. As judges and prominent members of the legislature and executive, they can use state power to grant an exclusive jurisdiction to legal institutions (over civil and criminal adjudication, divorce, adoption, and probate), complicate the task beyond lay competence, and even award themselves a legal monopoly (representation, drafting, advice, real property transfers). Having commodified legal services, lawyers must limit the number of producers by prohibiting lay competition and regulating entry to the profession by establishing educational qualifications and economic barriers, requiring apprenticeships and examinations, and by limiting opportunities to practice. Finally, lawyers must dampen competition among themselves.

This concept of the "professional project," adapted from Larson, can lead to several misunderstandings. It does not require deliberation or conspiracy—although lawyers and other professionals, in desperation or at unguarded moments, often expose their self-interested motives. (The Depression provoked Germany and Greece to limit the number of lawyers and American states to lower the pass rate on bar examinations.) Even a genuine dedication to ensuring quality inevitably promotes social closure. Because I viewed market control as pivotal, I equated its fluctuations with "professionalism."[4] Some commentators objected that law-yers in "declining" professions seemed to be doing surprisingly well—economically, politically, and socially.[5] This is true but irrelevant. I am concerned with the dramatic changes in the structure of legal occu-pations: the increase in market control from the nineteenth to the mid-twentieth century and its erosion in recent decades. That market con-trol has declined does not refute my theory—quite the contrary. Refuge from competition is always ephemeral, as shown by breaches in even the most powerful cartels. The very rewards of success—wealth, status, and power—spur outsiders to circumvent, surmount, or destroy the barriers. Neither am I troubled by the observation that market control is not equivalent to effective self-regulation.[6] Professional regulators are less so-licitous of clients than of peers. And it is notoriously difficult to enforce anticompetitive rules against the self-interest of practitioners.

Some of the chapters in the original volumes on the legal profession in other countries (notably Canada, Australia, and New Zealand) adopted the framework I advanced in my chapters on England and the United States and my attempts at synthesis.[7] The volumes also included two kinds of demurrers, however. Alan Paterson maintains that within the common law world, Scotland did not fit my model.[8] Yet his own histor-ical account repeatedly reveals efforts by legal professionals to control production of and by producers. As early as the seventeenth century, ad-vocates sought to limit their numbers and raise their social status by re-quiring a written examination in civil law, a thesis written in Latin and defended in Latin before the entire faculty, and a public lesson in Latin to the Court of Sessions. Dismayed by their increasing numbers in the late nineteenth century, Writers to the Signet imposed a £500 entrance fee, a five-year apprenticeship, and the requirement of a liberal education. As late as 1980 the profession added the requirement of a one-year Diploma in Legal Practice, knowing that government would only fund 410 places. Paterson acknowledges that qualification as an advocate is still limited by the requirement of an unremunerated nine months as a "devil" (ap-prentice) followed by another nine months without income. Moreover, some of his rebuttals seem insubstantial: Scottish solicitors lack a mo-nopoly over the administration of estates or conveyancing of real prop-erty because others can do these tasks—without pay!

If common law professions are united by the necessity to mediate the relation of their members to the market, civil law professions have expe-rienced a different history in their relations to private employers, the uni-versity, the state, and, therefore, the market.[9] Sociologists and historians have stressed these differences in writing about a wide variety of profes-sions.[10] Continental lawyers (and their colonial counterparts) have been trained in universities, rather than through apprenticeship, ever since those institutions separated from the Church.[11] Professional associations developed late and tended to be local. The state set the rules for entry and practice, with little professional input.[12] And most jurists became employees of the state or, more recently, large businesses. Indeed, the several categories of law graduates—judges and prosecutors, civil servants, corporate employees, advocates, notaries and so on—do not see themselves as a single profession and even lack a common name. I belatedly recognized the magnitude of the divide between civil and common law professions.[13]

But although I acknowledge that Larson's framework, developed to analyze the United States and England, is inappropriate for the histories of Continental European legal professions, there is evidence that common and civil law professions are converging as a concomitant of the globalization of the economy.[14] Many of the divisions within civil law professions are disappearing, while the centrality of private practice in common law professions is being eroded by the growth of public and private employment. Universities play increasingly similar roles in training lawyers throughout the world. And civil lawyers have had to adapt some of the traits of common law competitors or risk losing their most lucrative work. Even lawyers in the former communist world, who are doubly removed from common law lawyers by their civil law heritage and state-dominated economy, are exhibiting the struggle for market control. Although Michael Burrage continues to deny the centrality of the market, his observations on the contemporary Russian *advokatura* resonate well with Larson's theory. One informant told him that "the colleges don't want to hire more people because their incomes would be reduced. In Bukhara, Uzbekistan, they have taken a decision to freeze the number of advocates."[15] Eastern European countries such as Poland, Hungary, the Czech Republic, and Slovakia are witnessing contests between advocates and jurisconsults (former house counsel to state enterprises) to service the newly privatized economy.[16]

Although Terence Halliday tendentiously titled his book about the Chicago Bar Association *Beyond Monopoly*, lawyers and other professionals remain deeply concerned about their relation to the market.[17] English solicitors have strenuously fought to retain their monopoly over conveyancing (real property transactions), and, in turn, have challenged the Bar's monopoly of advocacy in the higher courts.[18] More than half a century after the American legal profession erected the present entry barriers, it continues to repel new challenges. The administrators of the bar in the nation's capital became concerned that law graduates were finding easy admittance to the District of Columbia bar through the Pennsylvania bar exam: Those who correctly answered 133 of the 200 multiple-choice questions on the multistate examination gained exemption from the essay portion. An official complained, "It's the Tijuana of the law admissions world." The District resolved to eliminate this loophole while shaming Pennsylvania into requiring entrants to pass the essay examination as well.[19] About the same time the American Bar Association refused to accredit the Massachusetts School of Law, rejecting the argument that it cut tuition to less than half that of elite law schools used practitioners as adjunct professors and electronic data bases and interlibrary loans to save the large capital investment in law books. The school has threatened an antitrust action against the ABA.[20]

The health care industry exhibits even more numerous and intense battles over turf as subordinate occupations challenge the dominance of doctors. In the 1930s nurses could not take blood pressure; in the 1950s they could not perform EKGs. In Arizona today, however, nurse practitioners can make their own diagnoses, charging thirty-five dollars a visit, and can write prescriptions; twenty other states also allow nurse practitioners to write prescriptions. A 1986 report by the Office of Technology Assessment of the U.S. Congress estimated that 60 to 80 percent of basic health care could be performed by nurses. A 1993 study by the American Nurses Association found that nurse practitioners gave more accurate diagnoses and took more comprehensive medical histories than doctors. The American Medical Association's senior vice president for medical education dismissed these studies as "inconclusive" because they looked at "a limited number of services": "We draw our sword and make our line in the sand at nurses practicing independently."[21] (Perhaps he meant the staff of Asclepius. In any case, the metaphor, overused by George Bush following Iraq's invasion of Kuwait, seems inconsistent with Hippocrates' exhortation to "first do no harm"; apparently this applies only to patients, not rebellious subordinates.) Nurses are making inroads elsewhere, especially areas in which doctors apparently have little interest: women's health, service in rural communities, care for urban homeless. Cost is a primary reason—the average income of nurses is just one-fourth that of doctors. Yet the AMA insists that "replacing physicians with lesser prepared personnel may increase the medical risk to patients and the ultimate cost of care." Medical association PAC fundraising brochures refer to all competitors as "quacks" and warn, "Don't let reform fowl [sic] up health care."[22] Optometrists, psychologists, pharmacists, and physician's assistants seek the right to prescribe medicine. Psychologists note that 87 percent of psychotropic drugs are prescribed by doctors with no training in mental health. Yet the California Medical Association continues to justify its opposition to increasing nurses' responsibility in terms of the "extraordinarily large differences" in "educational requirements."[23]

In developing my theoretical framework I argued that the market imperative compels service producers to seek not only to control supply but also to stimulate demand. The latter strategy has grown in importance as supply control has eroded with the expansion of university education (and its increasing centrality as the entry route into professions), movements for gender and race equality, and attacks on restrictive practices. I agree with critics that professional motives for stimulating consumption are complex and ambiguous.[24] Just as professionals justify supply control as ensuring quality, so they justify demand creation as increasing access (while disregarding the tension between these two goals). Furthermore, the investment in and manifestations of demand creation vary across time and national cultures. Professions that still enjoy a decent competence can afford to indulge the gentleman's disdain for trade.[25] Yet English solicitors, who sneered at American "cowboys" for advertising and contingent fees, now indulge in the former and flirt with the latter.

Law enjoys distinct advantages in creating demand, just as it does in controlling supply. As judges, legislators, administrators, and advocates, lawyers construct the rules they later mobilize on behalf of clients. The revolving door between government and private practice allows lawyer regulators to turn around and sell their knowledge of how to evade the law (although this may be less common in civilian countries). Fame (or notoriety) as an innovator often brings repeat business, as did the first poison pill defense to a corporate takeover and the first successful palimony claim.[26] In adversary systems, work by one lawyer usually makes work for others. (Indeed, although legal scholars and policy makers often invoke Weber for the proposition that law creates the certainty and predictability essential to commerce, lawyers actually foster uncertainty on behalf of their clients and themselves. If law were certain, after all, lawyers would be superfluous.)[27]

Yet demand creation has significant drawbacks, which may explain the reluctance of many lawyers to engage in it. What the profession touts as altruism can appear to outsiders as self-interest, especially given the deep public ambivalence toward the act of litigating and the content of many legal rights.[28] Whereas supply control tends to benefit all professionals, demand creation advantages entrepreneurial lawyers, forcing all to become more competitive. Some forms of demand creation also tend to concentrate demand and thus the dependence of producers on corporate consumers or governmental third-party payers (for legal aid).[29]

Common law professions display an increasing commitment to creating demand. American lawyers have launched prepaid insurance plans, established clinics to offer mass-produced routine services, and invested heavily in advertising.[30] English lawyers have documented "unmet legal need" to justify increases (or prevent decreases) in the legal aid budget. The Law Society launched the Accident Legal Advice Scheme to encourage victims to file tort claims.[31]

The profession remains deeply ambivalent about such activity, however. A New York lawyer had to sue his bar association to obtain permission to use client testimonials, which only three other states allow.[32] A decade after their fourteen founders met secretly for the first time, the National Association of Law Firm Marketing Administrators has a thousand members, who compete for the ABA's "Dignity in Advertising" awards.[33] Yet, what offers economic rewards to individual lawyers may impair the profession's collective status. A personal injury lawyer in Birmingham, Alabama, promoted himself by emblazoning his name on wrist watches, baseball caps, and chairs donated to churches and by offering bumper stickers warning: "BACK OFF! MY LAWYER IS ROBERT NORRIS." He went too far, however, when he sent a twenty-five dollar wreath to the funeral of a nineteen-month-old baby who died when a day-care worker left him in a closed van for four hours. Attached was a card to the family: "Please accept our deepest sympathies in the loss of Randy. We know you are presently being faced with many difficult decisions and will soon be faced with others. If we may be of assistance to you in any regard, do not hesitate to contact us at 870-8000." He was suspended for two years.[34] Even the American Trial Lawyers Association, whose 65,000 members have the greatest interest in seeking individual clients, was so embarrassed after several prominent lawyers flew to Bhopal that it passed a resolution condemning lawyers "who go, uninvited, to the scene of a disaster and advertise for prospective clients." A District of Columbia lawyer who had rushed to both Bhopal and the DuPont Plaza fire in San Juan responded contemptuously that the ATLA leaders "would love to wake up and find they'd gone to Harvard and been asked into a partnership at Cravath, Swaine & Moore."[35] The California Trial Lawyers Association has sponsored a bill that would significantly restrict television advertising. Larry H. Parker, who makes extensive use of that medium, complained that "those country club lawyers don't like guys like me taking cases from them."[36]

Health services providers have been pioneers in stimulating demand, perhaps because the potential rewards are so enormous. Public relations firms, representing 60 percent of Los Angeles doctors and all New York hospitals, ensure that their clients appear in newspapers and on television. A New Orleans urologist sent a *Time* magazine article about a new prostate cancer test to all his patients with a note proclaiming: "We offer this!"[37] Doctors ordered tests at laboratories in which they had a financial interest until Medicare refused reimbursement. A General Accounting Office study found that doctors were three to five times more likely to order CAT scans, MRIs, ultrasound, and other diagnostic procedures when they had invested in the firm providing the service. The AMA senior vice-president and general counsel rationalized: "If you have the equipment at your fingertips and you operate it yourself, you have complete confidence in the results, and you're more likely to use it. . . . the real issue for patients is whether they will get the tests they need, not whether they are getting too many." T² Medical Inc. has been helping doctors set up home health care companies, promising profits of up to $20,000 a year from referrals for an initial investment of about $3,000. Medicare and Medicaid, however, have stopped reimbursing for physical therapy, radiology, home health services, or hospital services in which the doctor has an interest.[38]

Nevertheless, Tokos Medical Corp. has been pushing its "Dr. Deal" program, in which doctors invest in companies leasing its fetal monitoring device and get 15 percent of the payments from patients for whom they prescribe it. A $1,000 investment produces an average annual income of $5,000 and the prospect of up to $22,500.[39] Although pharmaceutical companies long have offered doctors incentives to prescribe their products (free samples, expensive family vacations), they now seek to speak directly to consumers. An ad by the Glaxo Institute for Digestive Health asked rhetorically: "It's only heartburn. I should learn to live with it . . . right? Attention heartburn sufferers. It's time to talk to your doctor." The National Mental Health Association ran a media campaign to "increase public awareness" about depression, without revealing that it was paid for by Eli Lilly and Co., the makers of Prozac. The Marion Merrill Dow Pollen Forecast Hotline not only gave pollen counts to allergy sufferers but also warned that over-the-counter medicines, unlike its own, could cause drowsiness. Searle Pharmaceuticals developed a "Day-to-Day Dialogue on Arthritis" to promote its Daypro medicine.[40] CIBA-Geigy pushes Actigall for gallstones; only the small print reveals that the expensive pills must be taken twice daily for years and fail to dissolve most gallstones. The company maintained: "The ads are a source of information just like a newspaper article or a TV news report." Upjohn promotes Rogaine for baldness and Seldane for allergies. Burroughs Wellcome took full-page ads urging readers to be tested for HIV—without mentioning that it makes AZT.[41]

A wide variety of commentators on the professions have made the market the core of their analyses, focusing on efforts at social closure, endogenous and exogenous influences on supply and demand, and the growing role of the state in subsidizing consumption.[42] Nevertheless, critics of the original volumes of *Lawyers in Society* (and my two books on American and English lawyers) have advanced a number of objections to market control theory.

Several felt I overemphasized the economics of social closure while neglecting the other dimension of Larson's "professional project"—collective mobility. I accept the criticism. I may have been misled by my starting point—an attempt to understand American lawyers, who were preoccupied for decades with material improvement, which they pursued through state bar associations. Now that most enjoy comfortable incomes (and some are obscenely wealthy) the profession has become increasingly concerned with honor. In the summer of 1993 a disgruntled former client went on a rampage in a San Francisco law firm, killing three lawyers, a law student, a legal secretary, a client, two trust company employees, and ultimately himself. The California State Bar president responded with a call for a "cease-fire" on lawyer jokes, which were "nothing more than hate speech." He also advocated heavier penalties for ordinary crimes when the victims were lawyers (as occurs for crimes against police, judges, and political officials). In response, the Miller Brewing Co. withdrew its popular television commercial showing cowboys roping lawyers carrying briefcases.[43] Opposition from professional associations to law firms engaging in "ancillary practice" or lawyers entering multidisciplinary partnerships appears to be motivated less by economic concerns than by the fear of losing status from being subordinated to the much larger, better organized Big Six accounting firms.[44] Mark Osiel and Michael Burrage go much further, insisting that the professional project was *exclusively* concerned with status and indifferent to money.[45] This is both historically incorrect (as my chapters and books demonstrate) and theoretically incoherent (since status and wealth are inextricably connected). In a capitalist society, personal impoverishment tends to undermine professional status (as suggested by the fate of the clergy), and the acquisition of wealth confers its own status (however vehemently those mired in genteel poverty may contemn the nouveau riche).

Others have criticized the notion of a "project" for treating the profession as too monolithic and for obscuring internal tensions.[46] I not only agree but also feel that the identification of professional fractions helps explain the interplay between market control and collective mobility (which possess different salience for each subgroup). Theodore Schneyer has charted the complex factional politics shaping the ABA's Model Rules of Professional Conduct.[47] Ronen Shamir, refining Christine Harrington, has made a convincing argument that upper and lower strata American lawyers displayed very different reactions to the emergence of the regulatory state during the New Deal. Solo practitioners, suffering both falling demand during the Depression and growing numbers as legal education expanded, sought to bar nonlawyers from practicing administrative law. Elite lawyers, who derived more business from regulation, sought to judicialize administrative action to preserve the symbolic integrity of the rule of law.[48] Some personal injury lawyers demand the right to chase ambulances, while their professional organization, ATLA, seeks to distance itself from notorious vulgarity. Professional stratification also emerges in Seron's finding that younger lawyers, generalists, and those in the inner city favor advertising, whereas older lawyers, specialists, and suburban practitioners oppose it.[49]

II. KNOWLEDGE AND JURISDICTION

The most ambitious revision of sociological theories of the professions since we completed our comparative project is Andrew Abbott's emphasis on the relationship between knowledge and jurisdiction.[50] Abbott makes two claims: interprofessional competition for market shares is the central feature of the system of professions; and competition is conducted through the medium of knowledge claims. This reorientation has several virtues. It directs attention away from the social structural characteristics (associations, credentialing, self-regulation) professions share with other occupations and toward the distinctiveness of what professionals do.[51] Abbott thereby problematizes the structural-functional claim that professionals deploy expertise, just as social closure theory problematized the structural-functional claim that self-regulation was necessary and sufficient to ensure quality and altruism.

At the end of our three volumes (chapter 8 in this volume) we commended such a redirection, and we welcome the studies that have begun to emerge. Many concern the ways in which lawyers transform client experience and motivation into legal claims and remedies—mostly in family disputes,[52] but also in commercial matters[53] and civil litigation generally.[54] Others look at the role of lawyers in negotiation.[55]

Competing claims to knowledge often illuminate fluctuations in the market for legal services: for instance, the rivalry between English solicitors and accountants since the mid-nineteenth century,[56] the success of employed German jurists in retaining their role in banking while being reduced to paralegals in the insurance industry,[57] the efforts of Rechtsanwälte to retain corporate work,[58] and the campaign by Parisian judges to expand their role in economic disputes.[59]

I do have reservations about Abbott's theorization, however. First, his emphasis on knowledge is far from original. More than twenty years earlier two French sociologists stressed the importance of knowledge in analyzing university hospitals, as did two American lawyers in mapping competition between lawyers and others in the United States and England.[60] Second, Abbott explains a fairly narrow segment of professional life. Most professionals are not engaged in competition with outsiders most of the time. As Abbott clearly states, professional jurisdictions tend to be entrenched for lengthy periods, both in law and, to a lesser extent, in public opinion.

Third, it is very difficult to ascertain what professionals know and how they are using that knowledge. This indeterminacy imbues the theory with a strongly postmodern quality, allowing it to explain everything (and therefore, perhaps, nothing). The elusiveness of any independent measure of knowledge tempts the analyst into circularity and tautology—the attribution of knowledge to professions that have secured their jurisdictions. Mark Osiel, for instance, asserts that common lawyers enjoy a broader jurisdiction than their civilian counterparts because the former must exercise practical judgment in the absence of code and theory.[61] I find this both empirically dubious and virtually untestable.

The theory of social closure insists that professions justify their anti-competitive practices by demonstrating a connection to quality. Because knowledge claims are so hard to test, theorizations based on them can lose their critical edge (another trait often associated with postmodernism), lapsing into structural-functional complacency. Shapiro, for instance, asserts that professions are defined "by the quantities and qualities of knowledge they acquire and practice." "Lawyers . . . are specialists in a particular language who gain that special knowledge by training. What they do is speak that language as a means of representing individuals."[62] Sterett maintains "it is clear that whether or not practitioners study or use 'the law,' society does expect and take account of some presumed expertise."[63] Halliday ascribes the authority of professional organizations to "knowledge mandates."[64] But lawyers may actually speak jabberwocky and claim knowledge that is either factitious or irrelevant. Abbott cannot be blamed for this misreading. He consistently characterizes professional knowledge as a social construct, offering a nuanced analysis of how knowledge claims are advanced and challenged, succeed and fail. Others have described the role of professional ideology in shaping and defending jurisdictions and the differences between knowledge claimed and deployed by both teachers and practitioners.[65]

Perhaps the best antidote to mistaking professional pretensions for proficiency is to look at the knowledge actually deployed. Many professions have supplemented entry barriers with mandatory continuing education. Once again, medicine is in the forefront. But consider this advertisement.[66]

The 4th I.A.C.D. Conference on
CONSCIOUS IMMORTALITY
Continuing Education credits for medical professionals
CME approved 7.5 hours for physicians, Category I;
CEU approved 7.5 hours for Registered Nurses;
Certificates issued to all conference attendees.
Lectures understandable to the General Public.

RAYMOND A. MOODY, JR., M.D., Ph.D.,
     Author of *Life After Life, Reflections on Life After Life, The Light Beyond*
     and *Reunions*. (The Latter is about Encounters with the Departed
     Loved Ones, which he will talk about at the seminar.)
KENNETH RING, Ph.D.
     Author of *Life at Death, Heading Toward Omega*.
BRUCE GOLDBERG, D.D.S., M.S.
     Author of *Past Lives-Future Lives*.
DONINGA L. REYES, Ph.D.
     Author of *Two Souls* (an Out-of-the-Body Experience).
CLAUDIA JENSEN, M.D.
     Counselor on Consciousness Awareness.
SUSAN STORCH, RN, BSN, M.A.
     Lecturer on Conscious Dying, a thanatologist practicing hospice
     nursing, working in L.A. HIV/AIDS community.

The rapid expansion of the global economy is creating new markets for professional services, which offer an excellent opportunity to test theories about knowledge and jurisdiction.[67] I want to enter a preliminary caveat, however. Clients include multinational corporations, foreign governments, and parastatals. Transnational practice possesses the exotic allure earlier enjoyed by exploration, colonialism, diplomacy, the Grand Tour, and jet-setting. Material and social rewards are high. Yet for all but the smallest legal professions, transnational practice will remain an esoteric specialization, preoccupying only a small minority of members (while perhaps accentuating professional stratification).

Globalization shifts economic activity from within states to their interstices or across their borders, where rules are either absent or new and unclear. National cultures clash, upsetting and obstructing informal understandings among entrepreneurs. Conflicts can be taken to a variety of forums, each using different techniques and requiring appropriate expertise. With established jurisdictions dislocated, competition thrives among nations and disciplines. The knowledge on which new jurisdictional claims can be based is transitory and fluid. Consumers (corporations, financial institutions, and states) are expert. The stakes are high: the formation and termination of large enterprises (mergers and acquisitions, bankruptcy and reorganization), deal-making, and relations with and among national and transnational states (licensing, regulation, antitrust, and government contracts).

The principal competitors in this domain are lawyers, accountants, management consultants, and, to a lesser extent, investment bankers. The struggle is most intense in Europe and the Far East. Accountants have significant advantages: numeracy, computer literacy, the size and international character of the Big Six, existing ties with multinational corporations (for which they conduct audits), expertise in tax, and a strongly entrepreneurial attitude.[68] But lawyers make the rules. American lawyers (and to a lesser extent English solicitors) have the advantages of firm size, a focus on corporate work, and aggressiveness; many, however, lack knowledge of civil law systems and European languages. European lawyers have sought to update their knowledge by forging links with innovative legal academics and acquiring further education in the United States. Competition has forced national legal professions to close ranks against outsiders: French *avocats* and *conseils juridiques* finally united some twenty years after a failed attempt in 1971; German *Rechtsanwälte* defied the ban on multistate partnerships; the distinction between English solicitors and barristers is eroding. European firms, increasingly multinational (and even multidisciplinary), are emulating the size and structure of American firms.

But knowledge is not the only terrain of contestation and is often little more than a rationalization. National legal professions have resorted to a wide variety of protectionist strategies: limiting practice to citizens; demanding a lengthy, unpaid apprenticeship; setting an examination in the local language or law; excluding outsiders from certain functions (litigation, land transfers, probate, and family matters); demanding extortionate payments to local compensation and indemnity funds; insisting on reciprocity from the lawyer's home jurisdiction (and every subjurisdiction in federal polities); limiting advocacy by employed lawyers; and prohibiting multinational and multidisciplinary partnerships. Status concerns may be as important as market share: All lawyers fear dominance by accountants, and all other lawyers fear dominance by Americans.

III. THE IDEAL OF PROFESSIONAL INDEPENDENCE

A number of writers have sought to reclaim the ideal of lawyer independence from the static functionalism of Parsons or Carr-Saunders and the apologetics of professional associations. Robert Gordon's revisionist account of the emergence of the American corporate bar in the late nineteenth and early twentieth centuries is the leading example.[69] As a critical legal historian, Gordon seeks to demonstrate the relative autonomy and importance of ideology as a counterweight to excessively materialist and necessitarian theories. He boldly proclaims his theoretical idealism: "Lawyers have slid into the modes of reaction, schizophrenia, and privatistic denial of any public role not from any innate depravity of the profession, but from the poverty of modern liberalism."[70] He argues that elite corporate practitioners exhibit several kinds of autonomy. Lawyers develop new legal forms, transactions, claims, and remedies, which can have unanticipated and even adverse consequences for their clients. Some lawyers display fidelity to the internal coherence of legal doctrine (expressed in terms of logic, science, or art), seeking to systematize and reform it. Some expose incompetence and corruption in legal institutions such as the lower courts or the police. Some expand the access of poor or immigrant clients to law through pro bono activities or legal aid offices. And some check illegal or unethical behavior by their clients.

I share many of Gordon's values.[71] But I become uneasy when he seems to confound exhortation with explanation. First, he focuses on the aberrational behavior of a small minority of lawyers—as if economists constructed a theory of entrepreneurial activity based on Mobil's funding of "Masterpiece Theater" or Ben and Jerry's efforts to save tropical rain forests. Second, much of the evidence for "independence" concerns not the core of the professional role, but the margin—what lawyers do *after* they have billed 2,000 hours a year. The public interest fellowships funded by Skadden & Arps are the perfect example of lawyers' schizophrenic ability to dissociate the most aggressive corporate representation from pro bono contributions.[72] Third, lawyers' charitable activities are quantitatively insignificant, whether measured in pro bono hours or cash contributions to legal aid, per lawyer or in the aggregate. Fourth, much of the activity promotes elite culture (museums, opera) rather than social change.[73] Fifth, legal academics may tend to exaggerate the potential of law schools to nurture the ideal of independence. But repeated studies have confirmed that law schools transform incoming law students who voice a (romantic and superficial) identification with social justice into lawyers who choose material rewards, professional prestige, career stability, and technical proficiency.[74]

Most perplexing, however, is Gordon's central claim that lawyers can and should independently evaluate the means and ends of their clients. The ideal of independence contains a basic ambiguity: Should lawyers substitute their own ends or only make strategic judgments about means? In Charles Derber's terms, should they resist ideological or only technical proletarianization?[75] The quixotic search for a universal class disinterestedly pursuing the common good has been repeatedly disappointed: Aristocrats rarely display noblesse oblige; the bourgeoisie are associated less with Enlightenment universalism than with the horrors of industrial capitalism; the proletariat may be classless, but they are also xenophobic, racist, and sexist; civil servants are petty bureaucrats; artists and intellectuals are self-absorbed.[76]

Corporate lawyers are particularly unlikely candidates for the role of universal class. Frank Munger's study of the emerging bar in nineteenth-century West Virginia mining towns reveals its strong class loyalties.[77]

Michael Katz, who operates an eviction mill for Los Angeles landlords and claims to have 10 percent of the market, boasted: "I'm a hired gun, bottom line. Somebody pays me money to go out there and fight their battle with this tenant. I like the fight." He threatens tenants with a bad credit rating to make them pay, even if they are not legally obligated because the premises are uninhabitable.[78] Recent exposés of large firms reveal little to inspire respect.[79] Ronald Gilson offers an economic explanation for why lawyers cannot restrain clients from engaging in strategic litigation.[80] Robert Nelson's study of four Chicago firms revealed that individual lawyers derive 20 to 60 percent of their income from a single client—surely a strong disincentive for "independence." Their identification with clients was so strong that few had *ever* perceived an ethical dilemma in representation.[81] Two leading American law firms paid fines of $45 million and $50 million to settle government charges of complicity in the savings and loan scandal (which cost Americans hundreds of billions of dollars).[82] Recent research has shown how solicitors take advantage of errors or incompetence by adversaries and find or carve loopholes in regulatory and tax regimes.[83]

The situations where lawyers do shape, resist, or even disregard client wishes are even more troubling. Heinz and Laumann found that lawyer claims of independence varied inversely with firm size.[84] Recent research has shown that family lawyers transform their clients' goals while counseling them about divorce.[85] Small-town American lawyers are more likely than their urban counterparts to dominate one-shot clients and refrain from alienating repeat players.[86] Personal injury plaintiffs' lawyers sell out their clients in cutting package deals with insurance adjusters.[87] Legal aid lawyers and public defenders also may display greater loyalty to repeat players in the courtroom (judges and opposing counsel) than to their one-shot clients.[88] Between the wars, Japan and Germany required lawyers to place the public good above representation of clients.[89] Communist states granted legal aid only to promote "governmental and social interests."[90] There is no escape from the basic paradox that lawyers who enjoy the greatest rewards of money, status, and power also are the most heteronomous, while those at the bottom of the professional hierarchy are most autonomous.[91] Ironically, the principled refusal to promote immoral ends is *less* likely to be found among lawyers, who claim to be professionals, than advertising models, who have no such pretensions but may refuse to promote cigarettes or alcohol.[92]

Those claiming to oppose from within—prosecutors solicitous of defendants' rights, environmentalists purporting to keep their corporate employers honest—may have access to power, but they rarely exercise it.[93] Too often the protestations of public interest sound like rationalizations for a comfortable life. If Gordon and others are looking for sites of resistance to public and private power, surely it makes more sense to study their opponents (trade unionists, civil rights organizations, feminist groups, environmentalists, consumer and welfare advocates), oppositional lawyers (in legal aid and public defender offices and public interest firms), and dissident professional associations (National Lawyers Guild, National Legal Aid and Defenders Association).[94] Many of these lawyers emphasize their fidelity to oppressed and despised clients—not their independence.

Nor do professional associations urge independence. When Armand P. D'Amato was convicted of mail fraud for billing Unisys $32,500 for consulting work he never did as part of a scheme to influence his brother, Senator Alfonse D'Amato (R-NY), an amicus brief was filed on his behalf by the New York State Bar Association, National Association of Criminal Defense Lawyers, New York State Association of Criminal Defense Lawyers, New York State Trial Lawyers Association, New York Criminal Bar Association, and New York Civil Liberties Union. Arthur Liman, a leading Wall Street lawyer who wrote it, condemned the "overcriminalization of the law." Sentencing D'Amato to five months, U.S. District Judge Jacob Mishler acknowledged that only "one out of 100 would say 'no' to the deal that Mr. D'Amato entered into."[95]

Others defend the professional project in terms of its potential to permit and encourage lawyer altruism. English barristers justify their monopoly of higher court advocacy on the ground that only they have sufficient "independence"—an assertion most solicitors find insulting and unfounded. Solicitors, in turn, claim that the monopoly rents they reap from conveyancing are necessary to subsidize their undercompensated legal aid practice.[96] But most solicitors do hardly any legal aid work, and the few who do a great deal perform little conveyancing.[97] Terence Halliday argues that bar associations are "Beyond Monopoly" and have entered a "concordat" with society to do good works.[98] The metaphor seems inapt. Law (and other professions) is beyond monopoly only in the sense of such trendy phrases as postcolonial, postmodern, postindustrial, postcapitalist, postcommunist, and postapartheid. In each instance, the past is deeply embedded in the present (from which it may be barely distinguishable). Lawyers devote less energy to defending their monopoly today only because it is so well entrenched.

Alan Paterson closely follows Halliday but draws his metaphor from the Enlightenment, positing a "social contract" in which the state ensures the profession "reasonable rewards" in return for altruism.[99] He bemoans the fact that heightened competition in recent decades has made lawyers into hired guns. (It also cut conveyancing costs nearly in half—exposing solicitors' monopoly rents.)[100] But lawyers were hired guns long before competition intensified. Sir George Allen was eulogized on his 1952 retirement from Allen & Overy, the leading City firm he had founded: "He completely identified himself with his client . . . always gave himself wholeheartedly to the client's interests."[101] And the Law Society repaid state support of its anticompetitive rules not with an outpouring of altruism but by *opposing* salaried legal aid and law centres.[102]

Michael Burrage is most profoundly hostile to sociological critiques of the professional project.[103] He vigorously defends the efforts of lawyers to raise their status, attributing the "extremely high" "standard of honour" of the English Bar and its "non-competitive, disinterested style of work" to its high social standing. (Most barristers would be dismayed to be characterized as noncompetitive.) This is a peculiar argument to advance at the end of the twentieth century. The legal profession, perhaps more than others, pursued collective mobility by deliberately excluding aspirants on the basis of class, race, ethnicity, and gender. Lord Mansfield boasted in the nineteenth century about "keeping out the vermin." The explicit purpose of the Law Society's preliminary examination in Latin and Greek (required in 1835) was to exclude "men who have traveled up the gutter from Fleet Street to the Law Institution."[104] Harry S. Drinker, author of the first American code of legal ethics in 1908, echoed these sentiments, condemning "Russian Jew-boys" who had come "up out of the gutter [and] . . . were merely following the methods their fathers had been using in selling shoe-strings and other merchandise." Harlan Fiske Stone, Columbia Law School dean and Supreme Court Justice, deplored "the influx to the bar of greater numbers of the unfit," who "exhibit racial tendencies toward study by memorization" and "a mind almost Oriental in its fidelity to the minutiae of the subject without regard to any controlling rule or reason." (Racists have since inverted this anti-Semitic slur by denigrating Asian-American students for their resemblance to Jews.) Elihu Root (ABA president, founding partner of a leading Wall Street law firm, and Cabinet member) and Dean Swan of Yale Law School opposed the admission of immigrants, especially Jews.[105] The Lord Chancellor's Office limited the appointment of Jews and Catholics to the bench until well after World War II.[106]

Burrage is particularly distressed by the increasing role of universities as the entry route into the profession and the declining role of apprenticeship, which he endows with a unique capacity to instill ethical values. This is both ahistorical and without empirical foundation. The superior honor he attributes to barristers (compared with solicitors) cannot be explained by apprenticeship since, until recently, pupillage was a voluntary six months and articles a mandatory five years! (Articles still are twice as long as pupillage.) Nor is it clear how barristers' honor can be reconciled with the late return of briefs or perfunctory conferences with legally aided defendants prior to a plea bargain.[107] Barristers preserve their honorable contempt for trade only by relying on working-class clerks to tout for solicitors' business. And the apprenticeship Burrage values so highly has repeatedly been condemned as exploitative and lacking pedagogic value.[108] The one indubitable advantage of apprenticeship over the university is the opportunity for discrimination. Ethnoreligious minorities entered the American profession in significant numbers only when law schools displaced apprenticeship in the first two decades of the twentieth century. Women entered legal professions on the Continent (where university was the entry route) earlier than they did in England (where apprenticeship barred the door). And women and racial minorities have entered the common law professions in the last two decades through the university door.[109] A recent study confirmed that solicitors' firms strongly discriminate against black law graduates in granting articles.[110]

IV. ECONOMIC INTERPRETATIONS

Several decades after first applying their discipline to analyze substantive law, economists have belatedly addressed legal institutions and processes, including the profession itself. They have posed both micro issues (such as structures of production) and macro (the relation between lawyers and economic productivity).

The large law firm has attracted disproportionate interest, perhaps because of its social prominence, economic rewards, rapid growth, and dramatic transformation.[111] Several competing interpretations have been advanced. Charles Derber has adapted class analysis to argue that professionals are subjected to ideological proletarianization (by being forced to embrace the goals of their clients or superiors) while successfully resisting technical proletarianization (by being permitted to retain artisanal control over instrumental decisions about how to realize those goals).[112]

More recently, however, other researchers have observed a more conventional proletarianization. Oversupply (the result of poor articulation between the rigid qualification process and economic cycles of expansion and contraction) has forced lawyers to perform highly routinized tasks for German insurance companies, with no prospect for advancement.[113] Increasing numbers of American law graduates can find only part-time or temporary work that is brokered by employment agencies.[114] Greater use of computers to conduct research and generate legal forms has led to either the replacement of lawyers by paralegals or the creation of a substratum of lawyers with little decisional responsibility or client contact.[115] John Hagan and his associates have portrayed these developments as the emergence of class relations within the legal profession, highlighting the overrepresentation of women in the lower classes.[116] It is noteworthy that accountants—often the precursors of change in the legal profession—have adopted the corporate form, selling equity interests to raise capital for expansion, and hiring nonaccountant subordinates (including lawyers).[117]

Critical observers have interpreted the emergence and growth of large firms as the exploitation of subordinated labor, noting that fee-earning employees (paralegals, contract lawyers, associates, and salaried partners in America; articled clerks, assistant solicitors, nonequity partners, and legal executives in England) generate substantially more in billings than they cost in salary or overhead. Neoclassical economists, not surprisingly, interpret the same facts in terms of efficiency. Some explain the lengthy apprenticeship and denial of partnership to all but a small fraction as deterrents to opportunism and shirking.[118] Galanter and Palay argue that partners own surplus "reputational capital," which they rent to associates,[119] but, although they portray law firms as pyramid schemes where partner greed drives unsustainable growth, firms actually grow at very different rates.[120] One problem with economic models is that they disregard the complexities of human behavior. Growth may be motivated by competition for social status or the lack of other accepted measures of quality and success. The 1994 dissolution of Shea and Gould, which had more than 350 lawyers at its zenith, was attributable less to quarrels about money (although these were acute) than to struggles for status and power within the firm and personality conflicts among inflated egos.[121]

It may not matter much whether some large-firm lawyers are exploiting others—few observers are deeply troubled by the suffering of lawyers who earn more than $100,000 a year. It is more important to develop and test models of the relation between lawyers and the economy. What generates the demand for lawyers? Why do they seem so much more numerous and prominent in some societies than others—the United States and Japan usually being represented as the extremes. What is their impact on the economy? Do they enhance productivity and facilitate exchange (as Willard Hurst argued nearly half a century ago)? Or are they parasites, not just unproductive but actually a drag on the economy? An extreme and poorly substantiated case for the latter view (a classic "big lie" popularized by Dan Quayle) has prompted a barrage of criticism, which may have the desirable effect of stimulating more sophisticated economic analysis of the profession.[122]

V. CONCLUSION

Although many of these theoretical controversies were joined after the initial publication of the empirical data presented in the following

national and synthetic essays, the exchanges can be illuminated and refined by comparative study of legal professions. Indeed, such comparison is indispensable. Furthermore, these debates point to the kinds of additional information necessary to test the theories. I hope readers will be
encouraged to formulate their own theoretical frameworks for understanding the legal profession, test them against the accounts presented
here, and be provoked to conduct the research suggested by lacunae and
ambiguities.

NOTES

*Once again I am grateful to Philip Lewis for thoughtful and detailed criti-
cism of this essay.

1. Royal Commission on Legal Services, 1979; Abel, 1982; the conference
papers appeared in Thomas, 1982. I offered a critical synopsis of Larson, 1977 in a
review essay, Abel, 1979.

2. Hence the criticism of Larson's theory—that professions long antedate
the triumph of modern capitalism—is beside the point. See Sterett, 1990; Sugarman, 1993: 262. Nevertheless, capitalism vastly expands and utterly transforms
the market for lawyers' services.

3. In 1979, New York City's Taxi and Limousine Commission allowed me-
dallion owners to lease their vehicles. In the next ten years, the value of a medal-
lion tripled, to $140,000. Drivers now pay owners about $90 for a twelve-hour
night shift and spend another $20 on gas. Most do not start earning any money
for themselves until they have worked seven hours. More than 90 percent are
foreign-born. Dangerous driving has emerged as the leading consumer complaint,
up 166 percent from 1985 to 1992 (Fragin, 1994).

4. Abel, 1986.

5. Berends, 1992: 177; Schurr, 1990; Shapiro, 1990: 689. Public lecturing failed
to professionalize in the nineteenth century (Scott, 1983), yet some people today
make an excellent living giving lectures or hosting or appearing on radio and
television talk shows.

6. Pue, 1989, 1990.

7. Abel, 1985a, 1986, 1988a; Arthurs et al., 1988; Murray, 1988; Weisbrot, 1988,
1990.

8. Paterson, 1988.

9. See the criticisms of Berends, 1992: 166 and Shapiro, 1990: 697–698.

10. See, e.g., Brante, 1990; Collins, 1990a; Fox, 1984; Geison, 1984b; Gelfand,
1984; Goldstein, 1984; Hellberg, 1990 (Swedish veterinarians); Kocka, 1990; McClelland, 1990 (Germany); Ramsey, 1984; Siegrist, 1990b; Torstendahl, 1990b; Weiss,
1984.

11. On contemporary differences between American and German legal education, see Ostertag, 1993.

12. On the role of the state in the development of the legal profession, see
Karpik, 1988 (France); Konttinen, 1991 (Finland).

13. Compare Abel, 1985a with Abel, 1988b.

14. On the lack of historical fit, see Siegrist, 1986; on the differences among contemporary European legal professions, see Tyrrell and Yaqub, 1993.

15. Burrage, 1990a: 445; for a picture of the very different situation before perestroika, see Huskey, 1986; Shelley, 1991.

16. See Abel, 1994. On the unified Germany, see Blankenburg, n.d.

17. Halliday, 1987.

18. Abel, 1989a; Bishop, 1989.

19. *New York Times* B12, May 15, 1994. The reference to Tijuana recalls the era when Mexico offered quick divorces to Americans unable to obtain them at home because of the fault requirement.

20. *New York Times* B10, February 4, 1994; A13, February 9, 1994.

21. *New York Times* A1, November 22, 1993.

22. *Los Angeles Times* A1, January 1, 1994.

23. *Los Angeles Times* E1, September 7, 1993.

24. E.g., Dzienkowski, 1989: 470.

25. This is the answer to Osiel's insistence on "the remarkable reluctance of lawyers in many countries to seize the new opportunities that private industry offered them," 1990: 2039.

26. See, e.g., Powell, 1993.

27. Sarat and Felstiner (1986; 1995) nicely capture the tension between the individual client's fervent hope for legal certainty and the lawyer's self-interested manipulation of uncertainty.

28. For a critique of aggressive lawyering, see Kagan, 1994.

29. See, e.g., Goriely and Kempson, 1995. American corporations have deliberately reduced the number of law firms they use in order to increase their leverage in fee negotiations. *New York Times* §3 p5, July 4, 1993; B10, July 9, 1993.

30. See, e.g., Seron, 1992, 1993, 1996. Germany long has had far more widespread legal expense insurance.

31. Abel, 1989a. Legal need studies have been conducted in many other countries, including the United States, the Netherlands, Canada, and Australia.

32. *New York Times* B11, March 1, 1991.

33. *New York Times* B11, March 26, 1993.

34. *New York Times* B14, June 7, 1991; see also *Los Angeles Times* A3, February 22, 1993: "Injured? Larry Parker got me $2.1 million," "Accidente? Call 1-800-7-DINERO."

35. *New York Times* B11, May 25, 1990.

36. *Los Angeles Times* A3, August 22, 1994.

37. *New York Times* C1, December 11, 1991.

38. *New York Times* A11, April 13, 1994 (GAO statistics based on analysis of 2.4 million claims); *New York Times* A10, March 19, 1993 (T² Medical Inc.).

39. *New York Times* §3 p1, February 14, 1993.

40. *New York Times* §4 p2, April 10, 1994.

41. *New York Times* 17, March 3, 1991.

42. Abbott, 1991; Åmark, 1990; Bishop, 1989; Brazier et al., 1993; Collins, 1990a, 1990b; Goodrich, 1990; Murphy, 1988, 1990; Ramsay, 1993; Rosen, 1992; Sander and Williams, 1989; Stager and Foot, 1989; Stephen, 1995; Sugarman, 1995; Thomas, 1992; Willock, 1992.

43. *Los Angeles Times* A1, July 6, 1993, A1, July 8, 1993; *New York Times* B10,

July 9, 1993. A Virginia lawyer, angered by the Miller ad, wrote, produced, and paid to run a spoof in which a cowgirl lassos "Philip Millerd" (a play on Philip Morris, Miller's parent company) and condemns him for the health effects of cigarettes. *New York Times* B12, January 21, 1994.

44. See Ripps, 1993; Schneyer, 1993. On the role of elite bar associations in elevating status, see Powell, 1989.

45. Burrage, 1995; Osiel, 1990: 2027.

46. Arthurs et al., 1988; Dingwall, 1989; Ledford, 1990; Pue, 1989: 73–74; Siegrist, 1990a. On the tortuous path to collective action, see Halliday et al., 1993.

47. Schneyer, 1989, 1992.

48. Shamir, 1993, 1994; Harrington, 1983.

49. Seron, 1992, 1993, 1996; see also Cain, 1994; Van Hoy, 1993.

50. Abbott, 1988; see also Karpik, 1990. Kritzer (1991a) urges that professions be compared in terms of relative institutionalization, a concept that appears to combine social structural and cognitive variables. Auerbach (1990) suggests that Jewish preoccupation with religious law is related to Jewish overrepresentation among secular lawyers.

51. That this usefully forces comparison across occupational categories is shown by Heinz et al. (1993), who study Washington lobbying by lawyers and other representatives.

52. Erlanger et al., 1987; Felstiner and Sarat, 1992; Ingleby, 1992; Kressel, 1985; McEwan et al., 1994; Sarat and Felstiner, 1986, 1988a, 1988b, 1995. Berends (1992) both urges such studies and has conducted them, but unfortunately they are available only in Dutch.

53. McCahery and Picciotto, 1994; Sugarman, 1993, 1994b; Wheeler, 1991.

54. Kritzer, 1990.

55. Kritzer, 1991b; Flood, 1991.

56. Sugarman, 1994a.

57. Hartmann, 1993, 1994.

58. Rogowski, 1994.

59. Bancaud and Boigeol, 1994.

60. Jamous and Peloille, 1970; Johnstone and Hopson, 1967. Abbott, 1988 cites both of these but also makes strong claims for the novelty of his own schema.

61. Osiel, 1990: 2055–2056.

62. Shapiro, 1990: 703, 709.

63. Sterett, 1990: 369.

64. Halliday, 1987: 28–43.

65. Harrington, 1994; Torstendahl, 1990a; Larson, 1990; Svensson, 1990; Becher, 1990; Elzinga, 1990.

66. *Los Angeles Times* A18, February 19, 1994. For a critique of lawyer self-regulation, see Wilkins, 1992.

67. See Abel, 1994; Dezalay, 1990, 1991, 1992, 1994a, 1994b, 1994c; Dezalay and Trubek, 1994; Flood, 1994, 1995; Flood and Skordaki, 1992, n.d.; Miller and Power, 1992, 1994; Olgiati, 1994; Trubek et al., 1994; Veenswijk, 1994; Whelan and McBarnet, 1992.

Local legal professions within federal polities have sometimes engaged in similar competition.

68. On the interaction between law and accounting, see Bromwich and Hopwood, 1992.

69. Gordon, 1983, 1984, 1988, 1990; Gordon and Simon, 1992; see also ABA Journal, 1994; American Bar Association, 1986; Brint, 1994; Croft, 1992; Elkins, 1992; Glendon, 1994; Harrington, 1994; Indiana Law Journal, 1988/89; Kelly, 1994; Kronman, 1993; Linowitz, 1994; Luban, 1984, 1988, 1993; Nelson and Trubek, 1992a; Simon, 1988, 1993.

70. Gordon, 1984: 67.

71. Abel, 1989b, 1989c.

72. Caplan, 1993. Nelson and Trubek (1992b) offer legal services as evidence of professionalism; once again, however, fewer than one percent of American lawyers provide legal services, and they are paid by the state, not the profession.

73. Handler et al., 1978.

74. Erlanger and Klegon, 1978; Stover, 1989; Granfield, 1992; Granfield and Koenig, 1992.

75. Derber, 1982. Freidson (1992) leaves this ambiguity unresolved. On the possibility of a "universal class," see Derber et al., 1990.

76. Osiel actually titles a section of his review essay "Lawyers as Aristocrats" (1990).

77. Munger, 1994.

78. *Los Angeles Times* §1 p1, June 10, 1985.

79. Lisagor and Lipsius, 1988; Kumble and Lahart, 1990; Eisler, 1990; Caplan, 1993. On the role of lawyers in helping clients evade law, see McBarnet, 1984, 1988, 1991a, 1991b, 1994.

80. Gilson, 1990. See also an unpublished paper by economists Orley Ashenfelter and David Bloom, "Lawyers as Agents of the Devil," described in *New York Times* B12, March 25, 1994.

81. Nelson, 1988: 251.

82. They were Jones, Day, Reavis & Pogue (the largest law firm in the United States, excluding the multinational Baker & McKenzie) and Kaye, Scholer, Fierman, Hays & Handler (two of whose name partners are a judge on the U.S. Court of Appeals for the Second Circuit and a Columbia Law School Professor). *New York Times* C1, September 29, 1993.

83. Wheeler, 1991, 1994; McBarnet and Whelan, 1991, 1993; see also Mann, 1985.

84. Heinz and Laumann, 1982: chap. 4, 1994.

85. Sarat and Felstiner, 1986, 1988a, 1988b, 1995; Felstiner and Sarat, 1992; McEwan et al., 1994.

86. Landon, 1985, 1988, 1990; Engel, 1987; see also Johnsen, 1992.

87. Rosenthal, 1974.

88. Katz, 1982; McIntyre, 1987; Flemming, 1989.

89. Haley, 1982; Reifner, 1982.

90. Yugoslavia and Bulgaria. See Abel, 1985b: 531.

91. Solomon (1992) details the contradiction between lawyers' search for autonomy and their obsession with money. The latest example is an entrepreneurial California lawyer who, for $300 and proof that the buyer has obtained a $1 million recovery, will send "a handsome certificate, printed on heavy cream paper

and complete with gold scales-of-justice seal and a legend attesting to 'exceptional skill, experience and excellence in advocacy.'" In the first nine months he had seventy-five takers. The Inner Circle of Advocates, founded for the same purpose twenty years ago, has preserved its exclusivity through a numerus clausus of 100. *New York Times* B18, May 6, 1994.

92. Compare *Los Angeles Times* §IV p1 (May 2, 1989), *New York Times* 17 (July 13, 1988) (models refusing cigarette and other advertisements) and *New York Times* C1 (April 25, 1994) (pharmacists refusing to stock cigarettes) with *New York Times* A1 (November 20, 1992) (the 175 lawyers at Shook, Hardy & Bacon of Kansas City devote 20 percent of their time to tobacco company liability defense and fought to oppose the Surgeon General's warnings). U.S. Trade Representative Mickey Kantor boasted that the Clinton Administration abandoned the Reagan and Bush Administration's policy of aggressively promoting American tobacco exports. When asked how he reconciled this with his own representation (in private practice) of the Beverly Hills Restaurant Association in its fight against an anti-smoking ordinance, he replied: "I see no contradiction in that and I'm not defensive about it at all. Obviously when you're a lawyer in a corporate practice, in 99.9 percent of the cases, there is no ideology or philosophy involved." *The Nation* 556, April 25, 1994.

93. Salokar, 1992 (Solicitor General). Gordon and Simon (1992) find solace in Rosen's (1989a) claim that some house counsel restrain clients. The dilemma of the good lawyer in a bad role is a staple of media presentations, see Chase, 1986; Post, 1987; Rosen, 1989b.

94. Alfieri, 1993; Aron, 1989; Cain, 1994; Cain and Harrington, 1994b; Greenberg, 1994; Kessler, 1987; Lawrence, 1990; López, 1992; Schärf, 1994; Scheingold, 1988, 1994; Tushnet, 1994. For an account of Santa Monica City Attorney Robert M. Myers, who was fired for refusing to draft and enforce an ordinance criminalizing homelessness, see Fulton, 1993. His replacement, Marsha Jones Moutrie, announced: "I come in the door with no particular substantive agenda. I intend to work hard at being a very good lawyer for the city." *Outlook Mail* A1, December 29, 1993.

95. *New York Times* B12, March 21, 1994.

96. Osiel (1990: 2013–2014) makes this argument more generally.

97. Abel, 1989a; Goriely and Kempson, 1995.

98. Halliday, 1987. Does he really mean to hold up the concordat between the Papacy and the Italian state as something to be emulated?

99. Paterson, 1995. This extends Panglossian law and economics to the macro-level.

100. Domberger and Sherr, 1989.

101. Quoted in Flood, 1995.

102. Goriely and Kempson, 1995.

103. Burrage, 1990b.

104. Both quoted by Sugarman, 1995.

105. Abel, 1989d: 85; Auerbach, 1976: 107, 127.

106. Stevens, 1987, 1988.

107. Abel, 1988c: 188; Baldwin and McConville, 1977; McConville et al., 1994.

108. Abel, 1988c: 53–56, 149–156.

109. The literature on discrimination against women in the legal profession is enormous. For some recent accounts, see Chambers, 1989; Drachman, 1989, 1993; Eaves et al., 1989; Epstein, 1993; Gellis, 1990/91; Hagan, 1990a, 1990b; Hagan and Kay, 1995; Hagan et al., 1991; Mattesich and Heilman, 1990; Menkel-Meadow, 1994; New York Law School Law Review, 1990; Roach, 1990; Scott, 1987; Skordaki, 1995b; Stanford Law Review, 1988; Weiss and Melling, 1988. A recent survey by the Women Lawyers Association of Los Angeles (427 respondents out of 1100 members) found that three out of five believed women received less desirable work than did men and three out of four felt that women were held to higher standards. *Los Angeles Times* D1, March 10, 1994.

110. (Johannesburg) *Weekly Mail & Guardian* 37, April 29, 1994.

111. See Flood, 1995; Lee, 1992; Thomas, 1992.

112. Derber, 1982.

113. Hartmann, 1993.

114. *New York Times* B13, May 3, 1991.

115. Calhoun and Copp, 1988; Clark, 1992; Clark and Economides, 1988; Katsh, 1989; Sherr, 1990.

116. Hagan, 1990a, 1990b; Hagan et al., 1988, 1991; Hagan and Kay, 1995.

117. *New York Times* C1, June 14, 1990.

118. Gilson and Mnookin, 1985, 1989; see also Carr and Mathewson, 1990. Daniels (1992, 1993) offers a more complicated account, which I find more satisfactory; see also Nelson, 1994.

119. Galanter and Palay, 1992. I find this hypothesis unfalsifiable because the authors offer no index of "reputational capital" other than the partnership income it purports to explain.

120. Sander and Williams, 1992.

121. *New York Times* 17, January 29, 1994; A1, February 7, 1994.

122. Compare Magee et al., 1989 and Magee, 1992, n.d. with Clark, 1991; Cross, 1992a, 1992b; Epp, 1992a, 1992b; Gilson, 1984, 1992; Heymann, 1991; Olson, 1992; Sander, 1992.

REFERENCES

ABA Journal. 1994. "Identity Crisis," 80 *ABA Journal* 74 (December).

Abbott, Andrew. 1988. *The System of Professions: An Essay on the Division of Expert Labor*. Chicago: University of Chicago Press.

———. 1991. "The Order of Professionalization," 18 *Work and Occupations* 355.

Abel, Richard L. 1979. "The Rise of Professionalism," 6 *British Journal of Law and Society* 82.

———. 1982. "The Politics of the Market for Legal Services," in P. A. Thomas, ed., *Law in the Balance: Legal Services in the Eighties*. Oxford: Martin Robertson.

———. 1985a. "Comparative Sociology of Legal Professions: An Exploratory Essay," 1985 *American Bar Foundation Research Journal* 1.

———. 1985b. "Law Without Politics: Legal Aid under Advanced Capitalism," 32 *UCLA Law Review* 474.

———. 1986. "The Decline of Professionalism?" 49 *Modern Law Review* 1.

———. 1988a. "United States: The Contradictions of Professionalism," in Richard L. Abel and Philip S. C. Lewis, eds., *Lawyers in Society, Vol. 1: The Common Law World*. Berkeley: University of California Press.

———. 1988b. "Lawyers in the Civil Law World," in Richard L. Abel and Philip S. C. Lewis, eds., *Lawyers in Society, Vol. 2: The Civil Law World*. Berkeley: University of California Press.

———. 1988c. *The Legal Profession in England and Wales*. Oxford: Basil Blackwell.

———. 1989a. "Between Market and State: The Legal Profession in Turmoil," 52 *Modern Law Review* 285.

———. 1989b. "The Contradictions of Legal Professionalism," in School of Justice Studies, Arizona State University, eds., *New Directions in the Study of Justice*. New York: Plenum.

———. 1989c. "Taking Professionalism Seriously," 1989(1) *Annual Survey of American Law* 41.

———. 1989d. *American Lawyers*. New York: Oxford University Press.

———. 1994. "Transnational Law Practice," 44 *Case Western Reserve Law Review* 737.

Åmark, Klas. 1990. "Open Cartels and Social Closures: Professional Strategies in Sweden, 1860–1950," in Burrage and Torstendahl, 1990.

American Bar Association, Commission on Professionalism. 1986. '. . . In the Spirit of Public Service': A Blueprint for the Rekindling of Lawyer Professionalism. Chicago: ABA.

Alfieri, Anthony V. 1993. "Impoverished Practices," 81 *Georgetown Law Journal* 2567.

Aron, Nan. 1989. *Liberty and Justice for All: Public Interest Law in the 1980s and Beyond*. Boulder, Colo.: Westview Press.

Arthurs, Harry W., Richard Weisman, and Frederick H. Zemans. 1988. "Canadian Lawyers: A Peculiar Professionalism," in Richard L. Abel and Philip S. C. Lewis, eds., *Lawyers in Society, Vol. 1: The Common Law World*. Berkeley: University of California Press.

Auerbach, Jerold S. 1976. *Unequal Justice: Lawyers and Social Change in Modern America*. New York: Oxford University Press.

———. 1990. *Rabbis to Lawyers: The Journey from the Torah to the Constitution*. Bloomington: Indiana University Press.

Baldwin, John, and Michael McConville. 1977. *Negotiated Justice: Pressures to Plead Guilty*. London: Martin Robertson.

Bancaud, Alain, and Anne Boigeol. 1994. "A New Judge for a New System of Economic Justice?" in Dezalay and Sugarman, 1994.

Becher, Tony. 1990. "Professional Education in a Comparative Context," in Torstendahl and Burrage, 1990.

Berends, Miek. 1992. "An Elusive Profession? *Lawyers in Society*," 26 *Law & Society Review* 161.

Bishop, William. 1989. "Regulating the Market for Legal Services in England: Enforced Separation of Function and Restrictions on Forms of Enterprise," 52 *Modern Law Review* 326.

Blankenburg, Erhard. n.d. "The Purge of Lawyers: After the Breakdown of the East German Communist Regime" (unpublished).

Brante, Thomas. 1990. "Professional Types as a Strategy of Analysis," in Burrage and Torstendahl, 1990.

Brazier, Margaret, Jill Jovecy, Michael Moran, and Margaret Potton. 1993. "Falling from a Tightrope: Doctors and Lawyers between the Market and the State," 41 *Political Studies* 197.

Brint, Steven. 1994. *In an Age of Experts: The Changing Role of Professionals in Politics and Public Life.* Princeton: Princeton University Press.

Bromwich, Michael, and Anthony Hopwood, eds. 1992. *Accounting and the Law.* Hemel Hempstead: Prentice Hall; London: Institute of Chartered Accountants in England and Wales.

Burrage, Michael. 1990a. "*Advokatura:* In Search of Professionalism and Pluralism in Moscow and Leningrad," 15 *Law & Society Inquiry* 433.

———. 1990b. "Introduction: The Professions in Sociology and History," in Burrage and Torstendahl, 1990.

———. 1995. "Looking Backwards into the Future: Of the Status of Solicitors," in Skordaki, 1995a.

Burrage, Michael, and Rolf Torstendahl, eds. 1990. *Professions in Theory and History: Rethinking the Study of the Professions.* London: Sage.

Cain, Maureen. 1994. "The Symbol Traders," in Cain and Harrington, 1994a.

Cain, Maureen, and Christine B. Harrington, eds. 1994a. *Lawyers in a Postmodern World: Translation and Transgression.* Buckingham: Open University Press.

———. 1994b. "Introduction," in Cain and Harrington, 1994a.

Calhoun, Craig, and Martha Copp. 1988. "Computerization in Legal Work: How Much Does New Technology Change Professional Practice?" 4 *Research in the Sociology of Work* 233.

Caplan, Lincoln. 1993. *Skadden: Power, Money, and the Rise of a Legal Empire.* New York: Farrar, Straus & Giroux.

Carr, Jack, and Frank Mathewson. 1990. "The Economics of Law Firms: A Study in the Legal Organization of the Firm," 33 *Journal of Law and Economics* 307.

Chambers, David L. 1989. "Accommodation and Satisfaction: Women and Men Lawyers and the Balance of Work and Family," 14 *Law & Social Inquiry* 251.

Chase, Anthony. 1986. "Lawyers and Popular Culture: A Review of Mass Media Portrayals of American Attorneys," 1986 *American Bar Foundation Research Journal* 281.

Clark, Andrew. 1992. "Information Technology in Legal Services," 18 *Journal of Law and Society* 13.

Clark, Andrew, and Kim Economides. 1988. "Technics and Praxis: Technological Innovation and Legal Practice in Modern Society," 15 *Sociologia del diritto* 41.

Clark, R. 1991. "Why So Many Lawyers? Are They Good or Bad?" 61 *Fordham Law Review* 275.

Cocks, Geoffrey, and Konrad H. Jarausch, eds. 1990. *German Professions, 1800–1950.* New York: Oxford University Press.

Collins, Randall. 1990a. "Changing Conceptions in the Sociology of the Professions," in Torstendahl and Burrage, 1990.

―――. 1990*b*. "Market Closure and the Conflict Theory of the Professions," in Burrage and Torstendahl, 1990.

Croft, Colin. 1992. "Reconceptualizing American Legal Professionalism: A Proposal for a Deliberative Moral Community," 67 *NYU Law Review* 1256.

Cross, Frank B. 1992*a*. "The First Thing We Do, Let's Kill All the Economists: An Empirical Evaluation of the Effect of Lawyers on the United States Economy and Political System," 70 *Texas Law Review* 645.

―――. 1992*b*. "Law versus Economics?" 17 *Law & Social Inquiry* 653.

Daniels, Ronald J. 1992. "The Law Firm as an Efficient Community," 37 *McGill Law Journal* 801.

―――. 1993. "Growing Pains: The Why and How of Law Firm Expansion," 43 *University of Toronto Law Journal* 147.

Derber, Charles. 1982. *Professionals as Workers: Mental Labor in Advanced Capitalism*. Boston: G. K. Hall.

Derber, Charles, William A. Schwartz, and Yale Magrass. 1990. *Power in the Highest Degree: Professionals and the Rise of a New Mandarin Order*. New York: Oxford University Press.

Dezalay, Yves. 1990. "The *Big Bang* and the Law: The Internationalization and Restructuration of the Legal Field," 7 *Theory, Culture & Society* 279.

―――. 1991. "Territorial Battles and Tribal Disputes," 54 *Modern Law Review* 792.

―――. 1992. *Marchands de droit*. Paris: Feyard.

―――. 1994*a*. "Professional Competition and the Social Construction of Markets," in Dezalay and Sugarman, 1994.

―――. 1994*b*. "Technological Warfare: The Battle to Control the Mergers and Acquisitions Market in Europe," in Dezalay and Sugarman, 1994.

―――. 1994*c*. "The Forum Should Fit the Fuss: The Economics and Politics of Negotiated Justice," in Cain and Harrington, 1994*a*.

Dezalay, Yves, and David Sugarman, eds. 1994. *Professional Competition and the Social Construction of Markets*. London: Routledge.

Dingwall, Robert. 1989. Review of "The Legal Profession in England and Wales," 23 *Sociology* 309.

Domberger, Simon, and Avrom Sherr. 1989. "The Impact of Competition on Pricing and Quality of Legal Services," 9 *International Review of Law and Economics* 41.

Drachman, Virginia G. 1989. "'My "Partner" in Law and in Life': Marriage in the Lives of Women Lawyers in Late 19th- and Early 20th-Century America," 14 *Law & Social Inquiry* 221.

―――. 1993. *Women Lawyers and the Origins of Professional Community in America: The Letters of the Equity Club, 1866 to 1890*. Ann Arbor: University of Michigan Press.

Dzienkowski, John S. 1989. "The Regulation of the American Legal Profession and Its Reform" (review of *American Lawyers*), 68 *Texas Law Review* 451.

Eaves, David, I. P. L. Png, and J. Mark Ramseyer. 1989. "Gender, Ethnicity and Grades: Empirical Evidence of Discrimination in Law-Firm Interviews," 7 *Law and Inequality* 189.

Eisler, Kim. 1990. *Shark Tank: Greed, Politics, and the Collapse of Finley Kumble*. New York: St. Martin's Press.

Elkins, James R. 1992. "The Moral Labyrinth of Zealous Advocacy," 21 *Capital University Law Review* 736.

Elzinga, Aant. 1990. "The Knowledge Aspect of Professionalization: The Case of Science-based Nursing Education in Sweden," in Torstendahl and Burrage, 1990.

Engel, David M. 1987. "The Ovenbird's Song: Insiders, Outsiders, and Personal Injuries in an American Community," 18 *Law & Society Review* 551.

Epp, Charles R. 1992*a*. "Do Lawyers Impair Economic Growth?" 17 *Law & Social Inquiry* 585.

———. 1992*b*. "Toward New Research on Lawyers and the Economy," 17 *Law & Social Inquiry* 695.

Epstein, Cynthia Fuchs. 1993. *Women in Law*, 2d ed. Urbana: University of Illinois Press.

Erlanger, Howard S., and Douglas A. Klegon. 1978. "Socialization Effects of Professional School," 13 *Law & Society Review* 11.

Erlanger, Howard S., Elizabeth Chambliss, and Marygold S. Melli. 1987. "Participation and Flexibility in Informal Processes: Cautions from the Divorce Context," 21 *Law & Society Review* 585.

Felstiner, William L. F., and Austin Sarat. 1992. "Enactments of Power: Negotiating Reality and Responsibility in Lawyer-Client Interactions," 77 *Cornell Law Review* 1447.

Flemming, Roy B. 1989. "If You Pay the Piper, Do You Call the Tune? Public Defenders in America's Criminal Courts," 14 *Law & Social Inquiry* 393.

Flood, John. 1991. "Doing Business: The Management of Uncertainty in Lawyers' Work," 25 *Law & Society Review* 41.

———. 1994. "The Cultures of Globalization: Professional Restructuring for the International Market," in Dezalay and Sugarman, 1994.

———. 1995. "Conquering the World: Multinational Practice and the Production of Law," in Skordaki, 1995*a*.

Flood, John, and Eleni Skordaki. 1992. *Corporate Failure and the Work of Insolvency Practitioners: Professional Jurisdiction and Big Corporate Insolvencies*. London: ACCA.

———. n.d. "The Role of Informal Rule-Making by Accountants and Lawyers in Mega-Insolvencies" (unpublished).

Fox, Robert. 1984. "Science, the University, and the State in Nineteenth-Century France," in Geison, 1984*a*.

Fragin, Sheryl, 1994. "New York's Terror Taxis, Explained," *New York Times*, August 21, §3 p9.

Freidson, Eliot. 1992. "Professionalism as Model and Ideology," in Nelson et al., 1992.

Fulton, William. 1993. "Saint Bob," *California Lawyer* 51 (February).

Galanter, Marc, and Thomas Palay. 1992. *Tournament of Lawyers: The Transformation of the Big Law Firms*. Chicago: University of Chicago Press.

Geison, Gerald L., ed. 1984*a*. *Professions and the French State, 1700–1900*. Philadelphia: University of Pennsylvania Press.

———. 1984*b*. "Introduction," in Geison, 1984*a*.

Gelfand, Toby. 1984. "A 'Monarchical Profession' in the Old Regime: Surgeons, Ordinary Practitioners, and Medical Professionalization in Eighteenth-Century France," in Geison, 1984a.

Gellis, Ann. 1990/91. "Great Expectations: Women in the Legal Profession, a commentary on state studies," 66 *Indiana Law Journal* 941.

Gilson, Ronald J. 1984. "Value Creation by Business Lawyers: Legal Skills and Asset Pricing," 94 *Yale Law Journal* 239.

———. 1990. "The Devolution of the Legal Profession: A Demand Side Perspective," 49 *Maryland Law Review* 869.

———. 1992. "How Many Lawyers Does It Take to Change an Economy?" 17 *Law & Social Inquiry* 635.

Gilson, Ronald, and Robert Mnookin. 1985. "Sharing among the Human Capitalists: An Inquiry into the Corporate Law Firm and How Partners Split Profits," 37 *Stanford Law Review* 313.

———. 1989. "Coming of Age in a Corporate Law Firm: The Economics of Associate Career Patterns," 41 *Stanford Law Review* 567.

Glendon, Mary Ann. 1994. *A Nation Under Lawyers: How the Crisis in the Legal Profession Is Transforming American Society.* New York: Farrar, Straus & Giroux.

Goldstein, Jan. 1984. "'Moral Contagion': A Professional Ideology of Medicine and Psychiatry in Eighteenth- and Nineteenth-Century France," in Geison, 1984a.

Goodrich, Chris. 1990. "A Problematic Profession" (review of *American Lawyers* and three other books), *The Nation* 205 (February 12).

Gordon, Robert W. 1983. "Legal Thought and Legal Practice in the Age of American Enterprise, 1870–1920," in Gerald L. Geison, ed., *Professions and Professional Ideologies in America.* Chapel Hill: University of North Carolina Press.

———. 1984. "'The Ideal and the Actual in the Law': Fantasies and Practices of New York City Lawyers, 1870–1910," in Gerard W. Gawalt, ed., *The New High Priests: Lawyers in Post-Civil War America.* Westport, Conn.: Greenwood Press.

———. 1988. "The Independence of Lawyers," 68 *Boston University Law Review* 1.

———. 1990. "Corporate Law Practice as a Public Calling," 49 *Maryland Law Review* 255.

Gordon, Robert W., and William H. Simon. 1992. "The Redemption of Professionalism," in Nelson et al., 1992.

Goriely, Tammy, and Elaine Kempson. 1995. "Access to Social Justice: The Development of Legal Aid and Advice Services in the Area of Poverty Law," in Skordaki, 1995a.

Granfield, Robert. 1992. *Making Elite Lawyers: Visions of Law at Harvard and Beyond.* New York: Routledge.

Granfield, Robert, and Thomas Koenig. 1992. "Learning Collective Eminence: Harvard Law School and the Social Production of Elite Lawyers," 33 *Sociological Quarterly* 503.

Greenberg, Jack. 1994. *Crusaders in the Courts: How a Dedicated Band of Lawyers Fought for the Civil Rights Revolution.* New York: Basic Books.

Hagan, John. 1990a. "The Gender Stratification of Income Inequality Among Lawyers," 68 *Social Forces* 835.

———. 1990b. "Gender and the Structural Transformation of the Legal Profession in the United States and Canada," in D. M. Klein and J. Glass, eds., *Changes in Societal Institutions*. New York: Plenum.

Hagan, John, and Fiona Kay. 1995. *Gender in Practice: A Study of Lawyers' Lives*. New York: Oxford University Press.

Hagan, John, Marjorie Zatz, Bruce Arnold, and Fiona Kay. 1991. "Cultural Capital, Gender, and the Structural Transformation of Legal Practice," 25 *Law & Society Review* 239.

Hagan, John, Marie Huxter, and Patricia Parker. 1988. "Class Structure and Legal Practice: Inequality and Mobility Among Toronto Lawyers," 22 *Law & Society Review* 9.

Haley, John Owen. 1982. "The Politics of Informal Justice: The Japanese Experience, 1922–1942," in Richard L. Abel, ed., *The Politics of Informal Justice, Vol. 2: Comparative Studies*. New York: Academic Press.

Halliday, Terence C. 1987. *Beyond Monopoly: Lawyers, State Crises, and Professional Empowerment*. Chicago: University of Chicago Press.

Halliday, Terence C., Michael J. Powell, and Mark W. Granfors. 1993. "After Minimalism: Transformations of State Bar Associations from Market Dependence to State Reliance, 1918 to 1950," 58 *American Sociological Review* 515.

Handler, Joel F., Ellen Jane Hollingsworth, and Howard S. Erlanger. 1978. *Lawyers and the Pursuit of Legal Rights*. New York: Academic Press.

Harrington, Christine B. 1983. "The Formation of a New Specialty: The Administrative Bar." Presented at the Annual Meeting of the Law and Society Association, Denver (June 2–5).

———. 1994. "Outlining a Theory of Legal Practice," in Cain and Harrington, 1994a.

Hartmann, Michael. 1993. "Legal Data Banks, the Glut of Lawyers, and the German Legal Profession," 27 *Law & Society Review* 421.

———. 1994. "Bank Lawyers—A Professional Group Holding the Reins of Power," in Dezalay and Sugarman, 1994.

Heinz, John P., and Edward O. Laumann. 1982. *Chicago Lawyers: The Social Structure of the Bar*. New York: Russell Sage Foundation; Chicago: American Bar Foundation.

———. 1994. *Chicago Lawyers: The Social Structure of the Bar*, rev. ed. Evanston, Ill.: Northwestern University Press.

Heinz, John P., Edward O. Laumann, Robert L. Nelson, and Robert H. Salisbury. 1993. *The Hollow Core: Private Interests in National Policy Making*. Cambridge, Mass.: Harvard University Press.

Hellberg, Inga. 1990. "The Swedish Veterinary Profession and the Swedish State," in Torstendahl and Burrage, 1990.

Heymann, Philip. 1991. "Considering the Costs and Benefits of Lawyering in Drafting Legislation or Establishing Precedents," 36 *Villanova Law Review* 191.

Huskey, Eugene. 1986. *Russian Lawyers and the Soviet State: The Origins and Development of the Soviet Bar 1917–1939*. Princeton, N.J.: Princeton University Press.

Indiana Law Journal. 1988/89. "Symposium: The Growth of Large Law Firms and Its Effect on the Legal Profession and Legal Education," 64 *Indiana Law Journal* 423–600.

Ingleby, Richard. 1992. *Solicitors and Divorce*. Oxford: Clarendon Press.

Jamous, H., and B. Peloille. 1970. "Professions or Self-Perpetuating Systems? Changes in the French University-Hospital System," in J. A. Jackson, ed., *Professions and Professionalisation*. Cambridge: Cambridge University Press.

Johnsen, Jon T. 1992. "Rural Justice: Country Lawyers and Legal Services in the United States and Britain," 17 *Law & Social Inquiry* 415.

Johnstone, Quintin, and Dan Hopson, Jr. 1967. *Lawyers and Their Work: An Analysis of the Legal Profession in the United States and England*. Indianapolis: Bobbs-Merrill.

Kagan, Robert A. 1994. "Do Lawyers Cause Adversarial Legalism? A Preliminary Inquiry," 19 *Law & Social Inquiry* 1.

Karpik, Lucien. 1988. "Lawyers and Politics in France, 1814–1950: The State, the Market, and the Public," 13 *Law & Social Inquiry* 707.

———. 1990. "Technical and Political Knowledge: The Relationship of Lawyers and Other Legal Professions to the Market and the State," in Torstendahl and Burrage, 1990.

Katsh, M. Ethan. 1989. *The Electronic Media and the Transformation of Law*. New York: Oxford University Press.

Katz, Jack. 1982. *Poor People's Lawyers in Transition*. New Brunswick, N.J.: Rutgers University Press.

Kelly, Michael. 1994. *Lives of Lawyers: Journeys in the Organizations of Practice*. Ann Arbor: University of Michigan Press.

Kessler, Mark. 1987. *Legal Services for the Poor: A Comparative and Contemporary Analysis of Interorganizational Politics*. Westport, Conn.: Greenwood Press.

Kocka, Jürgen. 1990. "'Bürgertum' and Professions in the Nineteenth Century: Two Alternative Approaches,' in Burrage and Torstendahl, 1990.

Konttinen, Esa. 1991. "Professionalization as Status Adaptation: The Nobility, the Bureaucracy, and the Modernization of the Legal Profession in Finland," 16 *Law & Social Inquiry* 497.

Kressel, Kenneth. 1985. *The Process of Divorce: How Professionals and Couples Negotiate Settlements*. New York: Basic Books.

Kritzer, Herbert M. 1990. *The Justice Broker: Lawyers and Ordinary Litigation*. New York: Oxford University Press.

———. 1991a. "Abel and the Professional Project: The Institutional Analysis of the Legal Profession," 16 *Law & Social Inquiry* 529.

———. 1991b. *Let's Make a Deal*. Madison: University of Wisconsin Press.

Kronman, Anthony T. 1993. *The Lost Lawyer: Failing Ideals of the Legal Profession*. Cambridge, Mass.: Harvard University Press.

Kumble, Steven J., and Kevin J. Lahart. 1990. *Conduct Unbecoming: The Rise and Ruin of Finley, Kumble*. New York: Carroll & Graf.

Landon, Donald. 1985. "Clients, Colleagues, and Community: The Shaping of Zealous Advocacy in Country Law Practice," 1985 *American Bar Foundation Research Journal* 81.

———. 1988. "LaSalle Street and Main Street: The Role of Context in Structuring Law Practice," 22 *Law & Society Review* 213.

———. 1990. *Country Lawyers: The Impact of Context on Professional Practice*. New York: Praeger.

Larson, Magali Sarfatti. 1977. *The Rise of Professionalism: A Sociological Analysis.* Berkeley: University of California Press.

———. 1990. "In the Matter of Experts and Professionals, or How Impossible It Is to Leave Nothing Unsaid," in Torstendahl and Burrage, 1990.

Lawrence, Susan. 1990. *The Poor in Court: The Legal Services Program and Supreme Court Decision Making.* Princeton, N.J.: Princeton University Press.

Ledford, Kenneth F. 1990. "Conflict Within the Legal Profession: Simultaneous Admission and the German Bar, 1903–1927," in Cocks and Jarausch, 1990.

Lee, R. G. 1992. "From Profession to Business: The Rise and Rise of the City Law Firm," 18 *Journal of Law and Society* 31.

Linowitz, Sol, with Martin Mayer. 1994. *The Betrayed Profession: Lawyering at the End of the Twentieth Century.* New York: Charles Scribner's Sons.

Lisagor, Nancy, and Frank Lipsius. 1988. *A Law Unto Itself: The Untold Story of the Law Firm of Sullivan & Cromwell.* New York: Morrow.

López, Gerald P. 1992. *Rebellious Lawyering: One Chicano's Vision of Progressive Law Practice.* Boulder, Colo.: Westview Press.

Luban, David. 1984. "The Adversary System Excuse," in David Luban, ed., *The Good Lawyer.* Totowa, N.J.: Rowman & Allenheld.

———. 1988. *Lawyers and Justice: An Ethical Study.* Princeton, N.J.: Princeton University Press.

———. 1993. "Are Criminal Defenders Different?" 91 *Michigan Law Review* 1729.

Magee, Stephen P. 1992. "The Optimum Number of Lawyers: A Reply to Epp," 17 *Law & Social Inquiry* 667.

———. n.d. The Invisible Foot and the Waste of Nations: Lawyers vs. the U.S. Economy.

Magee, Stephen P., William A. Brock, and Leslie Young. 1989. "The Invisible Foot and the Waste of Nations: Lawyers as Negative Externalities," in *Black Hole Tariffs and Endogenous Policy Theory: Political Economy in General Equilibrium.* Cambridge: Cambridge University Press.

Mann, Kenneth. 1985. *Defending White-Collar Crime: A Portrait of Attorneys at Work.* New Haven: Yale University Press.

Mattesich, Paul, and Cheryl Heilman. 1990. "The Career Paths of Minnesota Law School Graduates: Does Gender Make a Difference?" 19 *Law and Inequality* 59.

McBarnet, Doreen. 1984. "Law and Capital: The Role of Legal Form and Legal Actors," 12 *International Journal of the Sociology of Law* 233.

———. 1988. "Law, Policy, and Legal Avoidance: Can Law Effectively Implement Egalitarian Policies?" 15 *Journal of Law and Society* 113.

———. 1991a. "It's Not What You Do But the Way You Do It," in David Downes, ed., *Unravelling Criminal Justice.* London: Macmillan.

———. 1991b. "Whiter Than White Collar Crime: Tax, Fraud Insurance and the Management of Stigma," 42 *British Journal of Sociology* 323.

———. 1994. "Legal Creativity: Law, Capital and Legal Avoidance," in Cain and Harrington, 1994a.

McBarnet, Doreen, and Christopher Whelan. 1991. "The Elusive Spirit of the Law: Formalism and the Struggle for Legal Control," 54 *Modern Law Review* 848.

———. 1993. "Beyond Control: Law Management and Corporate Governance," in Joseph McCahery, Sol Picciotto, and Colin Scott, eds., *Corporate Control and Accountability*. Oxford: Clarendon; New York: Oxford University Press.

McCahery, Joseph, and Sol Picciotto. 1994. "Creative Lawyering and the Dynamics of Business Regulation," in Dezalay and Sugarman, 1994.

McClelland, Charles E. 1990. "Escape from Freedom? Reflections on German Professionalization, 1870–1933," in Torstendahl and Burrage, 1990.

McConville, Mike, Jacqueline Hodgson, and Lee Bridges. 1994. *Standing Accused: The Organization and Practices of Criminal Defence Lawyers in Britain*. Oxford: Oxford University Press.

McEwan, Craig A., Lynn Mather, and Richard J. Maiman. 1994. "Lawyers, Mediation, and the Management of Divorce Practice," 28 *Law & Society Review* 149.

McIntyre, Lisa J. 1987. *The Public Defender: The Practice of Law in the Shadows of Repute*. Chicago: University of Chicago Press.

Menkel-Meadow, Carrie. 1994. "Culture Clash in the Quality of Life in the Law: Changes in the Economics, Diversification and Organization of Lawyering," 44 *Case Western Reserve Law Review* 621.

Miller, Peter, and Michael Power. 1992. "Accounting, Law and Economic Calculation," in Bromwich and Hopwood, 1992.

———. 1994. "Calculating Corporate Failure," in Dezalay and Sugarman, 1994.

Munger, Frank. 1994. "Miners and Lawyers: Law Practice and Class Conflict in Appalachia, 1872–1920," in Cain and Harrington, 1994*a*.

Murphy, Raymond. 1988. *Social Closure: The Theory of Monopolization and Exclusion*. Oxford: Clarendon Press.

———. 1990. "Proletarianization or Bureaucratization: The Fall of the Professional?" in Torstendahl and Burrage, 1990.

Murray, Georgina. 1988. "New Zealand Lawyers: From Colonial GPs to the Servants of Capital," in Richard L. Abel and Philip S. C. Lewis, eds., *Lawyers in Society, Vol. 1: The Common Law World*. Berkeley: University of California Press.

Nelson, Robert. 1988. *Partners with Power*. Berkeley: University of California Press.

———. 1994. "The Futures of American Lawyers: A Demographic Profile of a Changing Profession in a Changing Society," 44 *Case Western Reserve Law Review* 345.

Nelson, Robert L., and David M. Trubek. 1992*a*. "Introduction: New Problems and New Paradigms in Studies of the Legal Profession," in Nelson et al., 1992.

———. 1992*b*. "Arenas of Professionalism: The Professional Ideologies of Lawyers in Context," in Nelson et al., 1992.

Nelson, Robert L., David M. Trubek, and Rayman L. Solomon, eds. 1992. *Lawyers' Ideals/Lawyers' Practices: Transformations in the American Legal Profession*. Ithaca: Cornell University Press.

New York Law School Law Review. 1990. "Symposium on Women in the Lawyering Workplace: Feminist Considerations and Practical Solutions," 35(2) *New York Law School Law Review* (special issue).

Olgiati, Vittorio. 1994. "Process and Policy of Legal Professionalization in Europe: The De-Construction of a Normative Order," in Dezalay and Sugarman, 1994.

Olson, Mancur. 1992. "Do Lawyers Impair Economic Growth?" 17 *Law & Social Inquiry* 625.

Osiel, Mark J. 1990. "Lawyers as Monopolists, Aristocrats, and Entrepreneurs," 103 *Harvard Law Review* 2009.

Ostertag, Jürgen R. 1993. "Legal Education in Germany and the United States—A Structural Comparison," 26 *Vanderbilt Journal of Transnational Law* 301.

Paterson, Alan A. 1988. "The Legal Profession in Scotland: An Endangered Species or a Problem Case for Market Theory?" in Richard L. Abel and Philip S. C. Lewis, eds., *Lawyers in Society, Vol. 1: The Common Law World*. Berkeley: University of California Press.

———. 1995. "Professionalism and the Legal Services Market," in Skordaki, 1995*a*.

Post, Robert C. 1987. "On the Popular Image of the Lawyer: Reflections in a Dark Glass," 75 *California Law Review* 379.

Powell, Michael. 1989. *From Patrician to Professional Elite: The Transformation of the New York City Bar Association*. New York: Russell Sage Foundation.

———. 1993. "Professional Innovation: Corporate Lawyers and Private Lawmaking," 18 *Law & Social Inquiry* 423.

Pue, W. Wesley. 1989. "'Trajectories of Professionalism?': Legal Professionalism After Abel," 1989 *Manitoba Law Annual* 57.

———. 1990. "Moral Panic at the English Bar: Paternal vs. Commercial Ideologies of Legal Practice in the 1860s," 15 *Law & Social Inquiry* 49.

Ramsey, Ian M. 1993. "What Do Lawyers Do? Reflections on the Market for Lawyers," 21 *International Journal of the Sociology of Law* 355.

Ramsey, Matthew. 1984. "The Politics of Professional Monopoly in Nineteenth-Century Medicine: The French Model and Its Rivals," in Geison, 1984*a*.

Reifner, Udo. 1982. "Individualistic and Collective Legalization: The Theory and Practice of Legal Advice for Workers in Prefacist Germany," in Richard L. Abel, ed., *The Politics of Informal Justice, Vol. 2: Comparative Studies*. New York: Academic Press.

Ripps, Stephen R. 1993. "Law Firm Ownership of Ancillary Businesses in Ohio—A New Era?" 27 *Akron Law Review* 1.

Roach, Sharon L. 1990. "Men and Women Lawyers in In-House Legal Departments: Recruitment and Career Patterns," 4 *Gender and Society* 207.

Rogowski, Ralf. 1994. "German Corporate Lawyers: Social Closure in Autopoietic Perspective," in Dezalay and Sugarman, 1994.

Rosen, Robert. 1989*a*. "The Inside Counsel Movement, Professional Judgment, and Organizational Representation," 64 *Indiana Law Journal* 479.

———. 1989*b*. "Ethical Soap: *L.A. Law* and the Privileging of Character," 43 *University of Miami Law Review* 1229.

Rosen, Sherwin. 1992. "The Market for Lawyers," 35 *Journal of Law & Economics* 215.

Rosenthal, Douglas E. 1974. *Lawyer and Client: Who's In Charge?* New York: Russell Sage Foundation.

Royal Commission on Legal Services. 1979. *Final Report*. London: HMSO (Cmnd 7648).

Salokar, Rebecca M. 1992. *The Solicitor General: The Politics of Law*. Philadelphia: Temple University Press.

Sander, Richard H. 1992. "Elevating the Debate on Lawyers and Economic Growth," 17 *Law & Social Inquiry* 659.

Sander, Richard H., and E. Douglass Williams. 1989. "Why Are There So Many Lawyers? Perspectives on a Turbulent Market," 14 *Law & Social Inquiry* 431.

———. 1992. "A Little Theorizing about the Big Law Firm: Galanter, Palay, and the Economics of Growth," 17 *Law & Social Inquiry* 391.

Sarat, Austin, and William L. F. Felstiner. 1986. "Law and Strategy in the Divorce Lawyer's Office," 20 *Law & Society Review* 93.

———. 1988a. "Law and Social Relations: Vocabularies of Motive in Lawyer/Client Interaction," 22 *Law & Society Review* 737.

———. 1988b. "Legal Realism in Lawyer/Client Communication," in Anne Walker and Judith Levi, eds., *Language in the Judicial Process*. New York: Plenum.

———. 1995. *Divorce Lawyers and Their Clients: Power and Meaning in the Legal Process*. New York: Oxford University Press.

Schärf, Wilfried. 1994. "Para-legals and Prefiguration: Working in Black Townships towards a Post-Apartheid South Africa," in Cain and Harrington, 1994a.

Scheingold, Stuart. 1988. "Radical Lawyers and Socialist Ideals," 15 *Journal of Law and Society* 122.

———. 1994. "The Contradictions of Radical Law Practice," in Cain and Harrington, 1994a.

Schneyer, Theodore. 1989. "Professionalism as Bar Politics: The Making of the Model Rules of Professional Conduct," 14 *Law & Social Inquiry* 677.

———. 1992. "Professionalism as Politics: The Making of a Modern Legal Ethics Code," in Nelson et al., 1992.

———. 1993. "Policymaking and the Perils of Professionalism: The ABA's Ancillary Business Debate as a Case Study," 35 *Arizona Law Review* 363.

Schurr, Carolyn. 1990. "Monopoly" (review of *American Lawyers*), 76 *American Bar Association Journal* 100.

Scott, Donald M. 1983. "The Profession That Vanished: Public Lecturing in Mid-Nineteenth Century America," in Gerald L. Geison, ed., *Professions and Professional Ideologies in America*. Chapel Hill: University of North Carolina Press.

Scott, Joan Norman. 1987. "A Woman's Chance for Law Partnership," 71 *Sociology and Social Research* 119.

Seron, Carroll. 1992. "Managing Entrepreneurial Legal Services: The Transformation of Small-Firm Practice," in Nelson et al., 1992.

———. 1993. "New Strategies for Getting Clients: Urban and Suburban Lawyers' Views," 27 *Law & Society Review* 399.

———. 1996. *The Business of Practicing Law: The Work Lives of Solo and Small-Firm Attorneys*. Philadelphia: Temple University Press.

Shamir, Ronen. 1993. "Professionalism and Monopoly of Expertise: Lawyers and Administrative Law, 1933–1937," 27 *Law & Society Review* 361.

———. 1994. *Managing Uncertainty: Elite Lawyers in the New Deal*. Durham: Duke University Press.

Shapiro, Martin. 1990. "Lawyers, Corporations and Knowledge," 38 *American Journal of Comparative Law* 683.

Shelley, Louise. 1991. "Lawyers in the Soviet Union," in Anthony Jones, ed., *Professions and the State: Expertise and Authority in the Soviet Union and Eastern Europe*. Philadelphia: Temple University Press.

Sherr, Avrom. 1990. Review of "The Legal Profession in England and Wales" (and three other books), 53 *Modern Law Review* 406.

Siegrist, Hannes. 1986. "Professionalization with the Brakes On: The Legal Profession in Switzerland, France and Germany in the Nineteenth and Early Twentieth Centuries," 9 *Comparative Social Research* 267.

———. 1990*a*. "Professionalization as a Process: Patterns, Progression and Discontinuity," in Burrage and Torstendahl, 1990.

———. 1990*b*. "Public Office or Free Profession? German Attorneys in the Nineteenth and Early Twentieth Centuries," in Cocks and Jarausch, 1990.

Simon, William H. 1988. "Ethical Discretion in Lawyering," 101 *Harvard Law Review* 1083.

———. 1993. "The Ethics of Criminal Defense," 91 *Michigan Law Review* 1703.

Skordaki, Eleni, ed. 1995*a*. *Social Change and the Solicitors' Profession*. Oxford: Oxford University Press.

———. 1995*b*. "Glass Slippers and Glass Ceilings: Women in the Legal Profession," in Skordaki, 1995*a*.

Solomon, Rayman L. 1992. "Five Crises or One: The Concept of Legal Professionalism," in Nelson et al., 1992.

Stager, D., and D. Foot. 1989. "Lawyers' Earnings under Market Growth and Differentiation, 1970–80," 22 *Canadian Journal of Economics* 235.

Stanford Law Review. 1988. "Project: Gender, Legal Education, and the Legal Profession: An Empirical Study of Stanford Law Students and Graduates," 40 *Stanford Law Review* 1209.

Stephen, Frank H. 1995. "Assessing Post-War Growth: Factors Affecting the Number of Practising Solicitors," in Skordaki, 1995*a*.

Sterett, Susan. 1990. "Comparing Legal Professions," 15 *Law & Social Inquiry* 363.

Stevens, Robert B. 1987. "A View from the Lord Chancellor's Office," [1987] *Contemporary Legal Problems* 181.

———. 1988. "The Independence of the Judiciary: The View from the Lord Chancellor's Office," 8 *Oxford Journal of Legal Studies* 222.

Stover, Robert V. 1989. *Making It and Breaking It: The Fate of Public Interest Commitment during Law School*. Urbana: University of Illinois Press.

Sugarman, David. 1993. "Simple Images and Complex Realities: English Lawyers and Their Relationship to Business and Politics, 1750–1950," 11 *Law and History Review* 257.

———. 1994*a*. "Who Colonized Whom? Historical Reflections on the Intersection between Law, Lawyers and Accountants in England," in Dezalay and Sugarman, 1994.

———. 1994*b*. "Blurred Boundaries: The Overlapping Worlds of Law, Business and Politics," in Cain and Harrington, 1994*a*.

———. 1995. "'The Best Organised and Most Intelligent Trade Union in the Country': The Private and Public Life of the Law Society, 1825–1914," in Skordaki, 1995*a*.

Svensson, Lennart G. 1990. "Knowledge as a Professional Resource: Case Studies of Architects and Psychologists at Work," in Torstendahl and Burrage, 1990.

Thomas, Philip A., ed. 1982. *Law in the Balance: Legal Services in the Eighties*. Oxford: Martin Robertson.

———. 1992. "Thatcher's Will," 19 *Journal of Law and Society* 1.

Torstendahl, Rolf. 1990a. "Introduction: Promotion and Strategies of Knowledge-Based Groups," in Torstendahl and Burrage, 1990.

———. 1990b. "Essential Properties, Strategic Aims and Historical Development: Three Approaches to Theories of Professionalism," in Burrage and Torstendahl, 1990.

Torstendahl, Rolf, and Michael Burrage, eds. 1990. *The Formation of Professions: Knowledge, State and Strategy*. London: Sage Publications.

Trubek, David M., Yves Dezalay, Ruth Buchanan, and John R. Davis. 1994. "Global Restructuring and the Law: Studies of the Internationalization of Legal Fields and the Creation of Transnational Arenas," 44 *Case Western Reserve Law Review* 407.

Tushnet, Mark V. 1994. *Making Civil Rights Law: Thurgood Marshall and the Supreme Court, 1936–1961*. New York: Oxford University Press.

Tyrrell, Alan, and Zahd Yaqub. 1993. *The Legal Professions in the New Europe*. Oxford: Blackwell.

Van Hoy, Jerry. 1993. "Prepackaged Law: The Political Economy and Organization of Routine Work at Multi-branch Legal Services Firms." Ph.D. dissertation, sociology, Northwestern University.

Veenswijk, Virginia Kays. 1994. *Coudert Brothers: A Legacy in Law: The History of America's First International Law Firm 1853–1993*. New York: Truman Talley Books/Dutton.

Weisbrot, David. 1988. "The Australian Legal Profession: From Provincial Family Firms to Multinationals," in Richard L. Abel and Philip S. C. Lewis, eds., *Lawyers in Society, Vol. 1: The Common Law World*. Berkeley: University of California Press.

———. 1990. *Australian Lawyers*. Melbourne: Longman Cheshire.

Weiss, Catherine, and Louise Melling. 1988. "The Legal Education of Twenty Women," 40 *Stanford Law Review* 1163.

Weiss, John H. 1984. "Bridges and Barriers: Narrowing Access and Changing Structure in the French Engineering Profession, 1800–1850," in Geison, 1984a.

Wheeler, Sally. 1991. "Lawyer Involvement in Commercial Disputes," 18 *Journal of Law and Society* 241.

———. 1994. "Capital Fractionalized: The Role of Insolvency Practitioners in Asset Distribution," in Cain and Harrington, 1994a.

Whelan, Christopher, and Doreen McBarnet. 1992. "Lawyers in the Market: Delivering Legal Services in Europe," 18 *Journal of Law and Society* 49.

Wilkins, David. 1992. "Who Should Regulate Lawyers?" 105 *Harvard Law Review* 799.

Willock, Ian D. 1992. "Tomorrow's Lawyers in Scotland," 19 *Journal of Law and Society* 146.

2

England and Wales: A Comparison of the Professional Projects of Barristers and Solicitors

RICHARD L. ABEL

This chapter traces the contours of the rise and decline of the English legal profession during the last century and a half. I do not use the word "decline" pejoratively—to signify a lowering of ethical standards. Rather, I view professionalism as a specific historical formation in which the members of an occupation exercise a substantial degree of control over the market for their services, usually through an occupational association. I have chosen this concept of professionalism over others that stress technical expertise, or standards of competence and ethical behavior, or altruism because it seems to me to illuminate a great deal of the history and contemporary experience of English lawyers. There can be little doubt that nineteenth century solicitors consciously and energetically sought market control, and it is painfully clear today that both branches of the profession are deeply upset about threats to their continued exercise of such control. At the same time, English lawyers offer an especially apt context for exploring fluctuations in this concept of professionalism (a cycle that is visible in other countries as well). First, English lawyers professionalized earlier than did lawyers in other common law countries and also may be deprofessionalizing sooner. Second, the divided English legal profession offers a natural laboratory for observing the choice of tactics in the professional project and their relative success or failure.

All occupations under capitalism are compelled to seek control over their markets. The only alternative is to be controlled *by* the market—a situation that is fraught with uncertainty at best and may lead to economic extinction at worst. Of course, no occupation controls its market totally, and none is wholly without influence; control is a question of degree and constantly changes. The foundation of market control is the regulation of supply. Occupations that produce goods may pursue this goal by seeking to restrict raw materials or technology, but occupations that produce services constrain supply principally by regulating the production *of* producers. Professions are distinguished from other closed occupations by their requirement of demonstrated mastery of a body of formalized knowledge. Although advocates of control invariably portray their object as improving the quality of services, we should not let this claim blind us to the fact that any improvement necessarily also limits entry. At one extreme of the spectrum of control, the profession (often backed by the state) imposes a numerus clausus—illustrated by some nineteenth century continental legal professions, notaries in certain countries today, and elite advocates, such as Queen's Counsel in England and avocats of the Conseil d'Etat and the Cour de Cassation in France. At the other extreme, entry to the occupational category is governed by market forces: demand for professional services on one hand and the distribution of ability, energy, and inclination on the other hand. Examples include gardeners in Los Angeles, drivers of non-medallion cabs in New York, or window cleaners in London. Market control is inextricably related to occupational status, not only symbolizing status but also enhancing it instrumentally, both by restricting numbers (because scarcity is an intrinsic measure of status as well as a means of increasing income) and by controlling the characteristics of entrants. Professions pursue market control and status enhancement through collective action. Having erected barriers to entry, professional associations seek to protect their members from competition, both external and internal. In order to avert external surveillance, they engage in self-regulation. This chapter will examine the contrasting careers followed by barristers and solicitors in pursuit of the professional project.

ENTRY TO THE PROFESSION

In order to trace the dramatic fluctuations in the kind and degree of supply control that English lawyers have exercised during the last century and a half, it is useful to choose as a baseline the entry barriers that prevailed at the beginning of the nineteenth century. Barristers and solicitors differed significantly in the extent to which each branch emphasized ascribed or achieved qualities—the character of the whole person or narrow technical skills—and in whether controls were formal or informal, visible or invisible.

THE PREMODERN HERITAGE

The Bar entered the nineteenth century with stringent constraints on the kind of person who might become a barrister, constraints that had been in place for several hundred years. The benchers (judges and senior barristers) who governed the four Inns of Court had complete discretion to admit or reject a student; applicants had to state their "condition in life" and provide references from two barristers. The Inns of Court extended a preference to university graduates, shortening the number of years they had to keep terms from five to three and the number of dinners they had to eat each term from six to three, so that the burden on nongraduates was more than three times as onerous. Partly for this reason, half of all barristers were university graduates at a time when this privilege was enjoyed by only a tiny fraction of the population and restricted to upper-class members of the Established Church. Once called to the Bar, the fledgling barrister was expected to serve a pupillage (apprenticeship) of one to two years with an established barrister or other legal professional. Thereafter, fully qualified barristers had to open their own chambers, for in the early nineteenth century most practiced alone.

Two things about this entry process are striking, although perhaps not immediately apparent. First, it was extremely expensive. For the majority who attended university, there was the cost of tuition and three years of maintenance. The Bar student then had to pay a fee of £30 to £40 for admission to his Inn of Court and deposit an additional £100, which was refunded without interest only after call. During his three to five years as a student, while forbidden to work at most trades, he incurred annual expenses of £5 to £10 for hall dinners, £6 to £8 for books, and about £150 for maintenance. Call fees were £70 to £80, to which must be added about 8 guineas for a wig and gown. The premium for pupillage was 200 guineas, and the pupil had to maintain himself for another two years. Once established in his own chambers, the barrister could not expect to earn enough from practice to support himself for several years (if ever), although he might make ends meet by "deviling" (salaried work for an established barrister), tutoring, marking examination papers, law reporting, or editing. A midnineteenth century estimate put the one-time costs at £300 and the annual maintenance at £250 from entering university to reaching economic self-sufficiency, which could be as long as ten years. These financial demands strongly reinforced the ascriptive criteria that influenced the university and the Inn to admit a student, the barrister to accept a pupil, and the client or solicitor to brief a fledgling barrister.

The second noteworthy feature of this lengthy and arduous process of qualifying is that it had relatively little to do with the acquisition of technical skills. Those who attended university did not study English law because it was not taught. The Inns had abandoned any pretense of education two centuries earlier. In addition, although we know little about the content of pupillage, certainly many barristers must have accepted pupils for the substantial premiums the latter paid rather than out of dedication to teaching. The Bar selected those who aspired to be "gentle-

men" (regardless of whether their fathers were landed gentry); colleague-
ship at university and within the Inns may have reinforced such gentility;
but neither selection nor training ensured technical competence in law.

Because solicitors lacked the lengthy traditions of the Bar, they initially
subjected entrants to fewer ascriptive criteria and, consequently, imposed
fewer entry barriers of any sort. Nineteenth century solicitors were not
expected to attend university; indeed, only 5 percent of enrolled solicitors
were graduates as late as the 1870s. But solicitors were required by law to
serve a five-year apprenticeship (articles). This was an ascriptive barrier in
two senses: the apprentice obtained his place through personal contacts,
often with a solicitor who was a relative, family friend, or business acquaint-
ance; and articles were expensive—about £100 for stamp duty and £200
for the premium paid to the solicitor. Yet, unlike the Bar student or pupil,
the articled clerk could minimize his expenses by living at home, since
articles were available all over England, not only in London (where all
barristers had their chambers at the beginning of the nineteenth century).
And at the end of his apprenticeship, the qualified solicitor could attain
immediate economic self-sufficiency through salaried employment with a
firm and could look forward to joining the partnership or setting up his
own practice.

Even at the beginning of the nineteenth century, barristers and solicitors
thus diverged in their exercise of supply control. The Bar used rigorous
ascriptive criteria and demanded substantial economic sacrifices, effectively
limiting numbers. Yet, these barriers were both informal (pupillage was not
a legal requirement, for instance) and invisible (no person or institution
decreed that a newly qualified barrister would fail to obtain sufficient
business). Solicitors also employed ascriptive barriers, but these were less
elaborate and seem to have been more closely related to the acquisition of
legal knowledge. Because articles lasted several times as long as pupillage
and because the supervising solicitor generally expected to employ the
apprentice thereafter, it seems plausible that the experience conferred at
least a modicum of technical skill.

CONSTRUCTING MODERN CRITERIA

These differences between the branches became considerably more pronounced during the next hundred years. The Bar retained and indeed
strengthened its ascriptive criteria. In 1829, Inner Temple (one of the four
Inns of Court) required all students who had not matriculated at university
to pass an examination in history and either Latin or Greek; although this
requirement was abandoned briefly when the other Inns failed to adopt it,
the examination had become universal by the last quarter of the nineteenth

century. In any case, almost three-quarters of all Bar students were university graduates by this time. However, the Bar moved very slowly to ensure that entrants possessed technical knowledge. It resisted the example of physicians, solicitors, and colonial lawyers, all of whom had adopted formal examinations, for the Bar feared that this might facilitate entry rather than restrain it, thereby admitting the wrong kind of person. The examination finally required in 1872 was ridiculously easy. Graduates sat it a few months after leaving university, and 80 percent to 90 percent were passing at the end of the nineteenth century. The Bar was even less interested in preparing students to practice law than in examining their competence. Although the Inns created the Council of Legal Education in the midnineteenth century, it had a minimal teaching staff and relied heavily on practitioners. It is not surprising that the majority of Bar students preferred private crammers. Thus the barriers to becoming a barrister remained much the same until after World War II: cost and the particularistic decisions of universities, pupilmasters, and (later) heads of chambers.

Solicitors pursued a very different path toward controlling the production of producers. In the absence of substantial ascriptive barriers, the number of solicitors seems to have doubled in the first third of the nineteenth century. Partly in response, one of the early acts of the Incorporated Law Society (a voluntary association formed by solicitors in the 1820s, following the demise of the Society of Gentlemen Practisers) was to impose a professional examination in 1836, nearly four decades before the "senior" branch (barristers) did so. This decision to use achievement rather than ascription as the principal entry barrier seems to have had its desired effect: the issuance of new "practicing certificates" dropped by almost a quarter over the next fifteen years, and the number of solicitors stabilized for four decades (although other factors, such as falling demand, also may have contributed to this decline). Twenty-five years after initiating professional examinations (and ten years before the first Bar Final), the Law Society added a second hurdle: the Intermediate Examination, taken by articled clerks during their apprenticeship. (Although law graduates were exempt, there were very few during this period.) Then, in 1906, the Society required a third examination in trust accounts, accounting, and bookkeeping. Although the pass rates for each examination were very high when it first was introduced, all of them declined fairly steadily and were approaching 50 percent at the beginning of World War II; since all *three* had to be passed, their cumulative effect was even greater.

The Law Society also was more serious about professional education: it instituted lectures for articled clerks in 1833, three years before the first professional examination, and progressively expanded the offerings at its Chancery Lane headquarters. Nevertheless, attendance was low: articled clerks, like Bar students, preferred private crammers; and little instruction was available outside London and a few major provincial cities. In response, the Law Society made two major changes in 1922: it required a compulsory year of lectures prior to the Intermediate Examination, and it subsidized such instruction at provincial universities.

By contrast with its concern for technical competence, the Law Society did little to raise ascriptive barriers. Individual exemptions were granted freely from the preliminary liberal arts examination imposed in 1861 (thirty years after Inner Temple had required a similar examination of Bar students), and categorical exemptions rapidly proliferated, not just for university matriculates but also for those who passed a host of other exams. The proportion of solicitors with university degrees remained small: less than a fifth of all entrants in the first decade of the twentieth century (when three-quarters of all new barristers were baccalaureates), less than a third as late as World War II. At the same time, it must be recognized that preparation for the three professional examinations itself was costly and became an important, if indirect, barrier to those who could not afford to study full time or pay the crammers.

FLUCTUATIONS IN ENTRY

How effective were the divergent strategies of barristers and solicitors in controlling the production of producers? In answering this question, it is essential to bear in mind the impact of extraneous events, the most important of which were World Wars I and II. Nearly a quarter of all solicitors served in World War I; 588 were killed and 669 seriously wounded (nearly a tenth of all practitioners). The next generation of solicitors was affected even more seriously: more than half of all articled clerks served, of whom 358 were killed and 458 seriously wounded (perhaps a third of all clerks). Although these losses were inflicted *on* the profession, it also bears some responsibility for failing to respond to them by admitting more solicitors after the war (even though pass rates on the professional examinations did increase dramatically). In addition to those killed and disabled, there was a shortfall in production of 1,700 solicitors, if the ten years beginning in 1914 are compared to the previous decade. The experience of World War II was similar: more than 500 solicitors and clerks were killed, and there was a shortfall in production of more than 1,500.

Together, professional supply control and extraneous tragedies had a dramatic effect on the number of solicitors (see table 1). The rapid increase in the production of solicitors in the first third of the nineteenth century (an annualized rate of 3.1 percent) halted abruptly in 1835—which happened to be the year before the first professional examination was administered, although it would be dangerous to infer causality. The profession remained virtually static for the next third of the century. Although there was some growth in the 1870s and 1880s, it slowed to almost nothing in the next twenty-five years. The number of solicitors declined at an annualized rate of 1.7 percent between 1913 and 1920 and remained virtually static between 1939 and 1952. As a result, solicitors entered the postwar period (1948) with almost *exactly* the same number (15,567) that had been in practice more than half a century earlier (15,090 in 1890). Statistics for the practicing strength of the Bar before the 1950s are sadly inadequate. Nevertheless, available data show the number of barristers doubling between the first and the last quarters of the nineteenth century, declining by a fourth following World War I, and remaining at that depressed level until well after World War II.

THE POSTWAR TRANSFORMATION

The period since World War II, and especially the last two decades, have witnessed a major transformation in both the means and the extent of control over the production of producers. The distinctive characteristics of barristers and solicitors continued to color their different responses, but the overwhelming changes that both branches confronted induced a significant convergence between them. Some ascriptive barriers to the Bar were lowered, and achievements were emphasized. The £100 deposit required before admission to an Inn was eliminated for most students, the £50 stamp duty on call to the Bar was abolished in 1947, and other fixed fees became less burdensome as a result of inflation. Although the Bar formally required a university degree in 1975, the growth of tertiary education and, more importantly, government grants to undergraduates made it easier to obtain this credential (which nearly 90 percent of entrants already held in any case). Nine years later the Bar added the requirement of at least a lower-second-class degree (although few students with an inferior degree had been passing the Bar examination and finding a pupillage and tenancy).

The Bar also began to relate entry barriers more closely to technical competence. Students without a law degree now must spend a year studying law in a polytechnic (often without further government support) and pass an additional examination. Not surprisingly, 84 percent of intending practitioners called to the Bar in 1983 were law graduates. Legal education thus has become the principal barrier to qualifying as a barrister, a point to which I return below. All entrants must take a year of vocational training prior to the final examination, and the number of places available at the Inns at Court School of Law has been limited in recent years (although students can study elsewhere). Final examination pass rates remain high, however: nearly 90 percent of intending practitioners succeeded on their first try in the early 1980s, although the proportion has fallen significantly in the last few years.

Yet, the Bar certainly has not relinquished all control to the academy. Three major entry barriers remain, which traditionally have been more ascriptive and less subject to external influence. First, the Bar mandated a one-year pupillage in 1959 (previously pupillage had been voluntary though very common); six years later, it prohibited pupils from taking briefs during their first six months. Although the pupillage fee declined in importance after World War II and was abolished in 1975, maintenance during this year remains a serious problem, since no government grants are available, Inn scholarships are few in number and inadequate in amount, and briefs are difficult to obtain even in the second six months. Furthermore, a bottleneck has developed as the number seeking pupillages has multiplied rapidly while the number of barristers willing to act as pupilmasters has remained constant. Although the Bar maintains that every intending practitioner is placed, competition has intensified, and personal contacts and ascriptive characteristics clearly weigh heavily.

Second, and more important, the Bar requires every private practitioner to obtain a tenancy (a place in chambers from which to practice). Like pupillage, this became a problem only recently. In the nineteenth century, fledgling barristers simply opened their own chambers; this would be prohibitively expensive today, and in any case a new barrister practicing alone would attract very little business. In the early twentieth century, natural attrition in a relatively static profession created space for all who wished to enter; however, the rapid growth in the number of Bar students and pupils in the last two decades has disrupted this accommodation. The problem of tenancies is unique to England as well as to the postwar period: advocates in Scotland and barristers in some Australian states practice individually, and office space and assistance by a pool of clerks are available to all new entrants. By contrast, the present shortage of tenancies in London is both severe and chronic. Until recently, all London chambers were located in one of the Inns; even now only five of the more than 200 London sets have moved outside, and several of those also are "outsiders" in terms of political orientation or racial composition. Chambers within the Inns are grossly overcrowded, however, partly because the Inns traditionally have leased much of their space to residential or other commercial tenants. In the six years between 1975 and 1981, when the Bar grew by 28 percent, available space in the Inns expanded only 8 percent. As a result, every year since 1965 there has been a shortfall in the tenancies available to barristers completing their pupillages, sometimes by as much as 50 percent. More than 100 qualified barristers (approximately a third of the number starting practice annually) have occupied the amorphous status of floaters ever since the Senate (the umbrella association of barristers) began keeping records in 1974. This physical shortage of space (which is largely the Bar's own doing) has greatly intensified competition for entry, increasing the weight that heads of chambers give to ascriptive qualities in accepting tenants and discouraging many students and pupils from entering private practice.

The third barrier confronting the qualified beginner also is peculiar to the Bar: because private practitioners cannot be employed, they must find business on their own. The difficulties of doing so remained acute in the early postwar period: most barristers lost money in their first year and made only a nominal amount in their second. Not surprisingly, almost a third of those who entered practice in 1950/51 had abandoned it five years later. And between 1955 and 1959, the number of barristers with less than ten years of experience who left practice ranged from half to three-quarters of the number entering practice that year. In this respect (and others), barristers resembled small-scale entrepreneurs, most of whose businesses fail, rather than professionals, who make a lifetime commitment to a career (although some barristers who leave private practice continue to use their legal skills as employees in the public or private sectors). Yet, the situation of the novice improved dramatically in the 1960s and 1970s as a result of the growth of legal aid, which ensured at least a minimum level of subsistence. Juniors (barristers who are not Queen's Counsel) with less than nine years of experience, practicing at the family, common law, or criminal Bars in London, or on circuit, obtained between 59 and 72 percent of their incomes from public sources (both legal aid and prosecution briefs) in 1974/75. Consequently, departures from practice of those with less than ten years of experience dropped dramatically after 1959; although absolute numbers have risen slightly since 1976, they still represent only a tenth to a quarter of those starting practice.

Solicitors responded differently to the postwar environment. The principal ascriptive barrier to becoming a solicitor—articles—underwent significant change. Out-of-pocket costs fell when Parliament abolished the stamp duty on articles in 1947 and premiums gradually disappeared about 1960. The length of articles was reduced by a year for both graduates and nongraduates; however, since the former now greatly outnumber the latter, the effective period of apprenticeship has been cut from five years to two. More importantly, clerks began to receive salaries: £200 in the 1950s, £500 in the 1960s, £1,600 in 1976, and £3,000 to £4,000 today, although this still is insufficient for maintenance. However, obtaining articles (like finding a tenancy for a pupil) has become a significant problem for the first time. Because the number of law graduates seeking articles increased rapidly, while the number of solicitors qualified and willing to take on clerks remained fairly constant, competition for articles intensified. Firms today receive dozens of applications for each position, students write even more letters in order to obtain a place, and those with contacts fare far better than do those who use more universalistic methods, such as the Law Society Register or a university appointments board. The scramble for articles serves both to distribute law graduates across the hierarchy of solicitors' firms and to discourage those with poorer degrees earned at less prestigious institutions from seeking to enter private practice.

Primarily for symbolic reasons, the Law Society has refrained from formalizing the academic barriers to entry. It still is posssible for mature students to become solicitors without obtaining A levels (examinations taken at the end of secondary school), although the proportion of entrants who do so is insignificant. Similarly, a university degree is not required, although more than 90 percent of new solicitors now are university graduates, and almost all of these are law graduates (compared with only a quarter in 1949). The two branches thus have converged in fact, if not in rule. All aspiring solicitors, like all barristers, must complete a vocational year; but almost three-quarters of the students at the Law Society's College of Law in 1980 had received local authority grants (although the proportions have dropped as the Thatcher Government has placed ceilings on local taxes and cut grants to local authorities). The rapid growth in the prevalence of legal education also has reduced the significance of professional examinations in controlling quality and numbers. The nine out of ten entrants with law degrees are exempt from the Common Professional Examination (CPE), which replaced the Intermediate Examination in 1980 and which, despite its name, is taken only by aspiring solicitors. More importantly, the high proportion of examinees with a legal education seems to be correlated with a rise in the pass rate on the Final Examination from an all-time low of 48 percent in 1952 to a high of 74 percent in 1977—a level approaching that of the Bar Final, which historically has been much easier. Yet solicitors still are more serious than barristers about ensuring technical competence. The Law Society has imposed a requirement of forty-eight hours of continuing education in the first three years of practice; the Senate, on the other hand, told the Royal Commission that postqualification education would not be "appropriate" to the circumstances of the Bar.

Both branches of the profession thus have lost to academic legal education much of their control over the production of producers. It would be difficult to overestimate the importance of this transformation. First, it is a transfer of the locus of control: from professionals and their associations to universities and polytechnics and the governmental bodies that determine their enrollments and funding. Second, because public education consistently has been more universalistic than private associations or individuals, this transfer largely eliminated the principal ascriptive barrier to the profession: the exclusion of half the population on the basis of gender (just as the growth of American law schools in the early twentieth century opened that profession to the sons of immigrants). Half a century before Parliament compelled the profession to admit women and long before the academy became the principal mode of professional qualification, University College, London, allowed women to read law. In 1967, when women constituted 5 percent of the Bar and 3 percent of solicitors, they were 17 percent of entering law students at university and 11 percent at polytechnics. They were 45 percent of all domestic undergraduate law students enrolled in universities in 1983/84 and 47 percent of full-time domestic law students admitted to polytechnics for the fall term in 1984. Women thus reached virtual parity with men inside the academy in about two decades.

The third element of this transformation in the institutional structure of control is the growing heterogeneity of the academy. Prior to World War II, academic legal education was concentrated at Oxford, Cambridge, and the three London colleges, which together enrolled three-quarters of all students; the remainder (mostly articled clerks preparing for Law Society examinations) were distributed among the seven older provincial universities. By 1980/81, Oxbridge had fallen to 12 percent, London (even with two more faculties) had 9 percent, the older provincial universities enrolled 24 percent, eleven other universities (both pre- and postwar) had launched law courses with 22 percent of the students, and the twenty-four new polytechnic law programs enrolled a third of all students. Not surprisingly, the convergence of three factors—a government eager to provide social services (of which education was a relatively inexpensive example), universities and polytechnics interested in expanding, and women determined to pursue careers—produced a dramatic increase in law enrollments, perhaps the most dramatic ever experienced in *any* country (see table 1). In 1938/39 there were 1,515 undergraduate law students; in 1980/81 there were 12,603 full-time students (and another 3,375 part-time, external, or mixed-degree students)—more than an eightfold increase. In the United States, law school enrollment expanded more slowly even during its period of most rapid growth (1890 to 1927) and has increased only threefold since World War II.

Although supply control had been transformed, it still was being exercised—if now by the academy. Law departments received between ten and twenty applications per place in the 1970s; although much of this imbalance is explained by multiple applications, little more than 40 percent of all applicants obtained a place anywhere. Furthermore, admission is not tantamount to graduation. Although at least nine out of ten university law students graduate (perhaps as many as nineteen out of twenty), only three-quarters of full-time and about a third of part-time polytechnic students complete their courses.

UNPRECEDENTED EXPANSION

Let me summarize these changes in control over the production of producers as a preface to examining their consequences. Out-of-pocket fees, which had been a significant barrier in the nineteenth century, diminished in importance in both branches. The formal educational requirements of the two branches converged in a law degree and a year of professional training, while local government grants became widely available to defray the cost of the former, if not always the latter. The solicitors Final Examination came to resemble the Bar Final as a hurdle that most law graduates could expect to overcome. In addition, the attrition of qualified barristers during the early years of practice because of insufficient business declined with the growth of legal aid. Nevertheless, significant differences still separated the two branches. If it was difficult to obtain apprenticeships in both, it was more difficult to find a pupillage. Articled clerks could expect to live on their salaries; pupils had to rely on other sources of income. More importantly, there were enough jobs for most who wanted to be assistant solicitors but not nearly enough tenancies for beginning barristers.

These changes in the structure of supply control had an extraordinary impact on the rates of entry into the two branches after World War II (see table 1). Although there was some catch-up in starts at the Bar for the first five years, the numbers began to decline by 1950. The efficacy of supply control is visible in the fact that the Bar actually *shrank* each year from 1955 to 1961, a total decline of 5 percent, and the 1950 rate of entry was not attained again until 1965. Then the transformation described above began to take effect as the number of first law degrees increased from 1,072 in 1965 to 3,564 in 1980, or 232 percent. Starts at the Bar, which averaged 104 a year between 1955 and 1964, rose to 150 between 1965 and 1969, 246 between 1970 and 1974, and 317 between 1975 and 1984—a threefold increase. The total number of barristers in private practice, which declined at an annualized rate of 0.7 percent between 1954 and 1961, increased at 3.5 percent a year between 1961 and 1969 and at a staggering 8.2 percent a year between 1969 and 1978, before slowing to 3.2 percent a year between 1978 and 1984. The number of private practitioners increased from 1,918 in 1961 to 5,203 in 1984, or 171 percent. Yet, the lower rate of growth in the last five years suggests that the Bar did not entirely lose control over supply, and the decline in the ratio of starts to calls (among barristers domiciled in the United Kingdom) after 1975/76 is consistent with my contention that the Bar's restriction on the number of tenancies remains a significant barrier.

Solicitors display a pattern of growth that is similar in gross but different in detail. The postwar catch-up, during which an average of 900 solicitors were admitted a year, ended in 1950. For the next fourteen years, average annual admissions fell to 701, as a result of which the profession grew at an annualized rate of only 1 percent during the 1950s. Thereafter admissions increased rapidly: an average of 1,120 a year between 1965 and 1969, 1,777 between 1970 and 1974, 2,391 between 1975 and 1979, and 3,380 for the first two years of this decade, before declining to 2,522 between 1982 and 1984. As a consequence, the profession grew at an annualized rate of 2.4 percent between 1959 and 1968 and 5.9 percent between 1968 and 1982, although growth has fallen off in the last two years. The total number of solicitors increased 139 percent between 1959 and 1984.

Although barristers and solicitors have shown similar periods of stasis and change in the last four decades, the differential impact of the postwar environment on their strategies of supply control also is apparent. Because the Bar relied so heavily on ascriptive criteria, it could offer less resistance to the increasing dominance of meritocratic ideology; and given its much smaller base, its rate of growth inevitably was much higher. However, control over the number of tenancies by the Inns and by heads of chambers was able to slow the growth of the Bar five years before the growth of solicitors began to decline. The same forces that produced the unparalleled rate of expansion in both branches during the 1960s and 1970s also explain why that expansion has levelled off. Law student enrollments, which have become the principal bottleneck, are relatively flat (see table 1). Whereas university enrollment increased at an annualized rate of 9.9 percent between 1961 and 1976, it increased at only 1.2 percent thereafter; polytechnic enrollment rose at an annualized rate of 65.9 percent between 1970 and 1976 but at only 7.0 percent between 1976 and 1980. Undergraduate enrollment in both university and polytechnic law departments declined slightly between 1982/83 and 1983/84. Furthermore, the entry of women into law departments, which explains much of the growth of these departments, has stabilized at just under half. We can expect both branches to continue to grow for several more decades because the rate of production will outweigh deaths and retirements in the much smaller cohort of older lawyers: over the last ten years an average of 2,540 solicitors have been admitted annually, but only 1,107 have left practice; 314 barristers have started but only 124 have left. The rate of growth will remain constant and gradually decline, however. In a sense, supply control has been reestablished through a new mechanism—formal education—and at a new level.

THE COMPOSITION OF THE PROFESSION

This new mechanism affects not only the size of the profession but also its composition. First, the radically different levels of recruitment before and after the 1960s have produced a small cohort of older lawyers and a much larger cohort of younger practitioners. Whereas only 34 percent of all barristers were within ten years of call in 1966, a decade later 57 percent fell in this category. Similarly, only 47 percent of solicitors were forty or younger in 1969, but a mere seven years later 58 percent had been in practice for less than sixteen years, almost all of whom would be under forty. It is noteworthy that this imbalance in age distribution is consider-ably more pronounced among barristers, a reflection of the fact that supply control, initially more stringent, was relaxed more profoundly, as well as of the smaller size of the Bar. Although I can only speculate, it seems plausible to suggest that the large cohorts of younger lawyers have been and will be increasingly dissatisfied with restrictive practices that favor older lawyers and with structures of governance that institutionalize gerontocracy.

When the academy displaced the profession as principal gatekeeper, explicit reliance on ascribed characteristics gave way to an ideology of meritocracy. The great achievement of the academy has been to admit women in numbers that now approach those of male entrants. As late as half a century after Parliament ended the profession's formal exclusion of women in 1919, they still were only 3 percent of solicitors and 5.4 percent of barristers. With the growth of law departments and the even more important changes in consciousness wrought by the feminist movement, the Bar began to change in the late 1950s. Although the proportion of women grew steadily, it also grew slowly and seems to have peaked in the mid-1970s at about 15 percent to 20 percent of starts, only half the proportion of women law students. The number of women solicitors, by contrast, did not begin to grow markedly until the 1970s; but by 1980, the proportion of new solicitors who were women equaled the propor-tion of law graduates who were women. These differences between the branches cannot be explained in terms of the Bar's claim to be more demanding, for women law graduates are, if anything, more capable than men law graduates. Incomplete statistics suggest that the proportion of women applicants admitted to law departments is less than half that of men (although women perform better in secondary school), and women law students do just as well as their male counterparts in obtaining honors degrees.

Two factors seem responsible for the difference and are difficult to separate. First, barristers still make more particularistic decisions about entrants. Women encounter greater problems than do men in securing pupillages and many more obstacles in obtaining both tenancies and business during the early years of practice. The first two decisions are controlled by heads of chambers, most of whom are elderly men likely to retain prejudices against women barristers. The third is influenced significantly by senior clerks, also mostly men, whose patriarchal views may be reinforced by the belief that women tenants will charge lower fees than men and thus earn the clerk less income. Where, as in Scotland, advocates practice individually rather than in chambers and are served by a common pool of clerks, women have come to represent half of all new advocates.

The second explanation for the low proportion of women barristers turns on structural factors rather than individual prejudices. It is extremely difficult to combine a career at the Bar with family responsibilities, either by working part time or by leaving practice and returning after child-rearing. By contrast, employment in a firm, a company, or a government office may open one or both possibilities to women solicitors. Whether individual or institutional biases are dominant, their effect is visible in the fact that women law students express a stronger preference than men for becoming solicitors and a weaker preference for the Bar.

The experience of black lawyers has been almost the opposite of that of women. Blacks from the colonies have been called to the Bar since at least the early nineteenth century, although few, if any, practiced in England. Indeed, in 1960, three-quarters of all Bar students were from overseas. With the growth of both law faculties and nationalism in the newly independent countries, however, this proportion rapidly declined. At the same time, as the black population of England increased, so did the number of black barristers, which now approximates 5 percent of the Bar. Blacks have responded to discrimination in the allocation of tenancies and briefs by forming all black chambers serving a largely black clientele. By contrast, there is no tradition of black solicitors; indeed, noncitizens were not admitted to this branch until 1974. For this reason, and also because of the greater difficulty of the solicitors' examinations and the larger size of the solicitors' branch, the approximately 200 black solicitors now in practice represent only 0.25 percent of the profession. The Bar, which relies more heavily on ascriptive criteria, paradoxically has been more open to racial minorities. The shift to qualification through the academy also has led to a second paradox. On one hand, the academy has admitted—indeed, actively recruited—an increasing number of overseas law students, whose tuition payments subsidize the cost of educating domestic students (just as the fees of overseas Bar students subsidized the Inns in the 1950s and 1960s, most of whose benefits were enjoyed by domestic white barristers). On the other hand, heightened competition for places in law departments has made legal education less accessible to domestic black applicants disadvantaged by inadequate primary and secondary schooling. The move from professional ascription to academic meritocracy thus has not greatly eased the path for racial minorities.

Nor has that transformation significantly affected the class composition of the profession. The traditional claim by barristers that they enjoy a superior social status was derived partly from the higher proportion of university graduates among them and the Bar's more exclusive ascriptive barriers. Yet the emergence of common qualifications for the two branches, and particularly the expectation that entrants to both will possess a law degree, seem to have erased these differences. Several independent studies in the late 1970s confirmed that Bar students and articled clerks had very similar class backgrounds. Convergence has been achieved by *narrowing* class composition, however, not broadening it. One reason is the centrality of the academy, which always has selected disproportionately from the upper social stata and continues to do so even after the creation of the polytechnics. This bias, ironically, was amplified by the elimination of another ascriptive barrier—gender. As the numbers seeking entry to law departments effectively doubled, competition for places intensified. Indeed, because women still must overcome substantial social and cultural barriers, those who succeed tend to come from even more privileged backgrounds than men law students.

The emergence of the academy as the principal gatekeeper to the legal profession thus made a major contribution to eliminating gender as an ascriptive barrier but, simultaneously, magnified the barrier of class and provided a new legitimation for the barrier of race. Furthermore, although we lack the data to test these hypotheses, it seems plausible to expect that class and race influence which academic institution a student attends and the quality of degree the student attains and that these, in turn, determine the nature of the apprenticeship and the first position the student obtains after qualifying. The academy thus not only is more selective but also performs the indispensable function of allocating graduates to positions within the professional hierarchy and justifying that allocation in meritocratic terms.

LIMITING COMPETITION

In order to control the market for its services, a profession must seek to regulate not only the production *of* producers but also production *by* producers. This occurs only at a later stage of the professional project: an occupational category that limited the competitive energies of its own members before they had demarcated themselves from other service providers quickly would succumb to outside competitors who were not similarly restrained. Control of production *by* producers also can enhance the status of the profession by disclaiming crass economic motives. We can distinguish two types of control over production by producers: the definition and defense of the professional monopoly against external competitors and the elaboration of restrictive practices limiting internal competition. These tend to occur sequentially.

MONOPOLY

The legal profession's attempt to define its monopoly was complicated by the existence of two branches concerned with patrolling the boundaries that divide them as well as those that exclude other occupations. During the course of the nineteenth century barristers and solicitors reached an accommodation (although not without considerable dissension): solicitors ceased to challenge the Bar's exclusive right of audience in the higher courts, and barristers relinquished any claim to perform conveyances (real estate transactions) or to serve clients without the intermediation of solicitors. The Bar has been very successful in defending its turf, perhaps because advocacy occupies the core of the legal profession's identity and is a highly visible activity, whose elaborate ritual and arcane language proclaim the esoteric qualities of law. Furthermore, solicitors share with barristers a common interest in excluding outsiders from the courts.

On the other hand, barristers and solicitors are opposed in their struggle over the right of audience in the higher courts, which traditionally also has conferred eligibility for appointment to the bench—not only a prize for those few who attain it but also an important foundation for the Bar's collective assertion of superior status. The greater difficulty of justifying a monopoly against fellow lawyers may help to explain the vigor with which the Bar opposed nineteenth-century proposals for common training with solicitors. Yet, the recent convergence of the two branches in terms of background, education, and qualifications may weaken the Bar's defenses. At the same time, the erosion of supply control among solicitors may stimulate the latter to press their claims more strongly. The historic compromise between the branches survived the Royal Commission inquiry of the late 1970s, in which the Law Society (unsuccessfully) sought only a modest expansion of solicitors' rights of audience. However, the recent threat of losing the conveyancing monopoly led to an immediate demand for equality with barristers. Although the Government summarily rejected this claim, its concern to cut costs, together with the fact that it presently pays for half of all barristers' services, renders the Bar's monopoly precarious. Even if it is not abolished, the monopoly still may be eroded through the progressive expansion of lower-court jurisdiction, increased use of employed lawyers (solicitors as well as barristers), and the grant to solicitors of specific, if not general, rights of audience. Nevertheless, barristers may preserve a good deal of the market for higher-court advocacy by means of informal conventions despite the demise of formal rules.

Solicitors always have had greater difficulty defining and defending their monopoly. Much of what they do is less visible and less obviously technical than higher-court advocacy. Unlike lawyers in the United States and some Canadian provinces, English solicitors never claimed a monopoly over legal advice. Furthermore, whereas solicitors have been quite restrained in challenging the Bar, lay competitors have been far more aggressive in invading the domain of solicitors. Banks and trust companies, accountants, real estate agents, companies, and trade unions all perform solicitors' work for their customers, employees, and members. The lay public also seems less tolerant of the solicitors' monopoly than they are of the barristers' exclusive right of audience, perhaps because consumers encounter the former more often and more directly. Public resentment was most visible, of course, in the long-standing critique of the conveyancing monopoly. Recent legislation has forced solicitors to share it with a new paraprofession of licensed conveyancers; however, there is continuing uncertainty about the role of banks and building societies (savings and loan associations). On first impression this incursion, which solicitors vigorously resisted, appears to be an awesome loss, without precedent in the annals of any other profession, for solicitors derive half of their incomes from conveyancing. Yet, the ultimate consequences are unpredictable. The change will be felt more heavily by smaller firms, which typically earn a higher proportion of their income from conveyancing. In order to remain competitive, they will have to expand their volume through advertising, routinize conveyancing through computerization, and transfer work to paraprofessionals, all of which will foster concentration and render solicitors more like their lay competitors—that is, less professional. At the same time, solicitors may find themselves challenged from another direction for the first time in a century. Barristers, pressed by their own loss of supply control, threatened by solicitors, and perhaps concerned with allaying criticism about the wastefulness of the divided profession, may renew their demands to deal directly with other professionals (such as accountants and employed barristers) and possibly even with lay clients.

The monopoly of each branch is threatened not only by the other branch and by outsiders but also from within: by employed barristers and solicitors, whose numbers are expanding because private practice is able to absorb a declining proportion of the influx of new entrants produced by the erosion of supply control (see table 2). The significance of these emergent categories is threefold. First, the demarcation between employed barristers and employed solicitors is far more tenuous than the line that separates the branches in private practice. Both categories not only share a common training but also may work for the same employer and perform similar tasks. Consistent with this, their monopolies have converged: employed barristers lack a right of audience in the higher courts. Second, employed lawyers are less protected from competition with other occupational categories, such as accountants, civil servants, and city managers. Third, the number of employed lawyers is augmented by reason of heightened demand as well as greater supply: clients (public and private) may prefer to employ lawyers rather than retain private practitioners because the former are less expensive and more easily controlled. Moreover, having put lawyers on their payroll, employers are likely to add their own voices to the call for expanding the rights of audience of employed lawyers and for allowing all employed barristers to perform conveyances and to brief barristers in private practice without the intervention of a solicitor.

INTRAPROFESSIONAL RESTRICTIONS

Private practitioners seek to control their market not only by regulating the production of services by outsiders (laypersons, the other branch, and employed lawyers) but also by limiting competition from fellow professionals. Just as barristers were first to control the production *of* producers, so they anticipated solicitors in elaborating a set of restrictive practices. Initially informal, these progressively were formalized during the nineteenth century as the Bar grew in size and subgroups declined in importance (such as the circuits—barristers who traveled with high court judges when they sat outside London). Formalization also publicized the rules, rendering them more vulnerable to external criticism. Consequently, the Bar recently has been forced to relax several of its more conspicuous restrictive practices: the two-counsel rule (a Queen's Counsel always must be assisted by a junior barrister), the two-thirds rule (a junior barrister who assists a Queen's Counsel must be paid two-thirds of the latter's fee), and barriers to practice on the circuits (extra fees that must be charged by a barrister who appears in a circuit but is not a member of that circuit).

This sequence illustrates the peculiar situation of the Bar: on one hand, the nature of its market makes the restriction of competition particularly urgent; on the other hand, its internal structure facilitates such restriction through informal means. The production and sale of barristers' services resembles the ideal of the free market more than do most such exchanges. The performance of barristers in court is highly visible to potential consumers (i.e., solicitors), and the measures of success or failure are superficially clear (if actually ambiguous). More importantly, the solicitor-consumers are themselves professionals and thus unusually well equipped to judge quality. Also, at least some of those consumers—the larger firms—possess considerable economic leverage by virtue of the amount of business they can offer. In the absence of restrictive practices (and without professional control over the production *of* producers), barristers would be driven to compete vigorously in terms of price and quality.

The Bar has minimized this danger in several ways. First, it has drastically curtailed competition between younger and older age cohorts by means of an artificial barrier between Queen's Counsel and juniors, which grants each a submonopoly (Queen's Counsel over advocacy in "heavier" cases, juniors over the preliminary stages of litigation). The production of Queen's Counsel, unlike the production of barristers, remains tightly controlled by the Lord Chancellor (who himself is a barrister). Second, the Bar has dampened horizontal competition among juniors. Although barristers still cannot form partnerships with each other (much less with solicitors or other professionals), the Bar is not simply an aggregation of 5,000 individual competitors. Rather, it is grouped into about 200 sets in London and another 100 in some two dozen provincial cities; there is little competition between barristers in different cities. London sets are prevented from proliferating by the formal requirement of a clerk, the informal but effective restriction to the Inns, and the limited accommodation available within each Inn. Third, the London market is differentiated further by subject-matter specialization. Fourth, the homogeneity of social background and function among barristers and their geographic concentration within the Inns (and within similar settings in most provincial cities) facilitate informal control. To the extent that the Bar has grown more hetereogeneous, the newer elements—especially black barristers—tend to form distinct markets. Finally, barristers are subject to hierarchic controls that reward conformity to restrictive practices: pupils are subordinate to pupilmasters and to those who allocate tenancies, younger barristers are subordinate to their heads of chambers and clerks, juniors who aspire to become Queen's Counsel are subordinate to judges who advise the Lord Chancellor, and even Queen's Counsel who seek appointment to the bench remain subordinate to the Lord Chancellor and the judges who advise him.

The very characteristics that allowed the Bar to establish control over the production *of* producers in the first place and to reassert it after the academy introduced more meritocratic entry criteria thus also allow it to preserve control over production *by* producers through informal means, even after the demise of formal rules. A Queen's Counsel still insists that a junior be briefed, and the junior still demands two-thirds of the leader's fee. Barrister's clerks establish ongoing relationships with solicitors' firms, which allow the clerk to refer work to other chambers (because no barrister is free or because the set does not handle that speciality) without fear of losing the firm as a future client. A barrister will decline to accept a client who already has briefed another barrister unless the latter consents. Barristers continue to charge and receive the full brief fee even if the case is settled (as most are) and to bill separate fees for multiple clients in a single matter even if their representation does not increase the complexity of the task. Perhaps most importantly, the small number of chambers, and thus of barrister's clerks, and the intimate relations among the latter allow them to reach informal understandings about the level of fees.

The restrictive practices of solicitors are different in several respects. First, the market for solicitors' services is less freely competitive. Although there are many more productive units (because solicitors outnumber barristers by almost ten to one and firms are smaller than chambers on average), the market for individual consumers is highly localized. Furthermore, unlike the solicitor who selects and evaluates barristers' services, the individual consumer of solicitors' services is a layperson who is likely to have little prior experience with law or lawyers. Such a client's relationships with solicitors generally are sporadic rather than continuous, and the lay consumer will encounter extreme difficulty in obtaining accurate information about price or quality. Consequently, not only does the solicitor-consumer have distinct advantages in purchasing barristers' services but the solicitor-producer also has distinct advantages in selling services to individual consumers (although not, of course, to companies or other institutions). It is striking that the relationship of each branch to its market is the obverse of the stereotype: solicitors paradoxically are *more* "independent" than barristers. Perhaps, then, one function of restrictive practices is to correct this disparity: to make barristers more "independent" of consumers and solicitors less so. Such an interpretation draws support from the fact that one of the most important restrictions on solicitors —the regulation of fees in contentious matters (litigation)—is imposed externally.

Because solicitors, when compared to barristers, are more numerous, geographically dispersed, and heterogeneous in background, organization, and function, restrictive practices also must be more formal. The Law Society promulgated ethical rules long before the Bar felt the need to formalize its own etiquette, therefore, and it regulated subjects, such as advertising and fees in noncontentious matters, that the Bar still leaves to informal controls. These rules and others—the limitation on the number of partners in a firm, the prohibitions on practicing another occupation, forming a partnership with other professions, or even sharing office space with other occupations, and the restriction on employed solicitors accepting private work from fellow employees—all served to dampen intra-professional competition. Several of these restrictive practices, like those of barristers, have succumbed to attack in recent years, however. The ceiling of twenty partners was lifted in 1967, with the result that forty-six firms now exceed that number; of these, two have at least sixty partners, three have fifty to fifty-nine, five have forty to forty-nine, and thirteen have thirty to thirty-nine. Scale fees (minima) were abolished five years later, although prices stayed level or even rose. And in 1984 the Law Society relaxed its ban on advertising, under pressure from external critics.

It seems unlikely that solicitors can continue to suppress competition by relying on the informal understandings that have worked so well for barristers. First, the same market characteristics that allow solicitors to dominate individual clients also encourage a firm that wishes to increase its market share to establish branch offices, merge with other firms, cut prices, and engage in aggressive advertising. Legal clinics successfully have pursued such strategies in the United States. Second, even if solicitors themselves are averse to such marketing strategies, they may be forced to adopt them by the threat of lay competition, especially now that the conveyancing monopoly has been diluted and perhaps broken. Whereas barristers may continue to control production by producers through informal understandings, solicitors thus seem likely to face increasingly unconstrained competition from outside the profession as well as within.

STIMULATING DEMAND

Historically, lawyers sought to control their market by limiting supply before they turned to the alternative strategy of creating demand. True, lawyers are at least partly responsible for the fact that substantive and procedural laws are so complex that laypersons must hire professionals both to litigate and to perform noncontentious transactions, such as conveyances and the distribution of estates. However, neither the institutional infrastructure nor the legitimating ideology for large-scale demand creation existed before the emergence of the welfare state after World War II. Furthermore, it is the recent erosion of professional control over the production *of* and *by* producers that motivated lawyers to seek to stimulate demand. But I do not want to overstate the argument that professions have shifted from supply to demand as the principal locus of market control: lawyers have done so slowly, reluctantly, and ineffectively. Once again, the two branches diverge in their strategies.

BARRISTERS AND THE PUBLIC SECTOR

In many ways, the Bar has encountered greater difficulty in influencing demand. Few people can be persuaded to engage in litigation voluntarily. Indeed, the principal sources of increased demand for barristers' services— criminal and matrimonial cases—are matters over which the profession has no control whatsoever. Barristers may, however, be the passive beneficiaries of solicitors' efforts to stimulate demand for their own services. All that barristers realistically can do to influence demand is seek to ensure that those who must litigate actually do retain counsel (a decision that often is made by the solicitor rather than the lay client). In pursuing this goal, barristers enjoy certain advantages: the state's obligation to provide legal assistance is less problematic in court than outside and less problematic in criminal proceedings than in civil; and there are no functional equivalents to barristers as advocates (as there are for solicitors as advisors, drafters, and negotiators).

The means of guaranteeing representation, of course, has been legal aid. Yet, the impetus for its creation cannot be attributed to the professional project of market control. First, the inspiration for civil legal aid originated with a Labour Government, not with the legal profession. Second, the institution emerged at a time when the supply of barristers actually was declining and traditional restrictive practices were firmly in place. Nevertheless, the growth of the Bar from the early 1960s clearly is inseparable from the expanding legal aid budget generated by rising crime and divorce rates, regardless of whether legal aid is seen as the cause of eroding supply control—encouraging law students to enter the Bar confident that they would be able to survive the early years of practice—or as a response to numbers that were augmented by other causes. Barristers derived more than a quarter of their incomes from legal aid in 1974/75—43 percent from all public funds (which also includes fees for prosecution). For all juniors, the proportions were almost a third and almost a half; indeed, juniors with a London criminal practice derived about two-thirds of their incomes from legal aid in 1976/77—more than 90 percent from all public funds.

The state thus paid for the doubling of the Bar. Furthermore, it did so without much effort on the part of barristers. Although the Bar has advocated greater client eligibility and more generous payments to barristers, much of the growth of the legal aid budget is attributable to the extrinsic social phenomena that generate demand for legal services, such as crime and divorce. Nor has the Bar had to worry about the impact of these new sources of demand on the distribution, and particularly the concentration, of business. Legal aid work is allocated to barristers in much the same fashion as are briefs from private clients: by solicitors dealing with barrister's clerks. Nevertheless, the dependence of the Bar on legal aid does pose new and significant problems. First, the state is both more powerful than many private clients and less willing to acquiesce in the Bar's restrictive practices: it sets the fees for criminal legally aided work, and legal aid committees decide whether a Queen's Counsel is required and whether the latter needs the assistance of a junior. These externally imposed conditions may become the conventions for private clients as well. Second, a Bar that derives half of its income from the state no longer can make as persuasive an argument for its independence and altruism—and thus for its claim to be a profession. Ironically, the very foundation of the Bar's strength—its monopoly of advocacy—has become a source of dependence.

SOLICITORS AND THE PRIVATE MARKET

In one respect, the situation of solicitors is similar. They also are unable to influence the single most important source of demand. Conveyancing, which has provided half of the income of solicitors for at least a century, rises and falls with the economy. Fortunately, the dramatic growth in the production of solicitors during the last two decades coincided with an equally pronounced (if considerably more erratic) increase in the value of housing, superimposed on a long-term rise in the prevalence of home ownership and the geographic mobility of the population. This may be part of the reason why solicitors have been so passive in the face of incursions by accountants and members of other occupations in the fields of tax advice, government regulation, and general business counseling. As real estate values stabilize or decline and solicitors lose some or all of their conveyancing monopoly, however, they will have to look elsewhere for new demand.

Unlike barristers, solicitors have not relied heavily on legal aid. One reason is that solicitors have earned only a quarter of their incomes from contentious work and only a small proportion of this from cases that are likely to be legally aided, such as criminal defense (4 percent), personal injuries (3 percent), and matrimonial matters (5 percent). Although solicitors render virtually all the legal advice defrayed by public funds, this generates a trivial proportion of their earnings. In 1975/76, legal aid accounted for only 6 percent of gross solicitor income. Solicitors remain less interested than barristers in legal aid because they find such work relatively unprofitable. Since solicitors have rights of audience only in the lower courts, the cases that they can handle are less serious and consequently command smaller fees; and the legal advice scheme also discourages lengthy or elaborate consultations. Legal aid matters can be processed profitably only when they are mass-produced. Consequently, whereas most barristers do a fair amount of legal aid work, at least in the early stages of their careers, and thus share a collective interest in the institution, only about a third of all solicitors' firms earn even a tenth of their incomes from this source.

Other forms of demand creation also pose serious problems for solicitors. It is not much easier to encourage individuals to use law facilitatively than it is to induce them to litigate. Moreover, whereas the intermediaries who select barristers are solicitors, the potential clients of solicitors are laypeople. Even if the latter may be more impressionable (a dubious assumption), they also are more difficult to reach because they are more numerous, more anonymous, and much less interested in legal services. Solicitors thus face a dilemma. They can engage in advertising directed at their mass market—indeed, the Law Society launched several institutional campaigns in the 1970s and recently allowed individual solicitors to advertise. Such efforts are likely to be expensive and relatively unprofitable, however, at least unless the investment is substantial and continuous over a long period. Alternatively, they can focus their informational activities on populations likely to need and want solicitors' services. This strategy also has substantial drawbacks. Even more than advertising, it smacks of commericalism and thus endangers the claim of solicitors to professional status. And it runs the risk of encouraging dependence on the favor of occupations that channel clients to solicitors—police, for instance, who advise criminal accused, or real estate agents who counsel home buyers. (Barristers, by contrast, fully control the subordinated occupational category that performs a similar function for them—the barrister's clerk.)

But the greatest problem is that successful efforts to create demand inevitably tend to affect its distribution. Cost-effective demand creation thus not only impairs the solicitors' image of noncommercialism but also intensifies intraprofessional competition. Advertising by an individual firm probably is a good deal more productive than the institutional campaigns of the Law Society, but it benefits only that firm. Direct solicitation of clients is even more efficient but has even fewer spill-over effects. The problem becomes more acute when public resources are used to create demand, for then all qualified producers seem to feel an entitlement to share equally in the additional business generated. Such a belief may underlie the Law Society's dissemination of lists of solicitors willing to handle legal aid matters, the rapid proliferation of Duty Solicitor schemes (which provide an initial solicitor contact to all those arrested), the rosters of solicitors who volunteer to work at or take referrals from Citizens Advice Bureaus, and the initial hostility of solicitors to law centers (legal aid offices) thought to concentrate publicly subsidized work among employed lawyers. Whereas the Bar runs the risk of losing its independence when it turns to publicly created demand, solicitors thus run the risk of intensifying intraprofessional competition when they seek to stimulate demand in the private market.

THE SOCIAL ORGANIZATION OF THE PROFESSION

Both the strategies and the successes of the professional project of market control influence, and are affected by, the social organization of the two branches. We can trace these linkages by examining differentiation within the legal profession, the nature of the productive unit, and the consequences of both for stratification.

INTERNAL DIFFERENTIATION

The nineteenth century was a period of professional consolidation, the end product of which was the present division into two main branches. The separate category of serjeants (from which judges had been drawn) was abolished in 1873. That same year the merger of law and equity reduced the distinctiveness of the Chancery Bar and formally eliminated the demarcation between solicitors and attorneys. Doctors of Law and proctors disappeared with the closure of ecclesiastical and admiralty courts. Special pleaders and conveyancers, who had emerged several hundred years earlier in response to the enormous complexities of pleading and of encumbering and transferring land, had vanished by the end of the nineteenth century. Therefore, the rationalization of courts and the decline in certain legal functions reduced professional differentiation.

The fundamental division of the profession into two branches persisted and even rigidified (although it did not fully survive transplantation to any of the colonial legal systems whose inspiration was English). For the relationship between barristers and solicitors, although often tense, ultimately is symbiotic. Solicitors, for their part, enjoy greater economic leverage. Larger firms wield considerable patronage through the distribution of briefs. Smaller firms derive economic power (if less legitimately) from their ability to delay payments to barristers, although the Bar recently has begun to retaliate. Barristers, however, can decline or return briefs and control the scheduling of work. Furthermore, the greater economic security of solicitors is counterbalanced by the superior social status of barristers—itself a composite of history, ascribed characteristics, functions, conventions of deference, the visibility of a few stars, and an exclusive relationship with the bench.

If the division into two branches seems relatively fixed, there have been significant changes in differentiation within each. The Bar always has been more centralized. Until recently, the higher courts in which barristers practice sat primarily in London and made only brief forays outside. The principal educational institutions—the Inns of Court (and later their School of Law)—also are located in London. Moreover, barristers' clients were either London solicitors or the London agents of provincial solicitors. Consequently, virtually all barristers practiced in London until the end of the nineteenth century. With the growth of provincial courts and the decline of circuits, however, provincial chambers expanded rapidly, containing a quarter of the Bar by the 1950s and nearly a third today. Solicitors, by contrast, serve clients who are scattered throughout the country (especially given the dominant role of residential conveyancing). They are excluded from the higher London courts. By the end of the nineteenth century they had established a number of provincial training centers for articled clerks, who naturally are found wherever there are solicitors. It is not surprising, therefore, that the distribution of solicitors for the last hundred years has been the inverse of the present distribution of barristers: two-thirds have practiced in the provinces and only a third in London. On this measure, as on others, the Bar enjoys greater social cohesiveness (although less than it had in the past), a fact that may help to explain the different role of professional associations in the two branches.

A second parameter along which differentiation has increased is employment (see table 2). Although we lack adequate data, it seems unlikely that any barristers were employed until the beginning of the twentieth century, at the earliest. Today, approximately half of those called to the Bar are employed by government or private enterprise. Some solicitors always have been employed in private practice; more recently, they have been employed by government (especially local government) and by commerce and industry. Consequently, employed solicitors rose from a quarter of those holding practicing certificates in 1939 to a third in 1957 and a half today. Furthermore, since many employed solicitors do not take out practicing certificates, the proportion must be even larger. Nevertheless, although a larger proportion of solicitors than barristers are employed, employment creates greates divisions within the Bar. Employed barristers need not complete a pupillage, they lack rights of audience, they do not observe Bar etiquette and are not subject to Bar discipline, and few ever enter private practice (although movement in the other direction is possible). Solicitors, by contrast, suffer no disabilities by virtue of employment. Moreover, although there is relatively little mobility between private practice and employment by public or private entities, *all* private practitioners spend at least three years as assistant solicitors employed by firms, and most spend the bulk of their professional lives as partners employing assistant solicitors. The growth of employment, like the geographic shifts described above, thus has had a greater effect on the social integration of the Bar than on that of solicitors.

The category of private practitioners is further differentiated in terms of clients served and subject matter handled. Here, again, the Bar has changed more profoundly. Not only is the Bar as a whole more dependent on public funds, but the degree of dependence varies greatly with the barrister's age and specialty, from 1.5 percent of the income of London Chancery and specialist Queen's Counsel to 91.7 percent for London juniors with a criminal practice. Even many "independent" practitioners thus are virtually employed by the state at the beginning of their careers. Most solicitors, by contrast, earn little or none of their incomes from legal aid; but the 5 percent who specialized in such matters earned a third of the £100 million in public funds paid to solicitors for contentious business in 1980/81. Both branches thus are witnessing the emergence of a dual market, one public and the other private, although the lines of division are very different.

Barristers and solicitors also differ in the nature and extent of subject-matter specialization. Barristers' chambers tend to specialize, rejecting briefs that fall outside their expertise. Most solicitors' firms are more generalist, although individual lawyers will specialize within the larger firms. Indeed, almost all smaller firms (which contain the vast majority of private practitioners) perform the same broad range of work, the core of which is conveyancing; in this they resemble the local greengrocer, chemist, or stationer, whose market niche depends on geographic convenience. This difference between the branches presumably reflects the fact that the clients of barristers are solicitors, who can channel work to specialist chambers, whereas the clients of solicitors are laypeople, who must be offered a full range of services in order to attract and retain their business. Therefore, a profession that had only three main divisions at the turn of the century—the bench, the Bar, and solicitors—now has many more— employed barristers and solicitors, private practitioners who rely largely on public funds, and specialist chambers. (In addition, academic lawyers have increased in numbers and prominence as a result of the new role of formal education.)

STRUCTURES OF PRODUCTION

When we turn from the social organization of the profession as a whole to the structure of the units within which private practitioners produce services, we find further changes in both size and composition, as well as significant differences between the branches. As a result of changes in the market for their services (in both supply and demand), solicitors' firms have grown, and their membership has altered. In 1802 the median solicitors' firm had 1.2 principals. A century and a half later the median firm had only 2.5 principals, three-quarters of all firms had fewer than four principals, and 93 percent had fewer than six. Even in 1979, 58 percent of all firms had only one or two principals, and 82 percent had fewer than five. Thus the bulk of solicitors' services still are produced within relatively small units. To the extent that this situation reflects the comfortable market niche secured by the conveyancing monopoly, it is likely to change as a result of incursions by licensed conveyancers and the competition that this fosters among solicitors (consequences that will be even more pronounced if banks and building societies are allowed to perform conveyances). As the erosion of market control makes it more difficult to extract the customary profits from clients, solicitors will be forced to intensify the extraction of surplus value from subordinates, a development that I discuss further below. Competition also fosters concentration. One likely trend is the expansion of firms through the creation of suburban branch offices; in 1978, for instance, a third of all firms already had at least two offices, and a tenth had three or more.

Furthermore, even if the median productive unit has remained small, a few large firms have emerged since World War II. I found none with more than ten principals prior to the war and only a dozen with as many as five. Yet, five firms had ten or more principals by 1950, twelve had reached this level by 1960, ten had at least twenty principals by 1970, and forty-six are this large today; the largest contains more than 200 solicitors. More than 3,000 solicitors, or 7 percent of those holding practicing certificates, belong to these forty-six large firms. Among the twenty-nine City firms with at least twenty principals, twenty had offices abroad—an average of 2.6 branch offices per firm.

The growth of these larger firms is partly a response to the size of their corporate clients and the need to specialize in order to handle more complex and more varied legal problems. But it also is related to changes in the use of subordinated labor, the explanation for which is both historical and economic. During the 1960s, managing clerks waged a partly successful campaign to professionalize. Legal executives, as they now were called, made somewhat awkward employees, for they were of the same age and gender as their employers and often from a similar social class, some were just as well trained, and they stayed long enough to expect advancement. The tensions within this relationship have been ameliorated in two ways. First, the role of legal executive has been significantly feminized: almost half of the "fellows" admitted by the Institute of Legal Executives (ILEX) in 1983/84 were women. The sexual division of labor and the patriarchal subordination of women both reinforce the male employer's authority. Second, some legal executives have been replaced by assistant solicitors; although 60 percent of the latter still are male, all are temporary employees, moving either up to partnerships or out to other positions. Their transitory subordination is more easily justified as training. The enormous increase in the production of solicitors, together with the rule requiring all new entrants to work as employees for three years before setting up on their own or in partnership with another, have provided a constant supply of eager recruits. There has been a concomitant decline in the number of new ILEX fellows since the 1960s and in the numbers of new ILEX students and associates since the 1970s. In the ten years during 1966 to 1976, the number of legal executives remained constant, while the number of articled clerks increased by a third, and the number of assistant solicitors grew almost 90 percent, with the result that the ratio of assistant solicitors to principals rose while the ratio of legal executives to principals fell.

These changes in the labor force may have been motivated by considerations of profitability as well as the fact that trainee solicitors were more available and perhaps more docile. The difference between the cost of labor to firms and its price to clients (i.e., the surplus value extracted) is greatest for assistant solicitors and least for legal executives, with articled clerks falling in between. The profitability of using the labor of assistant solicitors also increases with firm size; so does the ratio of assistant solicitors to principals. In 1976 the average firm with ten principals or more had twice as many assistants per principal as the smaller firms (although only a third again as many legal executives); in 1984/85, the average firm with sixty principals or more had two and a half times as many assistants per principal as did the firm with twenty to thirty principals. This more intensive and extensive exploitation of subordinated labor undoubtedly is part of the reason for the higher incomes enjoyed by principals in the larger firms. At the same time, only the larger firms can increase at a rate that holds out to assistants the possibility of a partnership whose rewards outweigh the sacrifices of a prolonged apprenticeship. If I am correct in attributing the growth of solicitors' firms to the relative availability, pliancy, and profitability of assistant solicitors as subordinates, we can expect further divergence between small and large firms in terms of the labor they employ. Solicitors may be fissioning into the two hemispheres whose polarization characterizes the American legal profession.

The structure of practice at the Bar has changed even more radically, but in different directions. Although most nineteenth century barristers (like most solicitors) practiced alone, by the late 1950s the average set contained more than seven barristers in London and five in the provinces. These figures have grown steadily to more than sixteen barristers per set in London today and twelve in the provinces. The emergence of large sets is a recent phenomenon: only 5 percent of London sets had more than fifteen barristers in 1965, whereas half did so by 1976. Today, nearly three-fourths of London sets contain at least fifteen barristers (excluding those in Lincoln's Inn, where Chancery practices tend to be smaller), and so do more than half of all provincial sets. Furthermore, unlike solicitors, few barristers still practice in small groups: a quarter of all London sets and half of all provincial sets contained fewer than six barristers in 1961, but now only 3 percent of London sets and 9 percent of provincial sets contain fewer than five barristers. Only 2 of the 336 sets have thirty barristers or more, however, and the largest, with forty-five barristers, does not begin to approach the size of the larger solicitors' firms.

Chambers have grown for some of the same reasons that impelled the expansion of solicitors' firms. Size confers its own prestige; together with internal diversity or "balance" among the members of a set (in terms of subject-matter specialization, length of experience, and reputation), it attracts and keeps business. Like firms (if to a lesser degree), chambers can benefit from economies of scale in the use of computerized billing and word processing. But the central dynamic of growth has been different because of the absence of subordinated labor: barristers in private practice cannot be employed (although young barristers may devil for older members of their chambers); and the barristers' clerk is an independent contractor, not an employee. Partners in solicitors' firms have a profound interest in the clerks they accept for articles and the assistant solicitors they hire: both will be performing work for which the partners are responsible and also are candidates for partnership. Barristers who accept pupils and heads of chambers who fill tenancies undoubtedly are concerned with the quality of those they select, but not for these reasons. Young barristers are acutely affected by the prominence of the older barristers in their chambers and the entrepreneurial skills of their clerk, however, for it is these that attract most of the work the new recruit is likely to obtain.

However, the greatest difference between chambers and firms is the role of the barristers' clerk. Whereas the work of legal executives closely resembles that of solicitors, the barristers' clerk performs *no* legal functions. Furthermore, whereas the legal executive is only minimally differentiated from the solicitor in terms of class and training and even may aspire to become a solicitor, the barristers' clerk generally comes from a working class background, has no education beyond secondary school, and never becomes a barrister. Despite these differences, the clerk is less subordinated than the legal executive or trainee solicitor and is a petty bourgeois rather than an employee. Barristers' clerks wield considerable power over the younger members of chambers: allocating briefs when solicitors have not specified a barrister or when the preferred barrister cannot accept the brief or has returned it; and influencing the selection of tenants, particularly from among pupils. Barristers' clerks also earn substantial incomes— more than most of the junior barristers in their chambers.

Most importantly, whereas solicitors' firms have grown, in part, because partners seek to enhance their profits through subordinated labor, the expansion of barristers' chambers redounds primarily to the economic benefit of senior clerks. Since most are paid a proportion of the brief fee and each set contains only one senior clerk (although the senior clerk may have to pay the salaries of the junior clerks), the senior clerk's income varies directly with the number of barristers in the set. Consequently, clerks certainly have not been unhappy about the lack of space in the Inns, which has inhibited the fission of sets. Given this space shortage, economies of scale, the self-interest of clerks, the prestige that attaches to growth and size, the commercial advantages of internal differentiation, and the relative absence of economic tensions within chambers because barristers do not share profits, we can expect further expansion. Although the unit of production has grown in both branches, this growth has very different meanings. For solicitors, it signifies the intensification of capitalist relations of production and a widening division between the larger firms that have followed this route and the smaller firms that have not. Although the prohibition of partnerships and employment at the Bar precludes this development, the growth of chambers does signify an intensification of hierarchy as greater power accrues to both the head of chambers (advised by other senior tenants) and the senior clerk.

STRATIFICATION

Inevitably, the forms of differentiation traced above also structure inequality within the profession. It is essential to distinguish stratification that is relatively permanent, and therefore threatens professional cohesion, from situations where assignment to a stratum is temporary, and mobility can strengthen professional integration. Geography affects the power, wealth, and status of practitioners in both branches, but these differences appear to generate more tension among solicitors, perhaps because the majority are located in the provinces while professional advantages are concentrated in London. The principal division among solicitors is firm size, however, which reflects clients served and functions performed and affects solicitor income and status. There appears to be little movement between large and small firms. Furthermore, recruitment to the larger firms seems to be influenced strongly by the academic institution attended and the degree attained, both of which correlate with background variables such as class.

This form of stratification is almost certain to intensify with the proliferation of large firms and their continued growth. Although barristers' chambers also differ by size and specialty, these variables do not appear to define as strongly the status of individual barristers within them, and there is increasing movement between sets. A very significant exception to both generalizations, however, are the so-called ghetto chambers occupied primarily by black barristers—a phenomenon that contradicts the universalistic pretensions of the Bar.

Other professional divisions are characterized by varying degrees of mobility. Although barristers still enjoy higher social status than do solicitors, the entry requirements of the two branches have converged, and transfer between them is far easier than it once was, if few avail themselves of the opportunity. Like all professions, those of the law hold out to their members the hope of attaining higher income, status, and power with age. But whereas most articled clerks become assistant solicitors and end as principals, and any solicitor who wishes can play a role in the local, if not the national, law society, the career ladder at the Bar is unusually long and steep, and progress up it far less certain. Not all pupils obtain tenancies; not all fledgling barristers earn their keep and remain in private practice; not all juniors become Queen's Counsel; not all Queen's Counsel become judges; and not all older barristers become heads of chambers or benchers. These status differences are reflected in income. Whereas the highest decile of solicitors earn only two-thirds more than the median and those forty years or older, only two-thirds more than those under thirty, the highest decile of barristers earn more than twice the median and those forty years or older, almost three times as much as those under thirty.

For solicitors, therefore, the problem posed by stratification is to explain the relatively permanent distribution that occurs at the beginning of legal careers: of law students among apprenticeships and of clerks who have completed their articles among law firms and other forms of employment. For the Bar, by contrast, the problem is to explain cumulative success and failure throughout a lifetime of testing. The early and irrevocable assignment of position within the system of stratification would seem to pose greater problems for the unity of solicitors than the later, more gradual, and apparently more reversible assignment of status to barristers. Stratification among solicitors has not been associated overtly with racism because there are so few blacks (although this is changing), and women have been hired by some of the larger firms in proportion to their representation among law graduates (if few have been given partnerships). At the Bar, however, it is clear that blacks, and to a lesser extent women, are severely disadvantaged. Although stratification at the Bar may be more fluid than it is among solicitors, the pretense that it simply reflects meritocratic principles—that success rewards ability and effort—thus is more thoroughly undermined by the visible correlation between the stratum attained and the race and gender of the aspirant.

PROFESSIONAL ASSOCIATIONS

In tracing the trajectory of the professional project among barristers and solicitors, I have not yet discussed the instrument through which they pursued their goals—the professional association. I will begin by describing the emergence and consolidation of structures for collective action during the nineteenth and early twentieth centuries before examining their responses to the challenges of the postwar period.

THE INSTITUTIONAL FRAMEWORK

Barristers entered the nineteenth century as a fully mature profession. They controlled entry and enjoyed an unchallenged monopoly over advocacy. Indeed, these privileges had been won so far in the past that they had acquired the unquestionable legitimacy of tradition. At the same time, the Bar's demographic and organizational characteristics facilitated informal social control. The Bar was small (less than a thousand actual practitioners), extremely homogeneous, and concentrated within a few square blocks of London. Because solicitors insulated barristers from direct client contact, the Bar was less subject to the centrifugal pressures of client loyalty. Barristers encountered fewer temptations to engage in financial misconduct, for they did not handle clients' money. Since most of their professional activities occurred in open court, they constantly were subject to the scrutiny of both judges and their fellow barristers.

Consequently, it is not surprising that formal structures for self-governance were relatively weak and highly decentralized. Each of the four Inns admitted its own students, called them to the Bar, and was responsible for discipline; however, there is no evidence that they exercised any real scrutiny over admissions or calls or took their disciplinary functions seriously. There was no official written code of conduct. The Inns had great difficulty in agreeing on common policies and generally acted independently. Each Inn was governed by its benchers—an elderly, self-perpetuating oligarchy. Content with the professional status of the Bar, they sought to contain change rather than foster it. Consequently, although the Inns cooperated in forming the Council of Legal Education in 1852, the Council had hardly any full-time staff until after World War II and attracted few students. And the Inns adopted a Bar examination in

1872 only as a reluctant concession to the example of solicitors and the threat of fusion.

During much of the nineteenth century, the circuits may have exercised more significant social control; however, their authority over entry and behavior was entirely informal and their actions even less coordinated than those of the Inns. Furthermore, their influence declined as the circuits grew in size and ultimately were supplanted by provincial bars. The only centralized professional association was the Bar Council, created at the end of the century at the initiative of younger barristers who feared that solicitors were threatening their market. More than either the Inns or the circuits, it actively sought to promote the economic interests of barristers and may have helped to formalize such restrictive practices as the two-counsel and two-thirds rules. The Bar Council derived all its financial support from the Inns, however, which were extremely parsimonious, and it enrolled only a small proportion of all barrristers. Until well after World War II, therefore, barristers were governed by a miscellany of uncoordinated institutions but actually relied on tradition and informal understandings to control their market and regulate professional behavior.

Solicitors present a marked contrast in almost every respect. At the beginning of the nineteenth century they were not a profession. It was not they, but the courts, that regulated entry, established restrictive practices, and exercised discipline. Informal controls were ineffective, for there were too many solicitors (approximately five times the number of barristers), and they were too dispersed (two-thirds were scattered across England) and heterogeneous (in both background and function). Nor did they have a viable institutional structure through which to act collectively. The eighteenth century Society of Gentlemen Practisers was moribund, and the only vital organizations were local law societies in a few provincial cities. It was precisely in order to professionalize that solicitors founded the Incorporated Law Society in the 1820s. Like all professional vanguards, the Society began as an elite organization, composed of a few London practitioners. It retained both characteristics throughout the nineteenth century: London solicitors dominated (although they were a minority of the profession); and fifty years after its inception only 25 percent of practitioners had joined. Provincial solicitors continued to invest primary loyalty in their local law societies, which formed federations that competed with the national organization until well into the twentieth century.The Law Society also was governed by elderly solicitors (the median age of council members in 1899 was sixty) who, once elected, generally served for life.

But even if the institutional structure was flawed, the Law Society energetically mobilized whatever resources it possessed to pursue the professional project. First, as we have seen, it erected the formal entry barrier of professional examinations. Although judges initially administered these, the Law Society soon took over. Solicitors were less successful in controlling production *by* producers, for the courts, rather than the Society, regulated fees and demonstrated their solicitude for the public interest by establishing maxima rather than minima. In response, the Law Society promulgated a practice rule prohibiting fee cutting and encouraged local law societies to set minimum fees at or near the judicial maxima.

Second, solicitors sought to persuade the courts to hand over disciplinary powers. The Society was authorized to present charges of misconduct to the Supreme Court in 1873, to conduct a preliminary hearing in 1888, and finally to constitute the disciplinary tribunal in 1919, although solicitors still could seek judicial review. Unlike barristers, solicitors did not rely on traditional conventions about proper behavior; ethical precepts were embodied in judicial decisions and, after the Law Society obtained statutory authority in 1933, in its practice rules.

Third, the Law Society responded to a problem that uniquely threatened the collective status of solicitors—financial misconduct. In 1901 alone, fifty-five solicitors declared bankruptcy, betraying the faith of clients whose money they held in trust accounts. In response, the Law Society successfully sought legislation making such conduct criminal; five years later it secured the right to suspend a practicing certificate on the same ground and required newly qualified solicitors to pass an examination in accounting. It also started to make ex gratia payments to clients who had suffered financial loss. In 1935, under legislative compulsion, it required solicitors to keep and report client accounts (although these rules were widely flouted and largely unenforced), and in 1942 it compelled solicitors to contribute to the compensation fund. Whereas barristers preserved their traditional decentralized institutions and relied heavily on informal control, solicitors thus created a new central institution that constantly sought to expand its formal control.

POSTWAR CHALLENGES

The changes the legal profession has experienced since World War II have induced some convergence in the structures and processes of governance in the two branches, but significant differences remain. The Bar, as we saw, has become more heterogeneous in terms of race and gender, more youthful, and more dispersed (more than a fourth of all barristers now practice primarily in provincial cities); however, governance of the Inns hardly has changed in response. There are no black benchers, although blacks constitute at least 5 percent of the Bar. Women constitute only 2 percent of the benchers, although they represent 12 percent of the Bar. In the mid-1970s, juniors constituted only 5 percent of the benchers, although they represented 90 percent of the practicing Bar. The doubling in the median size of chambers also has altered the structure of governance. On one hand, larger sets may shield their members from external influence, both formal and informal. On the other hand, the sets themselves may have become more important loci of control. Because the vast majority of heads are elderly white males, the hierarchy within chambers reinforces traditional authority. Extensive socializing among the small number of barristers' clerks strengthens this informal control. Yet a few may be able to retain some autonomy from informal influences because they have physically isolated themselves from the Inns or because their members, head, and clerk are predominately black, female, youthful, or politically dissident.

The greatest institutional transformation in the governance of barristers was the creation of the Senate of the Inns of Court and the Bar in 1966. Unlike the Bar Council (which it absorbed eight years later), the Senate enjoys both substantial resources and significant authority. Although membership is voluntary, more than 80 percent of private practitioners subscribe. In order to enhance its legitimacy, it has coopted laypersons onto certain committees, most notably those charged with discipline. Its governance still is not much more representative than that of the Inns (which continue to appoint twenty-four benchers to the Senate), however, for there are only three women and no blacks in the Senate. Furthermore, within that moiety of all barristers who are employed, probably no more than half belong to the Senate, and only 8 serve on its governing body of more than 100. In addition, although the Senate has centralized the disciplinary powers previously exercised by the four Inns, the new structure—like all forms of professional self-regulation—seems intended more to shield barristers from criticism than to change behavior or punish misconduct. Barristers, who are in the best position to observe their peers, file only 8 percent of all complaints. More than half of the complaints are dismissed without a hearing, and another quarter are either withdrawn or handled summarily. Only 3 percent of complaints between 1968 and 1982 led to disbarment, and only 1 percent led to suspension; the other 96 percent resulted in no significant penalty. In addition to these institutional changes in its structures of governance, the Senate formalized the substantive rules of ethics by promulgating the first Code of Conduct in 1980. Furthermore, dictum in a 1969 case exposing barristers to the threat of malpractice liability for noncontentious activities has led insurers to settle several claims and convinced the Senate to require barristers to carry professional indemnity insurance. Barristers today thus operate under a structure of formal, centralized self-regulation and the specter of increasing external regulation—a situation similar to that of prewar solicitors.

The Law Society also has had to cope with growing diversity in the background of solicitors, the functions that they perform, and the structures

within which they practice. Although almost all private practitioners now
belong to the Society, its governing council is not remotely representative
of the general membership. Women presently hold more than 10 percent
of practicing certificates and constitute more than 40 percent of newly
admitted solicitors, but the first woman was appointed to the seventy-
person council only in 1977. Most solicitors today are at the beginning of
their careers, but most council members are at the end of theirs. London
solicitors make up a minority of the profession, but they continue to
dominate the council. Nearly one out of every ten solicitors is a sole
practitioner, but there are none on the council; two-partner firms contain
16 percent of all principals, but such principals represent only 4 percent of
council members. Employed solicitors are underrepresented within the
Society and even more so on the council.

This disenfranchisement not only has caused tension and apathy within
the Society but also has led to the emergence and growth of rival organizations. Local law societies continue to champion the parochial interests of
their members. There are specialized associations representing London
litigators, criminal solicitors, local government solicitors, employed solicitors, and now legal aid practitioners. The creation of the British Legal
Association in the 1960s and its survival for two decades reflects the
persistent dissatisfaction of younger solicitors, provincial solicitors, and
solo and small firm practitioners. In addition, two other organizational
structures threaten to compete with and perhaps even to supplant the professional association. Large firm principals, although still a minority, are
likely to insist on governing their own domain, resisting interference
by professional associations. At the other end of the status hierarchy,
articled clerks, assistant solicitors, and junior employees in government or
industry may prefer trade unionism to professionalism. That hallmark of a
profession—the capacity to act collectively through a single organization
—which solicitors struggled to attain during the nineteenth century,
appears to be fragmenting as the interests of discrete and sometimes
antagonistic segments are expressed through forms that may be antitheti-
cal to professionalism.

The institutions of self-regulation created by the Law Society in the
early twentieth century have been strained by postwar changes. Although
complaints per solicitor appear to have increased, many instances of misconduct still are overlooked. Solicitors, who are best situated to detect
misconduct, file only 14 percent of the complaints. Clients also are reluctant to make accusations; only a third of those with grievances complained
to anyone, and only 6 percent of complainants (or 2 percent of all ag-
grieved clients) addressed the Law Society. Even so, there are more than
five times as many complaints per solicitor as there are for each barrister,
probably because solicitors have so much more client contact. Yet Law

Society discipline, like that of the Senate, exculpates far more than it punishes. More than two-thirds of all complaints are found unjustified by the investigative body (the Professional Purposes Committee), and others are terminated with only a reprimand. In those cases sent to the Disciplinary Tribunal, less than half of the solicitors are struck from the roll or suspended. In summary, the Society punished less than 1 percent of all solicitors who were the object of complaints between 1973 and 1979. Public dissatisfaction with this record, together with periodic scandals, have led the Society to appoint lay members to the Disciplinary Tribunal, establish a Lay Observer to hear complaints about the disciplinary process, and, most recently, add laypersons to the Professional Purposes Committee (in response to the Glanville Davies affair); however, these reforms appear to have achieved neither a significant voice for the laity nor the restoration of public confidence.

Self-regulation has been threatened from other directions as well. First, although the Society hired a staff to investigate solicitor accounts in 1945 and has enlarged it steadily, the compensation fund has had to make increasingly greater payments to the clients of defaulting solicitors, rising from about £100,000 a year in the 1960s to nearly £2,000,000 in 1984 —an increase that far outstrips the combined effect of inflation and the growth of the profession. Given the sums involved, it is not clear how long the Law Society can preserve this as an ex gratia scheme rather than a legal liability. Second, more clients are charging solicitors with malpractice. In the 1960s, only about half of all solicitors carried malpractice insurance, and less than 10 percent were sued each year. The Law Society required insurance in 1976, and one index of the greater frequency, magnitude, and success of malpractice claims is the fact that premiums doubled in the next four years. Furthermore, the apportionment of the Law Society's master premium among solicitors recently became a point of bitter contention between the larger City firms and small firms and sole practitioners, leading to an upsurge in support for the position of the British Legal Association. Competence increasingly is evaluated by the courts rather than the Law Society, therefore, and there is a real danger that the latter also will lose some or all of its authority to punish ethical violations and to deal with financial misconduct.

THE TRAJECTORY OF PROFESSIONALISM

BARRISTERS AND SOLICITORS AS ALTERNATIVE MODELS

The history of barristers and solicitors during the last two centuries offers unparalleled insights into the trajectory of professionalism. These two branches must resolve similar problems because they perform overlapping functions within a common social, economic, and political environment. Yet, they entered the period with different endowments, have pursued different strategies, and confront different futures. At the beginning of the nineteenth century, barristers already were an established profession, legitimated by traditional warrants. Solicitors, by contrast, still had to carve out their place within the division of labor and weld disparate occupations into a unified whole, while trying to legitimate the new entity by reference to utility rather than history. The Bar was a small, homogeneous, geographically centralized collectivity performing a limited repertoire of functions. Solicitors (who lack any similar collective label) were a much larger aggregation of heterogeneous, geographically dispersed individuals performing a wide variety of functions.

These attributes and resources help to explain the divergent strategies adopted by the two branches in pursuing the professional project of market control and collective mobility. As long as possible, barristers sought to evoke an aristocratic ideal, employing ascribed characteristics—qualities of the whole person—as the principal, sometimes the sole, criterion for entry. Solicitors, by contrast, initiated their struggle for supply control by imposing measures of technical competence, which they gradually made more rigorous. Whereas the barriers to becoming a barrister were relatively informal and invisible—most notably pupillage (which was not required until after World War II), tenancy, and the difficulty of obtaining business—the professional examinations that the aspiring solicitor had to pass were highly formal and visible. The restrictive practices by which barristers limited intraprofessional competition—for instance, membership in a circuit, the role of chambers and clerks, or relations between seniors and juniors—were traditional and initially informal, although they were gradually formalized toward the end of the nineteenth century. By contrast, solicitors' scale fees were not only formal but imposed externally. The Bar saw no need to promulgate an ethical code and governed itself through a multiplicity of traditional institutions. Solicitors devoted considerable energy to refining ethical rules, created a single, formally representative, professional association, and publicly sanctioned the most egregious forms of misconduct.

At the beginning of the postwar period, therefore, the Bar had preserved largely intact a premodern profession that sought its warrant in gentility and tradition and controlled its market through relatively informal, invisible mechanisms, whereas solicitors had created a modern profession that derived its legitimacy from claims of meritocracy and utility and controlled its market through highly formal, visible mechanisms. Given these divergent histories, it was inevitable that the two branches would respond differently to the challenges of the last few decades. Both suffered an erosion in their control over supply, as a result of the growth of higher education and the decline of gender as an entry barrier. We might have expected solicitors to retain greater control through their reliance on more stringent, formal, visible, and meritocratic criteria; however, the reverse seems to be true. Although the increase in the number of barristers was earlier and proportionally greater, the Bar also has been able to reassert control first by continuing to apply its more traditional, informal, invisible, and ascriptive criteria in the selection of pupils, the grant of tenancies, and the allocation of business. Both branches also have responded to the erosion of supply control by diverting entrants away from private practice and into employment in government or industry and commerce, but once again this has done more to relieve the pressure of numbers within the private Bar. Half of all barristers now are employed; and because they lack a right of audience, they cannot compete with those in private practice (although both barristers and solicitors in employment can compete with private solicitors). Employed barristers are less well integrated within the profession, however, as shown by their lower rate of subscription to the Senate.

The erosion of supply control also undermines the professional project by increasing heterogeneity within the profession, thereby endangering both its unity and its collective status. The response of the Bar has been twofold. First, there has been some segregation of blacks, women, and political activists into separate chambers, as a result of both discrimination and self-selection. Although this may help to quarantine potential dissidents, it also publicly reveals internal disunity. Second, the Bar holds out to all entrants the promise of ascending a lengthy career ladder: earning more, handling weightier matters, representing more prestigious clients, taking silk, and becoming a head of chambers, a Senate member, a bencher, or a judge. This simultaneously controls and integrates recent entrants, who are both more diverse and less socialized than their predecessors; it also preserves the status of those at the top from taint by association with those at the bottom. But the legitimacy of this hierarchy depends on preserving an image of equal access to the apex: to the extent that strata become visibly associated with the race, gender, or class origins of their members, the hierarchy may become a source of internal tension and public opprobrium. Solicitors have had to confront the problem of integrating more women, but fewer blacks. Their solution has been an apprenticeship that is both longer—two years of articles and at least three as an assistant—and more intensively supervised. In the course of this, solicitors distribute new entrants fairly permanently to professional strata defined by firm size, specialty, and geographic location. Here, again, the legitimacy of the hierarchy will depend on whether partnerships and firms are perceived as equally open to all—especially to women.

Weakened control over the production *of* producers also endangers control over production *by* producers. Here, too, the Bar's restrictive practices have been more resilient. Although some rules had to be repealed when formalization exposed them to hostile public scrutiny, barristers still were able to dampen intraprofessional competition through informal understandings. Because advocacy constitutes the core function of the legal profession and contains a good balance of technicality and indetermination, the Bar's exclusive rights of audience have survived largely intact. But much of solicitors' work occupies the periphery of the lawyer's role; although tasks are technical, many also are determinate and thus can be performed by nonprofessionals. Just as solicitors constantly ceded ground to other occupations, so now they have lost their monopoly over conveyancing and with it their ability to set the fees for those conveyances they continue to perform. Barristers also have been more successful in creating demand because, as mediators between citizens and the most visible forms of state power, they perform a core function that the polity feels obligated to subsidize. Economic survival has been attained at considerable cost, however; when half the income of the Bar is derived from public funds, professional control over the market is problematic, indeed.

Both branches have had to respond to heightened competition and the consequent pressure to rationalize the market for their services. As barristers' chambers have grown in size, they have become increasingly significant as the unit of production, notwithstanding the prohibition against sharing fees. Especially in lesser matters, solicitors often send briefs to chambers rather than to specified barristers, and clerks enjoy considerable discretion in distributing them. By performing much of the dirty work of getting and allocating business, clerks relieve barristers of the need to engage in such patently commercial practices as advertising. Subject-matter specialization by chambers and informal understandings among the small number of senior clerks also suppress competition between chambers. Consequently, despite the increased size and importance of chambers and the growth of hierarchy within them, at least the more senior barristers remain independent professionals.

Solicitors have responded to competition differently. Previously, although most firms produced a similar range of services, they divided the market geographically. The rapid growth in the size of firms, the proliferation of branch offices, and now the possibility of advertising all foster concentration within markets that are becoming increasingly regional, if not yet national. Solicitors no longer can rely on conveyancing to assure themselves a comfortable living, and continuing incursions by lay competitors will compel solicitors to reach out toward new clients, subject matters, and functions, thereby increasing differentiation within the profession. However, the most significant development is likely to be the increasing employment of both solicitors and paraprofessionals. First as an employee and later as an employer, the solicitor is being transformed from an independent professional into a worker and then a capitalist; in both cases, the solicitor is inextricably enmeshed within capitalist relations of production.

The last problem confronting lawyers is their capacity to engage in the self-regulation that is both the privilege and the responsibility of all professions. Neither barristers nor solicitors satisfactorily have responded to the challenges of the postwar transformation. Their structures of governance remain unrepresentative, driving some lawyers to form alternative institutions while breeding apathy in others. In any case, the official associations have lost significant power over their members—to both the state and the ever-larger and more bureaucratic units of production, such as public and private employers, barristers' chambers, and solicitors' firms. Attempts to restore popular legitimacy by coopting laypersons onto governing bodies and disciplinary boards have produced no measurable increase in public respect. Self-regulation is being circumvented by malpractice claims. It is unclear whether either branch today can govern or discipline itself effectively.

THE FUTURE OF PROFESSIONALISM

In light of the experience of recent decades, what does the future hold for the English legal professions? The dilemma of prediction is that its stimulus typically is some unanticipated change but its technique remains the extrapolation of existing trends. At the risk of falling into just this error, I will refrain from trying to forecast further shifts as abrupt and unprecedented as the expansion of higher education and the entry of women, which initiated the present era of change, and content myself with speculating about the cumulative effect of recent tendencies. Barring a drastic contraction of academic legal education, which seems politically unfeasible even if it might be attractive to the present Government, both branches will continue to grow until the cohorts of older lawyers all have retired. Each branch will expand by about half before the end of the century and then grow at a lesser rate for another ten years. Women will constitute a fifth of the Bar and two-fifths of all solicitors. Because private practice cannot absorb these numbers, government and industry and commerce will employ the excess, with the result that legal education will become less a professional qualification and more a credential for membership in the administrative class (broadly conceived as including all those who exercise managerial functions in either the public or the private sector). Competition will intensify among those who persist in aspiring to be true professionals (as I have used that term)—that is, private practitioners.

Younger barristers will continue to be almost entirely dependent on public funds and, in that way, subject to state control. Younger solicitors will have little choice but to seek employment in increasingly hierarchical and bureaucratic firms, attracted by an ever-receding prospect of partnership. Moreover, all solicitors must resign themselves to losing more business to lay competitors; to the extent that firms respond by increasing their use of paraprofessionals, this will displace even more solicitors. If, as a result, the Law Society turns its attention in the other direction and renews its attack on barristers' exclusive rights of audience, the similarity of academic education and professional training in the two branches will make it increasingly difficult for the Bar to resist. The consequence may be fusion, although some lawyers will continue to specialize in advocacy in response to consumer choice rather than professional rules. Neither the Senate nor the Law Society will be able to represent or govern this increasingly heterogeneous collection of occupations. In any case, such professional associations will be largely irrelevant to employed lawyers (who will constitute a majority of both branches); and collective self-regulation will be supplanted by both direct state control and bureaucratic controls within the units of production.

Professionalism—in the sense in which both champions and critics have used that concept during the last two centuries—will not disappear. It will persist as both a nostalgic ideal and a source of legitimation for increasingly anachronistic practices, although it will lose considerable credibility. It will continue to reflect the experience of a dwindling elite—some profit-sharing partners in solicitors' firms and the handful of more successful barristers—who will remain largely impervious to state control and continue to dominate their markets and govern their professional associations. For the mass of lawyers, however, occupational life will mean either employment by a large bureaucracy, dependence on a public paymaster, or competition within an increasingly free market. Whichever they choose, these lawyers no longer will enjoy the distinctive privileges of professionals—control over the market for their services and high social status. The age of professionalism is ending.

Tables

2.1. Barristers, Solicitors, and Law Students

Year	Barristers					Solicitors		Education[c]	
	Census	Private practice	Starting practice	Calls to bar[a]	Census	Practicing certificates	Admitted to roll[b]	Law students	Law degrees
1985		5,367	335	945		46,490	2,687		
1984		5,203	325	902		44,837	2,728		
1983		5,032	323	1,052		42,984	2,596	14,362	3,816
1982		4,864	282	936		41,738	2,241		
1981		4,685	270	904		39,795	3,223		
1980		4,589	309	862		37,832	3,538	12,603	3,564
1979		4,412	302	896		34,090	2,552	12,105	3,411
1978		4,263	285	954		32,864	2,538	11,817	3,328
1977		4,076	326	843		32,812	2,480	11,430	3,102
1976		3,881	382	857		31,250	2,184	11,136	2,635
1975		3,646	364	902		29,850	2,203	10,273	2,374
1974		3,368	299	741		28,741	1,849	9,223	2,180
1973		3,137	321	913		27,379	1,764	8,259	2,004
1972		2,919	275	1,011		26,327	1,713	7,335	1,817
1971		2,714	222	979		25,366	1,682	6,574	1,709
1970		2,584	241	935		24,407	1,877	5,998	1,558
1969		2,448	137	688		23,574	1,365		1,558
1968		2,379	139	525		22,787	997		1,451

2.1. Continued

Year	Barristers				Solicitors			Education[c]	
	Census	Private practice	Starting practice	Calls to bar[a]	Census	Practicing certificates	Admitted to roll[b]	Law students	Law degrees
1967		2,333	206	559		22,223	1,107		1,306
1966		2,239	129	528		21,672	1,123		1,161
1965		2,164	138	751		21,255	1,009	4,204	1,072
1964		2,118	80	729		20,683	663	3,838	
1963		2,073	158	792		20,269	805	3,543	929
1962		1,964	110	737		19,790	766	3,401	
1961		1,918	108	687		19,438	685	3,169	
1960		1,919	85	682		19,069	711	3,070	876
1959		1,923	88	692		18,740	784	3,002	
1958		1,947	91	626		18,522	673	3,041	821
1957		1,968	97	546		18,344	734		
1956		1,973	111	523		18,165	745		
1955		2,008	114	601		18,143	695		
1954		2,010	136	513		17,831	603		
1953		1,907	155	536		17,687	649	2,640	
1952			165	597		17,628	588		
1951	3,084		174	501	19,689	17,396	717		
1950			156	551		17,035	926		
1949			196	514		16,318	895		
1948			177	481		15,567	877		576
1947			131	372		15,348	904		
1946				308			441		

Year						
1945		180	12,979		169	
1944		117	13,063		92	
1943		122	13,340		105	
1942		104	18,835		97	
1941		194	14,430		156	
1940		323	15,884		192	
1939		567	17,102		319	
1938	1,515	932	16,899		294	
1937		831	16,478		290	
1936		751	16,299		312	
1935		630	16,132		293	
1934		655	15,941		332	
1933	1,804	595	15,783		319	
1932		695	15,616		345	
1931		615	15,668	15,777	321	2,966
1930		680	15,418		354	
1929		610	15,297		342	
1928		580	15,168		342	
1927		440	15,143		336	
1926		455	15,152		332	
1925		455	15,132		389	
1924		455	15,071		366	
1923		444	15,026		422	
1922		446	14,889		395	
1921		383	14,623	14,956	315	2,953
1920		606	14,767		254	
1919		335	14,380		298	

2.1. *Continued*

Year	Barristers				Solicitors			Education[c]	
	Census	Private practice	Starting practice	Calls to bar[a]	Census	Practicing certificates	Admitted to roll[b]	Law students	Law degrees
1918				149		14,040	81		
1917				136		13,846	95		
1916				176		14,362	111		
1915				203		14,988	158		
1914				344		15,887	351		
1913				503		16,788	485		
1912				414		16,759	494		
1911	4,121[d]			357		16,739	489		
1910				356		16,841	501		
1909				337		16,797	561		
1908				304		16,725	512		
1907				322		16,741	590		
1906				298		16,624	591		
1905				322		16,508	593		
1904				276		16,455	637		
1903				260		16,362	558		
1902				290		16,265	557		
1901	4,733[d]			245		16,136	584		
1900				210		16,006	593		
1899				291		15,950	633		
1898				260		15,810	581		
1897				241		15,629	698[e]		

Year				
1896	698[e]	15,518	264	
1895	698[e]	15,424	270	
1894	698[e]	15,402	299	
1893	698[e]	15,281	303	
1892	698[e]	15,165	270	
1891	662	15,167	275	4,823[d]
1890	716	15,090	271	
1889	842	14,896	230	
1888	829	14,788	259	
1887	882	14,311	266	
1886		13,893	257	
1885		13,592	256	
1884		13,390	246	
1883		13,066	233	
1882	808	12,961	268	
1881		12,565	256	4,792[d]
1880		12,688	272	
1879		12,263	262	
1878			187	
1877			252	
1876			204	
1875			259	
i874			270	
1873			280	
1872			259	
1871		10,576	244	
1870			227	

2.1. *Continued*

Year	Barristers				Solicitors			Education[c]	
	Census	Private practice	Starting practice	Calls to bar[a]	Census	Practicing certificates	Admitted to roll[b]	Law students	Law degrees
1869				228					
1868				203					
1867				182					
1866				211					
1865				189		10,200			
1864				178					
1863				165		10,418			
1862				179					
1861	3,071			121	11,386	10,029			
1860				120					
1859				137		10,047			
1858				132					
1857				113					
1856				113					
1855				119			347		
1854				140					
1853				157		10,200			
1852									
1851	2,816				11,350	9,957			
1850						10,087			
1849						9,943			
1848									

Year				
1847				
1846				
1845			10,188	
1844			9,042	
1843			9,939	391
1842				
1841	2,088	11,684[f]		
1840				
1839				
1838				
1837				
1836				
1835			10,436	
1834				
1833				
1832		8,702	8,061	
1831			9,083	

[a] Between 1948 and 1974 overseas students gradually increased from a third of all calls to three-fourths before falling back to a fourth. Almost none of these entered practice in England. Prior to 1948 the proportion of calls represented by overseas students is not available but must have been considerable. No calls to Gray's Inn were recorded before 1890.

[b] Figures for 1924–1934 inclusive are estimates.

[c] First degree full time; excludes mixed degree, part-time, external, and postgraduate students.

[d] Census combines solicitors and barristers; this figure is difference between census and solicitors with practicing certificates. It overstates number of barristers because many solicitors do not take out practicing certificates.

[e] Average for the years 1892–1897 inclusive.

[f] Includes law writers and law students.

2.2. Distribution of Solicitors Holding Practicing Certificates Among Practice Categories, 1939, 1955, and 1957–1985

Year (ends 10/31)	Partnership	Assistant solicitor	Sole practitioner	Sole practitioner and other employment	Sole practitioner and assistant solicitor	Sole practitioner and partnership	Partnership and assistant solicitor	Partnership and other employment	Commissioner for oaths	Consultant	H.M. Forces	Not in active practice, retired, unemployed	Commerce, industry, and nationalized enterprises	Central government[a]	Local government	Other full-time employment	Practicing abroad
1985	22,053	11,793	4,031	121	80	58	—	—	—	2,057	—	114	1,989	163	2,896	1,037	98
1984	19,875	12,610	3,840	269	24	60	—	—	—	2,034	—	22	1,829	100	3,000	1,175	12
1983	19,467	10,591	3,908	338	32	52	—	—	—	1,906	—	46	1,931	106	2,869	1,679	19
1982	19,065	10,860	3,398	337	46	117	18	166	2	1,773	1	44	1,799	66	2,899	1,005	102
1981	18,377	10,701	3,060	239	41	100	18	42	4	1,673	2	28	1,715	68	2,746	873	108
1980	17,922	9,580	2,815	305	16	96	16	92	6	1,590	3	15	1,636	166	2,627	869	78
1979	17,419	8,537	2,634	343	27	89	15	98	5	1,464	2	33	1,513	215	2,594	761	21
1978	17,061	7,645	2,478	184	16	89	14	66	4	1,382	2	32	1,238	258	2,520	771	104
1977	16,808	6,989	2,691	135	56	109	29	48	4	1,280	3	86	1,092	296	2,465	702	82
1976	16,400	6,223	2,895	131	65	153	22	39	2	1,031	1	33	952	336	2,370	561	36
1975	15,956	5,775	2,894	123	48	64	30	39	6	1,001	1	68	985	353	1,710	746	51
1974	15,387	5,226	2,778	163	66	89	24	69	9	965	2	49	1,143	428	1,965	344	34
1973	14,670	5,712	2,773	108	56	73	8	15	9	392	2	50	983	48	1,883	574	23
1972	13,657	5,860	2,719	143	131	139	11	11	7	381	1	42	851	48	1,804	484	38
1971	13,585	5,015	2,725	139	131	142	12	10	11	385	1	47	822	48	1,785	475	33
1970	13,401	4,252	2,738	127	128	133	12	10	8	391	1	52	795	49	1,776	501	33
1969	13,077	3,825	2,754	127	112	129	12	10	6	398	1	50	773	49	1,748	472	31
1968	12,784	3,474	2,769	112	95	119	12	9	6	380	1	50	745	47	1,721	430	33
1967	12,184	3,428	2,874	149	105	113	12	7	8	342	1	63	732	49	1,667	408	28
1966	11,686	3,367	2,987	181	122	120	17	28	7	296	1	71	677	47	1,672	363	30
1965	11,377	3,274	3,006	196	131	147	18	35	13	274	1	66	657	48	1,635	344	33
1964	11,099	3,142	3,014	161	135	141	15	43	8	230	2	62	632	49	1,592	327	31
1963	10,851	3,017	3,045	138	151	156	20	52	12	201	2	65	581	55	1,566	320	37
1962	10,539	2,943	3,057	124	139	167	12	53	8	198	7	47	523	54	1,544	336	39
1961	10,192	3,044	3,138	155	98	149	15	45	3	147	19	54	470	57	1,507	310	25
1960	9,897	2,887	3,289	163	104	122	17	43	7	122	28	57	458	46	1,464	351	14
1959	9,760	2,785	3,277	140	115	128	18	45	10	86	12	46	452	34	1,446	361	19
1958	9,717	2,704	3,245	138	113	117	18	43	5	68	40	48	407	35	1,413	347	18
1957	9,661	2,520	3,207	143	149	125	19	42	10	39	31	67	430	26	1,409	328	14
1955	9,500	2,500	3,500										404		1,375	309	
1939	6,937	2,256	3,986										512				

1991

a. ... ditioners were held to be ... not practicing certificates, in 1974 and in 1981.

NOTE

An earlier version of this chapter was presented as the Chorley Lecture in June 1985 and published in 49 *Modern Law Review* 1 (1986). The data on English lawyers that ground my argument are presented and documented thoroughly in my book *The Legal Profession in England and Wales* (Basil Blackwell, 1988). Consequently, I have omitted all references here. I have used the adjective "English" throughout as a shorthand reference to England and Wales; my comments do not apply to Northern Ireland or Scotland.

I have been assisted in this research by so many people and institutions that I cannot thank them all individually. The Law Department of the London School of Economics kindly offered me hospitality during the fall of 1982. The Academic Senate, the Law School Dean's Fund, and the Committee on International and Comparative Studies of the University of California, Los Angeles and the Law and Social Science Program of the National Science Foundation (Grant Numbers SES 81-10380, 83-10162, and 84-20295) all provided generous financial support. Aubrey Diamond helpfully arranged for me to present some of these ideas at a seminar at the Institute of Advanced Legal Studies, the participants at which offered invaluable comments and criticism. The Chorley Lecture provided a stimulus and opportunity to develop them more fully. Stuart Anderson, Philip Lewis, Simon Roberts, David Sugarman, and Michael Zander have read drafts and furnished essential information, and Geoffrey Bindman has patiently answered endless questions. My intellectual debt to the sociological writings of Eliot Freidson and Magali Sarfatti Larson will be obvious throughout.

3

German Advocates:
A Highly Regulated Profession

ERHARD BLANKENBURG
AND ULRIKE SCHULTZ

WHY THE CONCEPT OF A "LEGAL PROFESSION" IS MISLEADING IN THE GERMAN CONTEXT

THE ROLE OF ADVOCACY IN THE GERMAN LEGAL PROFESSION

If Germans talk about the "legal profession," they think first not about practicing lawyers but rather about all those who have passed two state examinations to become "full-fledged jurists" (*Volljuristen*). These are then qualified to become a judge, a public prosecutor, a civil servant, a company employee, or an advocate. Mobility between these careers is low. Legal education (which consists of university studies followed by an apprenticeship) is oriented not to the practice of law by *Anwälte*, or advocates who represent parties, but rather to the role of the judge who is above the parties. Fewer than half of those with law degrees actually practice as advocates. During the two-year apprenticeship before the second of two state examinations (which are written by boards at the Ministries of Justice of the sixteen *Länder*, or states), future lawyers spend just four months in an advocate's office.[1]

For two centuries, judges and civil servants have dominated the legal profession numerically, and advocates have been the minority. Their share has increased recently as higher education, and particularly legal education, have expanded. This disproportionate increase may reflect the limited number of salaried jobs more than a growing demand for legal services. In any case, the supply of new graduates has compelled advocates to try to create new markets. It also has led to relaxation of statutory fee schedules and restrictions on advertising and specialization; in order to increase cooperation with competitors, such as estate agents, advocates may have to relinquish their monopoly over legal advice.

Such a market perspective might surprise readers familiar with the literature on the German legal profession, which traditionally has concentrated on the roles of judges and civil servants and their orientation toward authority rather than on advocacy. That emphasis on law as government regulation rather than the assertion of individual rights accurately reflects the subordinate position of advocates within the occupational structure of the legal profession. The role of jurists in the ideology and institutions of the German state is shaped by statutory regulation of legal education and the legal profession. Contemporary changes may cause convergence with the more adversarial cultures of common law countries, a prospect that must be seen in the context of European integration and a general convergence of Western cultures.

THE HISTORICAL WEAKNESS OF ADVOCACY WITHIN THE LEGAL PROFESSION

Traditionally, legal training in Germany was education for the judiciary and civil service. Lawyers were expected to serve "the state" rather than represent citizens. The training of lawyers was strictly regulated by government, admission to the profession required passage of two state examinations, and careers open to jurists were regulated by admission quotas. The influx of law graduates could be adjusted to the perceived needs of the judiciary and civil service. In 1839, for instance, the Prussian Minister of Justice Mühler published the following warning:

> According to our survey of the yearly influx of graduates from the first and second state examinations there are only very distant prospects for anyone aspiring to join the judiciary and to find admission therein; parents and foster parents of such young men can only be advised to deter them from studying law, unless they show extraordinary qualifications and are able to provide themselves with the necessary means of subsistence for at least ten years.[2]

The 4,300 positions in the Prussian civil service at that time included both advocates and procurators (a distinction analogous to barrister/solicitor and later eliminated). (Advocacy became private practice only in 1879.) Three-fourths of law graduates who entered the civil service became judges, and only one-fourth became advocates (Weissler, 1905: 236–300).

There is ample historical evidence of the sovereign's deep distrust toward advocates. The Prussian King Friedrich Wilhelm I, enthroned in 1713, personally determined the number of lawyers admitted as advocates and prescribed the clothes they wore. The title of his 1739 edict vividly expressed his disdain for lawyers:

Edict that those advocates, procurators, and draftsmen [*Konzipienten*] who dare make people rebellious by having soldiers hand over to His Royal Majesty petitions on the most negligible matters or any other documents on justice, such as those asking for pardon, shall be hanged with a dog hanged at their side, granting neither mercy nor pardon.[3]

In 1713 the courts to which lawyers sought admission as advocates imposed examination requirements in order to reduce incompetence and malpractice and to control the number of entrants. In 1780 a Prussian Royal Order actually abolished the profession of advocate, prohibiting representation in court and replacing advocates with civil servants (*Assistenzräte*), who were charged with assisting the parties while helping the judges investigate the facts. Former advocates were allowed to work as Commissioners of Justice (*Justizkomissare*), offering advice and representation in noncontentious legal matters such as land registration, probate, guardianship, bankruptcy, drafting contracts, and notarial work.

This attempt to eliminate advocacy was bound to fail. Pressure from jurists restored advocates to judicial proceedings in 1783. The Corpus Juris Fridericianum (1793) permitted Commissioners of Justice to combine advocacy and notarial functions. The local courts, however, still exercised strict control over admissions because lawyers remained civil servants appointed by the state, even though private clients paid their fees.

After 1871, when unification of the Reich demanded uniform regulation, there were attempts to establish a true "free advocacy" with unrestricted admission and rights to practice, separation from notaries, and the elimination of apprenticeship.[4] These reforms were only partly successful. In 1877 the "Statute on the Constitution of the Judiciary" (*Gerichtsverfassungsgesetz*) made the judiciary autonomous, although it continued to regulate university education and apprenticeship, thereby strictly controlling access to the legal profession. In 1879 the Statute on Advocacy removed numerical limits, granting admission to the bar to all who had passed both state examinations. Continued ministerial supervision over the uniform legal education, together with the two state examinations, still prevented advocates from gaining control over entry to the profession under the Kaiserreich.

Soon after the 1879 deregulation of entry, complaints were made about oversupply. These peaked at the beginning of this century in numerous articles about the alleged "misery" of advocates. State examinations, however, remained a powerful means of restricting access. Just as the Prussian Ministry of Justice had responded to complaints about "a threatening supply of lawyers" in the 1840s and in 1858 by persuading examination boards to make examinations more difficult, encouraging students to drop out, and discouraging some from entering, so the Reich Ministry of Justice did the same thing in the 1910s (Kolbeck, 1978: 41, 55).

The reasons for fluctuations in the number of law graduates in the nineteenth century resemble those operating today. A prosperous economy, which allowed more to attend university, caused increases in the number of law students in the 1820s, 1840s, and 1860s. Quotas for entry to the civil service and judiciary compelled law graduates to resort to other careers during economic contractions, although advocacy clearly remained a second choice for many.

THE RECENT GROWTH OF ADVOCACY

Advocates have been multiplying faster than civil service lawyers and judges since the turn of the century. Between 1960 and 1994 the number of advocates increased almost fourfold, from 18,347 to 70,438. The advocates' journal *Anwaltsblatt* commented: "No profession shows a comparable development. The figures have never been more alarming" (1984/5: 254; see also 1985/5: 249). Yet competing professions exhibited even more rapid growth. During the 1980s the number of advocates increased 56 percent while that of approved business consultants grew 58 percent and tax accountants 78 percent.

The growth of the legal profession, especially advocates, has been more closely related to political changes than has the growth of other professions. Because legal education staffs the civil service, all legal occupations have been highly vulnerable to changes in political power. Throughout the Kaiserreich advocates had to fight for emancipation within the legal profession. Since the bar never gained control over entry, its membership remained a function of access to law schools and to the other legal occupations within the judiciary and the government. The distinction between practicing advocates and salaried lawyers in business remains nebulous.

Table 1 shows the trend toward long-term growth in the number of advocates in Germany once we discount political upheavals. Until the turn of the century, newcomers clearly were discouraged from becoming advocates rather than joining the civil service and judiciary. Examination standards were used to keep the expansion of the legal profession below the population increases resulting from natural growth and territorial occupation. In light of nineteenth-century industrialization and expansion of trade (even though Germany was a late bloomer), these limitations led to uncontrolled growth in the number of scriveners, law clerks, and unregistered paralegals (Gneist, 1867). Overcontrol of entry into advocacy thus led to a black market of unlicensed practitioners, who worked both clandestinely and as employees of and in the name of the few registered advocates. At the same time, the Prussian Minister of Justice was able to employ law graduates for years without pay by holding out the hope that they would gain entry into advocacy. This practice was unique among German states and sharply criticized in Parliament; nevertheless, it shows the extent to which the public administration controlled the careers of lawyers (Gneist, 1867; Kolbeck, 1978: 69ff.).[5]

Since the deregulation of entry to advocacy in 1879, the number of registered advocates has risen steadily (if we exclude the Nazi regime, with its suppression of free advocacy, and the German Democratic Republic [GDR], with the lower lawyer densities characteristic of socialist countries). The Weimar Republic saw further deregulation of entry and a consequent rise in the number of advocates; from its inception in 1933, however, the Third Reich expelled from advocacy political opponents, the few women who had been admitted, and Jews. Official statistics record 4,394 Jewish advocates in 1933, 2,550 in 1935, and none in 1938. Nazi ideology also stressed the advocate's duty to "guard the law" (*Rechtswahrer*) rather than to represent and defend the interests of clients. Conflicts were regarded as detrimental to the "welfare of the whole nation," and the purpose of advocacy was to persuade the parties to accept the wider interests of the state. In 1935 the "Act Against Misuse of Legal Advice" restricted admission as an advocate to "elements who are loyal to the State." The expulsion of Jews was one element of a general suppression of liberalism, which advocates increasingly had been championing during the Weimar Republic (Reifner, 1984). When the post-war Federal Republic of Germany (FRG) sought to re-create democratic political and adversarial legal institutions, it also reinstated advocates in public life. Together with the expansion of educational opportunities and the job market, this stimulated the number of advocates to grow 18 percent from 1955 to 1964 and then 36 percent, 75 percent, and 50 percent in each succeeding decade.

Advocates in the GDR were so severely restricted that they numbered only 600 in a country with 16.7 million inhabitants when the regime collapsed in 1989. During the brief year before unification in 1990 about 1,400 additional lawyers applied for registration: 300 from West Germany, and the rest from the East German judiciary, civil service, universities, or state industries (including a substantial number who had no future in the public sector because they had worked for or collaborated with the security police [Stasi]). After unification the number of advocates in the former East German states (including East Berlin) tripled, to about 5,500 in 1994. Most of the increase came from the former West Germany, since East German law students had to begin learning West German law, which was adopted at unification. West German law firms, which had been restricted to a single office, were allowed to open branch offices to fill the gap in legal services (Kirschner and Lienau, 1994).

PUSH AND PULL FACTORS

Educational production rather than demand for legal services stimulated the growth of German advocates. The number of entering law students increased from about 10,000 between 1973 and 1979 to 14,718 in 1981 and 16,000 in 1990. Following unification it reached 22,000 in 1992 (in the former West) and will continue to increase as law faculties are opened in the former East. A third of these entrants are expected to qualify after eight to ten years of university study and apprenticeship. Given a drop-out rate of about 65 percent, some 6,400 jurists now pass their second qualifying examination annually. In the 1960s and early 1970s 30 to 35 percent of newly qualified jurists obtained employment in the civil service, but this proportion fell to 10 percent in the 1980s and rose again only after unification (Bundestagsdrucksache 9/1939: 4). The creation of a new judiciary and civil service in the former East opened many new positions for those qualified in the former West, but these vacancies will soon be filled. Openings created by the predicted wave of retirements at the end of the century will most likely be offset by the tendency toward privatization resulting from Europeanization and deregulation, which may eliminate many civil service positions. In the 1980s lawyers' associations discouraged young people from studying law by warning of a "flood of lawyers." But the fear that recent entrants would not find enough clients and consequently become a "lawyer proletariat" remains unsubstantiated, although most do start as solo practitioners or partners in small firms they form themselves (Hommerich, 1988).

The influx into all professions has resulted from the general educational expansion of the 1960s, which always outran the job market in the expectation that rapid economic growth would continue indefinitely. In 1960 only 6 percent of the relevant age cohort passed the *Abitur*, qualifying them to enter the university. By 1982 this proportion had grown to 25 percent in the former Western states. Former East Germans were quickly approaching this proportion, although they started at a low level. By 1992 the nationwide proportion had reached 35 percent.

Disciplines with high per capita educational costs (such as medicine, science, and engineering) responded by restricting student numbers. Law faculties, with their low per capita educational costs, initially did not follow suit. Some still have not established quotas, and the new faculties in the former East continue to expand the number of places. Consequently, many denied admission to study their preferred subject enter law faculties; law is the second or third choice of at least 18 percent of all law students, almost half of whom preferred medicine, dentistry, or pharmacy (Heldrich and Schmidtchen, 1982: 15–16; Portele and Schütte, 1983: 98 ff.). The proportion of secondary school graduates with university qualifications entering law faculties has remained fairly stable during the last twenty years: about 5 percent of men and 6 percent of women.

As jobs for jurists in the civil service and judiciary were limited by the fiscal crises of the 1980s, jurists were forced into advocacy—the only lawyer job without entry limitations.[6] Because professional organizations could not control supply they sought to expand the scope of legal services by relaxing restrictive practices and enlarging the traditional clientele of advocates. But German advocates still defend their monopoly over legal advice and representation at the risk of remaining restricted to a small market. This may reflect their historical experience that government regulates advocates if they do not define their profession very narrowly. The constitutional court and competition from non-German lawyers, however, is forcing advocates to reconsider this defensive strategy and is transforming the composition of the profession (Winters, 1990).

THE JOBS OF GERMAN LAWYERS

Becoming a lawyer in Germany still means choosing a salaried career as often as it means practicing as an advocate: about half of all jurists enter salaried positions in government, the judiciary, or business. Judges and civil servants are seldom recruited from the bar; they have their own life-long career paths.

A professional qualification, thus, is the gateway to many different occupations; it requires a university education plus in-practice training in judicial and governmental institutions. This "uniform legal education," controlled by examination boards of the state Ministries of Justice, is a heritage of the time when legal education was predominantly the recruitment reservoir for higher positions in government administration. The state examinations still serve to channel aspirants for legal and managerial careers. Because the choice of career has to be made soon after the completion of legal education, we describe legal education before surveying the jobs that German lawyers do.

LEGAL EDUCATION

To become a German jurist, one first must enroll in a university law faculty. People often do so without clear motives: most of those who qualify enter university because of the status it confers. Law students are more uncertain than others about their careers (Heldrich and Schmidtchen, 1982: 15 ff.; Portele and Schütte, 1983: 98 ff.). Legal training traditionally has been an all-purpose choice. In 1992 there were 22,000 beginning law students in former West Germany alone and another 3,000 at the new law faculties in former East Germany. German universities are tuition-free, and about one-third of all students receive grants to help finance their studies (Statistisches Bundesamt Wiesbaden [BAFÖG]). Even though scholarships were replaced by loans in the 1980s, university study remains an attractive low-cost option for all those passing their secondary-school examinations.

There is widespread dissatisfaction with the quality of university legal studies, however. Before 1993 they took an average of almost six years, although only three and a half years are required. New regulations allowing students to take and fail the first state examination without penalty have reduced this period to nearly five years. University teaching consists mostly of lectures and concentrates on imparting knowledge of legal codes and their application to hypothetical cases. Considerable pressure is exerted by rigid marking of tests and examinations. The drop-out rate is about 50 percent during university studies (and about 25 percent during apprenticeship).[7] Final oral examinations have been described as a "conformity test" to see whether the candidate's thought processes fit the appropriate pattern of "perceiving, thinking, and judging" (Portele and Schütte, 1983: 32; Schütte, 1982). To prepare for these examinations, many students attend courses with a private tutor (*Repetitor*). Tutors offer a systematic, limited program oriented toward the examination and concentrate on case-solving techniques. Two types of tutor can be distinguished: the "impresario" who runs a one-person business, and the large firms with employed tutors and branch offices in many university towns. Some tutors distribute course notes. About 70 percent of law students take these private courses (Heldrich and Schmidtchen, 1982: 91), and almost all use some of their publications. Two out of three law students in 1980 used those of the largest establishment (Alpmann at Münster). Now, however, another law factory has surpassed it, and the market is less concentrated. Even private tutors cannot guarantee good results; to be successful, students must construct their own curriculum, and many form private study groups.

Students restrict their reading to legal dogmatics, and traditional training omits even a basic exposure to philosophy, sociology, economics, or political science (Wassermann, 1969, 1983). Neither the universities nor the tutorial "crash courses" offer training in the skills needed by an advocate. Students do not receive rhetorical training, legal clinics, or training in administrative skills, and there is no moot court. In the late 1960s both the neglect of social science and the perceived need for some skills training led to demands for reform. In 1971 educational programs were established combining university courses and in-service training;[8] in 1982 approximately 12 percent of all graduating lawyers had completed these programs. In 1985, however, all legal training returned to the earlier model despite its well-known deficiencies.

Professional in-service training requires two years and reinforces the judge-centered tendency of German legal education. The trainee has the status of a civil servant without tenure and receives a monthly allowance. Training consists of specified periods in a trial court, a public prosecutor's office, and a local government authority, and an obligatory four months with an advocate.[9] In addition, the trainee has to attend classes conducted by judges in civil and administrative law, by public prosecutors in criminal law, and by civil servants in administrative law. This training emphasizes the technical skills needed in the judiciary: giving preparatory opinions and writing judgments. There is little training in advocacy, drafting, negotiation, or legal advice. This orientation to the demands of judicial office is underlined by the fact that the examination panel consists mainly of judges, public prosecutors, and civil servants,[10] whose experience shapes the examination.[11]

THE ALLOCATION OF GRADUATES TO LEGAL OCCUPATIONS

Those who pass both examinations may choose among the different legal occupations largely on the basis of their performance on the second state examination, supplemented by the evaluation of their training judges. Very good grades (a *Prädikat*, which is achieved by fewer than one-sixth of examinees) open the door to a career in the judiciary or civil service. Advertisements for legal jobs generally demand "a young jurist, possibly with professional experience and [two] Prädikat examinations." A Prädikat always was a prerequisite for employment in the judicial service and often was demanded in the civil service, except between 1965 and 1975 and in the former Eastern states after unification, when graduates were in short supply. Given the current oversupply of graduates and the contraction of all civil service labor markets, even a Prädikat may not continue to assure entry to the judiciary or civil service.

Work as an advocate has become an alternative.[12] In the 1960s and 1970s it rarely was a deliberate choice, except for those who "inherited" contacts with practicing advocates through family or friends or made contacts as a trainee. Advocates traditionally were characterized by high self-recruitment and upper-middle-class backgrounds. In the 1980s, however, advocacy became the occupation for all jurists unable to find government or civil service jobs.

As we shall see, solo practice has been declining in recent decades, and young lawyers increasingly begin as law firm employees. With the supply of graduates increasing, starting salaries are decreasing, and it takes longer to become a partner. Multilingualism and specialization in economics, tax law, labor law, or commercial law give the applicant an advantage. There is a reputational ranking among the thirty-two established law faculties, but the university attended has little influence on one's career. If anything, the state in which the examinations are passed is more relevant. Bremen, for instance, has the most thoroughly reformist model and is the scapegoat for some discrimination in other states.[13]

JUDICIAL CAREERS

German legal culture is thoroughly judge centered. Among all developed formal legal systems, Germany traditionally has had the highest ratio of professional judges to population. This is due to a combination of high litigation rates, high appeal rates, and the inquisitorial system. Procedural law gives judges a dominant role: they control the proceedings, direct the inquiry, suggest settlements, pass judgment, and give detailed written reasons.

To be a judge is a lifelong career, starting immediately after the second qualifying examination (often as a public prosecutor, who is formally part of the judiciary). The status resembles that of a civil servant, and promotion to the higher courts is the usual expectation. Seniority strongly influences careers, although merit does determine the speed of advancement in the judicial hierarchy and is a prerequisite for achieving such senior positions as president or chairperson. Recruitment to all these posts is vertical; temporary exchanges between the judiciary and ministerial bureaucracies are the only observable types of lateral mobility (Lange and Luhmann, 1974).

LAWYERS IN THE CIVIL SERVICE

Most higher civil servants with any sort of administrative responsibility have been recruited from the pool of qualified lawyers. A "judicial qualification" opens the door to higher positions in the civil service and local government (Schmid and Treiber, 1975). Because of their employment status, civil servants cannot represent parties in most judicial proceedings.

Judicial qualification is particularly advantageous for public service careers. Jurists have a very strong position in both the executive and the ministerial bureaucracies. The judicial mode is deeply embedded in German administrative law: every public administrative decision is subject to judicial review on substantive as well as procedural grounds. Because public policy also relies heavily for its legitimation on a belief in legality, jurists play a central role in preparing new legislation (Lange and Luhmann, 1974). Since jurists with a rather homogeneous background dominate the civil service (Brinkmann et al., 1973), training in law has attained a central place in the idea of a "universal education" for public functions (Bleek, 1972).

In spite of uniform education, each legal occupation has its own career path, and mobility between occupations is difficult after a few years. The relatively high incomes produced by seniority and promotion practices in both the judiciary and public administration render transfer to private practice after the age of thirty-five a financial sacrifice. Civil servants and judges rarely leave to become advocates. Most mobility is a one-way movement of younger advocates into permanent civil service jobs. Having obtained the status of a permanent civil servant, most lawyers are reluctant to return to advocacy. In contrast to the average advocate, civil servants enjoy extraordinary security: life tenure, health insurance, generous pension schemes, and, after maternity leave, a guaranteed job and the possibility of part-time work. Many lawyers who have recently graduated have enrolled as advocates simply to wait for a job in the civil service.

UNIVERSITY TEACHERS

University teachers follow a separate career. Professors have to acquire a long series of academic qualifications, and many are actively involved in other legal functions. In 1994 there were 41 law faculties with 752 full professorships, 17 of which were held by women. Once they are recognized as authorities, professors exercise influence through their publications and their (often published) expert opinions on controversial questions in judicial proceedings. The only time most of them practice is during in-service training before the second qualifying examination.[14] Since professors are civil servants they cannot perform all the roles of advocates. They may defend those accused of crimes and represent parties before the Federal Administrative Court and Federal High Court. Some also gain prestige by appearing before the Federal Constitutional Court or as experts before any of the High Courts, where they can participate on the "frontiers" of innovative jurisdiction.

LAWYERS IN PRIVATE EMPLOYMENT (SYNDICI)

Larger German companies tend to have their own in-house counsel. We estimate that between 30,000 and 40,000 lawyers currently are working in companies, industry associations, and similar organizations (for a much lower estimate, see Hartmann, 1990). Some in-house lawyers are admitted as advocates. Official statistics estimate that 12 percent of all registered advocates are *Syndici*, but we believe the figure is more than twice as high. Statistics show that 30 percent of all registered advocates have no income from their practices. While a few are not practicing because of age or other reasons, the rest probably are employed. The dramatic increase in law graduates during the last two decades, however, has not increased the proportion employed in business. Employed lawyers may not represent their employer in court (*Bundesrechtsanwaltsordnung* [BRAO], art. 46). Many become advocates just to have the privilege of using the title; they see themselves as employees bound by contract to their employer rather than as independent lawyers in private practice. Most are found in the big city bars (A. Braun, 1987; Kolvenbach, 1979).

Large corporations have legal departments with fully qualified lawyers. Lawyers also work in personnel and administrative departments and exercise management functions. Professional associations, trade unions, and other organized interest groups employ lawyers as managers or legal advisers.

That so many lawyers work in salaried positions indicates a particular management style: rather than contracting with lawyers, consultants, or accountants for specific services, German businesses tend to incorporate these services within their permanent organizations. Company lawyers enter business firms at the beginning of their careers and tend to move up internal company ladders.

WHAT ADVOCATES DO

Advocates traditionally have been regarded as "part of the system of justice."[15] They have a monopoly not only of representation in court but also of legal advice (Legal Advice Act [*Rechtsberatungsgesetz*]). This "lawyer monopoly" has prevented any other type of adviser from penetrating the "legal market" and also has discouraged the development of any significant legal aid advocacy (Blankenburg, 1980; 1992). Because legal education is oriented toward the judicial service, young advocates see their role primarily as litigators. This consists mainly of preparing written statements; compared to common lawyers, civil lawyers play an insignificant role in collecting and presenting evidence (Kaplan et al., 1958; Merryman, 1968). Once an action has been filed, the inquiry is in the hands of the court, which directs the proceedings, decides what evidence to take, and hears the witnesses.

Even though several big law firms have been founded, those with more than ten partners still contain only 6 percent of registered advocates, and solo lawyers remain 50 percent of the bar. Even if we disregard the approximately 30 percent of bar members who do not practice, the *number* of solo practitioners has not decreased. Most attorneys, however, work in small partnerships. (In 1991, 80 percent of partnerships had fewer than four partners.) Because such lawyers are restricted to private clients with nonrepetitive needs, their income derives mostly from divorce cases. If they can routinize their litigation to increase volume, they may specialize in automobile accidents and traffic offenses, relying on continuing relations with legal expense insurance companies. Few advocates specialize in such administrative law matters as political asylum, admission to university, conscientious objection, and land development. Equally few manage to make a living doing social advocacy reimbursed by legal aid (Blankenburg, 1986). Only those who have acquired additional skills in commercial, tax, and company law and have built up a regular business clientele establish law firms that are larger, more prosperous, or both. Such specialists often are sought by companies for careers as in-house counsel or managers.

Legal advice outside litigation is not part of the lawyer's traditional image, but it is lucrative. Solo practitioners generally concentrate on litigation, but in larger law firms advice constitutes the bulk of legal work. Here, lawyers face vigorous competition from tax consultants and chartered accountants, who combine advice on business strategies, tax strategies, and management. Tax consultants increasingly form their own partnerships offering comprehensive business advice, including the drafting of contracts and wills. Advocates have lost much of the growing consultancy market by concentrating on the forensic areas in which they have a monopoly, and they are trying to regain it by joining interdisciplinary partnerships.

NOTARIES

Advocates are not the only lawyers in private practice—there also are notaries. In most of the former West German states, advocates can be admitted as notaries, a privilege dating back to a Prussian ordinance. In 1992 there were 8,657 advocates who could act as notaries.[16] In the state of Württemberg and in parts of Baden, notaries are civil servants, although they may collect private fees. In most of the states not previously ruled by Prussia, statutes long have provided for a profession of notaries in private practice, with strict entry controls enforced by the state. In 1990 there were 1,382 notaries who were not advocates (*nur-Notare*); three years later, the unified Germany contained 1,562.

German law permits notarial certification and attestation in a wide range of matters, but it is required only to validate some legal documents:

the purchase, sale, or mortgage of land; the decisions of company meetings; and the sale of shares in a private company. Other legal documents, such as a will (which is executed only if the testator wants to depart from the standard provisions of inheritance law), can be drafted by notaries.

Notaries hold public office and charge fees according to a fixed scale, but they are organized as an independent profession. They do their work under the supervision of their regional court of first instance, which controls admissions. Advocates who also wish to practice as notaries can only be admitted when it is determined that there is a need for their services and they can prove their personal competence (Wagner, 1993).

LEGAL ADVISERS WITHOUT UNIVERSITY LEGAL TRAINING

Paralegals are of little importance in contemporary Germany. The Legal Advice Act (*Rechtsberatungsgesetz*) outlaws unauthorized legal practice and requires judicial permission before anyone not qualified as a jurist may practice as a legal adviser. A small group of paralegal advisers with a nonuniversity law qualification (*Rechtsbeistände*) traditionally have enjoyed limited rights to give legal advice. In 1981, however, the Legal Advice Act (formerly the Act Against Misuse of Legal Advice) was amended to terminate the admission of new paralegal advisers. Now only specialist groups of nonlawyers (such as tax advisers) are admitted to practice under the Legal Advice Act.

Of much greater importance, however, are those legal advisers who, while not admitted to the bar, may give legal advice to a specific clientele on specific issues. Trade union secretaries can advise on social and labor law matters and may represent workers in labor courts; consumer organizations can advise and represent consumers; tenant or homeowner associations can advise their members about housing disputes; student advice bureaus can deal with student problems. Many of these organizations provide legal services by contracting with advocates for an annual retainer and are ideologically oriented toward representing collective interests as well as individual claims. Therefore, they are more capable than traditional advocates of changing the distribution of legal advantage by combining individual representation with the use of litigation and political lobbying (Blankenburg and Reifner, 1982).

UNIFORM EDUCATION AND DIVERSE OCCUPATIONS

As we have seen, all German jurists complete the same legal education; this professional uniformity is expressed by the concept of *Einheitsjurist*.

The coherence of the German "legal profession" is perceived as based on this common educational experience rather than a common occupational profile or membership in (predominantly occupational) associations, since subsequent career paths separate judges (including public prosecutors), practicing advocates and/or notaries, civil servants, and salaried company lawyers.

The distribution of jurists among these careers has undergone considerable change since the turn of the century. Until 1909 judges in the German Reich actually outnumbered advocates; the small number of civil servants and judges enjoyed the highest prestige, and other salaried lawyers were rare. Throughout the Weimar and Federal republics the proportions of judges decreased relative to advocates, civil servants, and especially salaried lawyers (while the entire profession grew). The number of jurists doubled between 1960 and the mid-1980s, but the growth rate was most rapid among advocates (see table 2).

In 1993 there were 67,562 registered advocates (25 to 30 percent of whom derived their incomes from sources other than private practice), 1,562 jurists working only as notaries, 18,913 judges, 4,920 state prosecutors, about 40,000 civil servants in federal, state, and local government, and about 40,000 who worked as business lawyers (12,000 of whom were registered as advocates).[17]

REGULATION OF THE PRACTICE OF ADVOCATES

If legal education in Germany seems highly regulated, so is the practice of advocates.[18] While admission as an advocate is a pure formality, the practice of advocates is strictly constrained. Until the early 1990s advocates were not allowed to combine with professionals offering other services, form law firms extending outside the district of the court to which they were admitted, advertise, or announce specializations. A 1987 decision of the Constitutional Court declared the Code of Ethics (*Richtlinien zur Ausübung des Rechtsanwaltsberuf*) unconstitutional for lack of a sufficient statutory basis, forcing amendment of the Statute of Advocates.[19] This led to a broad discussion of the rules and vigorous disputes between conservative and liberal advocates (the latter promoting the growing European and international legal market). The European Court and the German Constitutional Court and Federal Supreme Court decided several cases that permitted liberalization of several rules concerning the practice of advocates. A 1994 amendment to the Statute of Advocates[20] allows advocates to combine with some professionals offering other services (such as patent agents and tax advisers),[21] form national and international partnerships, inform potential clients about their services, and declare particular certified specializations.

Regulations not only affect the "product" advocates offer but also fix the "price" of their forensic representation. This was justified as necessary to prevent unfair competition and maintain a high standard of professionalism, but it also restrained innovations in legal services, which would have followed the more aggressive marketing strategies of lawyers who could work on contingent or hourly fees. (Advocates' fees are fixed by statute, BRAGO—*Bundesrechtsanwaltsgebührenordnung*, and were raised substantially in July 1994.)

ADMISSION

Application for admission is addressed to the court to which the advocate wants to be admitted and granted by the Court of Appeal of that jurisdiction. During the Cold War, the Federal Supreme Court (following the Supreme Court of the Weimar Republic) interpreted the Statute on Advocates (BRAO, art. 7) to allow the exclusion of members of the Communist Party. Even though the Federal Constitutional Court overruled this decision in 1983, a special "purge law" was passed in 1992 to allow exclusion for "unworthy conduct," especially collaboration with the GDR security police.[22]

JURISDICTIONAL AND TERRITORIAL RESTRICTIONS

Practicing lawyers must be admitted to a civil court. In most states they can be admitted to both trial and appellate courts; in some, however, they can only be admitted to one or the other (a hotly contested restriction). In civil matters advocates may represent parties only in the courts to which they have been admitted, although they may appear and be heard in another court if the party also is represented by an advocate admitted to that court. This territorial restriction does not apply to the local courts that handle small claims and most criminal matters nor to courts of special jurisdiction. This rule, which was the backbone of German advocacy, is due to be abolished in the year 2000 in the former West German states and five years later in the former East Germany, after which it will apply only to appeal courts and the highest federal court.

RESTRICTION AND MONOPOLY OF LEGAL SERVICES

In all family courts, district courts (which handle more important civil matters), and appellate courts, parties must be represented by advocates. Advocates also enjoy a monopoly of representation before State Labor

Courts, the Federal Labor Court, and the Federal Administration Court (Civil Procedure Code, art. 78; Criminal Procedure Code, art. 140). In local courts and minor criminal proceedings, parties may appear unrepresented.

DISCIPLINE

Discipline is exercised by the councils of the Chambers of Advocates, which are "autonomous courts under the legal supervision of the state Ministries of Justice" (Statute on Advocates). Appeal lies to a joint court of judges and lawyers and then to the Federal Supreme Court (BGH), where judges constitute a majority. An advocate can be reprimanded by the council for minor offenses, but courts hear more serious charges. The disciplinary bodies have very low caseloads, which have remained constant even as the number of advocates has grown rapidly. In 1992 there were 465 trials (representing 0.7 percent of all advocates), most dealing with problems of admission, such as the candidate's desire to combine membership in the bar with work as a salaried employee.[23] Once the advocate it admitted, *any* sanction is extremely rare, and disbarment is imposed only for serious misconduct, such as a criminal conviction (in 1969 drunk driving was viewed as insufficient) (Lehmann, 1984). The few decisions regarding professional misconduct have a good chance of being published; the journal of the Chamber of Advocates (*BRAK—Mitteilungen*) carries a regular column on such cases. Local chambers prefer to use informal admonitions to express their dissatisfaction with breaches of professional rules, such as those relating to advertising and unfair competitive advantage. Client complaints about service are rare, and advocates' associations and chambers try to deal with them informally. The slight recent increase in formal disciplinary measures only reflects the growing numbers of advocates.

PROFESSIONAL ASSOCIATIONS

All lawyers practicing within the jurisdiction of each court of appeal must belong to its "Chamber of Advocates" (*Anwaltskammer*) (BRAO, art. 60). In addition, there are a number of voluntary organizations. In 1990 about 36,000 advocates, or 60 percent of those registered, belonged to the Deutsche Anwaltsverein (DAV), which protects professional interests, gives practical assistance to its members, and organizes continuing education. It also publishes a journal (*Anwaltsblatt*), holds a biannual meeting (*Deutscher Anwaltstag*), maintains an institute advising lawyers about office equipment and managerial techniques, establishes committees and working groups on legislation and current problems, and promotes professional interest through publicity and lobbying. It increasingly is involved in continuing education, although a number of private entrepreneurs also offer courses for specialists. That there are only a few special interest groups for advocates, such as the leftist "Republican Lawyers" and the "Criminal Defense Lawyers Association," attests to the low differentiation within the bar.

DIVISIONS AND STRATIFICATION WITHIN THE PROFESSION

Preoccupation with preventing competition among practicing lawyers and defending the monopoly of legal advice has discouraged German advocates from extending their services into innovative areas and exploring the possibility of cooperation with neighboring professions. At the same time, it also has avoided the sharp income differences and stratification that typify American lawyers.[24] The social distance between solo practitioners (who still can make a decent living) and members of law firms (those with ten lawyers are still among the biggest), although considerable and growing, is far smaller in Germany than in the United States. There is not yet much "mega-lawyering" (Galanter, 1983) within the bar (but see Rogowski, 1994), nor are there "street-corner lawyers." German advocates still resemble a guild of craftsmen.

Differences in the size of practice and the clientele are evident, however. Senior practitioners in larger law firms prefer to serve companies and associations and rarely go to court, whereas juniors in law firms and solo practitioners tend to do more litigation for a clientele of individuals, relying on divorce cases for a larger proportion of their income. Stratification among advocates may increase if the influx of young lawyers continues. So far, the age, gender, and income distributions of German advocates have changed constantly but not rapidly.

SIZE OF PRACTICE

Advocacy traditionally has been the province of solo practitioners. Small partnerships of two to three advocates began to form in the 1960s. Although some have expanded, few contain more than ten lawyers (see table 3). The number of solo advocates is increasing absolutely and declining very slowly relative to the total number of advocates. According to our estimate, however, about a fourth are not practicing. The number of salaried lawyers employed by advocates (not included in official statistics) also has been increasing with the rapid expansion of the bar, which has motivated some young lawyers to accept long-term employment.

Because advocates employed in business have not been increasing as rapidly as private practitioners, the recent increase in admissions caused a (temporary) increase in the number of solo practitioners with no other source of income. If we exclude all advocates employed as *Syndici*, the practicing bar appears to be equally divided between solo practitioners and lawyers in law firms. Even with the recent increase in the number of partnerships, none is as large as those in the United States. In 1991 only 91 partnerships contained more than ten partners, although the largest had more than 100.

INCOME

When Rueschemeyer (1973) compared the income of practicing lawyers with that of other self-employed professionals for 1954, advocates ranked highest. Since then the incomes of dentists and medical practitioners have been growing faster than those of lawyers, even though the latter have kept pace with general economic growth. Table 4 shows that the average income of advocates now is considerably below that of physicians, dentists, and tax advisers–chartered accountants, and higher than that of engineers and architects. Notaries rank somewhat above advocates but below the medical professions.[25]

Thus far only the *relative* income of lawyers has been decreasing. With the growing influx of young lawyers in the 1980s and 1990s it was feared that their absolute income also might decline. This was delayed through the opening of the new legal market in the former East German states, which has caused at least a temporary growth in demand. When the ratio of lawyers to population in the East reaches that in the West, stratification within the profession will intensify once more as growing numbers of lawyers earn less. This will be the long-term effect of what the profession sees as the failure to limit access to legal education or to the bar; from another perspective, of course, it can be seen as a success in keeping the profession open to newcomers.

FEES

A compulsory fee scale for advocates is contained in the federal "Statute on Lawyers' Fees" (BRAGO). This regularly is negotiated between the lawyers' association on one side and the Ministry of Justice and the Parliamentary Committee on Legal Affairs on the other. Since any changes require legislation, the lawyers' lobby in each party represented in the committee is very influential. Fees in civil cases vary with the value of the object in dispute; there also are guidelines for fees for criminal defense. For consultation, advocates may charge a proportion of the fee for a litigated case, which varies with the kind of work involved. Until recently advocates charged on an hourly basis only in international matters. New legislation regulates fee contracts and hourly fees. Although these statutory fees do not vary in a linear manner with the monetary value of the case, the system still promotes very high fees in large cases, since these fees must compensate for the time spent on small claims, for which lawyers do not even recover expenses. Undercutting is forbidden and punished by the Chamber of Advocates. Contingent fees are not allowed, and legal expense insurance payments in litigated matters also must adhere to the fee scheme. Bargaining seems possible only in pretrial settlements, especially of traffic tickets.

The rigid fee system has a number of consequences:

1. A general litigation practitioner with a predominantly wage-earning clientele can barely make a living.
2. Legal aid income is insignificant except in divorce cases. Criminal defense advocates can do well since the inquisitorial system requires them to expend little effort in collecting evidence and their overhead is extremely low.
3. Some advocates specialize in routine matters, such as automobile and traffic offenses, and are paid by legal expense insurance; highly automated mass processing generates a good income.
4. Legal expense insurance is feasible because fees are predictable.
5. Law firms concentrating on business consultation not covered by the fee scheme earn high to very high incomes.
6. Notary-advocates, who often advise companies or land developers, earn the most.
7. The highest incomes are found in partnerships of four or more, characterized by internal specialization, consultation, a clientele composed almost entirely of businesses, and no debt collection (Oellers, 1982; A. Braun, 1986a).

LEGAL EXPENSE INSURANCE

The predictability of fees has allowed legal expense insurance to develop more extensively in Germany than in any other country. Because insurance companies may not give legal advice themselves but only reimburse the costs of legal advice and representation by advocates, this kind of insurance has become an important element in lawyer income.

Every other German household has a policy. As our own research has shown conclusively, however, legal expense insurance has not increased the likelihood of litigation: About the same proportions of insured and uninsured clients are advised by their lawyers to settle out of court and avoid litigation.[26]

SPECIALIZATION AND ADVERTISING

For decades there has been an official subject-matter specialization in tax law leading to a specialist title. Now public, labor, and social law specializations also are officially recognized and have to be certified by examination. Because the legal situation was very uncertain until the promulgation of new professional regulations in 1994, few advocates cared to qualify (see table 5). Some local advocates' associations informally generate "lists of specialists." They are of little value, however, since referral and advertising are prohibited. The revised Statute on Advocates allows lawyers to disseminate limited information about the scope of practice and specializations—legalizing what had already been occurring in recent years (BRAO §43b).

Most advocates, including those in smaller partnerships, remain generalists; large firms allow some specialization by individual partners but rarely portray the entire firm as specialized. The revised Statute on Advocates imposes a duty of further education without offering any specification.

THE VIRTUAL ABSENCE OF FREE LEGAL ADVICE

Compared to Anglo-American legal culture, there is remarkably little "social advocacy" in Germany. Few young left lawyers have taken the hard route of representing a poor clientele for little pay. Until 1981 the government did not subsidize legal advice outside court, which remained the province of pro bono programs organized by lawyer associations. Since 1981 there has been a very modest legal advice scheme (*Beratungshilfe*). The revised Statute on Advocates imposes a duty to participate in these programs.

The need to equalize representation *within* court had been recognized by German civil procedure as early as 1879 by the *Armenrecht*, or "poor person's law." Criminal defendants also have had a statutory right to a duty solicitor[27] since 1877, although only in the most serious cases. There is no legal aid for the large number of accused in the local criminal courts, nor is there any public defender service for those arrested by the police and detained by the courts. Most legal aid in civil matters (*Pro-*

zesskostenhilfe) concerns divorce for low-income parties. In comparison to Britain and the Netherlands, per capita, civil legal aid is slightly higher in Germany, criminal legal aid is considerably lower, since the duty solicitor scheme is available only in serious cases, and expenditures for out-of-court advice are insignificant (Blankenburg, 1983, 1986). In both East and West Germany the defensive attitude of the bar successfully obstructed the expansion of legal aid beyond fee waivers in divorce proceedings, and it also prevented institutional innovations, such as political represen-tation, neighborhood law centers, and university law clinics. The law-yers' lobby has sought to defend their monopoly over the traditional func-tions of advocacy rather than expand into new markets. Professions such as tax advisers and accountants, in which the government had never reg-ulated education, entry, or conduct (but which also never enjoyed similar monopoly privileges and price regulation), managed to expand their markets in response to the influx of younger entrants. Advocacy, which is open to any qualified legal graduate, now faces an increasing number of young lawyers demanding a share of the highly regulated market for legal services. The defense of monopoly turns out to be a suitable strat-egy when supply is stable but an impediment when a growing profes-sion must expand its market. Since continued adherence to that strategy is dysfunctional in terms of the collective economic interests of the legal profession, the explanation must be found in the traditional political functions of German jurists. The German legal profession may be on the verge of profound change because of the influx of law graduates (includ-ing women), who tend to come from less elite backgrounds.

CHANGING THE SOCIAL RECRUITMENT
OF PRACTICING LAWYERS

Sociological studies of the recruitment patterns of German jurists gen-erated much controversy in the 1960s. The relationship they revealed be-tween the class background and the ideologies of the judicial elite could not be ignored. Sociologists who situated this relationship in the context of the antidemocratic elitism of German political culture aroused public anger. Ralf Dahrendorf, in particular, argued that "the lawyers of the monopoly" were one of the structural factors that explained the blind obedience to authority and avoidance of overt conflict characteristic of traditional German political institutions (Dahrendorf, 1965).

The weak position of advocacy within the German legal profession is an additional reason for relating the respect of German elites for "state and authority" to their antidemocratic sentiments throughout the history of the Reich, as well as to the special dilemmas of an obedient judiciary and civil service during the Third Reich. In the Federal Republic, however, the continuities of German political culture coexisted with substantial changes, and this was true also within the legal profession. The role of German advocates now appears to be converging with that of lawyers in the less authoritarian cultures of the "Western victorious powers," which reshaped the Federal Republic after World War II. The schemes of planned ideological and institutional change advanced by "reeducation authors" such as Talcott Parsons (1954) have borne fruit. After the unification of 1990 they were replicated in the integration of former East German judges, prosecutors, and state company lawyers.

SOCIAL CLASS BACKGROUND

German jurists traditionally came from a rather homogeneous middle-class background in which there was a clear overrepresentation of parents in the civil service. Advocates deviate somewhat from this pattern, however, by being from more urban backgrounds, Protestant rather than Catholic, and the children of entrepreneurial rather than civil service parents (Kaupen, 1969).

In 1980, a third of younger advocates and judges (but only a fourth of law students) were children of civil servant fathers (although civil servants were only 11 percent of the labor force in that generation), while only 4 to 5 percent of younger advocates and judges (but 11 percent of law students) had worker fathers (although workers were 42 percent of the labor force in that generation) (Heldrich and Schmidtchen, 1982: 252). The fact that 19 percent of advocates come from professional backgrounds, compared to 11 percent of judges, suggests the strength of self-recruitment (see table 6), even though the proportion from jurist families is unavailable. The upward social mobility fostered by the overall increase in secondary and tertiary education is more pronounced in other faculties, such as education. Law faculties have been the last to reduce elite recruitment, just as they were the last (except engineering) to admit an increasing proportion of women.

The ideological climate of the 1970s had some impact on the political and social attitudes of the jurists of that generation, who were more critical of authority and emphasized the importance of social welfare for public policy and the legal profession. The cohort graduating in the 1980s and early 1990s, however, seems politically more conservative and also more instrumental in their attitudes toward their jobs. Changes in the recruitment of jurists, as well as in the political environment, may have been influential. The slight increase in working-class recruitment has amplified welfare-state liberalism, whereas the higher proportion of women students has intensified political conservatism (except on some feminist issues, such as employment discrimination and abortion). Law students have persistently been more conservative than those in liberal arts or social sciences.

WOMEN IN THE PROFESSION

In 1922, after long impassioned discussions, advocacy was opened to women (*Reichgesetz über die Zulassung der Frauen zum Richterberuf*, July 11, 1922). During the Weimar Republic the number of women advocates was insignificant. As part of their family policy, the National Socialists excluded women from the judiciary (edict of September 17, 1935), and after mid-1936 women no longer were admitted as advocates (Meier-Scherling, 1975). Gender discrimination in the professions ended in the 1950s in the GDR, but women slowly began to enter male domains in the Federal Republic only in the 1970s (see table 7).

In 1966, when women constituted 30 percent of all university students, they were only 10 percent of law students. This changed rapidly in the second half of the 1970s, and by 1980 women were a higher proportion of law students than of all university students (50 and 40 percent, respectively, in 1994) (Statistisches Bundesamt).

Today, legal studies are the second choice of women, surpassed only by medicine (although economics is catching up). The main reason for this dramatic change is declining career opportunities in other fields. Job prospects in teaching, traditionally women's first choice, are very dim at present. The increase in education graduates in the 1960s created an oversupply of teachers, while the declining birth rate and decreased public spending reduced demand. Women have traditionally preferred public sector jobs; for lawyers these were in the judiciary. Women in public service who are raising children are entitled to work part time and can take maternal leave for several years with guaranteed reemployment. Although there may have been some reluctance about employing women because of the organizational problems caused by maternal leave, public services have been particularly careful not to discriminate; nevertheless, women remain concentrated in the less prestigious courts (Wetterer, 1993: 89). Ambitious young men tend to seek prosperous regional law firms with international work. This raises the question of whether the judiciary is losing its paramount status because of the growing proportion of women judges and prosecutors (as is happening in France).

In 1992 women constituted 41.3 percent of jurists doing their in-practice training and 38.6 percent of those passing the second state examination. Approximately 45 percent were joining the judicial service, where they constituted 22 percent of judges (see table 8). Women judges and prosecutors express high job satisfaction, reflecting the high status and independence of the judiciary, good income, and favorable working conditions (Hassels and Hommerich, 1993: 333).

Their sisters working as advocates face a much more difficult situation. They encounter overt discrimination in seeking jobs, are more likely than men to occupy salaried positions in small firms, more often are underpaid or employed part time (for lack of other offers rather than family obligations), are less specialized, have fewer commercial clients, and earn less as partners (Hommerich, 1988: 40). Most women lawyers are convinced that their working style is distinctively feminine; women and men concur that women have to meet gendered demands and expectations (Schultz, 1990: 346; 1994).

RACISM

German lawyers hardly ever discuss racism. In 1933, however, one of every five advocates in the German Reich and every other lawyer in Berlin was Jewish.[28] As soon as they seized power, the Nazis began expelling Jewish advocates. The 1935 "Law Against Misuse of Legal Advice" prohibited those expelled from engaging in any kind of practice. The final official expulsion of Jews from the legal profession occurred in 1938. Only a few German Jewish lawyers returned to practice after the war.

Today Turkish, Italian, and Yugoslav lawyers are conspicuously absent, despite the high proportion of Mediterranean immigrants in the population and the increasing importance of immigration law. Since university entrance requirements and state examinations present such high barriers, we might ascribe this to "structural" discrimination rather than individual prejudice. Nevertheless, there are a few lawyers in the third generation of thoroughly assimilated immigrants.

CONCLUSION

The data on the recent growth of the legal profession in Germany are strikingly similar to those for all developed Western countries. Throughout the Western world the number of lawyers has been rising rapidly, and there has been a considerable influx of women into the profession, at least since the 1970s. The largest proportion of all entrants have begun in private practice, partly as a route to other lawyer jobs. Yet, despite the common training, lateral mobility among legal careers is much lower in Germany (and most of continental Europe) than in common law countries.

Legal services tend to be provided within public administrative and private corporate institutions rather than purchased from the professional market on a case-by-case basis. Consequently, the job of a practicing lawyer appears to be concentrated much more on traditional, forensic services than it is in the common law world. The bar, therefore, should be regarded as only a part of the profession of "jurists," even if it is increasing its share.

The German legal profession traditionally has been oriented toward public service rather than advocacy. Law schools teach judges to decide cases, not advocates to represent parties. Future lawyers serve most of their in-practice training with the judiciary and in public administration and little with advocates. Legal training in both university faculties and in-practice settings is highly regulated and controlled by the education boards of the state Ministries of Justice. The fact that legal education generates the recruits for the civil service explains their emphasis on uniformity. The legal profession has been the backbone of the legalistic-authoritarian state, and the need for a reliable, uniform elite of civil servants explains the high degree of state regulation of entry and education.

Yet this has not prevented the number of law graduates from rising sharply. Clearly, the growth of the legal profession in the last two decades was stimulated not by greater demand for legal services but by increased supply caused by the expansion of university training. To the degree that traditional careers for lawyers have not multiplied to meet the output of law graduates, more young lawyers have been pushed into advocacy. The composition of the legal profession is slowly changing as a result. Even though pressure within the profession diminished in the early 1990s through the opening of the new market in the former Eastern states, it will inevitably increase, especially now that legal education has been shortened by about two years.

One might expect such quantitative changes to produce a major reorientation of legal education. On the contrary, reforms by newly founded law faculties have been terminated by national legislation. The legal profession's reaction to expansion has been to defend established boundaries rather than expand the scope of legal services. It is highly doubtful, however, that such a defensive policy can be pursued for long. It is more probable that advocates will respond to overcrowding by seeking new markets. Reform is more likely to be produced by the self-interested actions of particular groups of advocates (backed by the pressure for deregulation from the European Union) than by the efforts of any other political lobby, especially since comparative studies of legal cultures show that the legal services market is influenced more by institutional determinants of supply than by changes in demand or "legal need" (Blankenburg and Verwoerd, 1991).

TABLES

1. Growth in the Number of Registered Advocates, 1880–1994

Political environment	Year	Number of registered advocates	Population per practicing lawyer
End of numerus clausus	1880	4,091	11,100
	1895	5,597	8,330
	1905	7,835	7,140
	1913	12,297	5,260
World War I	1914–1918		
	1919	12,030	5,260
	1925	13,578	4,550
Third Reich	1933	19,276	3,330
	1935	18,712	3,450
	1939	14,800	4,760
World War II	1939–1945		
Federal Republic	1950	12,844	3,850
	1955	16,824	3,120
	1960	18,347	3,030
	1965	19,796	2,860
	1970	22,822	2,630
	1975	26,854	2,270
	1980	36,077	1,690
	1985	46,927	1,300
Unification	1990[a]	57,082	1,110
	1994[b]	70,438	1,080

[a]There were 1,800 registered advocates in the former Eastern states or 8,800 people per practicing lawyer.
[b]There were 5,500 registered advocates in the former Eastern states or 2,900 people per practicing lawyer.
Sources: 1880–1928: Kneer, 1928: 61; Ostler, 1971: 60, 207. Population 1880–1913: Statistical Yearbooks; 1935–1939: Reifner, 1984: 386; 1950–1994: Bundesrechtsanwaltskammer (BRAK).

2. Distribution of Jurists in Labor Force, 1961–1990[a]

	Distribution (percentage)		
	1961	1984	1990
Judicial office (incl. pros.)	19	16	14
Government service	30	27	25
Private employment	21	27	26
Practicing advocates	30	30	35
N	62,000	125,000	160,000

[a]The official census of the Statistische Bundesamt found 113,000 persons in the labor force in 1970 who had passed at least one state examination in law, of whom 43.8 percent were advocates, 23.5 percent civil servants, 17.1 percent in the judiciary, 5.3 percent teachers, and only 3.2 percent in private business.

The Zentrale Forschungsgruppe für Juristenausbildung (1979) treats *Syndici* as advocates rather than "private employees"; therefore, they estimated a total of 95,000 jurists, 20 percent of whom are in the judiciary, 25 percent civil servants, 17 percent in private employment, and 37 percent advocates. Such figures misleadingly include all those admitted even if not actually practicing (an estimated 25 percent of all registered advocates). We estimate that 25 percent of all registered advocates were employed by private companies in 1984, based on federal income statistics showing that 30 percent of those who give their occupation as "advocate" derive more than half their income from salaries.

Sources: 1961: Rueschemeyer, 1973: 32–33 (recomputed); 1984: Statistisches Bundesamt Wiesbaden, combined with data of the Chamber of Advocates and the Bundesjustizministerium and personal estimates.

3. Number and Size of Law Firms, 1967–1991

	1967	1980	1991
1. Total number of advocates	20,543	30,077	59,455
2. Percent of those in partnerships	26.5	37.7	39.2
3. Percent not practicing (est.)	24	30	25
4. Percent solo [100 − (2) − (3)]	50	33	36
Fraction of practitioners solo [(4)/(2)]	≤2/3	≤1/2	≤1/2
Number of law firms with			
2–3 partners	2,185	4,440	6,557
4–9 partners	149	704	1,329
≥10 partners	0	14	91

Sources: Chamber of Advocates; Oellers, 1982; A. Braun, 1987, 1993.

4. Average Annual Net Pretax Income of Advocates Compared
to Other Self-Employed Professions, 1954–1980 (1,000 DM)

	1954	1961	1971	1980	1986
Dentists	12	28	110	239	239
Physicians	18	40	117	181	192
Advocates	18	38	79	123	121
Tax advisers/chartered accountants[a]	16	40	82	139	202
Engineers	NA	NA	72	86	88
Architects	NA	NA	60	92	83

[a]Only chartered accountants since 1980; this exaggerates the extent to which this profession
has surpassed advocates.
Sources: 1954 and 1961: Rueschemeyer, 1973: 64; 1971: Oellers, 1982: 151; 1980: A. Braun,
1986a: 67; 1986b; A. Braun & Jansen, 1992: 254.

5. Number of Advocates with Officially Registered
Specializations, 1991 (out of 70,881 advocates)

Tax law	2,260
Public law	413
Labor law	1,340
Social law	293

Source: Bundesrechtsanwaltskammer, annual statistics (January 1, 1994).

6. Family Background of Advocates Compared to Judges
and the General Population, 1965 and 1978 (percentage)

	1965		1978		
Father's occupation	Advocate	Judge	Younger advocate	Younger judge	General population
Self-employed profession	NA	NA	19	11	2
Civil servant	35	52	31	38	11
Worker	NA	NA	4	5	42

Sources: Kaupen, 1969: 192; Heldrich & Schmidtchen, 1982: 252–254.

7. Proportion of Advocates Who Are Women, 1925–1994

Year	Number of advocates		Percent women
	Women	Total	
1925	44	13,578	0
1932	79	19,000	0
1962	480	19,001	2.5
1972	1,035	22,882	4.5
1982	3,458	39,036	8.9
1985	5,651	49,927	12.0
1994	12,733	70,438	18.1

Source: Bundesrechtsanwaltskammer.

8. Representation of Women in Judicial
Careers, 1973–1993 (percentage)

	Law students	Probationary judges	Tenured judges	Appellate judges	Advocates
1973	15	13	9	NA	5
1977	25	18	11	6	6
1981	33	24	14	8	8
1989	45	37	18	8	15
1993	50	43	22	9	17.5

Sources: students: Statistisches Bundesamt; judges: Bundesjustizministerium; advocates: Bundesrechtsanwaltskammer.

NOTES

1. During the 1970s academic and practical training were amalgamated in some "reformist" law faculties, but these experiments have been terminated by national legislation. In the former Eastern states all new faculties are starting with the traditional model of legal education.

2. Justiz-Ministerialblatt (1839: 415–416), quoted in Kolbeck, 1978: 41. All translations are our own.

3. Quoted in Manstetten, 1967: 255.

4. See Gneist, 1867 for the ideological background and Magnus, 1929 and Weissler, 1905 for rather eulogistic historical sketches.

5. There are parallels with nineteenth-century England, where aspiring solicitors had to pay premiums up to £500 to serve five years in articles and newly-qualified barristers had to survive for years without paying briefs.

6. For parallels with other countries, see Abel, 1989.

7. In 1992 the failure rate was 22 percent in the first examination and 10 percent in the second.

8. In the 1970s and 1980s there was a flood of literature on the reform of legal education. For the first proposal, see Loccumer Arbeitskreis, 1970, 1973. For a proponent of the reform attempts and further literature, see Voegele, 1979 and M. Braun, 1980 (a useful overview). For the final evaluation, see Zentrale Forschungsgruppe für Juristenausbildung (1984). A revisionist mood presently prevails, especially in the new law faculties of the former East Germany. For the present state of discussion, cf. Giering et al., 1990.

9. Recent legislative changes allow law graduates to spend a total of eleven out of twenty-four months of in-service training with an advocate. There are not yet any statistics about who takes this opportunity and how it relates to later careers.

In the 1990s two universities (Bielefeld and FernUniversität Hagen) started to offer preparatory courses for young advocates and law students. FernUniversität, which teaches by correspondence courses, attracts about 450 participants a year (equivalent to 15 percent of newly admitted advocates) (Schultz, 1992, 1993).

10. In Northrhine-Westphalie in 1984, only 9 of 235 examiners were advocates or notaries according to information obtained from the Ministry of Justice at Düsseldorf.

11. In-service training recently was cut by about a year. (The actual training now takes two years instead of two and a half, and the examination period has been shortened.) Because the average length of university studies also decreased, German lawyers now start their professional careers two years earlier than before. However, they still enter professional life later than their foreign colleagues (Deutscher Juristentag, 1990). Although they complained that this put them at a competitive disadvantage, the real reason for the change was the "shortage" of lawyers. When the supply increases, legal education may be lengthened again. There were similar fluctuations in the 1970s, when in-service training was extended on the ground that the quality of young lawyers had declined.

12. For an overview of various legal occupations, see Kaupen and Werle, 1974.

13. Klausa (1981) showed that the state of Bremen had the lowest reputation among all German law faculties, even though it would have deserved an above-average rank on objective indicators, such as scholarly merit.

14. According to Klausa (1981: 151 ff.), only about 7 percent of the younger professors (thirty to forty-five years old) have practiced as advocates for a significant time. In this age group, 72 percent have served exclusively in university positions. The limited job experience of younger university teachers may, however, be generationally specific. With the fiscal crisis of the 1980s, few positions were available within universities, so that those who wished to become teachers had to begin their careers elsewhere.

15. The first article of the Statute on Advocates (BRAO) of August 1, 1959, states that they form an "organic part of the system of justice." For an empirically informed and less ideological analysis of the modern advocate's role, see Volks, 1974.

16. Annual statistics provided by the Bundesrechtsanwaltskammer and the Federation of Notaries.

17. Exact figures are not available. The sum of these figures is higher than the total shown in table 2 because 25 to 30 percent of the admitted *Anwälte* also are in private employment. Insurance companies alone employed 4,500 lawyer-advocates (Hartmann, 1990).

18. The legal provisions are described in English in Schultz, 1982 and Schultz and Koessler, 1980. Cohn (1960/61) provides the classic description for an English audience. Recent comprehensive accounts in German are Hartstang, 1986, 1991 and Gleiss, 1987. A collection of the existing rules for practicing advocates is Treffkorn and Koch, 1991.

19. Bundesverfassungsgericht, Urteil vom 14.7.1987, NJW 1988, 191; see also Kleine-Cosack, 1986.

20. BBG1 I 1994, 2278.

21. Bundesverfassungsgericht, Beschluß v. 4.11.1992, BB 1993, S. IV.

22. Bundesverfassungsgericht, Beschluß v. 8.3.1983-1Bvr 1978/80; NJW 83, 1535. The meaning of "unworthy" in the 1992 law was construed very narrowly.

23. 1986/3 *Anwaltsblatt* 148.

24. Nevertheless, a young lawyer can be offered 120,000 DM a year in one of the big law firms doing international work, compared to 40,000 to 50,000 DM in a smaller firm and still less in the least profitable firms.

25. The incomes of physicians and dentists have been reduced by new statutory regulations aimed at limiting health-care costs.

26. In 1979, surveys showed that 40 percent of all households were covered by such insurance: About a third of these were insured only for automobile accidents and traffic offenses and the remainder for all legal expenses. Since then insurance sales have increased. See Blankenburg, 1982.

27. This is a literal translation of "Pflichtverteidiger," although the functions are less limited than those of the British duty solicitor.

28. See Weinkauff and Wagner, 1968; Juristische Wochenschrift 2956 (1933). Jews represented 4,394 out of 19,500 advocates and 60 percent of Berlin advocates.

REFERENCES

(Unless expressly stated, the data in this article come from Statistisches Bundesamt, Bundesjustizministerium, and Bundesrechtsanwaltskammer.)

Abel, Richard L. 1989. "Comparative Sociology of Legal Professions," in Richard L. Abel and Philip S. C. Lewis, eds., *Lawyers in Society, Vol. 3: Comparative Theories.* Berkeley, Los Angeles, London: University of California Press.

Blankenburg, Erhard. 1982. "Legal Insurance, Litigant Decisions and the Rising Caseloads of Courts," 16 *Law & Society Review* 601–624.

———. 1983. "Evaluation der ersten Jahres Beratungshilfe," 1983 *Zeitschrift für Rechtssoziologie* 308–311.

———. 1986. "Subventionen für die Rechtsberatung im Rechtsvergleich," 1986 *Zeitschrift für Rechtspolitik* 108–112.

———. 1992. "Comparing Legal Aid Schemes in Europe," [1992] *Civil Justice Quarterly* 106–114.

Blankenburg, Erhard, ed. 1980. *Innovations in the Legal Services.* Kronstein and Cambridge, Mass.: Oelgeschlaeger, Gunn & Hain.

Blankenburg, Erhard, and Udo Reifner. 1982. *Rechtsberatung.* Neuwied: Luchterhand.

Blankenburg, Erhard, and Jan Verwoerd. 1991. *Prozeßflut.* Cologne: Bundesanzeiger.

Bleek, Wilhelm. 1972. *Von der Kameralausbildung zum Juristenprivileg.* Berlin: Colloquium.

Braun, Anton. 1986a. "Einkünfte und Praxiskosten von Rechtsanwälten 1977 bis 1983," 1986/2 *BRAK—Mitteilungen* 67.

———. 1986b. "Altersstruktur der Anwaltschaft," 1986/3 *BRAK—Mitteilungen* 150.

———. 1987. "Sozietäten," 1987/4 *BRAK—Mitteilungen.*

———. 1993. "Sozietäten," 1993 *BRAK—Mitteilungen* 185.

Braun, Anton, and Friedrich Jansen, 1992. "Einkünfte, Praxiskosten und BRAGO," 1992/6 AnwBl 254.

Braun, Manfred. 1980. *Juristenausbildung in Deutschland.* Berlin: de Gruyter.

Brinkmann, Gerhard, Wolfgang Pippke, and Wolfgang Rippe. 1973. *Die Tätigkeitsfelder des höheren Verwaltungsdienstes: Arbeitsansprüche. Ausbildungserfordernisse.* Opladen: Westdeutscher Verlag.

Cohn, Ernst J. 1960/61. "The German Attorney: Experiences with a Unified Profession," 9 *International and Comparative Law Quarterly* 580–599, 10 *International and Comparative Law Quarterly* 103–122.

Dahrendorf, Ralf. 1965. *Gesellschaft und Demokratie in Deutschland.* Munich: Piper.

Deutscher Juristentag, ed. 1990. "Welche Maßnahmen empfehlen sich - auch im Hinblick auf den Wettbewerb zwischen Juristen aus den EG-Staaten - zur Verkürzung und Straffung der Juristenausbildung?" Sitzungsbericht 0 zum 58. *Deutschen Juristentag München* 1990. Munich: Beck.

Galanter, Marc. 1983. "Mega-Law and Mega-Lawyering in the Contemporary United States," in Robert Dingwall and Philip Lewis, eds., *The Sociology of the Professions: Lawyers, Doctors and Others,* 152–176. London: Macmillan.

Giering, Heinz, Fritz Haag, Wolfgang Hoffmann-Riem, and Klaus Ott, eds. 1990. *Juristenausbildung erneut überdacht.* Baden-Baden: Nomos.

Gleiss, Alfred. 1987. *Soll ich Rechtsanwalt werden,* 2d ed. Heidelberg: Sauer.

Gneist, Rudolf von. 1867. *Die Freie Advokatur.* Berlin: Springer.

Hartmann, Michael. 1990. *Juristen in der Wirtschaft.* Munich: Beck.

Hartstang, Gerhard. 1986. *Der deutsche Rechtsanwalt. Rechtsstellung und Funktion in Vergangenheit und Gegenwart.* Heidelberg: C. F. Müller.

———. 1991. *Anwaltsrecht.* Cologne, Berlin, Bonn, and Munich: Heymanns.

Hassels, Angela, and Christoph Hommerich. 1993. *Frauen in der Justiz.* Cologne: Bundesanzeiger.

Heldrich, Andreas, and Gerhard Schmidtchen. 1982. *Gerechtigkeit als Beruf.* Munich: Beck.

Hommerich, Christoph. 1988. *Die Anwaltschaft unter Expansionsdruck.* Cologne: Bundesanzeiger.

Institut für Freie Berufe. 1978. *Struktur und Bedeutung der Freie Berufe in der Bayerischen Wirtschaft.* Nuremberg: Universität Erlangen.

Kaplan, Benjamin, Arthur T. von Mehren, and Rudolf Schaefer. 1958. "Phases of German Civil Procedure," 71 *Harvard Law Review* 1461.

Kaupen, Wolfgang. 1969. *Die Hüter von Recht und Ordnung.* Neuwied: Luchterhand.

Kaupen, Wolfgang, and Raymund Werle, eds. 1974. *Soziologische Probleme juristischer Berufe.* Göttingen: Schwartz.

Klausa, Ekkehard. 1981. *Deutsche und amerikanische Rechtslehrer.* Baden-Baden: Nomos.

Kirschner, Lutz, and Marc Lienau. 1994. "Rechtsanwälte im Übergang—Zur Situation des Berufsstandes in den neuen Bundesländern," [1994] *Zeitschrift für Rechtssoziologie* 66–81.

Kleine-Cosack, Michael. 1986. *Berufsständische Autonomie und Grundgesetz.* Baden-Baden: Nomos.

Kneer, August. 1928. *Der Rechtsanwalt.* Mönchen-Gladbach: Volksvereinsverlag.

Kolbeck, Thomas, 1978. *Juristenschwemmen—Untersuchungen über den juristischen Arbeitsmarkt im 19. und 20. Jahrhundert.* Frankfurt on Main: Lang.

Kolvenbach, Walter. 1979. "Die Tätigkeit der Syndikusanwälte im Unternehmen und ihre Zusammenarbeit mit frei praktizierenden Anwälten," 33 *Juristenzeitung* 458–460.

Lange, Elmar, and Niklas Luhmann. 1974. "Juristen, Berufswahl und Karrieren," 65 *Verwaltungsarchiv* 148–152.

Lehmann, Paul. 1984. "25 Jahre Ehrengerichtsbarkeit," in *25 Jahre Bundesrechtsanwaltskammer.* Munich: Beck (Schriftenreihe der Bundesrechtsanwaltskammer, no. 6).

Loccumer Arbeitskreis, ed. 1970. *Neue Juristenausbildung.* Neuwied: Luchterhand.

———. 1973. *Der neue Jurist. Ausbildungsreform in Bremen.* Neuwied: Luchterhand.

Magnus, Julius. 1929. *Die Rechtsanwaltschaft.* Leipzig: Moeser.

Manstetten, Fritz. 1967. *Vom Sachsenspiegel zum Code Napoléon.* Cologne: Wienand.

Meier-Scherling, Anne-Gudrun. 1975. "Die Benachteiligung der Juristen zwischen 1933 und 1945," *Deutsche Richterzeitung* (DRiZ) 10–13.

Merryman, John. 1968. *The Civil Law Tradition*. Stanford: Stanford University Press.

Oellers, Bernhard. 1982. "Einkünfte und Praxis(un)kosten von Rechtsanwalten, 1971–1979," 1982/4 *BRAK—Mitteilungen* 151.

Ostler, Fritz. 1971. *Die deutschen Rechtsanwälte 1878–1971*. Essen: Ellinghaus.

Parsons, Talcott. 1954. "The Problem of Controlled Institutional Change: Report on the Conference on Germany after the War," in *Essays in Sociological Theory*. Glencoe, Ill.: Free Press.

Portele, Gerhard, and Wolfgang Schütte. 1983. *Juristenausbildung und Beruf*. Hamburg: Interdisziplinäres Zentrum für Hochschuldidaktik der Universität Hamburg (AZHD) (Hochschuldidaktische Arbeitspapiere no. 16).

Reifner, Udo. 1984. "Die Zerstörung der freien Advokatur im Nationalsozialismus," 17 *Kritische Justiz* 380–393.

Rogowski, Ralf. 1994. "The Growth of Corporate Law Firms in Germany," in Yves Dezalay and David Sugarman, eds., *Professional Competition and the Social Construction of Markets*. London: Routledge.

Rueschemeyer, Dietrich. 1973. *Lawyers and Their Society: A Comparative Study of the Legal Profession in Germany and the United States*. Cambridge, Mass.: Harvard University Press.

Schmid, Günter, and Hubert Treiber. 1975. *Bürokratie und Politik. Zur Struktur und Funktion der Ministerialbürokratie in der Bundesrepublik Deutschland*. Munich: Fink UTB.

Schultz, Ulrike. 1982. "The German Rechtsanwalt: Images of a Unified Profession," 79 *Law Society's Gazette* 1210.

———. 1990. "Wie männlich ist die Juristenschaft?" in Ulrich Battis and Ulrike Schultz, eds., *Frauen im Recht* 319. Heidelberg: C. F. Müller (abridged as "Women in Law or the Masculinity of the Profession in Germany," in Alberto Febbrajo and David Nelken, eds., 1993 *European Yearbook in the Sociology of Law* 229).

———. 1992. "Weiterbildungsprogramm 'Einführung in den Anwaltsberuf' der FernUniversität und der Deutschen AnwaltAkademie," 1992/3 *BRAK—Mitteilungen* 152.

———. 1993. "Das Projekt 'Einführung in den Anwaltsberuf,'" in *Grundlagen der Weitersbildung. Praxishilfen*. 9.10.30.1. Neuwied: Luchterhand.

———. 1994. "Erwartungen und Erwartungserwartungen von und an Juristinnen. Frauen mit Recht als Beruf," 1, 2, and 3/1994 *Mitteilungen des Juristinnenbundes*.

Schultz, Ulrike, and Paul Koessler. 1980. "The Practicing Lawyer in the Federal Republic of Germany," [1980] *The International Lawyer* 531.

Schütte, Wolfgang. 1982. *Die Einübung des juristischen Denkens. Juristenausbildung als Sozialisationsprozess*. Frankfurt: Campus.

Statistisches Bundesamt Wiesbaden. 1987. *Berufs- und Bevölkerungszählung 1987* (special census series).

———. *BAFöG-Statistik*, Fachserie 11, Reihe 77 (annual series).

———. *Hochschulstatistik*, Fachserie 11, Reihe 44, 1 (annual series).

Treffkorn, Matthias, and Peter Koch. 1991. *Berufsrecht der Rechtsanwälte und Notare*. Freiburg, Berlin: Rudolf Haufe.

Voegele, Wolfgang. 1979. *Einphasige Juristenausbildung—zur Pathologie der Reform.* Frankfurt: Campus.

Volks, Holger. 1974. *Anwaltliche Berufsrollen und anwaltliche Berufsarbeit in der Industriegesellschaft.* Cologne: Diss.

Wagner, Paul. 1993. "Der Zugang zum Anwaltsnotariat," 1993/1 *BRAK—Mitteilungen* 6.

Wasilewski, Rainer. 1990. *Streitverhütung durch Rechtsanwälte.* Cologne: Bundesanzeiger.

Wassermann, Rudolf. 1983. "Zu den Prüfungsinhalten der ersten juristischen Staatsprüfung," 1983 *JuS* 703.

Wassermann, Rudolf, ed. 1969. *Erziehung zum Establishment.* Karlsruhe: C. F. Müller.

Weinkauff, Hermann, and Albrecht Wagner. 1968. *Die deutsche Justiz und der Nationalsozialismus.* Stuttgart: Deutsche Verlagsanstalt.

Weissler, Adolf. 1905. *Geschichte der Rechtsanwaltschaft.* Leipzig: Pfeffer (reprinted Frankfurt: Sauer und Auvermann, 1967).

Wetterer, Angelika. 1993. *Professionalisierung und Geschlechterhierarchie.* Kassel: Jenior und Preßler.

Winters, Karl-Peter. 1990. *Der Rechtsanwaltsmarkt. Chancen, Risiken und zukünftige Entwicklung.* Cologne: Verlag Dr. Otto Schmidt.

Zentrale Forschungsgruppe für Juristenausbildung. 1984. Mannheim: Zentrale Forschungsgruppe für Juristenausbildung.

4

The Present State of Japanese Practicing Attorneys: On the Way to Full Professionalization?

KAHEI ROKUMOTO

This chapter attempts to present an overall picture of Japanese lawyers in private practice and the legal services they deliver, drawing on a recent national survey (table 4.1).[1] I shall discuss some of the most salient features of the Japanese bar and its business, primarily on the basis of the survey, focusing on (1) the size of the bar, (2) the recruitment of its members, (3) the forms of their practice, (4) the kind of work they do and the clients they serve, and (5) their income. However, in order to interpret such an overall picture correctly, we must put it in an appropriate framework. So I shall start with a brief summary of the historical and institutional background of the profession.

HISTORICAL AND INSTITUTIONAL BACKGROUND

Before 1868 there was no distinct occupational group with special expertise in law.[2] Within the government of the central Tokugawa Shogunate, as well as those of the subordinate feudal domains, the judicial function constituted only one of the tasks of generalist administrators. Professional representation before the court was not recognized, although certain innkeepers and their clerks (called *kujishi*) were authorized to offer their knowledge of procedure and of the location of various offices to guests coming to Edo for litigation (Henderson, 1965: 167–169).

The Meiji Government created the entire modern, centralized legal system on the model of the imperial German legal system. This was done during the decades following the Imperial Restoration, through promulgation of a constitution and comprehensive substantive and procedural codes and the establishment of a system of courts distributed throughout the country. In the course of the gradual differentiation of the judicial branch within the governmental structure, the legal profession also emerged. Because it, too, was created by the government, it lacks autonomous authority rooted in tradition. Moreover, in the process of establishing the legal profession, emphasis naturally was placed on securing competent judges and prosecutors—career governmental officers charged with administering the imported systems of laws and courts—to the neglect of private attorneys.

In 1872 judges and prosecutors were recognized as legal officers distinct from ordinary government officials.[3] A certain amount of legal education (based mainly on the European law) was made a prerequisite for their appointment, and a government school was established for the purpose, which later was incorporated into an Imperial University. Beginning in 1890, the positions of both judges and prosecutors were firmly established through the formal examination system, the three-year apprenticeship, and the guarantee of tenure. Private attorneys, however, systematically were treated as the inferiors of judges and prosecutors, although their position gradually improved during the prewar period. Legal representation was recognized in civil cases in 1872 and in criminal cases in 1890, and the professionals who performed those functions officially were recognized in 1876. Their qualifications remained vague until 1893, when the first Practicing Attorneys Act introduced the present title of "bengoshi,"[4] together with a formal qualification based on an examination of legal knowledge. This examination, however, was separate from, and less demanding than, that for judges and prosecutors, and law graduates of Imperial Universities were exempt even from it until 1923. Apprenticeship was not required until 1936 (apprentices were paid by the state). Throughout the prewar period, private attorneys were under the control of the Minister of Justice and the prosecutors subordinate to him, and the activities of their organizations were closely supervised.

The general social and economic patterns determined by the precipitous modernization under the leadership of an authoritarian government also did not constitute a favorable environment for the development of a new profession. The traditional aversion toward "law" still prevailed among the population and was reinforced by the familistic nature of social organizations and governmental indoctrination of Confucian ethics emphasizing "harmony." The rise and growth of modern industry in an agrarian society that had been closed to the outer world for 300 years is attributable less to the workings of an impartial law protecting free entrepreneurial activities and more to active encouragement and protection by the government. Consequently, lawyers' services were not an indispensable element in the making of modern Japanese society and economy. The inquisitorial character of court procedures also narrowed the lawyers' role in civil matters. These circumstances led practicing attorneys to develop a characteristic professional self-image stressing their political role in representing criminal defendants oppressed by the state. They even called themselves the "opposition branch" of the legal profession, in contrast to the judges and prosecutors, who were labeled the "governmental branch."

It is only through the Practicing Attorneys Act of 1949 that Japanese practicing attorneys acquired formal equality with judges and prosecutors, in the sense that all are subjected to the same state legal examination and two-year apprenticeship and that the former were accorded full autonomy in governing their own affairs, including the matters of licensure and discipline.[5] Court procedures for both civil and criminal cases also have undergone substantial reforms to incorporate Anglo-American adversary principles, thus enhancing the role and status of attorneys in the courtroom.

Today, aspirants to the legal profession undergo a unitary state Legal Examination and a common two-year course of practical training at the Institute of Legal Training and Research (ILTR).[6] They decide whether to become judges, prosecutors, or practicing attorneys when they leave this institute.[7] Some efforts were made after the war to unify the legal profession, recruiting judges from among experienced private practitioners, but this effort failed, although a proportion of Supreme Court justices customarily are appointed from among eminent private attorneys.[8] Thus, only a few of those who choose private practice at the time of leaving the ILTR will enter the public sector, although a substantial number of judges and prosecutors resign to become private attorneys even before they reach retirement age.[9]

Within these and other new institutional frameworks, created as part of postwar democratization, the younger lawyers trained in the ILTR grew in number and the general quality and prestige of Japanese private attorneys significantly improved (table 4.2). Against the background of the postwar economic expansion, the importance of lawyers in civil matters gradually was recognized, and the public now accepts them as a major element in the administration of law and justice. Nevertheless, the status of practicing attorneys still reflects the historical handicaps described above. They rank somewhat lower than judges and prosecutors, and, in face-to-face interaction, the latter display their traditional sense of superiority, which is greatly resented by the former.

In analyzing the legal profession, we also have to note some of the distinctive features of the contemporary Japanese legal system. The judicial system resembles that of Germany, with each of the forty-seven prefectures having a district court, the principal court of first instance with general jurisdiction. Above the district courts there are eight high courts and one Supreme Court. Below, there are about 600 summary courts of limited jurisdiction (up to 900,000 yen [¥] in civil matters; about $4,500).

Unlike the German model, however, we also have separate family courts in each prefecture.

Mediation is an integral part of the judicial system. Lay mediators attempt to settle civil cases less formally, less expensively, and more quickly by assisting parties in reaching an agreement.[10] In family matters, a regular lawsuit can be filed only after mediation in the family court has failed. In other civil matters, the plaintiff can choose between mediation and adjudication regardless of the amount in controversy.

Legal representation is *not* compulsory, except in certain kinds of criminal cases (Code of Criminal Procedure, art. 290).[11] In contrast, a non-lawyer can represent a party only in summary courts (Code of Civil Procedure, art. 79). Both lawyers and lay representatives are allowed to participate in mediation.[12] There is no localization of practicing attorneys as in Germany, so that lawyers can represent their clients before any Japanese court. There also is no legal regulation of lawyers' fees. Each association of practicing attorneys establishes a standard fee schedule, in principle proportioned to the amount in dispute, but this has no binding force and is not strictly followed in practice.

SIZE

It is well known that both the Japanese legal profession as a whole and the practicing bar in particular are very small (see table 4.3). In 1979 there were 1,940 posts for regular judges and assistant judges,[13] 791 posts for summary court judges holding lower qualifications,[14] and 2,092 posts for regular and assistant prosecutors. As of January 1980 there were 11,466 registered practicing attorneys.[15] The ratio of practicing attorneys to the national population (about 116 million) is approximately one to 10,000 persons, only a sixth as high as in England and West Germany.[16]

The distribution of lawyers within the country is far from even. In 1980, 5,361 of the 11,466 lawyers (or 46.8 percent) had their offices in Tokyo and another 2,044 (17.8 percent) were practicing in Osaka or Aichi. Thus, almost two-thirds of all private attorneys are concentrated in the three largest industrial centers. Five other prefectures endowed with a high court contained 918 private attorneys (8.0 percent), and the remaining 39 prefectures with only a district court had a total of 3,143 lawyers (or 27.4 percent). The number of PAs per 10,000 people in each of the four survey areas is as follows: A = 4.58, B = 1.44, C = 0.64, D = 0.43. Therefore, in the peripheral areas there is an extreme shortage of practicing attorneys. Within these peripheral prefectures, lawyers' offices are concentrated in the city where the prefectural government and the district court are located, so that the nationwide maldistribution of lawyers is re-produced at the prefectural level.

These gaps are partly filled by the PAs who travel from urban centers to work on particular cases pending in local courts and by other cat-egories of law-related occupations, each of which has its own exami-nation, registration, and legally prescribed sphere of activities.[17] These include tax accountants (40,000), patent attorneys (2,500), judical scriv-eners (approximately 14,500 in 1980), and administrative scriveners (65,000).

Tax accountants are allowed to draft documents, give advice concern-ing tax matters, and represent clients in the administrative complaint pro-cedures against tax authorities; however, the number of such cases still is small in Japan. Patent attorneys may give legal opinions about patents and similar matters and represent clients in complaint or dispute pro-cedures concerning those matters before the competent authorities (the Patent Office and the Minister of International Trade and Industry) and, in certain matters, before the regular courts (Patent Attorneys Act, arts. 1, 9, 9-2). Patent, copyright, and taxation constitute highly specialized fields, in which only a very few lawyers could work confidently without the col-laboration of a patent attorney or a tax accountant. Not surprisingly, the distribution of patent lawyers and tax accountants resembles that of prac-ticing attorneys.

The activities of judicial scriveners are more general and somewhat overlap those of PAs.[18] The law authorizes them "to represent the client in the procedure concerning registration or deposit" and "to draw up doc-uments to be submitted to a court, a prosecutor's office, or a bureau of judicial affairs," among other functions (Legal Scriveners Act, art. 2).[19] The registration of real estate transactions and the creation or transforma-tion of commercial corporations makes up the bulk of the work of legal scriveners. The former includes the registration of many changes in the rights and duties concerning land and buildings, including transfer and mortgage. In Japan, these transactions normally are effected with the assistance of a real estate agent and a judicial scrivener and without the intervention of a PA. Furthermore, the judicial scrivener lawfully can pre-pare briefs and all the other documents submitted by the litigant in the course of a lawsuit. Judicial precedent has recognized that, in drafting such documents, the judicial scrivener must exercise legal judgment. It is almost impossible to separate the legal advice necessary to draft a document from the other advice a judicial scrivener may offer his client. Consequently, it is widely admitted that in most cases where the litigant is unrepresented a judicial scrivener is operating behind the scenes, not only drafting docu-ments but also advising the principal on how to conduct the litigation. They also frequently advise citizens in matters not related to the legitimate work of drafting a document and occasionally are prosecuted for violating the Practicing Attorneys Act.[20] Legal scriveners are much more evenly distributed geographically, partly compensating for the maldistribution of private attorneys.[21]

The work of administrative scriveners concerns the documents submitted to an administrative office (e.g., the application for a driver's license). This does not directly involve a legal transaction or dispute, however, and complaints against an administrative agency still are very rare in Japan. Therefore, administrative scriveners seldom are viewed as lawyer substitutes.

RECRUITMENT

The principal mode of recruitment to the legal profession is through the state Legal Examination, followed by two years of practical training at the Institute of Legal Training and Research. About 70 percent of attorneys practicing today are those younger, more competent lawyers who entered in this fashion. Within a few decades the others, who qualified under the older system, will completely disappear from the Japanese bar.

Practicing attorneys qualify rather late in life. Among those presently in practice, about 29 percent obtained their qualification before they were twenty-five, about 47 percent between twenty-five and thirty, and 20 percent after thirty. The average age of those who passed the Legal Examination was 27.69 years in 1965, 26.60 in 1970, 26.75 in 1975, and 28.07 in 1980 (Nihon Houritsuka Kyoukai, 1982: 139). (We have to add two more years in order to obtain the average age of qualification for each class.) This undoubtedly is due to the difficulty of the Legal Examination, which is notorious and often severely criticized by law professors. Each year, only 500 out of 29,000 candidates (or 1.7 percent) pass (see table 4.4). Since the normal age of graduation from the university is between twenty-two and twenty-four, those who pass have spent an average of three to five years preparing for the examination.[22] Many candidates attend cram schools, even while they are university students. There is no limit on the age of the candidates or the number of repetitions.

Although lawyers need not have a law degree or even a university degree, we found that only 1.6 percent of practicing attorneys were not university graduates and that 95.3 percent of university graduates had studied law.

Not all graduates aspire to enter the legal profession. Legal education is not offered in a professional school at the graduate level but is a two-year undergraduate course in a law faculty (following two years of general university education) and includes a wide range of subjects, such as political science and economics, as well as law.[23] In fact, those who pass the Legal Examination and go on to the ILTR constitute a small minority of law students (see table 4.5).[24] Others enter the civil service or business. The education in a law faculty, especially at one of the former Imperial Universities (which were founded mainly to recruit and educate civil servants), is considered the entrée to high positions in politics, government, and business. It cannot be said that the best law students become lawyers, either; for one thing, in order to pass the Legal Examination, one must devote two or three years almost exclusively to preparation.

Many law students enter large business corporations and become the "lawpersons" in the firm—employees who have acquired the basic knowledge of and skill in law and legal reasoning in the university and, without possessing the certificate of a lawyer, specialize in handling the legal matters of the firm. These people, of course, represent still another category of competitors with practicing attorneys.[25]

Our study of the social background of practicing attorneys revealed that 13.6 percent of their fathers were professionals, 12.6 percent were managers, 19.0 percent were clerical or technical employees, 28.1 percent were proprietors not in agriculture, 18.9 percent were farmers, 4.7 percent were workers, and 4.2 percent were in other categories. Overrepresentation of the professional and managerial classes on one hand and underrepresentation of workers and farmers on the other hand is clear. In order to ascertain accurately the implication of these data, however, we would need a detailed analysis of the social structure of Japanese society and its change over the past 100 years, particularly because it has undergone a fundamental transformation from a predominantly agrarian, static society into a highly industrialized, mobile society within a very short time (Dore, 1967).

FORMS OF PRACTICE

All Japanese practicing attorneys have or belong to one (and only one) law office, but their status varies with their relation to that office. Some lawyers are employed by another lawyer or lawyers (principals). Most employed lawyers earn a fixed salary (with annual raises) for the work they do for their principal,[26] and many also receive a percentage of the fee in cases they handle together with their employers or on their own (see table 4.6). A small number work entirely on commission. Most employed lawyers may take their own cases and work for their own clients using the office facilities and clerks of their employers. In this way, they acquire the necessary work experience to launch their own practices. These employed lawyers sometimes are called "Isoro-attorneys" ("Isoro" means one who hangs on a master and performs odd tasks). This term is a remnant from the time when practicing attorneys started their careers as personal apprentices of a senior lawyer. Even today, the relationship between principals and their young employees sometimes is colored by the paternalistic attitudes of the former and thus is not altogether free from friction.

Principal lawyers fall into two categories: those who are the only principal within their law office and those who share their office with other principals. The first group divides further into solo practitioners and sole principals who employ other lawyers. We call the latter "masters," in complementarity to the term "Isoro-attorneys." The second group also contains two subdivisions. One is the "office-sharers," who share only the rented office space, telephones, law books, and other equipment, as well as clerks. Sometimes they share employee lawyers, as well. Insofar as the management of the law practice is concerned, however, the members of a *Büro-Gemeinschaft*, as it would be called in Germany, are completely independent of each other. One has personal clients, works independently without consulting office companions, and pays a share of the office expenses out of separate fees. The other subdivision includes those who form a partnership with other lawyers and share not only the office expenses but also the clients, the work, and the fees, as well as responsibility for running the office. Many partnerships also have employee lawyers.

Thus, we can classify practicing attorneys into the following five categories (with the adjusted proportion of the total sample shown in parentheses): (1) "Isoro-attorneys," that is, employed lawyers (18.0 percent); (2) office-sharers (14.0 percent); (3) solo practitioners (50.0 percent); (4) "masters," that is, solo principals with employed lawyers (9.0 percent); and (5) partners (9.0 percent). The distribution of practicing attorneys across these categories by areas and age is shown in tables 4.7a, 4.7b, and 4.7c. On the basis of these tables, we can make the following observations.

Generally speaking, Japanese practicing attorneys start their careers as employed lawyers.[27] As they grow older, they try to practice independently, but some—especially in Tokyo where rents are higher—find it necessary to share an office in order to accumulate more capital before opening their own practices. After they have achieved independence, if their business prospers and the volume of their work both warrants and demands it, they hire younger lawyers to perform part of the work load. Thus, although Japanese attorneys may associate with others in various ways, their ultimate goal is to be on their own, "the master of a castle, however small it may be."

Partners, most of whom are in their thirties and forties, represent only a small minority among Japanese lawyers. They do not follow the traditional career pattern just described. In fact, partnerships are an innovation. According to our data, there presently are three types of partnership (apart from husband and wife or father and son). The first type comprises law firms specializing in international business transactions and adopting the work style and office organization of the larger American firms. These partners generally have had some legal education in the United States. Indeed, some of these firms were founded by American lawyers. Some have many patent attorneys among their partners. The employer and employee lawyers often are referred to by the English terms "partner" and "associate." Most firms send their young associates to Western countries (not always the United States) for legal studies and training. These firms are located almost exclusively in Tokyo and represent the largest and most modern law offices in Japan. In 1980 they contained eight to fifteen practicing attorneys, and some also had patent attorneys.

The second type of partnership consists of the law firms affiliated with left-wing political parties. They mainly represent labor unions in industrial disputes and defend union members and political leftists in criminal proceedings. In recent years, these lawyers have played an important role in cases concerning environmental pollution. Such cases often require cooperation among a number of committed lawyers sharing a common ideology. Specialization in union cases explains how these law firms can exist, even in the areas where the absolute number of practicing attorneys is very small.

The third type is made up of partnerships oriented to domestic business clients. Such partnerships are increasing in Osaka and Nagoya, and some make a conscious effort both to rationalize their practices through constant mutual consultation within the firm and to develop forms of legal services better adapted to the everyday needs of all Japanese business corporations, and not just the very large ones. These law firms generally are smaller than the first type and sometimes are formed on the basis of a former relationship between a master and an Isoro-attorney.

Most partnerships are fairly small (see table 4.8). One of our respondents belonged to a firm with 20 or more lawyers (partners and associates included), but this is a rare exception. The great majority of partnerships consist of two to five lawyers. This also is true of the offices of office-sharers, although here the average size is slightly larger (see table 4.9).

Table 4.10 shows the distribution of lawyers by area in terms of the number of lawyers in their offices, regardless of whether these lawyers are employed, office-sharers, masters, or partners. Half of Japanese lawyers are solo practitioners, 20 percent belong to a two-lawyer office, and another 20 percent belong to an office with three to six lawyers. In terms of management, however, office-sharers and masters both practice on their own account. In this sense, it can be said that 73 percent of all attorneys and 89 percent of all principal attorneys practice independently.

Law offices in Japan are small in another respect, too. The average number of clerks per lawyer is little more than one (see table 4.11). The occupation of law office clerk is not well institutionalized, either. There is no organized training or certificate system, as is the case in England and West Germany (Rechtsanwalt und Notar Gehilfe). Correspondingly, the work done by the clerks tends to be limited to secretarial and bookkeeping functions. Only a few regularly execute simple, patterned legal tasks. Practically no clerk is entrusted with work requiring independent legal judgment. Most are young women, who leave when they marry, or young men preparing for the Legal Examination, although a substantial minority of clerks are experienced men and women, who are indispensable to their employers. The average numbers of clerks per law office, by gender, education, experience, and area, are shown in table 4.12.

WORK AND CLIENTS

In order to ascertain the volume and content of the work of attorneys, we asked each respondent to list all open cases[28] and to classify them in terms of various criteria.

Table 4.13 shows that criminal matters account for 5 to 10 percent of the attorney's caseload, a proportion that increases as we go from area A toward area D, reflecting the lawyer shortage in peripheral areas (see also tables 4.14 and 4.15). The average number of cases open at the time of the survey (between thirty-two and forty-eight) is rather small; indeed, the national average of pending civil cases is only thirty-seven (see table 4.16). The volume is dramatically higher among the lawyers in their forties and fifties and also higher in peripheral areas, for the reason given above. Civil cases are heavily concentrated among the small number of masters and partners (see table 4.13). Only a few lawyers handle over 100 cases, most of whom are located in peripheral areas, and only 7.8 percent of all lawyers handle more than 80 cases (see table 4.15).[29]

There are four kinds of civil matters: (1) noncontentious (or preventive) cases; (2) disputes handled without the intervention of a court or other public agency (at least at the time of our inquiry); (3) cases brought before a public agency, such as an administrative tribunal; and (4) cases brought before a regular court for either mediation or adjudication. Formal litigation constitutes by far the greatest proportion of the civil work of Japanese practicing attorneys (see table 4.16). Noncontentious matters and out-of-court settlements represent only 15 to 30 percent of all civil cases (about 25 percent of the total work load of attorneys). Dispute settlement before administrative tribunals still is almost negligible. Only Tokyo differs significantly from this pattern because law firm partners specializing in international trade handle a larger proportion of noncontentious matters (see table 4.17).

When current civil cases are classified by subject matter (see table 4.18), the largest categories are debt collection (20 to 23 percent) and payment of debt (7 to 9 percent)—the gap between the two must be due to default cases. Closely related to these are executions of judgments (5 to 8 percent) and bankruptcy (2 to 3 percent). Together these categories account for about 35 to 40 percent. Next in importance are disputes involving rented houses or land (7 to 11 percent) and other cases involving real estate (9 to 15 percent); inheritance (4 to 5 percent) also primarily concerns houses and land. If we combine the three real estate categories, we get another 20 to 30 percent. A third major grouping consists of automobile accidents (4 to 7 percent), medical malpractice (1 percent), and other damages (6 to 7 percent), aggregating another 10 to 15 percent. Fourth place is taken by domestic matters (4 to 5 percent).[30] Those problems that arise in the everyday lives of most people— employment, environmental matters, consumer complaints, and grievances against the government—are not an important source of business for Japanese lawyers. Nor are those bodies of law that affect the daily affairs of larger business enterprises, such as company and economic law, patent and copyright law, and international trade law. Thus, Japanese lawyers depend heavily on debt collection and real estate matters, in which resort to court often is unavoidable.

Consistent with this subject matter emphasis, the main clientele of Japanese lawyers is individuals (who own property) and small and medium-sized enterprises, not large business firms (see table 4.19). Large business firms virtually are monopolized by master lawyers and partners in the major industrial centers (see table 4.20). Except for partners in Tokyo firms and masters everywhere, most Japanese lawyers rely heavily on new "one-shot" clients rather than on the return of habitual customers (see table 4.21).

Some lawyers have retainers (mostly oral) with an organization (very rarely an individual) whereby the lawyer offers daily consultation in return for a fixed annual fee. If the client also asks the lawyer to handle litigation, it will pay the lawyer a separate fee, although usually at a reduced rate. The retaining organization is not obligated to send its cases exclusively to its legal advisor, and some larger companies have several legal advisors (see tables 4.22 and 4.23). To create such relationships is one of the central goals of Japanese lawyers. Retainers ensure a regular income, which, although often rather small, at least covers the rent. They are important sources of work, for the retaining organizations not only give their advisor profitable cases but also refer other clients—and to be the legal advisor of a well-known firm enhances the prestige of a lawyer. Master lawyers have a distinct advantage in getting retainers (see table 4.22).

Very few clients come to the lawyer through public or private counseling bureaus, and only a small number come without any intermediary (see table 4.24). A potential client has to know the lawyer personally or else be able to mobilize a social network that can lead to a lawyer. This established pattern, which is accepted by both lawyers and the general public, undoubtedly limits the access of ordinary people to legal services.[31]

INCOME

It is difficult to determine the income of practicing attorneys accurately. We asked our respondents to reveal their gross and net income and certain expenses for 1979, as they reported these to the tax authorities (see table 4.25). The average net income of Tokyo Lawyers is ¥7,600,000 (or about $38,000) after deducting expenses of about 60 percent. In Area D, average net income is ¥6,140,000 (or about $30,700), and expenses are 53 percent of gross. These income levels are roughly comparable with those of British solicitors, but there is much greater variability in Japan than in England (see tables 4.26 and 4.27).

The average net income of lawyers peaks earlier in the more rural areas (see table 4.28). This table also can be used to compare the income of lawyers with the salaries of other occupational groups. Data on the income of company directors, independent entrepreneurs, and practicing physicians are not available. However, we do have reliable data on the salaries of employees of nongovernmental organizations (see table 4.29). This gives the impression that practicing attorneys earn much higher incomes than other white-collar employees but a little less than employed physicians.

The salaries of judges increase fairly regularly for each of the first ten years of their careers (as assistant judges) according to a schedule that, in 1980, rose from ¥147,500 to ¥319,600 per month. (Recall that in recent years the average judge has qualified at about age thirty.) In order to obtain a rough estimate of their yearly income, we may assume that they receive an annual bonus of five times their basic monthly salary, for a total of ¥2,510,000 to ¥5,430,000 per annum. Their salaries no longer are determined mechanically after they become full-fledged judges (see table 4.30). If we consider only ordinary full-fledged judges, whose compulsory retirement age is sixty-five (excluding the Chief Judges of District or High Courts and Supreme Court justices), their total yearly income ranges from approximately ¥6,530,000 to ¥14,530,000. It is difficult to draw a definite conclusion from these data, because these averages are not specified by age. Generally speaking, practicing attorneys in their forties and fifties appear to make a little more money than judges, but they do less well in their sixties and seventies, especially when we take into account the pensions judges receive after retirement.

The variation of lawyers' incomes is much greater within the same age group than that of salaries in other occupations, for those employed in organizations receive a similar salary at the same age. The enormous variation in the income of Japanese lawyers according to their status or form of practice is one of the central connotations of the term "free profession" (see table 4.31). The sole principals (masters) who employ one or more other lawyers are by far the richest, although there are very few. Partners in Tokyo, many of whom specialize in international trade, also are among the top profit-makers.

CONCLUSION

Our survey of the present condition of Japanese practicing attorneys reveals that they still play a limited role within the legal order. Their professional activities are largely confined to representation before courts. This partly reflects the traditional predominance of judges in the administration of justice. Noncontentious matters, where practicing attorneys would be the only authoritative representatives of the legal order, generally are not entrusted to them. Outside of court, lawyers also are surrounded by lay competitors. These distinct occupational groups of "quasi-lawyers," each with a legally recognized sphere of competence closely related to law, allegedly often serve as lawyer substitutes for individual citizens. Large business firms, in contrast, have their own "lawpersons," who handle the legal matters arising in the course of their daily business transactions (such as making a contract or resolving a dispute); they use their officially qualified "legal advisers" only when involved in litigation.

Practicing attorneys are not highly professionalized. Their heavy reliance on litigation is reflected in the fact that the bulk of their business involves debt collection or real estate—situations where litigation often is a last resort because the parties either are strangers or have terminated their relationships. These areas of legal practice do not require a very sophisticated level of expertise. The main clients of most lawyers—small and medium-sized business enterprises and propertied individuals—do not constitute a very stable clientele. There is little specialization in lawyers' work, except for the small minority who deal with patent law, international trade, or labor union matters. The great majority of Japanese practicing attorneys are generalists working, or aspiring to work, on their own, with minimal clerical help. The general style of their work and life closely resembles that of their main clients, small business proprietors.

In many respects the activities of Japanese practicing attorneys, and thus the legal system as well, touch only the surface of the social order. They still have not penetrated deeply into the everyday life of either ordinary citizens or the business world, nor have they managed to institutionalize the specifically legal ways of ordering human affairs.

TABLES

Areas	Population	Sample	Returned questionnaire	Return rate (%)	Weighted sample
A	5,361	1,340	507	37.8	789
B	2,044	679	326	48.0	301
C	918	459	234	51.0	135
D	3,143	1,558	622	39.9	463
Total	11,466	4,036	1,689	41.8	1,688

4.2. Admissions to and Graduations from ILTR and Graduates' Choice of Position[a]

Class (starting year)	Number of entrants	Number of graduates	Choice of position at graduation				
			Assistant judge	Summary court judge	Prosecutor	Practicing attorney	Others
1947	140	134 (2)	72 (1)		44 1)	18	
1948	245	240 (2)	106 (1)		54 (1)	78	2
1949	290	284 (3)	84 (2)		77	113 (1)	10
1950	245 (4)	246 (4)	57 (1)		79 (1)	97 (1)	13 (1)
1951	223 (4)	215 (4)	51 (2)		67	84	13 (2)
1952	234 (1)	226 (1)	45		48	131 (1)	2
1953	243 (7)	236 (7)	67 (5)		59	109 (2)	1
1954	214 (3)	216 (3)	73		50	89 (2)	4 (1)
1955	257 (9)	267 (9)	77 (2)		45	143 (7)	2
1956	256 (9)	256 (10)	65 (3)		45	144 (7)	2
1957	284 (16)	282 (14)	69 (3)		51 (1)	157 (10)	5
1958	291 (5)	291 (7)	81 (1)		44 (1)	166 (5)	
1959	354 (13)	349 (11)	83 (3)	1	48 (1)	216 (7)	1
1960	314 (10)	319 (10)	75 (4)		42	202 (6)	
1961	333 (15)	334 (14)	88 (3)		40 (2)	202 (8)	4 (1)
1962	374 (17)	365 (18)	56 (3)	1	45 (1)	261 (14)	2
1963	440 (23)	441 (23)	68 (6)	4	52 (1)	316 (16)	1
1964	485 (27)	478 (25)	63 (2)	3	47 (1)	359 (21)	6 (1)
1965	484 (25)	484 (26)	61 (2)	12 (2)	49	356 (21)	6 (1)
1966	513 (28)	511 (28)	77 (5)	8 (1)	49 (1)	369 (20)	8 (1)
1967	520 (18)	516 (18)	78 (2)	6	53	374 (16)	5
1968	513 (22)	512 (21)	61 (1)	3	38	405 (20)	5
1969	503 (37)	506 (37)	63 (1)	2 (1)	47 (3)	388 (30)	6 (2)
1970	503 (36)	495 (34)	58 (2)		59 (5)	370 (27)	8
1971	492 (34)	493 (33)	65 (3)	1	50 (4)	371 (23)	6 (3)
1972	510 (30)	506 (29)	85 (5)		47 (2)	367 (20)	7 (2)
1973	543 (26)	543 (27)	84 (2)		38 (2)	416 (22)	5 (1)
1974	538 (24)	537 (24)	78 (3)	1	74 (3)	376 (16)	8 (2)
1975	491 (22)	487 (21)	70 (3)	2	50	363 (18)	2
1976	461 (31)	463 (32)	76 (6)	2	58 (4)	325 (22)	2
1977	465 (40)	465 (40)	61 (4)	3 (1)	49 (4)	350 (31)	2
1978	454 (33)						
1979	485 (32)						

[a] The figure in parentheses indicates the number of women included.

Source: 700 *Jurisuto* 122–123 (1979).

4.3. Number of Judges, Prosecutors, and Practicing Attorneys, Absolute and in Relation to Population, 1896–1976

Year	Judges		Summary court judges		Prosecutors		Practicing attorneys		Population
	Number	Population per judge	Number	Population per judge	Number	Population per prosecutor	Number	Population per attorney	
1896	1,221	34,390			383	109,634	1,568	26,779	41,990,000
1916	903	59,236			389	137,506	2,665	20,071	53,490,000
1936	1,391	50,029			648	107,392	5,976	11,645	69,590,000
1956	1,597	55,254	730	120,877	1,717	51,392	6,040	14,609	88,240,000
1976	1,912	58,740	791	141,985	2,089	53,763	10,792	10,407	112,310,000

4.4. Pass Rates on ILTR Examination, 1949–1979[a]

Year	Taking	Passing	Percent passing
1949	2,570	265 (3)	10.3
1954	5,240	250 (10)	4.8
1959	7,858	319 (8)	4.1
1964	12,698	508 (25)	4.0
1969	18,453	501 (37)	2.7
1974	26,708	491 (23)	1.8
1979	28,622	503 (40)	1.8

[a] The figures in parentheses indicate the number of women included.

4.5. Pass Rates on ILTR Examination by University Attended, 1981

University	Taking	Passing	Percent passing
National			
Tokyo	1,920	101	5.3
Kyoto	868	44	5.1
Osaka	356	13	3.7
Tohoku	484	13	2.7
Nagoya	276	9	3.3
Hokkaido	284	4	1.4
Kyushu	432	6	1.4
Private			
Chuo	6,102	58	1.0
Waseda	2,887	56	2.0
Keio	1,128	19	1.7
Meiji	1,730	12	0.7

4.6. Mode of Remuneration of Employed Lawyers

Areas	Salary only	Salary and commission	Commission only	Other	Total
A	69	42	20	19	149
	(45.8)	(28.1)	(13.5)	(12.5)	(54.4)
B	44	15	2	6	67
	(66.7)	(22.2)	(2.8)	(8.3)	(24.2)
C	12	4	1	1	18
	(64.5)	(22.6)	(6.5)	(6.5)	(6.5)
D	30	7	2	2	41
	(72.7)	(16.4)	(5.5)	(5.5)	(14.9)
Total	154	68	25	28	275
	(56.1)	(24.6)	(9.3)	(10.0)	(100.0)

[a] Figures in parentheses are percentages within each area.

4.7a. Status of Lawyers, by Area[a]

Areas	Employed lawyer	Overhead-sharer	Solo	Master	Partner	Total
A	153	174	300	79	36	743
	(20.5)	(23.5)	(40.5)	(10.7)	(4.8)	
B	69	20	122	23	49	284
	(24.4)	(7.2)	(43.0)	(8.1)	(17.3)	
C	18	14	81	7	6	127
	(14.6)	(11.0)	(64.4)	(5.5)	(4.6)	
D	42	20	294	33	48	437
	(9.5)	(4.6)	(67.3)	(7.7)	(10.9)	
Total	287	229	798	143	138	1,590
	(17.7)	(14.4)	(50.2)	(9.0)	(8.7)	

[a] Figures in parentheses are percentages within area.

4.7b. Status of Lawyers, by Age[a]

Age	Employed lawyer	Overhead-sharer	Solo	Master	Partner	Total
20–29	55	6	4	2	5	73
	(75.7)	(8.8)	(5.9)	(2.1)	(7.5)	
30–39	173	70	171	9	66	489
	(35.3)	(14.4)	(35.0)	(1.7)	(13.5)	
40–49	29	73	242	56	41	442
	(6.6)	(16.6)	(54.7)	(12.7)	(9.3)	
50–59	12	54	135	47	15	262
	(4.4)	(20.8)	(51.5)	(17.8)	(5.6)	
60–69	2	11	96	15	5	129
	(1.2)	(8.8)	(74.3)	(11.9)	(3.8)	
≥ 70	11	11	140	15	6	182
	(6.0)	(6.0)	(76.9)	(8.0)	(3.1)	
Total	281	227	788	143	138	1,577
	(17.8)	(14.4)	(50.0)	(9.1)	(8.7)	

[a] Figures in parentheses are percentages within cohort.

4.7c. Status of Tokyo Lawyers, by Age

Age	Employed lawyer	Overhead-sharer	Solo	Master	Partner	Total
20–29	31	3	0	2	2	37
	(83.3)	(8.3)	(0.0)	(4.2)	(4.2)	
30–39	86	50	50	3	14	202
	(42.3)	(24.6)	(24.6)	(1.5)	(6.9)	
40–49	20	56	107	28	9	221
	(9.2)	(25.4)	(48.6)	(12.7)	(4.2)	
50–59	5	47	48	26	6	132
	(3.5)	(35.3)	(36.5)	(20.0)	(4.7)	
60–69	2	9	44	9	3	67
	(2.3)	(14.0)	(65.1)	(14.0)	(4.7)	
≥ 70	9	8	45	11	2	75
	(12.5)	(10.4)	(60.4)	(14.6)	(2.1)	
Total	153	173	294	79	36	735
	(20.8)	(23.5)	(40.0)	(10.8)	(4.9)	

[a] Figures in parentheses are percentages within cohort.

4.8. Number of Partners in Partnerships, by Area[a]

Areas	Number of partners					Total
	2	3–5	6–9	10–19	≥ 20	
A	19	15	0	0	2	36
	(52.2)	(43.5)			(4.3)	
B	20	18	9	2	0	49
	(41.5)	(35.8)	(18.9)	(3.8)		
C	4	2	0	1	0	7
	(60.0)	(30.0)		(10.0)		
D	22	18	5	1	0	46
	(48.4)	(38.7)	(9.7)	(1.6)		
Total	65	53	14	4	2	138
	(47.6)	(38.8)	(10.1)	(2.3)	(1.2)	

[a] Figures in parentheses are percentages within areas.

4.9. Number of Principals in Shared Offices, by Area[a]

Areas	Number of principals					Total
	2	3–5	6–9	10–19	≥ 20	
A	84	58	25	6	2	174
	(48.2)	(33.0)	(14.3)	(3.6)	(0.9)	
B	14	5	0	1	0	19
	(71.4)	(23.8)		(4.8)		
C	9	5	1	0	0	14
	(62.5)	(33.3)	(4.2)			
D	11	7	1	0	0	19
	(57.7)	(38.5)	(3.8)			
Total	118	74	26	7	2	227
	(51.9)	(32.7)	(11.5)	(3.0)	(0.8)	

[a] Figures in parentheses are percentages within areas.

4.10. Number of Lawyers in Law Office, by Area[a]

Number in office	Number of lawyers in offices of this size				
	A	B	C	D	Total
1	304 (40.5)	122 (42.2)	82 (64.3)	298 (68.0)	806 (50.2)
2	171 (22.8)	66 (22.7)	29 (22.6)	77 (17.5)	342 (21.3)
3	89 (11.8)	45 (15.7)	10 (7.7)	32 (7.3)	176 (10.9)
4	54 (7.3)	18 (6.1)	3 (2.3)	16 (3.7)	91 (5.7)
5	31 (4.1)	6 (2.2)	3 (1.8)	6 (1.4)	46 (2.9)
6	16 (2.1)	9 (3.2)	1 (0.5)	4 (1.0)	30 (1.9)
7	26 (3.5)	15 (5.1)	0	1 (0.3)	43 (2.7)
8	19 (2.5)	4 (1.3)	0	1 (0.2)	23 (1.4)
9	14 (1.9)	0	0	1 (0.3)	16 (1.0)
10	6 (0.8)	1 (0.3)	0	1 (0.2)	8 (0.5)
11	5 (0.6)	0	0	0	5 (0.3)
12	2 (0.2)	3 (1.0)	1 (0.5)	0	5 (0.3)
13	2 (0.2)	0	0	0	2 (0.1)
14	2 (0.2)	0	0	0	2 (0.1)
15	2 (0.2)	0	0	0	2 (0.1)
16	0	0	0	0	0
17	0	0	0	0	0
18	2 (0.2)	0	0	0	2 (0.1)
19	0	0	0	0	0
20	3 (0.4)	0	0	1 (0.2)	4 (0.2)
21	0	0	0	0	0
22	2 (0.2)	0	0	0	2 (0.1)
23	3 (0.4)	0	0	4	3 (0.2)
24	0	1 (0.3)	0	0	1 (0.1)
Total	750 (100.0)	289 (100.0)	128 (100.0)	439 (100.0)	1,606 (100.0)

[a] Figures in parentheses are percentages within area.

4.11. Number of Clerks per Lawyer, by Status and Area

Status	A	B	C	D	Total
Office-sharer	0.91	0.82	0.69	0.77	0.88
Solo	1.59	1.43	1.42	1.18	1.40
Master	1.09	1.17	1.15	1.01	1.09
Partner	1.50	1.00	1.10	1.12	1.18
Total	1.31	1.25	1.29	1.14	1.25

4.12. Number of Clerks per Law Office, by Characteristics of Clerks and Area[a]

	A	B	C	D	Total
Male	0.88	0.84	0.38	0.42	0.69
	(32.5)	(34.9)	(21.8)	(26.3)	
Female	1.75	1.58	1.36	1.18	1.52
	(65.5)	(65.1)	(78.2)	(73.7)	
University graduates	1.23	1.04	0.60	0.56	0.88
	(45.4)	(43.2)	(34.5)	(35.0)	
Others	1.40	1.37	1.14	1.04	1.33
	(54.6)	(56.8)	(65.5)	(65.0)	
≥ 7 years in office	0.58	0.45	0.41	0.35	0.46
	(21.4)	(18.7)	(23.6)	(21.9)	
3−6 years in office	0.93	0.91	0.63	0.62	0.81
	(34.3)	(37.8)	(36.2)	(38.8)	
< 3 years in office	1.12	1.05	0.70	0.63	0.94
	(44.3)	(43.6)	(41.4)	(39.4)	
All clerks	2.63	2.41	1.74	1.60	2.21

[a] Figures in parentheses are percentages within category and area.

4.13. Average Number of Open Criminal and Civil Cases, by Age and Area

	A		B		C		D		Total	
Years	Criminal	Civil	Criminal	Civil	Criminal	Civil	Criminal	Civil	Criminal	Civil
20–29	1.2	14.8	2.2	19.0	3.7	20.3	4.2	31.2	2.3	19.6
30–39	1.6	23.8	2.5	31.5	2.9	36.0	4.9	40.5	2.8	31.2
40–49	1.8	42.6	2.0	46.7	3.8	69.9	6.7	56.7	3.2	48.7
50–59	1.9	37.6	4.0	39.4	8.0	52.0	4.1	56.0	3.3	44.1
60–69	1.0	26.3	1.7	33.4	2.8	52.1	6.5	37.4	2.6	32.2
≥70	1.4	16.7	1.3	34.6	2.8	15.1	3.5	20.3	2.3	20.1
Total	1.6	31.0	2.3	36.8	3.9	44.7	5.1	43.3	2.9	36.6

Number of cases

4.14. Average Number of Open Criminal and Civil Cases, by Status and Area

| | | | | | Number of cases | | | | | | | |
| | A | | B | | C | | D | | Total | |
Status	Criminal	Civil	Criminal	Civil	Criminal	Civil	Criminal	Civil	Criminal	Civil
Employed	0.9	13.5	1.9	16.9	3.3	21.1	3.7	17.4	1.7	15.4
Office-sharer	2.3	33.4	1.8	32.6	2.6	29.1	4.4	43.7	2.4	34.0
Solo	1.6	29.4	2.6	35.5	4.3	48.1	5.0	41.9	3.3	36.9
Master	1.3	59.5	3.9	74.3	3.0	79.1	5.8	82.5	2.9	68.2
Partner	1.8	41.4	1.9	50.0	3.7	59.3	6.0	47.4	3.4	47.2
Total	1.6	30.7	2.4	36.5	3.9	44.3	5.0	43.2	2.9	36.4

4.15. Number of PAs with Different Civil Caseloads, by Area[a]

Areas	Civil caseload									
	0–5	6–20	21–35	36–50	51–65	66–80	81–100	101–120	≥121	Total
A	98	220	198	126	48	23	12	3	12	741
	(13.2)	(29.6)	(26.7)	(17.0)	(6.5)	(3.2)	(1.7)	(0.4)	(1.7)	(100.0)
B	31	64	66	63	28	18	8	3	6	286
	(11.0)	(22.3)	(22.9)	(21.9)	(9.7)	(6.5)	(2.9)	(1.0)	(1.9)	(100.0)
C	12	24	29	21	13	9	9	2	6	126
	(9.6)	(19.3)	(22.9)	(16.5)	(10.1)	(7.3)	(7.3)	(1.8)	(5.0)	(100.0)
D	42	90	91	76	49	33	33	12	16	442
	(9.6)	(20.4)	(20.5)	(17.2)	(11.1)	(7.4)	(7.6)	(2.7)	(3.5)	(100.0)
Total	184	399	383	286	138	84	63	20	40	1,595
	(11.5)	(24.9)	(24.0)	(17.9)	(8.6)	(5.3)	(3.9)	(1.4)	(2.5)	(100.0)

[a]Figures in parentheses are percentages within area.

4.16. Breakdown of PA Civil Work, by Type of Matter and Area[a]

| | Average number of civil cases per PA | | | | |
	A	B	C	D	Total
Noncontentious matters	3.26	2.47	2.29	1.95	2.68
	(10.4)	(6.6)	(5.1)	(4.5)	(7.3)
Out-of-court settlement	4.48	4.21	3.53	4.20	4.28
	(14.3)	(11.3)	(7.9)	(9.7)	(11.5)
Tribunal	1.32	1.18	1.48	1.09	1.24
	(4.2)	(3.2)	(3.3)	(2.5)	(3.4)
Court	22.30	29.32	37.56	36.11	28.60
	(71.1)	(78.9)	(83.7)	(83.3)	(77.7)
Total	31.36	37.18	44.86	43.35	36.80
	(100)	(100)	(100)	(100)	(100)

[a] Figures in parentheses are percentages within area.

4.17. Percentage of PA Civil Work Devoted to Litigation, by Status and Area

	A	B	C	D	Total
Employed	62.1	82.5	88.9	84.3	73.7
Office-sharer	77.8	83.0	86.4	80.1	79.1
Solo	69.2	80.7	83.2	83.7	78.3
Master	81.0	82.1	81.9	84.8	82.2
Partner	52.5	71.9	84.7	83.9	72.0
Total	72.3	79.3	83.3	83.6	

4.18. Subject Matter of PA Civil Work, by Area[a]

| | Average number of civil matters per PA | | | | |
	A	B	C	D	Total
Execution of judgment	2.52	2.50	2.77	2.12	2.47
	(8.5)	(6.1)	(6.3)	(4.9)	(7.0)
Bankruptcy	0.65	1.01	0.82	0.79	0.77
	(2.1)	(2.8)	(1.9)	(1.8)	(2.0)
International transaction	1.07	0.33	0.14	0.25	0.64
	(3.5)	(0.9)	(0.3)	(0.6)	(1.8)

4.18. (*continued*)

	Average number of civil matters per PA				
	A	B	C	D	Total
Family	1.54	1.58	1.77	2.61	1.86
	(5.0)	(4.4)	(4.0)	(6.1)	(5.2)
Inheritance	1.59	1.50	1.98	1.98	1.70
	(5.2)	(4.1)	(4.0)	(4.6)	(4.7)
Leased land or house	3.40	3.56	3.13	4.13	3.61
	(11.1)	(9.8)	(7.1)	(9.6)	(10.0)
Debt (creditor)	6.33	6.95	10.09	7.98	7.18
	(20.6)	(19.2)	(23.0)	(18.5)	(19.9)
Debt (debtor)	2.02	2.77	3.68	3.75	2.76
	(6.6)	(7.7)	(8.4)	(8.7)	(7.6)
Automobile accident	1.11	2.51	2.99	3.07	2.04
	(3.6)	(6.9)	(6.8)	(7.1)	(5.7)
Medical accident	0.34	0.44	0.74	0.52	0.44
	(1.1)	(1.2)	(1.7)	(1.2)	(1.2)
Labor, employment	0.67	1.02	1.41	0.84	0.84
	(2.1)	(2.8)	(3.2)	(1.9)	(2.3)
Environmental pollution	0.16	0.38	0.38	0.33	0.26
	(0.5)	(1.1)	(0.9)	(0.8)	(0.7)
Consumer	0.19	0.15	0.26	0.19	0.19
	(0.6)	(0.4)	(0.6)	(0.4)	(0.5)
Complaint against government	0.41	0.47	0.60	0.59	0.48
	(1.3)	(1.3)	(1.4)	(1.4)	(1.3)
Company or economic law	0.86	0.86	0.78	0.67	0.80
	(2.8)	(2.4)	(1.8)	(1.6)	(2.2)
Patent or copyright	0.55	0.51	0.19	0.14	0.40
	(1.8)	(1.4)	(0.4)	(0.3)	(1.1)
Other real estate	2.76	4.67	5.24	6.42	4.30
	(9.0)	(12.6)	(11.9)	(14.9)	(11.9)
Other damages	1.84	2.52	3.45	3.19	2.46
	(6.0)	(7.0)	(7.8)	(7.4)	(6.8)
Others	2.57	2.45	3.74	3.56	2.91
	(8.4)	(6.8)	(8.5)	(8.3)	(8.1)
Total	30.68	36.18	43.96	43.13	36.11
	(99.8)	(98.9)	(100.0)	(100.0)	

[a] Figures in parentheses are average percentage of total civil caseload within area.

4.19. Type of Client Served by PA in Civil Matters, by Area[a]

	Average number of civil matters per PA				
	A	B	C	D	Total
Individual	13.57	18.93	23.00	27.31	19.08
	(44.4)	(51.1)	(53.3)	(62.8)	(52.6)
Small- or medium-sized business	9.40	10.55	12.10	10.53	10.12
	(30.7)	(28.5)	(28.1)	(24.2)	(27.9)
Large business	5.50	5.31	4.45	2.68	4.61
	(18.0)	(14.3)	(10.3)	(6.2)	(12.71)
Government agency	0.42	0.52	1.57	0.85	0.66
	(1.4)	(1.4)	(3.1)	(2.0)	(1.8)
Other organization	1.68	1.70	2.00	2.14	1.83
	(5.5)	(4.6)	(4.6)	(4.9)	(5.0)
Total	30.57	37.01	43.12	43.51	36.30
	(100)	(100)	(100)	(100)	(100)

[a] Figures in parentheses are average percent of total clients within area.

4.20. Average Number of Matters Handled for Large Companies per Lawyer, by Status and Area

	A	B	C	D	Total
Employed	3.03	1.39	4.48	1.00	2.21
Office-sharer	2.89	3.50	1.13	0.81	3.24
Solo	3.57	5.63	1.91	2.27	3.35
Master	21.93	17.25	12.38	11.89	17.55
Partner	11.43	7.40	0.11	1.64	6.40
Total	5.53	5.35	4.48	2.63	4.82

4.21. Percentage of Lawyers Three-Fourths of Whose Civil Caseloads Are from New Clients, by Status and Area

	A	B	C	D	Total
Employed	47.4	55.7	61.3	77.8	54.8
Office-sharer	21.4	27.2	50.0	40.7	25.2
Solo	17.4	13.0	36.8	39.2	26.5
Master	11.7	6.7	0	8.8	11.5
Partner	4.8	21.3	44.4	47.5	26.3
Total	23.5	25.6	41.4	42.0	

4.22. Average Number of Clients Who Retain the Lawyer as Legal Advisor, by Status and Area

	A	B	C	D	Total
Employed	4.46	2.78	2.46	2.95	3.80
Office-sharer	9.05	9.24	8.64	9.17	9.05
Solo	9.37	10.98	11.92	9.56	9.95
Master	16.75	28.16	26.73	20.17	19.95
Partner	13.91	19.18	10.25	9.23	14.24
Total	9.68	12.84	11.66	10.19	10.54

4.23. Average Number of Clients who Retain the Lawyer as Legal Advisor, by Type of Client and Area[a]

	A	B	C	D	Total
Individual	0.85	1.15	0.87	0.84	0.91
	(8.6)	(8.9)	(7.3)	(8.1)	(9.0)
Small or medium-sized business	6.41	7.90	7.13	6.02	6.63
	(65.1)	(61.2)	(59.9)	(58.1)	(62.0)
Large company	1.76	2.59	2.36	1.53	1.89
	(17.9)	(20.1)	(19.8)	(14.8)	(17.7)
Government agency	0.11	0.22	0.41	0.43	0.24
	(1.1)	(1.7)	(3.4)	(4.2)	(2.2)
Other	0.72	1.04	1.14	1.54	1.03
	(7.3)	(8.1)	(9.6)	(14.9)	(9.6)
Total	9.85	12.90	11.91	10.36	10.70
	(100)	(100)	(100)	(100)	

[a] Figures in parentheses are average percentage of total retainers within area.

4.24. Route by Which the Client Came to the Lawyer in Civil Matters, by Area[a]

Route	A	B	C	D	Total
Kin or through kin	1.39	1.69	1.28	1.77	1.54
	(5.0)	(5.0)	(3.0)	(4.2)	(4.6)
Client in another case or through another case	6.26	6.30	8.96	8.78	7.17
	(22.6)	(18.5)	(20.9)	(21.0)	(21.2)
Retainer	8.65	12.20	14.77	10.51	10.28
	(31.3)	(35.9)	(34.5)	(25.2)	(30.4)
Other lawyer	1.91	2.33	4.05	2.57	2.33
	(6.9)	(6.9)	(9.5)	(6.2)	(6.9)
Other law-related person	0.47	0.75	1.02	1.29	0.79
	(1.7)	(2.2)	(2.4)	(3.1)	(2.3)
Private counseling bureau	0.37	0.76	0.65	0.77	0.59
	(1.3)	(2.2)	(1.5)	(1.8)	(1.9)
Public counseling bureau	0.43	0.82	0.99	1.17	0.74
	(1.6)	(2.4)	(2.3)	(2.8)	(2.2)
Other personal acquaintance	6.92	7.97	7.88	10.11	8.05
	(25.0)	(23.4)	(18.4)	(24.2)	(23.5)
Other	1.01	0.91	1.55	2.09	1.33
	(3.7)	(2.7)	(3.6)	(5.0)	(3.9)
No intermediary	0.26	0.26	1.43	2.70	1.02
	(0.9)	(0.8)	(3.3)	(6.5)	(3.0)
Total	27.67	33.99	42.58	41.76	33.82

[a] Figures in parentheses are percentage of source of all clients within area.

4.25. 1979 Gross and Net Annual Income of Japanese Practicing Attorneys (in ¥1,000)

	A	B	C	D	Total
Gross income	18,890	15,440	14,240	12,980	16,350
Net income	7,600	6,830	7,110	6,140	7,030
in U.S.$[a]	38,000	34,150	35,055	30,700	35,150
Rate of expenses (%)	59.8	55.8	50.1	52.7	57.6

[a] Assumes exchange rate of ¥200 = $1.00 (U.S.).

4.26. Net Annual Income of Japanese Practicing Attorneys (in ¥1,000), by Area[a]

	A	B	C	D
Highest decile	14,000 (2.37)	11,540 (2.16)	14,790 (2.62)	11,600 (2.30)
Third decile	8,000 (1.36)	7,500 (1.40)	8,440 (1.49)	7,200 (1.43)
Median	5,900 (1.00)	5,340 (1.00)	5,650 (1.00)	5,050 (1.00)
Seventh decile	4,290 (0.71)	3,930 (0.74)	3,440 (0.61)	3,160 (0.63)
Lowest decile	2,350 (0.40)	2,150 (0.40)	1,730 (0.31)	1,440 (0.29)
Average	7,600 (1.29)	6,830 (1.80)	7,110 (1.26)	6,140 (1.22)

[a] Figures in parentheses are ratios to median within area.

4.27. Net Annual Profit (in U.K. £) of
British Solicitors in 1976[a]

Highest decile	22,701 (1.94)
Third decile	15,224 (1.30)
Median	11,686 (1.00)
Seventh decile	8,862 (0.76)
Lowest decile	5,604 (0.48)
Average	13,581 (1.16)

[a] Figures in parentheses are ratios to
median.
Source: Royal Commission (1979,
2:477).

4.28. Average Net Annual Income (in ¥1,000), by Age and Area

Years	A	B	C	D	Total
20−29	3,470	3,030	3,020	2,740	3,200
30−39	5,480	5,010	5,730	4,800	5,210
40−49	8,380	8,530	9,400	7,910	8,360
50−59	11,340	8,030	9,460	8,780	10,050
60−69	8,420	11,580	9,160	5,860	8,320
≥70	5,300	5,910	3,750	3,830	4,690

4.29. Yearly Salary of University Graduates Employed in Various White-Collar Jobs by
Nongovernmental Organizations with Fifty or More Employees (1980) (in ¥1,000)

Clerk (average age 29.4 years)	3,236
Unit head (average age 36.17 years)	4,860
Section head (average age 42.9 years)	6,249
Department head (average age 48.9 years)	7,825
Medical doctor other than hospital or department head (average age 37.3 years)	9,342

4.30. Monthly Salaries of Full-Fledged Judges
(1980) (in ¥1,000)

Chief Justice of Supreme Court	1,550
Justice of Supreme Court	1,130
Chief Judge of Tokyo High Court	1,030
Chief Judge of other high court	950
Other full-fledged judge	
Class 1	855
Class 2	758
Class 3	708
Class 4	604
Class 5	521
Class 6	471
Class 7	423
Class 8	384

4.31. Average Net Annual Income (in ¥1,000) of Practicing Attorneys, by Status and Area

	A	B	C	D	Total
Employed	4,990	4,800	4,540	3,740	4,740
Office-sharer	7,280	5,610	6,630	5,510	6,950
Solo	7,160	6,340	7,270	5,900	6,580
Master	12,520	14,570	14,620	12,260	12,830
Partner	13,880	8,490	4,840	6,160	9,050

NOTES

1. In 1980 the Japan Federation of Practicing Attorneys' Associations (see note 5, below) undertook a survey of its members. This was the first systematic effort in Japan to ascertain empirically and statistically the actual state of legal practice. A thirteen-page questionnaire containing sixty-five questions covering a wide range of subjects was drawn up on the basis of preliminary interviews and sent to a stratified random sample of 4,036 practicing attorneys throughout Japan; 1,689 questionnaires were returned with valid answers to most of the questions asked (see table 4.1).

The total population of practicing attorneys was divided into four sub-populations corresponding to the following four areas: A, Tokyo; B, Osaka and Aichi; C, other prefectures with a high court (Hokkaido, Miyagi, Hiroshima, Fukuoka, and Kagawa); D, all the other prefectures where no high court is located. The prefectures in area C are local centers of legal activities because of their high courts; those in area D generally are rural, although they include some highly in-dustrialized prefectures adjacent to Tokyo and Osaka, such as Kanagawa and Hyogo.

Comparison of the respondents with the original sample with regard to the age, the year of registration as practicing attorney, the university attended, the method of qualification, and the prior occupation showed a statistically significant overrepresentation of younger lawyers, those registered more recently, those who passed the present legal examination, and those without any prior occupa-tion, and an underrepresentation of those over seventy years of age and those who attended the University of Tokyo. However, the overall distribution is not greatly distorted. For detail, see *Nichibenren* (1981: 43ff.)

2. For a general account of the history of the Japanese legal system and of the Japanese legal profession in particular, see Rabinowitz (1956), Takayanagi (1963), and Hattori (1963). A good introductory book on the Japanese legal system as a whole is Tanaka (1976), which also contains excerpts from the last two sources cited.

3. For the details of the history of the modern legal system of Japan, see note 2, above.

4. In this chapter the English term "practicing attorney" (sometimes abbre-viated "PA") is used to designate the title "bengoshi."

5. Practicing attorneys are required by law to set up a local association for each district court jurisdiction. Accordingly, there is one PA association in each prefecture, except that Tokyo has three, for historical reasons. The Japan Federa-tion of Practicing Attorneys' Associations (JFPAA), also a legally prescribed in-stitution, is constituted by all the PAs and all the local PA associations. All those associations are incorporated, and each PA must belong to one local association *and* the JFPAA. The purpose of both levels of association is "to perform the busi-ness in relation to the guidance, liaison and supervision of members in order to

maintain their dignity and to improve and develop the lawyers' business" (PA Act, art. 31).

Under the law, a person who has completed the legal apprentice course at the ILTR (see section entitled "Recruitment.") is qualified to become a PA. Those who were PAs under the former laws are regarded as having fulfilled this requirement. In addition, the law provides for some exceptional ways of qualifying as a PA (PA Act, art. 5), but only a small minority (less than 1 percent) of the present PAs have qualified in these ways. In order to become a PA, a person should be registered in the list maintained by the JFPAA. The applicant should request the registration through the local PA association, which has the power to refuse to forward this request to the JFPAA on certain grounds specified by the law (PA Act, art. 12). The complaint against the refusal eventually may be appealed to the high court (PA Act, art. 16).

Each PA Association has disciplinary powers over its members, which are exercised through a disciplinary committee whose members are selected from among PAs, judges, prosecutors, and persons of learning and experience (PA Act, arts. 52, 69).

6. For a general account of the examination system as well as of the content of the examination and of the training at the ILTR, see Tanaka (1976: 566–582).

7. The number who enter and leave the ILTR, as well as which branch of the profession they enter, are shown in table 4.2. The Legal Examination is not an entrance examination to the ILTR, and some of those who pass it choose not to enter the ILTR, at least immediately. Since those who have passed the Legal Examination can enter the ILTR whenever they choose, the entrants in a given year may include those who passed it some years previously. Those who enter the ILTR immediately after passing the Legal Examination actually do so the following year.

8. The regular judges may be appointed from among those with ten years' experience as an assistant judge, summary court judge, public prosecutor, practicing attorney, and others (Courts Act, art. 42). In actuality, however, most judges are promoted from the ranks of assistant judges. Only a handful of practicing attorneys are appointed to judgeships (Tanaka, 1976: 552).

9. In 1980, former judges and former prosecutors accounted for about 8 percent and 5.5 percent, respectively, of all private attorneys; both percentages were higher in areas C and D than in areas A and B. Some of these lawyers resigned their offices before retirement age, however. The reasons why judges abandon their careers have not been studied systematically, but the following factors are relevant. Judges usually are transferred from one place to another every few years, which causes increasing hardship when children begin to attend school. Some had chosen to serve as judges in order to get experience before becoming practicing attorneys later. After a period of service, some may feel that their career prospects within the judicial bureaucracy are not very bright. As to the relative income of judges and attorneys, see section entitled "Income."

With regard to the career structure of judges and prosecutors, the following account is relevant:

In Japan, most of the judges have chosen their position as their career job. This means that a typical judge is appointed to an assistant judgeship immediately after having received training for two years at the Legal Training and Research Institute, is promoted to the status of (full-fledged) judge after ten years, and intends (or is expected) to remain as a judge until the compulsory retirement age of sixty-five or seventy. Though it is guaranteed by Article 80 of the Constitution that judges "shall receive, at regular stated intervals, adequate compensation which shall not be decreased during their terms of office" and although the Courts Act provides that they cannot be dismissed or ordered to move to another post against their will, they in fact move from one position to another (usually every two to four years) as civil servants do. This practice is partly related to the graduated wage scale, which is not different in nature from the civil service wage scale, and partly related to tradition.

Public procurators also usually take the procuratorship as their career job. They, like other civil servants, not only in fact move from one position to another but are required by law to do so when requested. (Tanaka, 1976: 549–550; footnotes omitted)

10. In 1979, mediation cases constituted about 36 percent of all civil disputes brought before court, including family matters (General Secretariat, Supreme Court, 1979). For a discussion of the actual working of this system, see Henderson (1965) and Rokumoto (1981).

11. In ordinary civil litigation in courts of first instance, terminating in 1980, about 85 percent of the litigants in the summary court and about 40 percent of those in the district court were not represented by PAs (General Secretariat, Supreme Court, 1980).

12. In mediation cases terminating in 1975 in summary courts (where most mediation takes place), 25.6 percent of plaintiffs and 16.9 percent of defendants were represented by a lawyer and 14.6 percent of plaintiffs and 12.9 percent of defendants by a nonlawyer.

13. An assistant judge has limited power, cannot sit alone (see Tanaka, 1976: 462), and must serve ten years before being appointed to a regular judgeship.

14. According to Tanaka (1976: 556), summary court judges are appointed either (1) from among those who have served for not less than three years as an assistant judge, public procurator or practicing attorney or (2) from among those "who have the knowledge and experience necessary for carrying out the duties of a summary court judge, such as those who have engaged in judicial business for many years" and have been recommended by the Summary Court Judges

Selection Committee. As a matter of practice, about half of the nearly 800 summary court judges had previously served as court clerks for many years.

15. Changes in the size of the legal profession in Japan are shown in table 4.3.

16. In England there were 28,939 solicitors and 4,263 barristers in private practice in 1978 for a population of about 55 million (Royal Commission, 1979, 2:46), and in West Germany there were 36,081 private attorneys or attorney-notaries and 942 nonattorney notaries in 1980 for a population of about 60 million (*Anwaltsblatt*, 1980:145).

17. The PA Act (1972) grants practicing attorneys a monopoly in the delivery of legal services for pay.

18. Judical scriveners were recognized officially in 1919 and are distinct from notaries public. The latter also exist in Japan. They numbered about 444 in 1981 and were mostly retired judges or prosecutors. Their function is to authenticate legal actions and documents.

19. According to an official statistical report of the Japanese Association of Judicial Scriveners, they handled 17,577,686 cases in 1980, earning fees of about ￥107,043 million; drafting court documents accounted for 178,652 cases and earned the judicial scriveners about ￥1,800 million (124 *Geppo Shihoshoshi* [*Judicial Scriveners' Monthly*] 7 [March 1982]).

20. Judicial scriveners publicly admit that some of them specialize in litigation (ibid.). The relationship between private attorneys and judicial scriveners is naturally antagonistic, the former constantly and vehemently accusing the latter of violating the monopoly of legal services accorded to private attorneys by law (Practicing Attorneys Act, art. 72). In view of the scarcity and maldistribution of private attorneys and the high price of their services, however, the complementary functions of judicial scriveners are generally recognized as inevitable. Courts also tend to construe the attorney's monopoly clause rather narrowly. Some advocate recognizing judicial scriveners as a second private branch of the legal profession. Instances of a business association between an attorney and a judicial scrivener are rare but not unlawful. In our survey, about 6 percent of attorneys indicated that there was a quasilawyer (not always a judicial scrivener) in their office, and another 12 percent had an ongoing relationship with a quasilawyer, which produced referrals in both directions.

The judicial scriveners, for their part, always have been eager to enhance their status, and their effort bore fruit in the 1978 amendment of the Judicial Scriveners' Act, which formalized and unified the qualifying examination administered by the Minister of Justice, so that it now includes some basic legal subjects, such as civil, commercial, and criminal law, as well as procedures for registration, deposit, and litigation (Judicial Scriveners' Act, art. 5). In 1982, 15,103 candidates sat the examination and 382 passed (2.5 percent), of whom 76 percent had a college education (133 *Geppo Shihoshoshi* [*Judicial Scriveners' Monthly*] 16–17 [1982]).

21. In 1979 there were 1,373 judicial scriveners in Tokyo and 1,073 in Osaka. The ratio of practicing attorneys to judicial scriveners in these cities was 3.80 and 1.75, respectively. The national ratio was 0.77, ranging from 0.10 in Kagoshima Prefecture to 0.99 in Aichi Prefecture (Kaneko & Takeshita, 1978: 378).

22. Of the 486 successful candidates in 1980, 70 (14 percent) were university students, 8 were graduate students, 60 (12 percent) had a regular occupation (public servants, employees of private firms, clerks in a lawyer's office, etc.), and 348 (72 percent) had no occupation (Nihon Houritsuka Kyoukai, 1982: 140). A tenth were women.

23. For the curriculum of legal education at the University of Tokyo, a representative institution, see Tanaka (1976: 579–581).

24. In the Faculty of Law of the University of Tokyo, for example, only 90 to 100 students out of a graduating class of about 600 eventually enter the ILTR. For the variation in the success rate in the Legal Examination among universities, see table 4.5.

25. Growing foreign trade, government regulations, and consumer litigation have made Japanese corporations aware of the importance of having a staff specialized in legal matters, and many larger corporations today have such staffs. It seems safe to say that the legal section of the larger corporations have an average of about five employees with university legal education, and some large commercial companies have several dozen. A small proportion of these have passed the Legal Examination without going on to the ILTR. (Registered lawyers need to obtain permission from the Practicing Attorneys' Association before being employed regularly by a business firm, and there still are only a handful of such attorneys in Japan.) Some are sent abroad by the company for legal studies. Although they do not receive special treatment as professionals but are transferred to other sections as they ascend the career ladder within the company (a few may remain in the section for over ten years), these corporation "lawpersons" tend to form a distinct occupational group, conscious of their legal expertise and work ethos. An association called "Friends of Managerial Law" was formed in 1971 and now contains the legal section members of 365 companies.

26. About half of all employed lawyers earn between 2 and 3.5 million yen per year, and another quarter earn between 3.5 and 4 million yen. Today, those seeking employment demand a salary corresponding to that of their fellow graduates at the ILTR who enter the judiciary as assistant judges.

27. The lawyers in area D are an exception: even the youngest lawyers frequently are not employed. This is because in such peripheral areas the number of lawyers is so small that any association among them, including employment, reduces the number of law offices in the locality, which obviously is to be avoided. The scarcity of lawyers also means that newcomers will find clients much more easily than their colleagues do in central cities.

28. This index itself may reflect the characteristic pattern of Japanese legal practice, which is heavily dominated by litigation. Litigated cases can be counted easily and remain open longer in the lawyer's file than noncontentious matters. All litigation, therefore, may be slightly overrepresented in a survey based on this method, and criminal cases, many of which are terminated within a few months, may be underrepresented.

29. In a 1973 German study, by contrast, practicing attorneys reported that they handled 334 civil or criminal matters per year, of which 130 were litigated (Volks, 1974: 252, 265). Australian solicitors and barristers also report receiving larger numbers of briefs (Tomasic & Bullard, 1978: 310). The smaller number of cases generating the income of Japanese lawyers naturally raises the question of whether their work costs significantly more money.

This difference in the volume of lawyers' business reflects the difference in court caseloads. In 1979, there were only 386,563 civil cases in courts of first instance, whereas West German courts heard 2,001,664 similar cases in 1974 (Anwaltsblatt, 1976: 81).

30. Divorce by consent is an established Japanese legal institution, accounting for more than 89 percent of all divorces each year.

31. Criminal legal aid functions relatively well, but civil legal aid is only very weakly developed.

REFERENCES

Dore, Ronald P. 1967. "Mobility, Equality, and Individuation in Modern Japan," in Ronald P. Dore, ed., *Aspects of Social Change in Modern Japan*, pp. 113–150. Princeton, N.J.: Princeton University Press.

Hattori, Takaaki. 1963. "The Legal Profession in Japan: Its Historical Development and Present State," in Arthur von Mehren, ed., *Law in Japan*, pp. 111–152. Cambridge, Mass.: Harvard University Press.

Henderson, Dan F. 1965. *Conciliation and Japanese Law: Tokugawa and Modern.* Tokyo: University of Tokyo Press.

Kaneko, Hajime, and Morio Takeshita. 1978. *Saibanho [The Laws Concerning the Administration of Justice].* Tokyo: Yuhikaku.

Nichibenren. 1981. "Kihon-houkoku Jiyuu to Seigi [Preliminary Report on the Survey of the Economic Basis of the Japanese Legal Practice]," 32(10) *Nichibenren* 43.

Nihon Houritsuka Kyoukai, ed. 1982. *Shiho Shiken.* Tokyo: Gyosei.

Rabinowitz, Richard W. 1956. "The Historical Development of the Japanese Bar," 70 *Harvard Law Review* 61–81.

Rokumoto, Kahei. 1981. "Tschotei (Schlichtung)—eine Japanische Alternative zum Recht: Verfahren, Praxis und Funktionen" in Erhard Blankenberg, Ekkehard Klausa, and Hubert Rottleuthner, eds., *Alternative Rechtsformen und Alternativen zum Recht*, pp. 390–407. Opladen: Westdeutscher Verlag.

Royal Commission on Legal Services. 1979. *Final Report* (2 vols.) (Cmnd. 7648-I.) London: HMSO.

Takayanagi, Kenzo. 1963. "A Century of Innovation: The Development of Japanese Law, 1868–1961," in Arthur von Mehren, ed., *Law in Japan*, pp. 5–40. Cambridge, Mass.: Harvard University Press.

Tanaka, Hideo, ed. 1976. *The Japanese Legal System: Introductory Cases and Materials*. Tokyo: University of Tokyo Press.

Tomasic, Roman, and Cedric Bullard. 1978. *Lawyers and Their Work in New South Wales*. Sydney: Law Foundation of New South Wales.

Volks, Holger. 1974. "Anwaltliche Berufsrollen und anwaltliche Berufsarbeit in der Industriegeselleschaft." Inaugural dissertation, University of Cologne.

5
Legal Experts in Belgium

LUC HUYSE

This is not a chapter on lawyers in the narrow sense—that is, legal experts who represent clients in the courts. Reducing the scope of inquiry to what some see as the essence of lawyering—the representational function—would be the wrong strategy for describing the legal profession in Belgium. Such an approach would limit analysis to advocates, excluding almost 70 percent of the jurist population. It also would encourage a static perspective, since representation in court is not the most important function Belgian legal experts perform.

Therefore, I have begun by describing the jurist population as a whole and then have focused on the occupational groups that most closely fit the model of the legal profession, namely, advocates and notaries.

JURISTS IN BELGIUM: AN OVERVIEW

A HIGHLY DIVIDED "PROFESSION"

In Belgium, the terms for "lawyer" are *jurist/juriste* (all terms are given in their Dutch or Flemish/French versions), but they refer more to a statistical category of degree-holders (*dr./lic. juris*)[1] than to an occupational or professional group. Indeed, the differences between jurists are much greater than the traits they share.

Belgian folk conceptions make a rather sharp distinction between the highly visible legal practice of advocates, judges, notaries, and court clerks and the more "hidden" services of legal experts in the public sector (civil servants) and private employment (house counsel, jurists in nonprofit organizations, etc.).

Advocates, notaries, judges, and jurists in private employment and public administration also are profoundly differentiated in other ways.

168

First, the various categories are differently "bound" to the exercise of their legal expertise. Many who enter private firms or the public sector (except as judges) cease to be jurists in a narrow sense: they become managers or executives and only infrequently do legal work. By contrast, ethical codes prohibit advocates from combining their practice at the bar with "nonprofessional" activities, such as selling insurance or real estate. Second, lateral mobility is rare, except for occasional movements from the bar to the judiciary or private sector employment. Third, an overarching association of jurists never has existed, and, consequently, there has been no general professional project for "collective mobility," size control, self-regulation, or the formulation of universal ethical codes (Larson, 1977). The various categories of jurists have developed separate associations, of which the corporations of advocates and notaries are the oldest and most powerful. However, differentiation and decentralization also are the rule within each category. Advocates and notaries are organized in highly autonomous local associations, which have relinquished few powers to the national federation. Judges associate with each other on the basis of their positions within the judicial hierarchy. Finally, the battle for control over "production by producers" (Abel, 1988) is not primarily a struggle between jurists and nonjurists. Conflicts over market position often are challenges between neighboring occupations *within* the world of jurists: advocates against notaries against jurists in nonprofit organizations, and so on.

WHAT JURISTS DO

Membership in the bar (*balie/barreau*), which alone enjoys rights of audience in the courts, is reserved to jurists who are fully self-employed and who conform to the ideal of a legal profession (approximately 30 percent of all economically active jurists in 1984). The bar itself is divided into full advocates (70 percent) and apprentices (stagiaires—30 percent). In their external relations both groups operate as advocates (advocaten/avocats) and have the right to represent clients in court, but within the professional community (orde van advocaten/ordre des avocats) apprentices have the status of minors. The 7,500 advocates now in private practice are distributed among twenty-six local bars, although very unevenly. One in every three Belgian advocates belongs to the Brussels bar; nearly 60 percent practice in Brussels, Ghent, Antwerp, and Liège. Until 1967, advocates had to compete with a small number of *pleitbezorgers/avoués*—a soft version of the British solicitor.

Notaries (*notarissen/notaires*) are public office holders appointed by the Department of Justice. However, as an occupational group they claim the autonomy and status of a liberal profession. Sociologically they resemble advocates much more than civil service jurists. The function of the 1,200 notaries (5 percent of all practicing jurists) is to write, hold in trust, and deliver copies of contracts for the exchange and mortgage of land, wills, gifts, and marriage contracts. They also conduct public auctions of real estate and execute legacies. Finally, they advise about legal and financial affairs.

The careers of judges (*rechters/juges*) and prosecuting attorneys (*openbaar ministerie/ministères publics*) are closely intertwined. Both groups (which total 7 percent of jurists) are called by the same name: *magistratuur/ magistrature.*

The vast majority of jurists in government (15 percent of all practicing jurists) perform functions in the general administration (mostly national). A second group within this category are law teachers (in Belgium all types and levels of school, including "private" schools, are fully subsidized by the government). Both groups are civil servants.

By far the largest subgroup of jurists (approximately 40 percent) work in commerce, finance, industry, and private nonprofit organizations, but they are differentiated by function and degree of self-employment. The first variable divides this group into jurists practicing as lawyers in the narrow sense—house counsel (bedrijfsjuristen/juristes d'entreprise) and legal advisers in the private nonprofit sector—and jurists whose work is predominantly nonlegal (the larger subcategory). The other variable distinguishes a very large group of salaried employees from a tiny segment of legally trained employers or merchants. Privately employed lawyers are not subject to a professional code of ethics; they are responsible only to their employers.

Finally, there is a miscellaneous category of experts who lack formal credentials but perform legal functions: tax consultants, accountants, court and notary clerks, criminologists, and others. Some are included in the prevailing conception of legal personnel; others are not.

SOCIOGRAPHY OF LEGAL PERSONNEL IN BELGIUM

Quantitative Developments: Discontinuous Growth

In 1986 there were approximately 30,000 qualified jurists in Belgium, of whom more than 80 percent were economically active. Seen in relation to the total population, that is one jurist for 330 persons. In 1840 there were less than 1,800 legally trained people or one jurist for 2,300 persons. The jurist population thus has expanded considerably: sixteenfold in gross numbers, sevenfold in relation to the general population (see table 5.1).

The rate of change varied greatly during these 150 years. Three growth cycles can be discerned in the history of law school output (and in the accompanying increase or decrease of the jurist population) (see table 5.2). From 1875 to 1890 the annual output of law degrees rose considerably. This was followed by a very long period of decrease (1895–1932) and then stabilization at the level of 1890 (1932–1948). The second growth cycle was much shorter. There was a very high production of law graduates during the early 1950s. Again, this expansion was followed by a fall in output (1956–1963). The last growth cycle still is developing. At first the annual output of law school graduates increased spectacularly: from 496 in 1969 to 1,144 in 1975. Since then, production has stabilized but at such a high level that we may expect the jurist population to increase by half in the next fifteen years (see table 5.3).

The extraordinary growth of the jurist population conceals another development, however: there has been a real erosion of jurists as a proportion of university enrollment. Jurists were more than 20 percent of all persons with academic degrees in 1937, but they were 16 percent in 1961, and only 10 percent of all those graduating from a university in 1984 (see table 5.4).

Of course, figures do not speak for themselves: they must be confronted with other data if we want to understand patterns of quantitative development. The explanatory variables can be dichotomized into pull and push factors. Most research has been devoted to studying the elements that create conditions favorable to legal experts, generate business for jurists, and, thus, *pull* people into law schools and, subsequently, into legal occupations. These include the development of a market economy and the bureaucratization of political rule (Rueschemeyer, 1973: 5; Pashigian, 1977), legal activity (Grossman & Sarat, 1975), population increases (Abel, 1988), and the growth of state regulation (Pashigian, 1977). Various indices have been suggested: real gross national product, the number of active corporations and other measures of industrial and commercial activity, bankruptcies, automobile accidents, the divorce rate, the number and budgets of regulatory agencies, the number of laws and regulations, and the litigation rate. *Push* factors, by contrast, accelerate the influx of prospective students or jurists without the direct intervention of market demand. Measures that relax the entrance requirements for law schools and positive discrimination in the admission of students from minority groups are good examples.

More work needs to be done to understand both the production of lawyers and the demand for their services (Abel, 1988). This is not primarily a problem of gathering data. Many theoretical questions still have to be answered about the causal relation between variables. For example, does a rise in the volume of court cases pull more people into the legal profession, or does an increase in the number of lawyers lead to rising litigation rates? Why has an increase in the legal activity of notaries—238,041 notarized documents in 1899, 559,308 in 1968 (CRISP, 1974: 17)—been attended with a continuous decline in the number of notaries, with no concomitant loss of the original monopoly?

Two Push Factors

There can be no doubt about the influence of two push factors in the spectacular increase in the number of jurists after 1970. In 1964 a major reform of the entrance requirements for higher education dramatically opened the doors of universities: many high-school programs that previously did not allow access to colleges and universities were promoted to college-preparatory status. This reform, which enabled many more eighteen-year-olds to attend university, had a particularly strong influence on the recruitment pattern of law schools. Classical (Latin and Greek) studies in high school were dropped as an admission requirement. The impact on law school output was felt six to seven years later: an average of 374 law degrees were awarded annually in the 1960s, 671 in 1970, 781 in 1971, and 909 in 1972 (see table 5.2).

A second push factor is related to the emancipation of disadvantaged groups. The dramatic rise in the yearly output of law degrees, from 404 in 1968 to 1,220 in 1982, must be attributed largely to the breakthrough of female students, who received only 16 percent of law degrees in 1968 but 37 percent in 1983 (see table 5.2). Between 1968 and 1983, the number of law degrees earned by men increased 109 percent, but the number earned by women rose 540 percent. In the period following World War II, the Flemish population also attained greater equality (Huyse, 1982). Table 5.5 clearly shows that the recent rise in law school output also expresses the greater participation of Flemish youth in university education in general and legal studies in particular. The Flemish represented 47.5 percent of law graduates in 1968 but 58.1 percent in 1983. (They were about 65 percent of the general population both years.) The combined effect of the two push factors is visible in the fact that the ratio of French-speaking male law graduates to Flemish female law graduates declined from 7.7:1 in 1968 to 1.3:1 in 1983.

Older and Newer Types of Legal Experts

We learned in the preceding pages that the total body of legal expertise has vastly increased in Belgium. However, the incidence and rate of quantitative change vary substantially in the various occupations in which jurists are active. True, all branches have grown absolutely, but in proportion to general population, we find different types of development (see tables 5.6 and 5.7). One category of jurist—notaries—exhibited negative growth: there were 4,422 people per notary in 1841 and 8,000 in 1984. Until the 1960s the judiciary followed a somewhat similar pattern, from 7,350 people per judge in 1841 to 8,412 in 1960. This downward trend recently was reversed, when a major reform of the organization of judicial work dramatically increased the size of the judiciary. Three other branches undeniably display real growth. In the last 140 years the number of advocates grew eightfold in absolute terms and threefold relative to population. Jurists in government service realized a similar growth in less than fifty years (1937—1984). The fastest-growing occupation, however, is jurists in private employment, who numbered about 800 just before World War II but are about 10,000 today. Their breakthrough came in the 1950s. Almost 60 percent of the growth of the jurist population between 1947 and 1961 occurred in this branch, which expanded from about 1,500 to about 3,600, while the bar gained an additional 300 members.

The uneven development of the various occupations considerably modified their proportions of the jurist population. Looking at the distribution of jurists among practice settings (see table 5.7), we can see that the traditional categories (advocates, judges, and notaries) constituted more than three-fourths of the profession before 1940 but less than 45 percent in 1984. Jurists in private employment tripled their share in less than fifty years; they now are by far the largest category (about 40 percent of all jurists), followed by advocates (30 percent) and civil service jurists (about 15 percent).

One important consequence of this historical development is a major change in the size and type of the organizations within which most jurists practice. Before 1940, 80 percent of all jurists (advocates, notaries, and judges) worked alone most of the time. Today, 55 percent of all legally trained people unquestionably work in relatively large organizations, such as industrial, commercial, and financial firms and governmental agencies.

On the surface, the Belgian situation contrasts sharply with many common law countries, where most jurists are private practitioners—not salaried employees. It is questionable whether this signifies a substantial difference in the total amount of legal work accomplished and in the translation of legal functions into legal roles. Nevertheless, the margin for professional autonomy necessarily will be much smaller in Belgium than in some common law countries, given the preponderance of private and public salaried employment among jurists.

Increasing Participation of Disadvantaged Groups

The first woman jurist in Belgium, Marie Popelin, graduated in 1888. Having been denied entry to the bar, she fought a long court battle, which aroused great public controversy. She lost her fight and became a popular leader in the early feminist movement.

Women were admitted to the bar in 1922. However, demolition of the formal barrier did not immediately bring many more women to the law schools. They remained between 1 and 4 percent of the jurist population until the early 1950s. The low proportion of women among all undergraduates before 1950 is only part of the explanation, for other university branches attracted many more women (see table 5.8). When the number of women undergraduates abruptly started to grow in the 1960s, the law schools again were slow to catch up.

The breakthrough came in the 1970s. Between 1970 and 1984 the absolute number of women jurists rose almost fourfold, and their proportion of the profession doubled to about 22 percent (see table 5.9). Extrapolating from the figures in tables 5.2 and 5.3, we may expect that women will constitute more than a third of all jurists in the early 1990s. However, the earlier attitude of women toward legal studies persists: law schools still attract a smaller proportion of women than do the other university schools and departments (except civil and agricultural engineering) (see table 5.8).

What discouraged many educated women from becoming jurists? Formal discrimination ended with the admission of women to the bar in 1922, the judiciary in 1947, and the office of notary in 1950. One explanation may be that women choose studies that lead to jobs women traditionally have held (psychology, pedagogy) or to careers, such as teaching, where discriminatory practices are thought to be limited. If so, the allocation of careers within law may be based on women's expectations about discrimination. A closer examination of the proportion of women jurists in the various practice settings suggests other selection criteria (see table 5.9). There are few women jurists among notaries or in industrial and commercial firms, banks, insurance companies, and estate handling firms. Compared to the proportion of women among law graduates, women jurists also are underrepresented in the judiciary and civil service but slightly overrepresented in nonprofit organizations, legal education, and the bar. Thus, we may hypothesize that women jurists "feel good" in occupations where a career can be discontinuous, part-time work is available and socially accepted, and status devaluation is most probable (law teaching, the bar, and jobs in non-profit organizations). They will be less comfortable in occupations that are high status (the judiciary, notary offices) and where a career must be continuous and work performed full time (in the industrial, commercial, and profit-oriented service sectors and the civil service). The distribution of women, then, probably is not the product of deliberate choices about particular forms of legal work but a gender-bound allocation of career opportunities.

What effects will these demographic changes have on the way legal functions are performed? It would be unwise to expect to see substantial effects from the entry of women within the next twenty years or so. Recently, the proportion of women with law school degrees who remain unemployed (voluntarily or involuntarily) has been higher than that of men law graduates (see table 5.10; also Bonte [n.d.: 26]); more also work part time and have discontinuous careers. These occupational characteristics seriously diminish the influence of women jurists on the profession as a whole. In addition, women jurists still lack full access to influential positions within each occupation: in 1983, women were 15.5 percent of all judges (257/1,659) but only 8 percent in the courts of appeal and 3 percent in the highest court. That year women were about 25 percent of all advocates but only 7 out of the 325 members of the local disciplinary councils and 1 out of the 26 heads of local bars.

In yet another way the composition of the jurist population begins to reflect general emancipatory processes in Belgian society. Until the 1960s the Dutch-speaking Flemings, although a demographic majority, were underrepresented in the major political, economic, and cultural spheres of the country. The French-speaking Walloons and inhabitants of Brussels also dominated many professional groups, not least because of their higher participation in university education. Flemings obtained only 42.5 percent of the law degrees awarded between 1956 and 1965, although they were about 65 percent of the general population. By 1984, however, Flemings obtained 62 percent of law degrees. As a result, Flemish jurists slowly are taking over elite positions within the bar, the Royal Federation of Notaries, and the Belgian Association of House Counsel. This may effect changes in the organization of legal work. Flemish jurists look more to Dutch and Anglo-American models for their professional mores than do their French-speaking colleagues. The result well could be a shift from a Latin to a northern European legal culture. Signs of such a shift can be found in the differences in substance and form between the regional laws (*decreten/décrets*) of the Vlaamse Raad and the Conseil Wallon (the "parliaments" of the northern and southern regions), the divergent jurisprudence of the Flemish and francophone chambers of the Raad van State/ Conseil d'Etat (highest administrative court in Belgium), and the writings of Flemish legal scholars.

Class Origins Still Are Important

Class always has affected entry into the jurist population and allocation of law graduates to the various legal roles. The first threshold is access to legal studies. In 1965, 65 percent of all students at the University of Leuven Law School (which produces almost a third of all Belgian jurists) came from upper-class families (see table 5.11). The effects of positive discrimination (scholarships for working-class students and more flexible entrance requirements) are clearly visible in later years, which show a substantial decrease in the proportion of students from upper-class families and an even more pronounced rise in the participation of students with lower middle-class origins. This general trend was particularly strong between 1965 and 1973 but since then has slowed down or reversed, and the position of the lowest income group hardly changed. Law school today continues to draw from more privileged backgrounds than other university departments.

The class profile of jurists naturally reflects this situation. Advocates and notaries are even more privileged. Notaries display a particularly high degree of occupational heredity. Claeys (1974) surveyed a representative sample of Leuven law graduates in 1935, 1940, 1950, 1955, and 1960 and found that 67 percent of notaries and 41 percent of advocates had fathers with university degrees, 56 percent of notaries and 28 percent of advocates had grandfathers with university degrees, 43 percent of notaries and 14 percent of advocates had fathers in the same profession, and 18 percent of notaries and 3 percent of advocates had grandfathers in the same profession.

LEGAL EDUCATION AND SOCIALIZATION: THE MAJOR ROLE OF LAW SCHOOLS

Studies of legal education shed light on such crucial processes as the creation of legal expertise, recruitment into the various legal roles and occupations, preservation of a fairly homogeneous self-image among the branches of the jurist population, and maintenance of the prevailing definition of the professional situation. Ever since 1835, a university degree has been a formal requirement for advocates and judges. From the early years of the Belgian state, a law school degree also permitted entry to the civil service. Only notaries did not need a full academic training until much later.

Socialization of prospective jurists was and is a multiphase process. It starts in the family. We know that 40 percent of all law students at the

University of Leuven in 1981 had upper- and upper-middle-class origins; many were related to a legally trained person. We may assume that in these cases the assimilation of images about lawyers will have started well before the student crosses the doorstep of the university. The law school is the second—and for most future jurists probably the major—socializing influence. The facts that law schools have a monopoly over formal legal training and that there are no subsequent state or bar examinations give those schools considerable weight. Certain characteristics of Belgian law schools increase their impact: legal studies take five years (two undergraduate, three graduate); many faculty members are only part-time teachers and bring to the classroom their professional experience as advocates, notaries, judges, bankers, and similar functionaries; students have no opportunities to take summer jobs in law firms or to work in a government or nonprofit law office and consequently are totally dependent on the image of lawyers and the legal system presented in the classroom.

Other features reduce the socializing influence of the law schools, however: first-year undergraduates start their legal studies immediately after they leave high school and, therefore, often have no strong commitment to the subject; Belgian students return home every weekend; experiences that might encourage anticipatory socialization (such as membership in prestigious law reviews, early job hunting or preparation for a bar examination) are not available.

The first job is the third important socializing agent. In two of the legal roles (advocate and notary) this occurs during a relatively long period of apprenticeship, as we will see later in this chapter.

RECRUITMENT INTO LEGAL ROLES AND OCCUPATIONS

The allocation to legal roles is mediated by several steplike processes and intervening variables. Although we already have discussed who comes to law school, it is harder to know why they come. A study at the University of Leuven Law School suggests that many first-year students enroll because other subjects require quantitative skills they lack (De Neve, 1983).

In order to describe recruitment into legal roles during and after law school training, we may find it helpful to use Elliott's distinction between individual processes of choice and commitment and the selection mechanisms employed by the profession itself (Elliott, 1972: 75). "[T]he range of alternatives available to an individual is progressively limited until eventually choice takes place within a relatively narrow range" (ibid., 72). This process of reducing alternatives is affected by factors operating inside and outside the professional groups.

In all countries law school performance correlates with the type of law practice a graduate enters after leaving the university. In Belgium it has a much more direct effect: half of all first-year law students never earn a degree. There is no reason to assume that ascriptive characteristics significantly affect performance. Although students have a choice of courses only in their fifth (last) year, ascriptive elements, such as family background, may play a prominent role here.

The range of first jobs open to law school graduates is limited by a variety of factors. When the economy is stagnant and the output of newly graduated jurists is very high, as has been the case since 1970, obtaining *any* job is a victory. Getting *the* job one prefers often is postponed to better times. Law school performance is important, particularly for those who want to join private companies. Ascriptive elements are very influential for those who become advocates or notaries, however, as we will see later. The recruitment of judges and government jurists is based partly on examinations, partly on political patronage (Huyse, 1974). All cabinet ministers can influence who is recruited and promoted as a civil servant in the various administrative agencies that fall within their jurisdiction. They must, however, respect the principle of proportionality, which allocates civil service appointments among the partners of a coalition government. All this facilitates the emergence of political patronage in the recruitment of judges and civil service jurists.

WEAK SUPPLY CONTROL

It is difficult to speak of a professional project of supply control among the jurist population as a whole. Many of the usual goals of such a project (the elimination of nonacademic modes of entry, the imposition of high standards of training, the introduction of formal compulsory university examinations) already were in place in the early days of the Belgian state. University reforms (which may have affected supply) were not the product of a professional strategy but partly the initiative of medical and law school faculties and partly the resolution of a struggle between the two principal adversaries in Belgium: those who perceived the secular state as the main agency in the production of legal and medical experts and the Catholic party, which defended the autonomy of the denominational University of Louvain. The role of jurists was limited by the absence of an overarching association, and jurists also were divided along the same lines as other political actors. Consequently, restrictions on the production of legal experts never originated *within* the jurist population but rather expressed the characteristics of the political and educational system as a whole. Entrance requirements were rigid, fees were very high, sociocultural forces discouraged women from attending the university, and there was no secondary or higher education in Dutch (Flemish) before 1935. It is not surprising that the number of law students increased dramatically when these hurdles disappeared one after another, starting in 1960.

LAWYERING AS A LIBERAL PROFESSION: ADVOCATES AND NOTARIES

Most advocates and notaries work within the environment of a liberal profession. They are fully self-employed, they seek to control supply, and their associations have self-regulatory power granted by the state. A third occupational category, house counsel, recently has sought to obtain professional status. An association created at the end of the 1960s now contains half of the approximately 1,000 *juristes d'entreprise/bedrijfsjuristen*. Its short history is characterized by a continuous search for public and private measures that might accelerate the process of professionalization, such as official protection of the title of house counsel (a step toward monopoly and control over entry), self-regulation, and agreements with the bar that would allow house counsel to enter into partnerships with advocates.

THE SIZE AND SUPPLY CONTROL PROBLEM

Advocates continuously have patrolled the borders of their profession. Their strategy was threefold: establishing and defending their exclusive rights of audience, systematically excluding foreign advocates, and controlling the "production of producers" who formally qualify for the bar. Advocates obtained exclusive rights of audience early in the nineteenth century, although some of the functions of client representation remained the province of pleitbezorgers/avoués. The first real threat to the monopoly surfaced during a general reform of procedural law in the 1960s. The (local) associations of advocates countered this attack by mobilizing their members and fellow advocates in Parliament. A compromise was reached: non-advocates could represent clients before the labor courts, but the role of the pleitbezorger/avoué was eliminated. However, the importance of exclusive rights of audience is being reduced as litigation becomes a smaller fraction of the market for legal services.

The exclusion of foreign advocates from the bar has become an important and difficult task since the birth of the European Economic Community (EEC) and its advocacy of "free" trade for service occupations. Legal technicalities still prevent noncitizens from entering the Belgian bar (unless they hold a Belgian degree), but foreign law firms have bypassed the obstacles by hiring Belgian advocates.

The third goal, controlling the production of qualified producers, has proved to be the most difficult to realize, particularly the efforts to regulate size. Since 1950, advocates twice have confronted a serious growth problem: contraction between 1955 and 1970 and an extraordinary expansion since 1975. Advocates tried to correct underpopulation through a sort of promotion campaign and overpopulation through various techniques of discouragement and an informal numerus clausus for apprentices, but these endeavors were quite unsuccessful. One reason was the absence of a strong national association of advocates, which was created only in 1968. Another is the absence of a bar examination. Advocates also were constrained by their own public rhetoric of "openness" and "free access" for all who qualify. Finally, law schools have little power to reduce or expand their enrollments at the behest of the profession even if they wish to do so, since many of the forces that determine the size of the student body are exogenous (Pashigian, 1977).

The problems that advocates encounter in regulating their numbers do not prevent them from influencing *who* can become an advocate, thereby fostering the homogeneity of the bar. The major screening device here is apprenticeship, which gives the bar a strong voice concerning occupational entry. The disciplinary council of the local bar examines each applicant for inscription on the roll of apprentices for incompatibilities and to ascertain whether the candidate's conduct is flawless. It is impossible to appeal from a negative decision of the council. The apprenticeship itself is a particularistic training environment. The master–pupil relationship, on which it is based, tends to invest the full members of the bar with great moral authority and, thus, with substantial control over entry to the profession. It also is a setting in which universalistic or meritocratic qualifications for recruitment and occupational selection easily can be replaced by such criteria as "social skills," "character," and "social reliability." As an apprentice, the young jurist has the status of a minor within the professional community and a precarious financial position. Background characteristics, such as parental assistance in obtaining access to clients and direct financial support, may ensure that only the "proper" candidates for full membership survive. Yet, apprenticeship no longer can be an effective selection device if the number of apprentices exceeds that of patrons (who must be full advocates with a minimum of seven years seniority), and that is precisely what happened after 1975. Too many prospective advocates now slip through the apprenticeship period without being properly supervised, and their entry soon may bring greater heterogeneity to the bar. Thus, it is possible that the mere size of the law school population, rather than changes in its social composition, is the real threat to the homogeneity of the bar.

The legal occupation that most closely fits the model of the "professional project" (Larson, 1977) is the notary. Notaries originally were not jurists and enjoyed little prestige. They gained status and autonomy during the Napoleonic period, when the notary was redefined as a public office (and a source of taxes and political patronage) with a large degree of professional freedom. During part of the nineteenth century an official nomination by a public authority was needed, but candidates then were selected on the basis of a "moral examination" by the professional elite. No formal training was required. Today a notary must obtain a law degree, serve an apprenticeship, and be appointed by the Department of Justice. Here both the quantitative and qualitative dimensions of supply control have been very effective (as table 5.6 and the earlier description of occupational heredity clearly show). The successful formula seem to be a combination of appointment by a public authority (with which the profession forms an intimate alliance), limitation (by that authority) of the number of notary offices (which is strictly tied to population growth), the maintenance of apprenticeship as a screening device, the requirement of extremely high payments by those taking over an existing practice, and, finally, the early creation of an overarching association. The notary's present share of the market for legal services is only partly based on the original monopoly (writing, preserving, and delivering copies of notarized documents); notaries increasingly hold themselves out as general advisers in legal affairs.

APPRENTICESHIP AS A SOCIALIZATION AND RECRUITMENT PROCESS

After obtaining a law degree, those wishing to become advocates or notaries serve an apprenticeship (three years at the bar, one for notaries). During this period candidates undergo formal and informal training in two subroles: legal expert (e.g., how to represent a client in court) and entrepreneur (how to run an office). The patronage relationship with an older professional also maximizes the likelihood of socialization to a third subrole: member of the professional community.

To enroll as an apprentice at the bar seems to be a mere formality: the acolyte must swear allegiance to the constitution and laws and apply for inscription. However, we saw above that the disciplinary council of the local bar screens all applicants and that appeal is impossible. The members of the disciplinary council have unlimited discretion in defining the criteria for entry. Another hurdle is the search for a patron. Huyse and Cammaer (1982) found that in 1979, 25 percent of all applicants had to contact three or more advocates before they were accepted as apprentices. Ascriptive elements (such as kinship with lawyers) clearly affect such placements, which have an impact on the subsequent career of the apprentice.

In the United States, first jobs have a very strong influence on lawyer careers (Abel, 1988). That certainly is true for those Belgian lawyers who begin their careers as apprentices, which is based on sponsored, not contest, mobility. In Turner's (1961) definition, sponsored mobility is a process in which "the elite or their agents, who are best qualified to judge, call those individuals to elite status who have the appropriate qualities. Individuals do not win or seize elite status, but mobility is rather a process of sponsored induction into the elite following selection." Huyse and Cammaer (1982) found that the sponsored apprentices got the best and most powerful patrons, received a better training, were allocated more cases, and earlier obtained a decent share of the income they earned for their patron, while the non-sponsored apprentices were harassed with techniques of what Clark (1960) calls "cooling-out."

PROFESSIONAL ASSOCIATIONS

The organizational structure of the bar and the notariat has three striking characteristics: extreme localism, considerable self-regulatory powers, and problematic interest intermediation between the two branches and governmental agencies and between advocates or notaries and external occupations (see fig. 5.1). Advocates (and to a lesser degree notaries) are organized in highly autonomous local associations, which share little power with the national federation. The self-regulatory powers of the local corporations of advocates and notaries were not acquired through lengthy strenuous efforts by the profession, as was the case for American lawyers. Rather, these corporate associations were created by the state and endowed with their various competences as early as 1803 (notaries) and 1810 (advocates). It is almost impossible to overestimate the range of powers that local corporations exercise; within their judicial district they formulate ethical codes, discipline violators, mediate conflicts between *confrères*, and organize part of the training of apprentices. The national organizations have only secondary powers: they may try to streamline ethical codes, they deliver services the local corporations cannot afford, and they represent them at the national and international levels. The national corporation of advocates has been forced by its constituent elements to work with a Malthusian interpretation of its competences.

The decentralization of the associations of advocates and notaries was unproblematic as long as state intervention in professional activities was limited and sporadic. The absence of a strong national association became a serious handicap as soon as these professions regularly had to articulate their interests before the government, in competition with other occupations, and the internationalization of legal work made supranational contacts essential. The notaries were the first to fill the gap: their national federation, created in 1891 (in the middle of the "organizational revolution") (Schmitter, 1979), was revived in 1946. The advocates were in a more difficult situation. Their official national association (Nationale Orde van Advocaten/Ordre Nationale des Avocats) emerged only in 1968 and immediately was confined to ephemeral activities. True, there is another much older national association—the *Verbond van Belgische advocaten/ Union des avocats belges* (1886)—but its membership is small, it has no public law status, and it never was able to overcome the autonomy of the local corporations.

THE IMPACT OF RECENT DEVELOPMENTS IN LEGAL SERVICES DELIVERY

The demand for legal services has been modified recently in at least two important ways. Inexpensive legal aid for the less affluent has been requested with increasing frequency, and large bureaucratic organizations have multiplied their demands for expert advice concerning their legal contacts with individuals (as in the case of banking institutions, mail firms, and social security agencies), with other bureaucratic organizations (mainly government agencies, because of the rapid expansion of labor law, social security law, and economic regulations), and with corporate bodies on the international scene (because of the internationalization of governmental and commercial life). Both changes have led to transformations in the quantity and structure of supply.

Recent developments in legal aid have been analyzed by Breda (1983). Belgium has no state-supported system of public legal aid. Each local bar has a statutory obligation to provide representation to indigents (the pro deo system), a task usually performed by apprentices. The autonomy of local bar associations also extends to setting the income levels for free legal aid. In 1984 for the first time, the national government provided $800,000 to pay the pro deo work of apprentices ($10.08 per capita, compared to $3.20 in the United States). Law shops came into existence in the early 1970s, mostly in cities with a law school. They are staffed by volunteer law students and jurists but never succeeded in attracting the collaboration or even the sympathy of the bar associations. Their main function has been to articulate the issue of legal needs in the media and before policy makers. However, the greatest expansion occurred outside the state apparatus, the bar, and the law faculties. Private nonprofit organizations, such as trade unions and consumer movements, multiplied their activities in the field of legal aid. Labor unions, in particular, provide highly accessible, routinized, cost-effective legal services, which handle at least 100,000 cases a year (mostly rendering advice but also representing clients in labor court). Legal aid also is offered by local and national politicians (political patronage is widespread in Belgium) and by Public Assistance Agencies serviced and subsidized by local authorities. Breda (1983) concludes that Belgian legal aid combines characteristics that are very traditional (the pro deo system), Anglo-Saxon (the law shops), and Italian (clientelism and patronage).

The new demands, coming from large organizations, have been met by the organizations themselves, which have hired more jurists. Only a few law firms have emerged in the big cities, and American law firms have opened branch offices in Brussels.

Have there been meaningful changes in the conception of the lawyer's role? The most striking fact is the almost total absence of innovation on the part of advocates (still 30 percent of the profession). They could have used the law shops as ice-breakers (i.e., demand creators), as the British and Dutch private practitioners did, but they chose to fight them instead. They could have tried to reach agreements with other legal occupations to share the expanding markets. Again, advocates decided to antagonize these other occupations, sponsoring legislation that would have extended the advocates' monopoly to all legal advice. This conservation is difficult to understand. A more sympathetic attitude toward the legal aid movement, in particular, would have provided additional business for lawyers and enhanced the legal profession's reputation for altruism and the legitimacy of the legal system (Abel, 1988). Moreover, there was a very clear model: ten years earlier the Belgian medical profession succeeded in converting a major policy reform that made health care almost free into a mechanism for demand creation, without losing its professional autonomy.

The factors underlying the advocates' negativism are manifold. The Balkanization of the professional community into twenty-six local republics is responsible for the lack of a coherent strategy. However, there also is the fact that the bar elites, men in their forties and fifties, started their careers in the very comfortable market situation of the 1960s, when the bar was shrinking rapidly and demand was increasing. Consequently, they are well established in the market, monopolizing the most interesting clients (such as banking and insurance companies) and unmotivated to innovate. But profit margins are narrowing. Private firms and government agencies are hiring more jurists, who send advocates only the work that employed jurists cannot handle, namely, pleading a case in court. Even the elite members of the bar will learn the lesson soon: innovate or disappear, at least as a liberal profession. Notaries already have switched to demand creation, launching information campaigns, giving free advice to indigent people, and even "inventing" demands (such as the need for a cohabitation contract).

CONCLUSION

With one qualified jurist for every 330 inhabitants, Belgium seems to rest on a web of legal expertise. However, several factors make it extremely difficult to determine the precise social significance of all the legal expertise and its recent spectacular growth. It certainly would be unwise to regard that growth exclusively as a response to the demand for jurists in society. The output of law schools also is the product of what Larson (1989) calls "the autonomous logic of the market for educational services." In the 1960s and 1970s the political debate about equality of educational opportunity led to a policy of increasing access to the university (including the law schools) for disadvantaged groups such as women, Flemish speakers, and lower-middle-class youngsters. This substantially augmented the production of jurists. Furthermore, law schools are not merely vocational; they also are seen as the source of a liberal education, a ticket to the culture of the higher strata. The ratio of population to jurists also must take account of the fact that many legally-trained persons now are women, who are more likely than male jurists to work part-time and have discontinuous careers. Finally, we should note that the extraordinary growth of the jurist population conceals the rapid decline in the proportion of undergraduates studying law.

The mere fact that jurists share a common education and practical training and speak the same technical language facilitates their collective mobilization for purposes of social engineering. Yet, what divides jurists in Belgium is much greater than what unites them. In the past the heterogeneity of occupational forms and of the legal work performed was reflected in and reinforced by the folk conception of what jurists do and, equally, by the self-definition of the professionals. Strict incompatibility rules guarded the boundaries between the various legal occupations. Lateral mobility was rare. Moreover, localism and functional specialization of associations reduced the capacity of jurists for unified, collective action. Recent changes in the demography of the group have added new sources of heterogeneity. The influx of women, of Flemish speakers, and of persons with lower-middle-class origins has substantially reduced the dominance of men, French speakers, and those from upper-class backgrounds.

Before 1940, 80 percent of all jurists practiced solo. Today, more than half of all economically active jurists are either employees in relatively large organizations or, among advocates, members of associations and partnerships. Thus, more jurists than ever before now experience the division of labor and the problems of working together with paralegal and nonlegal experts.

TABLES

5.1. Total Number of Persons with Law or Notary Degree,[a] 1937–1985[b]

Year	Total	Average yearly percent increase	Total economically active	Percent economically active	Population per jurist	Population per economically active jurist
1937	8,460	—	7,360	87	988	1,136
1947	9,358	1.1	8,143	87	909	1,045
1961	13,701	3.3	11,554	84.3	670	795
1970	15,803	1.7	13,463	85.2	611	717
1985[c]	(30,000)	(6.0)	(24,900)	(83)	(330)	(400)

[a]Before 1969 a notary degree was received after two to four years of college and university training. Since 1969 a law degree is required before the year of notary training.

[b]Before 1937 the national census did not count degrees.

[c]Figures in parentheses are estimates.

Sources: 1937–1970—Department of Economic Affairs, National Census Reports; 1985—estimate.

5.2. Law Degrees, 1840–1984[a]

Year	Total		Men		Women		
	Number	Annual percent change	Number	Annual percent change	Number	Annual percent change	Percent of total
1840	44						
1850	90						
1860	96						
1865	98						
1870	81						
1875	136						
1880	186						
1885	185		184		1		0.5
1890	200						
1895	150						
1900	130						
1905	129						
1910	142						
1920	184						
1925	198						
1926	196	−1					
1927	197	0.5					
1928	205	4					
1929	229	18	214		15		
1930	240	5	225		15		6
1931	229	−5	220		9		
1932	222	−3	211		11		
1933	271	22	260		11		
1934	272	—	259		13		
1935	350	29	325		25		
1936	322	−8	295		27		
1937	317	−2	301		16		
1938	248	−22	235		13		
1939	246	−1	228		18		
1940	267	9	256		11		4
1941	241	−10	226		15		
1942	270						
1943	279						
1944	276						
1945	284		264		20		7
1946	335	18	313		22		
1947	340	1	314		16		
1948	273	−20	268		5		
1949	417	53	379		38		

5.2. (*continued*)

Year	Total Number	Total Annual percent change	Men Number	Men Annual percent change	Women Number	Women Annual percent change	Percent of total
1950	550	32					
1951	535	−3	474		61		
1952	495	−7	427	−10	68	11	
1953	514	4	444	4	70	3	
1954	494	−4	418	−6	76	9	
1955	511	3	449	7	62	−18	12
1956	495	−3	436	−3	59	−5	
1957	474	−4	410	−6	64	8	
1958	435	−8	380	−7	55	−14	
1959	418	−4	364	−4	54	2	
1960	415	−1	364	—	51	−5	12
1961	368	−11	313	−14	55	7	
1962	374	2	302	−4	72	31	
1963	301	−20	250	−17	51	−29	
1964	327	9	279	12	48	−6	
1965	343	5	293	5	50	4	15
1966	358	4	301	3	57	14	16
1967	360	—	302	—	48	−16	13
1968	404	12	340	13	64	33	16
1969	496	23	393	16	103	61	21
1970	671	35	509	30	162	57	24
1971	781	16	604	19	177	9	23
1972	909	16	706	17	203	15	22
1973	853	−6	617	−13	236	16	28
1974	977	15	714	16	263	11	27
1975	1,144	17	761	7	383	46	33
1976	1,188	4	768	1	420	10	35
1977	1,117	−6	730	−5	387	−8	35
1978	1,060	−5	711	−3	349	−10	33
1979	1,087	3	701	−1	386	11	36
1980	1,118	3	709	1	409	6	37
1981	1,170	5	756	7	414	1	35
1982	1,220	4	783	3	437	6	36
1983	1,121	−8	711	−9	410	−6	37
1984	1,205	7					

[a]1840−1935, 1942−1944—Belgians and foreigners; 1936−1941, 1945−1984—Belgians only.
Sources: 1840−1935—Department of Economic Affairs, *Annuaire Statistique de la Belgique*; 1936−1984—Universitaire Stichting/Fondation Universitaire, Dienst voor Universitaire Statistiek.

5.3. Law School Enrollment, 1936–1984[a]

Year	Total		Men		Women		
	Number	Annual percent change	Number	Annual percent change	Number	Annual percent change	Percent of total
1935–1936	1,024		947		77		8
1936–1937							
1937–1938	876		823		53		
1938–1939							
1939–1940	739		704		35		
1940–1941	832		790		42		5
1941–1942	923		884		39		
1945–1946	1,008		958		50		5
1946–1947	1,148	14	1,070	12	78	56	
1947–1948	1,417	23	1,302	22	115	47	
1948–1949	1,740	23	1,546	19	194	69	
1949–1950	1,877	8	1,648	7	229	18	
1951–1952	1,832		1,573		259		
1952–1953	1,788	− 2	1,544	− 2	244	− 6	
1953–1954	1,791	0.2	1,555	1	236	− 3	
1954–1955	1,750	− 2	1,533	− 1	217	− 8	
1955–1956	1,685	− 4	1,474	− 4	211	− 3	16
1956–1957	1,593	− 6	1,393	− 5	200	− 5	
1957–1958	1,507	− 5	1,313	− 6	194	− 3	
1958–1959	1,395	− 7	1,209	− 8	186	− 4	
1959–1960	1,294	− 7	1,107	− 8	187	0.5	
1960–1961	1,325	2	1,038	− 6	187	—	14
1961–1962	1,182	− 11	995	− 4	187	—	
1962–1963	1,132	− 4	957	− 4	175	− 6	
1963–1964	1,180	4	997	4	183	5	
1964–1965	1,221	4	1,025	3	196	7	

5.3. (*continued*)

Year	Total			Men			Women		
	Number	Annual percent change		Number	Annual percent change		Number	Annual percent change	Percent of total
1965–1966	1,341	10		1,127	10		214	9	16
1966–1967	1,491	11		1,231	9		260	21	17
1967–1968	1,847	24		1,462	19		385	48	21
1968–1969	2,321	26		1,811	24		510	32	22
1969–1970	2,866	24		2,239	24		627	23	22
1970–1971	3,036	6		2,329	4		707	13	23
1971–1972	3,327	10		2,487	7		840	19	25
1972–1973	3,572	7		2,534	2		1,038	24	29
1973–1974	3,907	9		2,692	6		1,215	17	31
1974–1975	3,980	2		2,649	−2		1,331	10	33
1975–1976	3,914	−2		2,585	−2		1,329	—	34
1976–1977	3,807	−3		2,512	−3		1,295	−3	34
1977–1978	4,069	7		2,744	9		1,325	2	33
1978–1979	3,993	−2		2,580	−6		1,413	8	35
1979–1980	4,106	3		2,648	3		1,458	3	36
1980–1981	4,119	0.3		2,671	1		1,448	−1	35
1981–1982	4,216	2		2,679	—		1,537	6	36
1982–1983	4,184	−1		2,607	−3		1,577	3	38
1983–1984	4,394	5		2,692	3		1,702	8	39

[a]Students in last three years of law school only (approximate equivalent of American law school training); Belgian students only.

Source: Universitaire Stichting/Fondation Universitaire, Dienst voor Universitaire Statistiek.

5.4. Jurists in the University-Trained Population, 1937–1984

	1937	1947	1961	1970	1984
A. Total number of persons with university degree	40,672	55,701	91,979	152,693	11,308[a]
B. Persons with law or notary degree	8,460	9,358	13,701	15,803	1,205[b]
B/A as a percentage	20.8	17.4	15.9	11.5	10.7

[a]Total number of persons graduating in 1984.
[b]Total number of persons graduating in law in 1984.
Sources: 1937–1970—National Census Reports; 1984—Dienst voor Universitaire Statistiek.

5.5. Law Degrees, by Language Group and Gender, 1956–1984[a]

	French			Flemish			Flemish (%)	
Year	Men	Women	Total	Men	Women	Total	Men	Women
1956	240	37	277	196	22	218	40	37
1965	171	34	205	122	16	138	36	32
1970	251	90	341	258	72	330	51	44
1975	292	185	477	469	198	667	62	52
1980	301	205	506	408	204	612	58	50
1983	284	188	472	429	222	651	60	54
1984			452			753		

[a]Belgian graduates only.
Source: Dienst voor Universitaire Statistiek.

5.6. Number of Advocates, Judges, and Notaries, 1841–1984

Year	Advocates	Decennial percent change	Population per advocate	Judges	Decennial percent change	Population per judge	Notaries[a]	Decennial percent change	Total
1841	920		4,498	563		7,350	980		2,463
1850	813	−12	5,444	537	−5	8,242	990	1	2,340
1860	983	21	4,814	561	4	8,435	995	0.5	2,539
1870	1,149	17	4,428	569	1	8,942	1,011	2	2,729
1880	1,356	18	4,070	625	10	8,832	1,025	1	3,006
1890	1,892	40	3,208	666	7	9,112	1,052	3	3,610
1900	2,184	15	3,064	708	6	9,455	1,087	3	3,979
1910	2,399	10	3,095	767	11	9,679	1,112	2	4,278
1920	2,132	−11	3,473	861	12	8,600	1,132	2	4,125
1930	3,023	42	2,677	820	−5	9,868	1,172	4	5,015
1940	3,694	22	2,245	813	−1	10,202	1,134	−3	5,641
1950	3,297	−11	2,625	1,116	37	7,754	1,128	−1	5,541
1960	3,579	9	2,564	1,091	−2	8,412	1,164	3	5,834
1970	3,827	7	2,521	1,586	45	6,085	1,202	3	6,615
1984	7,504	96[b]	1,313	1,669	5[b]	5,903	1,226	2[b]	10,399

[a]Before 1969 notaries did not need a full law degree but received a shorter legal training.
[b]Percent change over fourteen years.

Sources: 1840–1970—Van Houtte and Langerwerf (1977: 33–37). 1984—Nationale Orde van Advocaten, Ministry of Justice, Koninklijke Federatie van Belgische Notarissen.

5.7. Distribution of Jurists in Practice Settings, 1937–1984

	1937		1947		1961		1970		1984	
	Number	Percent	Number	Percent	Number	Percent	Number	Percent	Number	Percent
A. Advocates	3,627	49.3	3,309	40.6	3,641	31.5	3,827	28.4	7,504	31.3
B. Jurists in private employment	} 1,755	23.9	1,540	18.9	3,648	31.6	4,458	33.1	} 13,600	56.7
C. Jurists in government employment (judges excluded/educators included)			1,052	12.9	2,008	17.4	2,390	17.8		
D. Judges	813[a]	11.0	1,116[b]	13.7	1,091[c]	9.4	1,586	11.8	1,669	6.9
E. Notaries	1,165	15.8	1,128	13.8	1,166	10.1	1,202	8.9	1,226	5.1
Total	7,360	100.0	8,145	100.0	11,554	100.0	13,463	100.0	24,000	100.0
Total of "classical" legal professions (A + D + E)	5,605	76.1	5,553	68.1	5,898	51.0	6,615	49.1	10,399	43.3

[a] Figure is for 1940.
[b] Figure is for 1950.
[c] Figure is for 1960.

Sources: Advocates and notaries: 1937–1970—*Annuaire Statistique;* 1984—Nationale Orde van Advocaten. Judges: 1937–1970—Van Houtte and Langerwerf (1977: 33); 1984—Ministry of Justice. Jurists employed by government: 1947, 1961, 1970—National Census Reports. Jurists in private firms and government: 1937, 1984—figures are total minus categories A + D + E. Jurists in private firms: 1947, 1961, 1970: figures are total minus categories A + C + D + E. Total: 1937–1970—National Census Reports; 1984—estimate.

Luc Huyse

5.8. Women in University-Trained Population, 1937–1983

Degree	Percent women				
	1937	1947	1961	1970	1983[a]
Law	1.7	3.5	7.9	11.3	36.6
Philosophy and arts	16.8	27.8	39.3	40.4	61.7
Sciences	14.6	19.1	29.5	25.8	45.8
Medicine and other health, sciences ...	4.3	9.6	15.2	23.1	42.1
Civil and agricultural engineering	0.2	0.4	0.6	1.5	12.5
Social sciences, economics	4.2	6.5	10.8	15.1	31.2
Psychology, pedagogy	24.8	31.9	45.6	47.9	58.2

[a]Percentage of women graduating in 1983

Sources: 1937–1970—National Census Reports; 1983—Dienst voor Universitaire Statistiek.

5.9. Women Jurists in the Various Practice Settings, 1961–1983

Categories	1961		1970		1983	
	Number	Percent	Number	Percent	Number	Percent
A. Advocates	286	8.0	500	13.4	1,751	24.0
B. Lawyers in private employment					N.A.	N.A.
Primary sector	0	—	2	3.4		
Secondary sector	29	3.1	48	5.0		
Tertiary sector						
Commercial, banking, insurance, estate handling, and transport firms	83	4.6	129	5.6		
Nonprofit organizations	14	5.8	34	13.0		
International organizations	9	7.9	18	11.0		
C. Employment by government					N.A.	N.A.
General administration	N.A.	N.A.	114	6.8		
Education	87	19.9	157	23.4		
D. Judges	19	1.6	73	4.6	246	14.7
E. Notaries	4	0.3	12	1.0	44	3.6
Total	637	5.9	1,273	9.4	N.A.	N.A.

Sources: Advocates: 1961—CRISP (1971); 1970—Estimate; 1983—Nationale Orde van Advocaten. Lawyers in private and government employment: National Census Reports. Judges: communication from Ministry of Justice. Notaries: communication from Koninklijke Federatie van Belgische Notarissen.

5.10. University Graduates with Job, 1961 and 1970 (Percent)

	1961		1970	
Degree	Men	Women	Men	Women
Law	91.1	63.8	91.9	71.4
Philosophy and arts	90.8	76.6	91.9	77.1
Sciences	94.3	79.1	93.9	80.9
Medicine and other health sciences	95.3	78.6	95.8	81.4
Civil and agricultural engineering	85.0	70.0	87.0	65.0
Social sciences, economics	91.9	63.2	92.0	67.9
Psychology, pedagogy	89.9	72.4	91.6	74.5

Source: National Census Reports.

5.11. Social Stratification of Law Students[a] and All Undergraduates at University of Leuven, 1965–1981 (Percent)

	Law students			
Occupation of father	1965	1973	1981	All undergraduates, 1981
Upper (occupations requiring college or university degree, employers of 500 or more, top managers in public and private sector ...)	45.3	28.9	32.9	21.8
Upper-middle (junior-high-school teachers, employers of 500 or fewer, chief and senior employees ...)	19.3	25.8	18.1	17.2
Lower-middle (middle-rank clerks, primary-school teachers, artisans, farmers, skilled manual workers ...)	20.4	27.9	31.3	38.5
Lower (lower-rank clerks, small shopkeepers, shop assistants, servants and waiters, unskilled manual workers ...)	15.0	17.3	17.4	22.5

[a](Belgian) students in last three years of legal studies and last two years in criminology.
Source: Personal communication from I. De Lanoo, Center for the Study of Higher Education, Leuven.

FIGURE

	Orde van advocaten/Ordre des avocats	Kamer van notarissen/Chambre des notaires
I. Name of principal professional association		
1. Territorial base	Judicial district	Judicial district
2. Date of creation	1810	1804
3. Origin	Created by the state	Created by the state
4. Number	26	26
5. Corporate status?	Yes	Yes
6. Membership compulsory?	Yes	Yes
7. Authority	Self-regulatory power, licensed by the state (formulation of ethical codes, disciplining of all violators, regulation of conflicts between advocates, organization of apprenticeship, local interest intermediation, etc.)	Self-regulatory power, licensed by the state (formulation of ethical codes, disciplining of small violations, regulation of conflicts between notaries, organization of apprenticeship, etc.)
8. Structure	Chairman/general assembly/disciplinary council/chamber of young advocates	Chairman/general assembly/disciplinary chamber
II. National association		
1. Name	Nationale orde van advocaten/Ordre national des avocats	Koninklijke federatie van Belgische notarissen/Fédération royale des notaires de Belgique
2. Date of creation	1968	1891–1946
3. Origin	Created by the state	Created by the profession
4. Corporate status?	Yes	No

5. Membership — The only members are the local corporate associations — Notaries of local associations automatically become members of national federation

6. Authority — Unification of ethical codes/articulation and aggregation of common interests (de jure representational monopoly before the government) — Articulation and aggregation of common interests (de facto representational monopoly)/professional postuniversity training

7. Structure — Dean/general assembly of local chairmen — General assembly of local chairmen

III. Other national associations

1. Name — *Verbond van Belgische advocaten/Union des avocats belges*

2. Date of creation — 1886

3. Origin — Created by the profession

4. Membership compulsory? — No

5. Activities — Articulation of material and moral interests

IV. International associations

1. *Internationale unie van advocaten/Union internationale des avocats* (Brussels, 1927)

2. *Consultatieve commissie van de balies van de Europese Gemeenschap/Commission consultative des barreaux de la Communauté Européenne* (Brussels, 1960)

Union internationale du notariat latin (1952)

Fig. 5.1. Professional associations.

NOTES

I am grateful to Robert Dingwall and Filip Reyntjens for their comments on an earlier version of this chapter.

1. The degree lic. juris (dr. juris before 1971) is obtained after five years of university training in one of the seven Belgian law faculties. Students enter university at the age of eighteen or nineteen.

REFERENCES

Abel, Richard L. 1988. "United States: The Contradictions of Professionalism," in Richard L. Abel and Philip S. C. Lewis, eds., *Lawyers in Society*, vol. 1: *The Common Law World*, chap. 5. Berkeley, Los Angeles, London: University of California Press.

Bonte, André. n.d. *Universitaire studies in een economisch recessieklimaat [University Training in a Time of Economic Recession]*. Ghent: Rijksuniversiteit.

Breda, Jef. 1983. "Legal Aid in Belgium," 4 *Nieuwsbrief voor nederlandstalige rechtssociologen* 360–361.

Claeys, Urbain. 1974. *Universitair onderwijs als mobiliteitskanaal [University Education as a Channel for Upward Mobility]*. Louvain: Universitaire Pers.

Clark, Burton R. 1960. "The 'Cooling-Out' Function in Higher Education," 65 *American Journal of Sociology* 569–576.

Centre de Recherche et d'Information Socio-Politique (CRISP). 1971. *Le monde des avocats*. Brussels: CRISP.

―――. 1974. *Le monde des notaires*. Brussels: CRISP.

De Neve, Hubert. 1983. *Profiel van de opleiding in de rechtsgeleerdheid en in de criminologie [Law School and Criminology Students]*. Louvain: Dienst Universitair Onderwijs.

Elliott, Phillip. 1972. *The Sociology of the Professions*. London: Macmillan.

Grossman, Joel J., and Austin Sarat. 1975. "Litigation in the Federal Courts: A Comparative Perspective," 9 *Law & Society Review* 321–346.

Huyse, Luc. 1974. "Patronage en makelarij in het Belgisch benoemingsbeleid [Patronage in the Civil Service]," 10 *Civis Mundi* 222–229.

―――. 1982. "Political Conflict in Bicultural Belgium," in Arend Lijphart, ed., *Conflict and Coexistence in Belgium*, pp. 107-126. Berkeley, Los Angeles, London: University of California Press.

Huyse, Luc, and Hugo Cammaer. 1982. "Recrutering en selectie in de Belgische advocatuur [Recruitment and Selection of the Belgian Bar]," in André Hoekema and Jean Van Houtte, eds., *De rechtssociologische werkkamer*, pp. 41–63. Deventer: Van Loghum.

Larson, Magali Sarfatti. 1977. *The Rise of Professionalism: A Sociological Analysis*. Berkeley, Los Angeles, London: University of California Press.

————. 1989. "The Changing Functions of Lawyers in the Liberal State: Reflections for a Comparative Analysis," in Richard L. Abel and Philip S. C. Lewis, eds., *Lawyers in Society*, vol. 3: *Comparative Theories*. Berkeley, Los Angeles, London: University of California Press.

Pashigian, B. Peter. 1977. "The Market for Lawyers: The Determinants of the Demand for and Supply of Lawyers," 20 *Journal of Law and Economics* 53–85.

Rueschemeyer, Dietrich. 1973. *Lawyers and Their Society*. Cambridge, Mass.: Harvard University Press.

Schmitter, Phillipe. 1979. "Modes of Interest Intermediation and Models of Societal Change in Western Europe," in Phillipe Schmitter and Gerhard Lehmbruch, eds., *Trends Towards Corporatist Intermediation*, pp. 63–94. London: Sage.

Turner, Ralph. 1961. "Modes of Social Ascent Through Education: Sponsored and Contest Mobility," in Albert M. Halsey, ed., *Education, Economy and Society*, pp. 121–139. New York: Free Press.

Van Houtte, Jean, and Etienne Langerwerf. 1977. *Sociografische gegevens voor een studie van het gerechtelijk systeem* [*Sociographic Data for the Study of the Legal System*]. Antwerp: Kluwer.

6

The Venezuelan Legal Profession: Lawyers in an Inegalitarian Society

ROGELIO PÉREZ PERDOMO

INTRODUCTION: TERMINOLOGY AND HISTORICAL BACKGROUND

I will begin with a brief history of Venezuela. The territory of the present Republic of Venezuela was colonized by Spain during the sixteenth and seventeenth centuries. Its increasing prosperity led the Spanish crown to convert it into an autonomous administrative entity at the end of the eighteenth century. At the beginning of the nineteenth century the long-term effects of the French Revolution and the Napoleonic wars accelerated the independence movement within Latin America, and Venezuela became an important center of the struggle, providing leaders, politicians, intellectuals, and soldiers for the liberation of several other colonies. International difficulties, in part produced by the intense war of independence, as well as the lack of exports that would have integrated it within the capitalist system, combined to make Venezuela of the nineteenth and early twentieth centuries a poor and turbulent country. The population was more than 80 percent rural and sparsely distributed: approximately one million inhabitants at the beginning of the nineteenth century and three million at the beginning of the twentieth. In the last fifty years, the country has been incorporated into the world economy (especially through the export of petroleum, its major product); it has stabilized its political system and established a liberal democracy; it has urbanized and industrialized very rapidly; and its per capita income now is the highest in all of South America. The population has grown dramatically, partly through declining mortality rates achieved by improving sanitary conditions and partly through immigration. The country today has more than fifteen million inhabitants, over 80 percent of whom live in urban areas. Serious problems do exist, however, most notably the very unequal distribution of income and the strong dependence on the centers of world capitalism for the

201

export of the country's main product as well as for the import of foodstuffs and technology.

Manuals of comparative law include Venezuela and the rest of Latin America among the civil law countries. In fact, the country completed codifying its law around 1870 (generally by importing European codes), and legislation clearly dominates the production of legal rules today. Legal writings also are important and, in general, closely linked to the legal thought of the other Latin countries (Spain, Portugal, Italy, France, and other Latin American countries). The formal legal system thus can be considered entirely modern, but clearly there is considerable distance between the legislative models and the actual social practices.

There have been university law graduates in Venezuela since the beginning of the eighteenth century. Law teaching started in 1720, and a law professor occupied one of the first chairs in the Universidad Central de Venezuela (Caracas University). During the colonial period the university granted the degrees of *"bachiller," "licenciado,"* and *"doctor"* of civil law or canon law (or both). In the 100 years before independence in 1821, 372 persons took law degrees, but the number of law graduates in practice was somewhat greater because several graduates immigrated from other parts of the Spanish empire. The *Audiencia*—the highest court within the colony—granted the degree of "abogado" (lawyer) after a period of apprenticeship and an examination. For various reasons, less than a third of the law graduates aspired to the degree of "abogado," which was necessary to appear in the Audiencia but not before the *alcaldes* and the *tenientes de justicia* (lay judges).

Law graduates played an important role in the independence period. Many joined the independence party, and law graduates were well represented in the independence congresses. They had great influence in designing the institutions in the new Republic because they represented the *criollo* class (Spanish descendants born in America) and were experts in politics.

After independence the study of canon law declined and law teaching was enriched with such subjects as political economy, international law, and principles of legislation. By the middle of the nineteenth century the only degree that qualified for the practice of law was the doctor of political science. At this time the degree of "abogado" was granted by various courts after a period of apprenticeship. This degree was a mere formality; instead of a real examination, all that was necessary was certification by an established lawyer. Because an abogado no longer was burdened with the responsibilities that had accompanied the degree during the colonial era (such as the obligation to provide free assistance to Indians and the poor and to advise lay judges and other administrators), all graduates in law or political science also obtained the additional qualification. Between 1820 and 1930 only 1,800 degrees were awarded, or sixteen per year. By 1936, there were 740 law graduates (all of whom were both doctors of political science and abogados) in a country with 3,850,000 inhabitants. The legal profession could be considered established: the majority of law graduates had a private practice or eventually became judges, registrars, or notaries.

The year 1936 usually is specified as the beginning of contemporary Venezuela. The death of General Gómez, the dictator, the previous year initiated a period of political liberalization and rapid social change. The number of law graduates increased steadily, and growth became explosive after 1960 (see figs. 6.1 and 6.2).

During the 1950s the legal regime regulating professional qualification changed: the universities themselves granted the title of "abogado," which admitted the graduate to practice. The degree of "doctor" and the recently created titles of "*magister*" and "*especialista*" are granted after postgraduate studies and are relevant mainly for law teaching. However, because of heightened competition in the job market for lawyers, graduates are seeking these additional credentials as entree to the official bureaucracy or to enhance their prestige in private practice.

Thus, the word "abogado" (lawyer) designates all those who have earned the qualification as well as the much smaller category of title-holders who offer legal counseling, assistance, and representation to the public. Only about a third of law graduates are in private practice. Another third are judges and public officials within the legal system, and the last third occupy positions for which a law degree is not required. I shall use the word "lawyer" to designate law graduates in private practice, the word "jurist" for all law graduates, and the expression "legal professionals" (or sometimes just professionals) for those law graduates who have a full-time job in the legal system for which a law degree is required (including judges, lawyers, and notaries).

Historically, the relationship between formal legal qualifications, actual occupation, and sources of income has been complex. Even though there were people with the title of lawyer in the eighteenth and nineteenth centuries, legal occupations were not a stable source of income for many. There was far too little legal work to provide a sufficient income for people of high social status. Although the most important judges were qualified lawyers and political appointees, all other judges and all registrars were laypersons (*procuradores*).[1] Most jurists were *letrados* (learned people) rather than private practitioners, and their principal occupation was politics, where they discharged very important duties, even though they served *caudillos* and dictators. In twentieth-century Venezuela, in contrast, a true legal profession has emerged, although the political system continues to provide work for some jurists.

In the following pages I will analyze the current situation and will refer only occasionally to periods prior to 1935. Any statement made without a specific time reference pertains to the present day.

WHO ARE THE LEGAL PROFESSIONALS?

SELECTION

Law study is located within the university, which constitutes the only route into legal practice. Most students enter the university at eighteen, after completing a minimum of eleven years of mandatory schooling, although many enter later. There are two types of university: public, where tuition is free; and private, supported by student fees and, to a lesser degree, private foundations and the government. The four law schools in public universities enroll 65 percent of the law students—Caracas, Mérida, Maracaibo, and Valencia. There are two private universities in Caracas and a third in San Cristóbal. The total number of law students was 19,000 in 1981/82, or 5.7 percent of the entire university population.

Each school is allowed to set a maximum number of students (fixed by a national planning body for the public universities on the basis of budgetary considerations and physical capacity). Thus, there is selection at two levels: the capacity of the educational system as a whole and competition to enter schools that differ in prestige. In general terms, law schools are more selective than most other schools within the public universities, with the exception of computer science, architecture, engineering, and medicine. Entry to the Universidad de Venezuela (Caracas) is most highly competitive among universities.

The fact that the public universities are free might suggest that socioeconomic background plays no role. However, differences in attitude toward university study and selection and ranking at earlier stages of the educational system already have had had an effect. Few university students (about 5 percent) are of peasant or working-class origin because very few people from this social background are able to afford a long period of study or aspire to a profession in which their lack of personal contacts within the relevant milieu would make success very uncertain.[2]

Background variables other than class probably do not affect entry. The student bodies of both the university as a whole and the law schools are fairly equally divided between the sexes. The Venezuelan population is *mestiza* (a mixture of European, Indian, and black), any prejudice is covert, and race has no importance in the selection of the students. The vast majority of Venezuelans are Roman Catholic, but religion does not influence university selection or employment.

After admission there is a further screening by the law schools themselves. Although the data are inadequate, we know that student attrition is very high. In law—a subject that is not particularly difficult—less than 20 percent of entrants graduate. Many abandon their studies because they lack genuine interest (remember that tuition is free in most cases).[3] The significance of academic selection is unclear. In my judgment, the most obvious cases of intellectual incapacity are discarded, but creative students are lost as well. The dryness of the material, pedagogical rigidity, and the requirements of memorization probably exclude the most intellectually "alive" students.

INTELLECTUAL FORMATION

I will analyze briefly the content of the training the schools provide during the five or more years of the law course. This is relatively easy since there is an obligatory list of topics that varies little from one university to another.

The bulk of the assigned courses are designed for private lawyers involved in litigation (private law, procedural law, and legal practice constitute half of the curriculum). The remainder is divided between courses on public law, criminal law, and historical or complementary materials. Students are required to understand and often to memorize principles, concepts, and rules. Most critics feel that legal studies are irrelevant to, and an inadequate preparation for, the activities of professional life. The response (mistaken, in my view) has been to increase the number of courses useful for private practice, instead of modifying the teaching methods to develop the skills of factual investigation, legal reasoning, and problem-solving.

EDUCATION AFTER THE DEGREE: ON-THE-JOB TRAINING AND POSTGRADUATE WORK

Students most frequently seek to overcome the poverty of their formal legal education through training within the occupation itself. This is entirely informal, since there is no apprenticeship requirement for entry into the profession. Many students begin to work in courts, law firms, or public offices during the final years of their university careers. Others train after the degree by working with lawyers who are relatives, friends, fellow employees, or employers. Many graduates also pursue postgraduate studies, either in law schools (especially the Universidad Central de Venezuela, which has the largest and best organized program) or in other schools with interdisciplinary programs in administration, urban studies, planning, and similar fields. An increasing number seek a postgraduate degree abroad, usually in France, Italy, or the United States, generally in law but also in other disciplines that may be relevant to a bureaucratic career in a specialized area of public or private administration. Postgraduate degrees have gained importance in recent years, probably as a result of greater competition in the job market.[4]

PROFESSIONAL ORGANIZATIONS

I will now analyze the support systems available to legal professionals: the twenty-one colegios de abogados (bar associations), one in each state capital and one in Caracas, and the national institution that coordinates them, the Federación de Colegios de Abogados. The colegio de abogados was a colonial institution, created in 1788, which has some of the features of a medieval guild. Even though most lawyers belonged to the pro-independence party, the new Republic suppressed the colegios in 1822 as medieval corporations inconsistent with the prevailing ideology of liberalism. Nevertheless, the colegios were revived in 1883, principally as academic institutions to enhance public knowledge of law. Any law graduate can register in a colegio, without further examination, and almost all do so, although only a small group are active and pay their annual fees. Every law graduate who performs any legal professional activity must join a colegio and register with *Impreabogado*, a form of social security for lawyers. The colegios have multiple functions. Later I will analyze their role in enforcing the legal professional monopoly. They act as interest groups or trade unions to defend the working conditions of their members. Although they possess disciplinary authority and can suspend or expel a member, they almost never impose any sanctions or even reprimands. The colegio functions mostly as a meeting place for lower court judges and young or politically ambitious lawyers who seek to enhance their professional or political prestige or to establish friendships. The most active colegios organize professional refresher courses, publish a magazine and sometimes even books, and maintain a library. They also are social clubs and generally have a bar service and a swimming pool and organize sporting and cultural activities. Some colegios offer free legal assistance to low-income people, but such activity is marginal for both the colegio and the public. The colegio's president frequently is a judge, and political parties are involved in the election of a president. The Federación de Colegios de Abogados is merely an umbrella organization, as its name implies. Within it, judges, litigators, and women have organized their own special-interest groups (the Associación de Jueces, the Associación de

Abogados Litigantes, and the Federación de Mujeres Abogadas); none of these national groupings is very strong.

NUMBER, DISTRIBUTION, AND DIFFERENTIATION OF THE PROFESSION

The number of legal professionals in Venezuela has increased very rapidly: from 543 in 1926 (over 5,500 people per lawyer) to 15,000 in 1980 (1,000 people per lawyer).[5] Growth has been especially rapid since 1950. Approximately 65 percent of legal professionals are based in Caracas, which has 25 percent of the population of the country and is the center of political and economic decision-making (see table 6.1). Recently, however, there has been a redistribution toward the interior of the country, especially to the principal cities of the new areas of regional development.

The division by function is more difficult to determine. There are more than 1,000 courts, the vast majority of which are conducted by a legally qualified judge. Given that some courts have several judges and a number of court secretaries in the major cities are jurists, I estimate that approximately 1,500 professionals are employed in the judicial apparatus. Another 1,000 work in other public offices within the legal system as registrars, notaries, public defenders and prosecutors, and so on. There are approximately 600 law professors in the country, but they are not an important occupational category because less than 25 percent are full-time teachers. The remaining legal professionals are private lawyers, judges, or other officials who devote some time to teaching. We lack data with respect to two very important occupational categories whose size is particularly difficult to estimate: lawyers (i.e., private practitioners) and jurists who work as administrative officials within the government. I would guess that one-third of all law graduates, or about 5,000 people, are in each category. Finally, more than 1,000 law graduates are found in such diverse occupations as housewife, business executive, writer, and military officer. Declared unemployment is insignificant.

Each jurist in Venezuela traditionally occupies several different positions in the course of a lifetime. In analyzing the careers of those who graduated from law school in 1936, I grouped the positions into five categories: private practice; public officials, such as a judge, registrar, or notary; important positions in the political system (those who hold high governmental offices and diplomatic posts, legislators, leaders of political parties); literary activities (scholarship in law, history, literature); and law teaching. I found that 75.8 percent performed activities in three or more categories.[6] This tradition, which reflects the relatively undifferentiated nature of Venezuelan society until the middle of the present century and the absence of progressive careers within each sector, is undergoing modification.

Recent social and political changes have permitted functional specialization. Now a judge expects to remain on the bench throughout a professional career, rising within the judiciary until retirement. The same is true, to a lesser extent, of university professors, public officials, and private practitioners. Job security and the rewards of seniority encourage lawyers to remain within one occupational category (with occasional or part-time activity in another), which is producing a functional segmentation of the profession, such as exists in European countries.

WHAT DO LEGAL PROFESSIONALS DO?

Legal professionals have a monopoly over the following activities:

1. Representation and assistance of any individual or legal entity before the courts. Furthermore, no party may appear before a judge unless represented by a lawyer.[7]

2. Preparation of registered or notarized legal documents. All documents transferring property, establishing a company, or creating a lien must be prepared and signed by a lawyer.[8]

3. Legal consulting. Only legal professionals may publicly offer legal advice.

4. Important positions in the legal system. The Constitution of Venezuela requires that only law graduates may become members of the Supreme Court of Justice or serve as Contralor General, Fiscal General, and Procurador General.[9] Law is the only profession that enjoys a constitutional monopoly of high public office. The Organic Law of Judicial Power also reserves to legal professionals the position of judge, except in localities where there are no such professionals.[10] Other statutes and regulations require a law degree for the position of registrar, commercial registrar, notary, legal counsel, public defender and prosecutor and so forth.[11]

The colegios de abogados have added their own monopolistic practices to the laws reserving certain duties and positions to law graduates. Among the main ones are restrictions on advertising, the setting of minimum fees enforced by disciplinary action, and rules concerning the collection of fees.[12] Legal professionals do not limit themselves to activities over which they enjoy a monopoly but perform many others as well, most notably mediation and conciliation, business planning, negotiating, and politics.

SOCIAL AND PROFESSIONAL STRATIFICATION

In the "Introduction" I noted that Venezuelan society is highly inegalitarian. Each stratum retains a distinct type of legal professional and requires characteristic services. The manner of obtaining clients, the lawyer–client relationship, the structures of practice, and the type and quality of services vary with the type of professional. I will examine two extreme categories: the lawyers of the elite and lawyers for low-income people.[13]

LAWYERS OF THE ELITE

In this section I shall examine the organization and activities of lawyers who serve business and government—large units that require varied and continuous legal services. By including government within the economic elite, I am referring to the central administration, agencies, and public enterprises, which control substantial economic resources and are in frequent contract with entrepreneurs and investors, often adopting many of the forms of activity characteristic of private enterprise.

In-House Counsel (*consultoria jurídica*)

Almost all large companies and all public administrative bodies have an office of house counsel directed by one or more professionals. This type of practice may be inconsistent with the image lawyers have of themselves as independent professionals who offer their services to many clients and thus preserve their independence of judgment because they are not economically dependent on any one client. Although the number of lawyers employed is uncertain, it probably is 1,500 or more. The characteristic feature of the house counsel is that the professional really is an employee of a single "client," which actually is an employer. The service is rendered within the offices of the client, which provides all of the operating expenses and pays a salary (not a fee) to the professionals. The professional participates in the most important decisions, usually attends the meetings of the Board of Directors, and also handles routine matters: preparation of documents and contracts, employee relations, and interaction with companies or administrative bodies. When the volume of routine activities is very large, the in-house counsel employs additional professionals ranked within a bureaucratic hierarchy. The object of in-house counsel is to prevent conflicts. When litigation is unavoidable, the client usually will retain outside counsel, often through in-house counsel, although the latter may handle routine matters in court.

The prestige and salary of the employed lawyer will depend on the employer's importance and the employee's ranking among other lawyers within the office. The lower positions usually are occupied by women or by young lawyers seeking training. However, even the higher officials do not enjoy the prestige of elite private practitioners.

The "Big" Law Firm

There are no law firms in Venezuela as big as those found in the United States. The largest barely has thirty lawyers, and only ten have more than ten lawyers. I call these firms "big" because their model is the large American law firm. Their distinguishing feature is that the practice of law becomes a legal services company: the professional partners pool their work and share the earnings of the company in accordance with previously agreed rules. The company has employees: secretaries, students, messengers, accountants, and sometimes translators. Among the employees are other lawyers, generally recent graduates who expect to become partners of that firm or to establish themselves independently after completing an apprenticeship.

This organizational form appeared in Venezuela during the 1940s and is becoming more common among corporate lawyers. Currently there are many legal offices, containing five to ten lawyers, which have adopted this form with the intention of growing. I estimate the total number of lawyers in firms at about 300.

Some of these firms include litigantes (court lawyers), discussed below. But the basic activity of this type of firm is counseling and business planning. In the event of litigation, they frequently associate with a prestigious court lawyer.

The Interdisciplinary Service Firm with a Legal Component

This is a very recent development. To my knowledge, there are only two such firms, employing some twenty lawyers between them, although the phenomenon may proliferate. In these firms jurists, economists, engineers, accountants, sociologists, and other professionals collaborate to offer planning and counseling services to a group of related companies. Although these firms could operate independently, they gain expertise and efficiency by working for companies that encounter similar problems. Thus they combine the advantages of the corporate law firm with those of the inhouse counsel. Because they do not appear in court, they refer litigation and other unusual or complex legal matters to a court lawyer or a law firm.

The Prestigious Court Lawyers (Los Litigantes de Prestigio)

Although some lawyers known for their prowess as litigators have joined big law firms, most maintain individual offices or share expenses with other lawyers but not income or clients. Some of these court lawyers practice in the criminal area, which has acquired renewed prestige due to the greater frequency of cases of white-collar crime and of politically motivated prosecutions in a country where the judiciary is very independent of the executive (although not of the political parties, as we shall see later) and where the press enjoys considerable freedom.[14] There is no formal distinction between the litigante de prestigio and the ordinary lawyer. It is a specialization based on professional reputation, and often the distinction is difficult to draw. The category suggests what might happen in England if the barriers between solicitor and barrister were eliminated.

In summary, the most significant forms of economic activity, which are controlled by the ruling class, occupy the energies of the most qualified lawyers. They adopt different organizational structures, depending on the type of services they render. Because their services differ, they complement each other and frequently collaborate.

Finally, I want to highlight the way in which elite lawyers obtain clients. Some of the corporate law firms interested in representing foreign investors appear in the *Martindale-Hubbell Law Directory*. The majority of lawyers appear in the telephone directory, and a small percentage publish advertisements in the yellow pages of the telephone directory or in the major newspapers. Yet one of the oldest, largest, and most prestigious firms, Mendoza-Palacio-Acedo-Bórjas, does not appear even in the telephone directory. This is indicative of how clients are obtained in the majority of instances: through personal contacts within the shrinking Venezuelan elite, to which both the prestigious lawyers and their clients belong, or through contacts with American law firms. The common feature of elite lawyers is the small number of clients they serve, usually big national or multinational corporations. These lawyers generally have an excellent education and come from families of high social status. They earn substantially more than traditional lawyers: the median income of a senior partner in a big law firm is ten times that of any other lawyer.

LOW-INCOME CLIENTS AND THEIR LAWYERS

Before discussing this topic, I want to explain why I am not describing the lawyers used by clients of moderate means: individuals and small enterprises. These clients use general lawyers, who resemble those legal professionals described in the large literature in Spanish and in other languages. Another account would not reveal anything significant about the structure of Venezuelan society.

I indicated above that wealth and income is very unequally distributed in Venezuela. This has an obvious consequence: an important segment of the population cannot hope to purchase quality legal services from private providers. The usual rate for one hour of quality legal work (not by a lawyer who enjoys particular prestige) is approximately 500 bolivars, which is equal to the average family income for five days. However, the actual situation is even worse because informal mechanisms strongly influence decisionmaking in Venezuela. Much of the work of a lawyer is utilizing one's personal contacts, one's prestige, or the influence of one's client to achieve a favorable or at least a rapid decision. Low-income individuals not only cannot pay a lawyer but also lack the personal contacts necessary to persuade lawyers, judges, and administrators to pay attention to their cases.

Private Lawyers

Our research showed that in Caracas, and to a smaller extent in other large cities, a number of lawyers serve low-income clients. One group offer their services for ideological and political reasons. Lawyers active in politics, especially within the leftist parties, are involved in labor law, counseling and representing both unions and individual workers. The parishes of some Catholic churches, some universities, and some of the colegios de abogados also render legal services. Lawyers with ties to religious organizations are concerned with matters involving minors, the family, housing, and illegal immigrants. Those working with the Federación de Mujeres Abogadas tend to serve women and cases involving minors and the family.

Although the quality of the services varies from one institution to another, most lawyers serving low-income clients are dedicated to them. The number of lawyers rendering such services is low, and those who do are overworked. Therefore, although the services are little known, they are not publicized further in order to avoid aggravating the case overload.

Another group of private lawyers is motivated by profit, seeking to handle a large number of cases or documents at moderate prices. The offices of these lawyers are characterized by numerous secretarial employees who actually interview the client, make decisions, and prepare documents. The lawyer's role is limited to signing the document prepared by his employees after giving it a cursory reading.

The manner of attracting the client is illegal, or at least a violation of professional ethics. These lawyers advertise in the press, usually offering "free legal counseling" and listing the types of case handled, such as marriage certificates and requests for exemption from military service. The client finds that the "counseling" is free but payment will be demanded for the document prepared. Some lawyers contract with lay intermediaries who haunt places frequented by people with specific legal needs: jails, certain notaries' offices in downtown Caracas, and public offices that issue identity cards or other official documents. The intermediary looks for a confused or disoriented person and offers the services of the lawyer, telling the prospective client that the lawyer can resolve the problem. The intermediary then conducts the potential client to the lawyer's office and receives from the lawyer a percentage of the client's fee.

Public Lawyers

The Venezuelan government pays approximately 500 full-time legal professionals to render counseling, assistance, and representation to low-income clients. Although the duties of public lawyers are similar to those of private lawyers, the manner in which they relate to their clients differs significantly. Despite my reference to public lawyers, there is no such category within the Venezuelan legal system but only particular roles: public defenders, public prosecutors, procuradores de *menores* (minors), procuradores de *trabajadores* (laborers), procuradores *agrarios*, (farmers), lawyers from the Housing Regulation Office, lawyers with the Children's Institute, and so on.[15]

The most notable characteristic of these services reflects the basis fact that public lawyers are paid by the government, not by the client, and receive a fixed remuneration regardless of the quality of the services rendered. This, together with the very high caseload, tends to make the professional insensitive to the needs of the client. Thus, although particular lawyers are deeply dedicated to fulfilling their duties (especially those within the procuradores de menores), most have little motivation. Because the services are free, however, clients know that they cannot demand too much, even though the law requires the lawyer to be as diligent as possible and holds the lawyer responsible for negligence, if only on paper. Clients must queue up, often standing for extended periods, and the office personnel, including the receptionist and the secretaries, treat the clients with arrogance or condescension.

The services rendered by public lawyers are shaped by the interests of the lawyer, not the needs of the client. Thus, problems related to health, welfare, and education do not generate claims through the public lawyers. Low-income people do not perceive their problems as legal. The welfare system for Venezuelan workers, administered by the Social Welfare Institute, is an example. There are two million paying members and another six million dependents, who together account for more than half the population. However, we did not find any claims against the Institute made by the procuradores de trabajadores and very few made by other lawyers (Acedo Machado, 1986). This lack of claims is not testimony to the excellence of the welfare services, which generally are held in low esteem. Rather, it reflects the low quality of the legal services ostensibly rendered by public lawyers. Van Groningen (1980) evaluated the quality of the services performed by the public defenders and found them to be very poor. Among people accused of homicide, those represented received sentences averaging more than seventeen years, while upper-class defendants represented by private lawyers received an average sentence of 5.1 years.

Recently, a coalition of university researchers and politicians has proposed a radical restructuring of the delivery of legal services to the poor, based on an empirical investigation of the deficiencies of the present system (Pérez Perdomo, 1986). We advocated greater involvement by universities, colegios de abogados, unions, municipalities, and other intermediaries, supported by public funds and subject to government evaluation. The services provided by lawyers within these institutions progressively would replace much of the work presently performed by civil servants. Law students and recent graduates would be required to render free legal assistance as a prerequisite to qualifying as a lawyer, and qualified lawyers would be encouraged to do so. Mediation centers, staffed by specially trained legal professionals, would be given jurisdiction over many of the matters that concern poor people and would have the power to compel the parties to attend without their lawyers, even though the centers could not render judgments.

The proposal has elicited strong and widespread opposition. Public defenders and other public officials who provide legal assistance to the poor were deeply resentful of the highly critical evaluation of their work and anxious about losing their positions. Colegios de abogados and associations of trial lawyers (abogados litigantes) within the colegios also feared that these proposals would deprive them of paying clients. Although there has been little public discussion, discreet lobbying by both of these groups and the absence of countervailing support by equally powerful proponents has led to legislative inaction.

POLITICS AND THE LEGAL PROFESSION

I will conclude with an analysis of the place of the legal profession within the Venezuelan political system. I am consciously rejecting the commonly accepted distinction between professional and political activity. Legal professional activity, in the strictest sense, *is* political; its apparent neutrality and independence from the political system is a myth constructed by lawyers for their own purposes. Legal professionals are politically more active than other occupations because of their professional roles—and the political activity of lawyers is important for understanding the meaning of their professional roles.

Lawyers are viewed as independent of politics because their income is received from clients who choose lawyers on the basis of experience and professional prestige. As already mentioned, however, those who retain the more capable and prestigious lawyers are precisely the most powerful business executives. The resulting professional activity will favor those interests. However, those social sectors that cannot retain lawyers or can retain only the least prestigious will be at a disadvantage whether engaged in litigation or in actions designed to prevent conflict through mediation.

In the "Introduction" I pointed out that Venezuelan jurists have a long tradition of political participation, dating back to the end of the eighteenth century. This is not peculiar to Venezuela: jurists were prominent in the medieval and Renaissance Church, in the constitution of the national states, and in the bourgeois revolutions of the seventeenth and eighteenth centuries. In Spanish America, jurists have been the civil leaders par excellence. From 1936 to the present, five of the fourteen presidents of Venezuela were jurists and two were law students who abandoned their studies because of political persecution. Between one-third and two-thirds of all cabinet members have been jurists. Between 25 percent and 40 percent of the members of the National Congress are jurists. In the two major political parties, 47.4 percent and 36.7 percent of their Boards of Directors are jurists. In this regard we can speak of the law schools, especially those of the Universidad Central de Venezuela and, more recently, of the Universidad Católica, as centers of training and recruitment for the political elite. I will not speculate about the consequences for Venezuelan politics and government of the fact that so many leaders have had a legal background. I am concerned, rather, with the fact that the lawyers of the economic elite overlap with the political elite and that the two groups share common training and friendships. This is important for the study of the legal profession because the political contacts of legal professionals are an important factor in explaining the significance of law practice, especially in a country where the government wields such vast resources.

High government officials who usually are lawyers or are closely advised by lawyers maintain very close relationships with big-business lawyers. Consequently, lawyers are the main architects of a society that has been able to combine democratic political practices, the rule of law, and enormous social inequality.

FIGURES

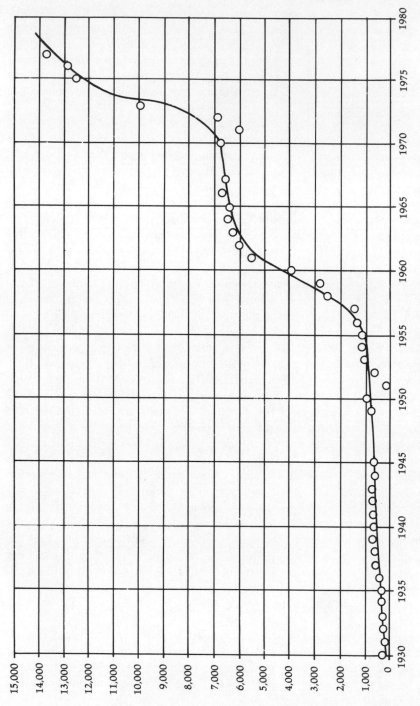

Fig. 6.1. Number of law students, 1930–1980. (*Source:* Pérez Perdomo [1981: 182].)

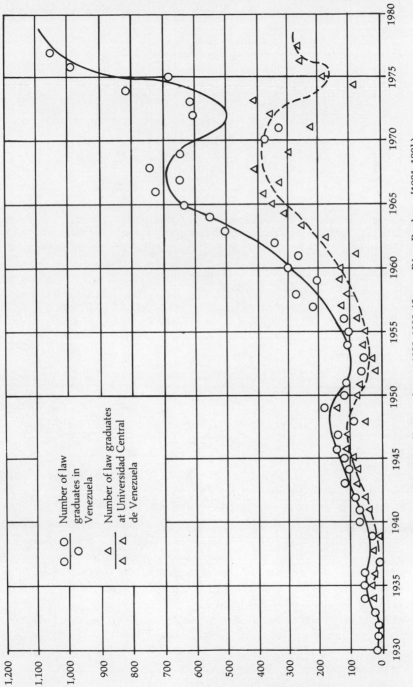

Fig. 6.2. Number of law graduates, 1930–1980. (*Source*: Pérez Perdomo [1981: 188].)

TABLE

6.1. Historical Trends in the Geographical Distribution of Law Graduates in Venezuela

Year	Population of the country (1,000s)	Law graduates in the country	Law graduates in Caracas (%)	Population of Caracas as percent of the country
1840	1,000	120	51.7	3.6
1894	2,445	246	48.4	3.0
1926	3,027	543	N.A.	5.5
1961	7,524	4.256	68.7	17.8
1971	10,722	8.102	63.0	20.4
1978	12,800	14.000	67.6	23.7 (est.)

Source: Pérez Perdomo (1981: figures 6, 7, 15, 16).

NOTES

The present chapter is based on my two books (Pérez Perdomo, 1981; 1986); for this reason, sources are not stated.

1. Registrars are public officials who record title to real property and maintain other public records. Today they are law graduates. In the nineteenth century, the term "procuradores" referred to laymen authorized to practice law. The category no longer exists and should be distinguished from procuradores agrarios, procuradores de menores, and procuradores de trabajadores—legally trained public officials charged with protecting the interests of disadvantaged groups (these are discussed further below).

2. A survey of university students (Instituto de Investigaciones Educativas, 1978) did not reveal a relationship between social background and academic achievement, probably because much of the selection occurs prior to entering university. Nevertheless, my personal experience as a teacher confirms that the best students are not from working-class origins.

3. There is no study of attrition, but the generally accepted view of student careers is as follows. After a year or two of school, most students begin working at one of a wide variety of jobs (wealthier students to gain experience, poorer students to support themselves and their families). Job pressures and university demands determine attrition. Many students who leave at this point return to the university after a few years, often to a different institution with lower academic standards, and graduate in law or another subject. The most desirable jobs from the point of view of law students are those in courts, in law offices, and with notaries. The number of good jobs that advance a student's career is limited, however, and usually only the well-connected students obtain them. At the same time, academic success in the Central University or the Catholic University makes demands on students that are compatible only with part-time work. These are the structural reasons for the high rate of failure and attrition.

4. I estimate that there were 400 postgraduate students and 1,000 jurists with postgraduate training in a population of 15,000 law graduates in 1980.

5. The estimates are very rough. Even if the number of law graduates could be calculated from university statistics and the registry of Impreabogado, that would tell nothing about their functional distribution. There are no figures for the number of private practitioners or for law graduates employed in government. Among the latter I have included law graduates in the central administration, the legislature, the Contraloria General, the Procuraduria General, and regional bureaucracies, even though not all those positions require legal training. For this reason I confine the category of "professional practice" to private practice and those positions in the judicial system and in other forms of employment that demand legal training.

6. Although I have no quantitative data on the sequence of positions, most lawyers begin as lower-court judges and lower- or middle-level administrative officials and either move up within those bureaucratic hierarchies or, following a political disgrace, return to private practice. Teaching and writing pay poorly and generally are part-time positions.

7. The profession's monopoly extends to administrative tribunals, with the exception of labor tribunals, which the petitioner can approach alone or with a lay assistant (usually a friend or trade union official).

8. A private lawyer must prepare the document, and the registrar or notary must read it and, unless it contains some obvious illegality, transcribe it in a public register of documents. Registrars and notaries are public functionaries and cannot practice privately.

9. The Contralor General oversees the legality and appropriateness of public expenditures. The Fiscal General is the head of the ministère public and performs some of the functions of an ombudsman. Both are elected by the National Congress for five-year terms. The Procurador General is legal advisor to the executive and represents the Republic in litigation in civil and administrative cases (hence equivalent to the solicitor general in common law countries). The Con-

tralor General is appointed by the President, subject to the approval of Congress, and is a member of the Cabinet.

10. In 1985 only ninety-two of the judges in the 1,064 tribunals were not law graduates.

11. Registrars keep records of transactions concerning real property, wills, and university titles. Commercial registrars maintain records of incorporation and other commercial transactions. Notaries record private documents and certify the signatures of those signing them. All three are public officials.

12. The minimum fee scale was established by the Federación de Colegios de Abogados in 1971, but not all colegios accepted it. At first, the Colegio of Caracas refused to enforce it. Following a change in the board of governors in 1983, the colegio promulgated a scale and required that a percentage of the charge be paid to it, justifying both as a means of allowing the colegio to provide legal aid. A group of members now has challenged the minimum fee scale as an unlawful monopoly, an improper use of funds, and an invasion of the constitutional rights of lawyers. In fact, the conflict is between low-status lawyers and judges, who control the colegio and use it for their own purposes, and elite lawyers and judges, who have no use for the colegio but resent their inability to control it.

13. There are no quantitative data on the stratification of private practitioners, so these remarks necessarily are more qualitative.

14. There is no overt political repression in Venezuela, and control of the government changes periodically through free elections. However, politicians, especially those challenging the incumbent, use the criminal process to disqualify their opponents. Recently, two former presidents, serveral cabinet ministers, and many high officials have been charged with a variety of economic crimes ("corrupción administrativa"), but few have been convicted.

15. The three types of procurador are public officials charged with representing minors, workers, and peasants in court and with giving them legal advice.

REFERENCES

Acedo Machado, Clementina. 1986. "Necesidades jurídicas y acceso a la justicia en un nuevo sector: Beneficiarios del Seguro Social," in *Estudios Laborales... en Homenaje al Profesor Rafael Alfonso Guzmán*, pp. 35–66. Caracas: Universidad Central de Venezuela.

Instituto de Investigaciones Educativas, Universidad Simon Bólivar. 1970. *El rendimiento estudiantil universitario*. Caracas: Equinoccio.

Pérez Perdomo, Rogelio. 1981. *Los Abogados en Venezuela: estudio de una élite intelectual y política 1780–1980*. Caracas: Monte Avila.

———, ed. 1986. *Justicia y pobreza en Venezuela*. Caracas: Monte Avila and Universidad Central de Venezuela.

Van Groningen, Karin. 1980. *Aplicación de la Ley Penal y Desigualdad Social*. Caracas: Ed. Jurídica Venezolana.

7
Feminization of the Legal Profession: The Comparative Sociology of Women Lawyers

CARRIE MENKEL-MEADOW

INTRODUCTION: COMPARATIVE FRAMEWORKS

One of the most dramatic changes in the legal profession in recent years has been the influx of women. In many countries women now constitute close to half of all law students, although it will be the turn of the century before this representation is fully mirrored among practitioners. This chapter explores the meaning of these changes for both the profession and women, using the description of common and civil law professions in the previous two volumes and various theoretical frameworks through which we can interpret these data. Because these developments are still relatively new and the theoretical terrain is shifting, I will offer some speculations about the complex relationships between legal professionalism and feminization.

I begin by addressing some of the problematic themes and tensions. First, there are the usual difficulties of scope. This chapter and the national reports define their subject matter as those with formal credentials who practice a legal occupation: independently or as employees in public and private settings (Freidson, 1986), or as judges or law teachers (the definition occasionally includes other legal functionaries, such as clerks and paralegals). But even these boundaries could be expanded to encompass police and other law-enforcement personnel, court adjuncts such as American custody conciliators, and new forms of private practice such as mediation—and perhaps they should be, especially if we wish to consider new entrants to the profession, such as women.[1]

Measuring the number of women should be easy enough, but the significance of gender in the professional context has become increasingly contested. Feminist theorists contrast the social construction of gender to the biology of sex (Kessler & McKenna 1978; Donovan, 1985). Further-

221

more, those who emphasize "equality" models and gender similarity (C. Epstein, 1970a, 1970b, 1987; Rosenberg, 1982) disagree with those who describe and value gender differences (Eisenstein & Jardine, 1985), and there is additional disagreement about the sources of difference (MacKinnon, 1987).

At the simplest level, we can consider the profession feminized simply because it contains more women. However, whether the profession will be changed by the presence of women is a different question. For those who attribute "feminine" qualities to women (or men), the legal profession becomes feminized when traits such as empathy, relatedness, nurturance, and collectiveness are recognized, valued, and expressed in the performance of legal tasks and functions (Lenz & Myerhoff, 1985; Sherry, 1986). For others, the profession becomes "feminized" not by stereotypic attributions of gender qualities (Olsen, 1986a) but by a "feminist" influence on the profession, which includes changes in both the practice of law (e.g., adaptations of work to family) and substantive rules (in areas ranging from employment discrimination to family law and criminal law). In this sense, feminism is the political and intellectual program of analyzing law from the point of view of women and working toward legal changes that will improve their material and cultural conditions. Indeed, it has been argued that the determination of some women reformers to change oppressive laws compelled them to seek admission to the bar in order to counteract the self-interest of male lawyers—an example is Caroline Norton's efforts to reform divorce and child custody in nineteenth-century England (Forster, 1984). This is a controversial project because what is "good" for women is neither obvious or agreed (MacKinnon, 1983, 1987; Wishik, 1985; Littleton, 1987). Even more controversial is the notion that the oppression of women has produced a particular feminist experience and epistemology (Harding, 1986; Belenky et al., 1986; Gilligan, 1982). If so, women's entry into the legal profession might transform legal processes and institutions (Menkel-Meadow, 1985; Menkel-Meadow et al., 1985; Frug, 1987). Will women who enter the profession conform to a "male" model of what it means to be a legal professional, or will the profession innovate and adapt to previously excluded entrants, who may have different perspectives on how to practice law (Menkel-Meadow, 1985, 1987)? Will women make contributions to the profession from their position as previously excluded outsiders (C. Epstein, 1981), or as dominated and oppressed beings (MacKinnon et al., 1985) who will reject the hierarchy and stratification of the profession, or as people with family responsibilities and interests who will insist on changes in the workplace (Spangler, 1986; Fenning, 1985)?

Most studies of women in the legal profession accept adopt the traditional sociological indicia of achievement (C. Epstein, 1981; Rhode,

1988; cf. Stacey & Thorne, 1985). By contrast, recent investigations of women in business have revealed that they are more "successful" and "satisfied" when working for enterprises they have created themselves than when employed by large hierarchical business organizations (*Wall Street Journal*, 1986). Yet another feminist school of thought would criticize this entire project as further strengthening and reifying gender categories. Is gender the significant variable here, or should we simply be looking at the structure of the legal profession and noting where the gender data seem to cluster without seeking to confirm our preconceptions about difference (C. Epstein, 1987, 1988; Frug, 1987)?

Women are overrepresented in those segments of the profession that traditionally have enjoyed the lowest status and income. A comparison with women in other male-dominated professions (medicine, architecture, business, and science) and female-dominated professions (nursing, teaching, and librarianship) should illuminate what, if anything, is distinctive about women's participation in the legal order. A historical perspective also helps to reveal whether nineteenth-century themes are being replayed in a modern voice or new patterns are emerging. Complementing these structural comparisons are psychosocial explanations that attempt to link structural and individual levels of analysis.

As women come to constitute half of the legal profession, will its status decline? Will the performance of more legal tasks by women affect the way these are regarded? Or might the status of lawyers rise as the entry of women transforms the profession into one that truly "helps" through warmer, less aggressive, more honest practices?

Once participation in the profession exceeds token levels (Kanter, 1978; Spangler et al., 1978; Halliday, 1986) new questions emerge. Will only "exceptional" women rise in the professional hierarchy (MacKinnon, 1987), or will average women do as well as average men? Are those exceptional women who act like men allowed to penetrate the restricted boundaries, while the majority who act more like women are excluded? What will happen when some women are not just "equal" to men but wield authority over them? Will objections be raised in the name of the same equality? As professional growth has slowed in the 1980s and occupational places become more limited, who are women "displacing"? As gender barriers are eliminated or reduced, class barriers may be raised; most women entrants are from the middle class (Abel, chap. 3, above). Is class discrimination more resistant to change than gender discrimination, in the professions and elsewhere? What is the relationship between gender and race in the practice of law (Sokoloff, 1987)?

To explore these questions in comparative perspective (Lewis, 1986) is to ask women, as well as lawyers, whether there will be adaptation and assimilation to the profession as currently constituted or innovation in and transformation of the practice of law.

A BRIEF HISTORY OF WOMEN IN THE PROFESSIONS

The story of women in the professions began quite recently. Entry to the so-called learned professions—law, medicine, and the ministry—was prohibited by law in many countries until well into the twentieth century. Even where entry was lawful (as in New Zealand), social and ideological barriers were substantial. Women generally participated in activities that had not yet been professionalized (such as midwifery before the physicians took over) or occupations that were losing economic and social status after an initial period of male dominance, such as teaching (Strober, 1976; Strober & Tyack, 1980; Graham, 1978) and office work (Davies, 1975). Women entering the professions in the nineteenth century generally assimilated to prevailing Western ideologies, such as the "cult of domesticity" and "women's separate sphere" (Harris, 1978), by arguing that women had special contributions to make (Leach, 1980) in medicine (Morantz-Sanchez, 1985), social work (Glazer & Slater, 1987), teaching younger children (Rosenberg, 1982), and nursing. This history suggests interesting parallels to contemporary debates between the "special contributions" of women and the "similar" values of male and female professionals, which should allow women to rise in the conventional hierarchies (Dubois et al., 1985). However, changes in context, including the increased bureaucratization of the professions (Larson, 1977), greatly complicate the analogies.

A small but important group of nineteenth-century feminists in England and the United States argued that women could and should participate in the professions on equal terms with men (Chester, 1985; Morello, 1986; Forster, 1984; Rosenberg, 1982; Weisberg, 1977). Concurrently, a core of activist practitioners and researchers began to demonstrate that sex differences were either nonexistent or irrelevant. While some historians have seen women gaining entry to the professions by accepting the dominant cultural doctrines about their innately nurturant qualities (Harris, 1978; Sklar, 1973; Cott, 1977; Antler, 1977), more recent interpretations suggest that there were several avenues for professional achievement. Penina Glazer and Miriam Slater (1987) have examined the role of American women professionals in academia, medicine, research science, and social work and have identified four different strategies: superperformance (female physicians who performed so brilliantly that their competence could not be challenged), separatism (female academics at women's colleges who forswore conventional domestic life), subordination (found in virtually all male-dominated professions but particularly pronounced in science, where women disproportionately staffed the lower levels of laboratories), and innovation (efforts to create or modify professions, such as psychiatric social work, by combining scientific training with more "conventional" caring values).

In the late nineteenth and early twentieth centuries, when women began to enter college and graduate school, some used the burgeoning social sciences to challenge the dominant ideology of sexual differentiation based on Darwinian, and then Freudian, variations on the theme of "anatomy is destiny" (Rosenberg, 1982). Researchers showed that woman's intelligence was not significantly different from man's, even if her brain was smaller; menstruation did not limit performance; and, most important, intrasex variation was greater than intersex variation.

Helen Thompson, a graduate student in psychology at the University of Chicago at the turn of the century, showed that, although women's average performance might differ from men's, the distribution of performances for the two sexes overlapped almost completely (Rosenberg, 1982: 72), a conclusion that has proved remarkably resilient over the years (Maccoby & Jacklin, 1974). Building on this work, early social scientists such as Jessie Taft and Margaret Mead argued that gender was socially constructed and gender divisions of labor were explained by social organization, not biological theories.

Feminist social theorists argued about whether women's "marginal" status endowed them with altruistic attitudes that would "purify" humankind if women were granted the vote, allowed to practice their separate professions of social work and teaching, and able to accomplish their social reform agendas of protective labor legislation. They were opposed by those who stressed the "homogeneity of the human mind" (Rosenberg, 1982: 170). Throughout the nineteenth century in both England and the United States most of the activists, but not all, stressed the "special qualities of women." Nevertheless, the history of women in the professions is peppered with strong individual achievers who do not fit easily into either camp (Hummer, 1979). This background is useful for understanding the efforts of the first pioneers who challenged male hegemony in the legal profession.[2]

Besides Shakespeare's Portia there are several historical examples of women who attempted to play legal roles long before they could contemplate formal admission to the profession. Margaret Brent was counsellor to the governor of Maryland in the early seventeenth century, while amassing her own real estate fortune and trying to obtain a seat in the Maryland Assembly. Her name appeared in over 100 lawsuits, and she acted as executor of a number of estates. She was called "Gentleman Brent" because colonists did not know how to address such a powerful woman. Karen Morello (1986) found that several black women argued their cases in early American courts.

On the other side of the Atlantic, Caroline Norton, a wealthy and talented writer, plunged into legal reform when she lost custody of her children following separation from an abusive husband who accused her of infidelity. When she learned that she had no legal existence under the doctrine of coverture, she became an avid student of the common law and began publishing pamphlets advocating reform of divorce and custody law and women's property rights. Her writings and activities influenced the 1857 reform of marriage and divorce law, although she did not live to see the passage of the Married Women's Property Act of 1882, which finally permitted married women to keep their own property. The doctrine of coverture, which barred married women from owning property in their own names and making contracts, prevented them from entering the legal profession, as well as others. Even when the impediment was removed with the passage of Married Women's Property Acts in many Eastern and Midwestern American states (Chused, 1983), however, courts drew on the "divine ordinance" to confine women to the home, ruling that their "proper delicacy and timidity" suited them to care for husbands and children but not to enter the rough-and-tumble of public life (*In re Bradwell,* 1870; *Bradwell v. Illinois,* 1873). In Great Britain these battles also were waged in the courts but initially by medical students (Pearson & Sachs, 1980).

Thus, in both the United States and Great Britain, the professions were deemed unsuitable for women because of their assumed biological and psychological differences from men, particularly their reproductive and nurturing capacities. Many men, including Virginia Woolf's uncle (a leading barrister), actually opposed women's entry into the professions because they feared competition and family breakdown. These notions were profoundly class biased. Working class women of all races and black American slaves had engaged in harsh, rigorous work for hundreds of years. It was the mark of upper-middle-class success that a woman should belong to a leisured world, in which she was relieved of most childrearing responsibilities by domestic servants. Ironically, when women finally did achieve admission to the bar, many worked in the environment least suited to women's "delicacy and timidity"—the criminal justice system—partly because men avoided such undesirable settings (Morello, 1986; Babcock, 1987; Menkel-Meadow, 1987). In California, for example, the first woman lawyer, Clara Shortridge Foltz, campaigned to reform the criminal justice system, creating a socially progressive probation program and a public defender system that may have been the first in the nation (Schwartz et al., 1985).

Women learned their law by trying to become lawyers. Most of the first American women lawyers read law with their husbands and fathers and encountered legal obstacles only when they sought to practice. In the common law countries they challenged these obstacles in court—although male lawyers made the actual arguments, the women applicants often wrote them. Yet, it was legislatures, not courts, that ultimately struck down the barriers in both the United States and Great Britain. In the United States extensive lobbying by women and sympathetic men gradually changed state laws, beginning with Iowa in 1870. In Great Britain the Sex Disqualification Removal Act of 1919 achieved the same result. But many American law schools continued to refuse to admit women, and Clara Shortridge Foltz had to sue the Hastings College of Law for her degree when the institution refused to recognize her attendance at classes (Schwartz et al., 1985; Babcock, 1988).

Women's experience in gaining entry to the legal profession was distinctive in that they had to work with men and present arguments concerning rights and equality that depended on applications of existing law. Although some women lawyers developed a reform culture emphasizing the need for protective labor legislation and women's special legal talents (Sklar, 1986; Babcock et al., 1975), women generally did not appeal to courts and legislatures on the basis of their "special" qualities, as strongly as they did in medicine and teaching (Rhode, n.d.). This may be one reason why the formal equality model is so strong among contemporary feminist lawyers.

The struggle in which women engaged in order to gain admission left an important legacy; they consistently have been overrepresented in legal reform efforts. Many of the earliest women lawyers in both the United States and England were suffragists who devoted their lives to the battle for the vote. Others, such as Myra Bradwell and Clara Shortridge Foltz, actively sought to reform labor legislation and juvenile and family law (Morello, 1986; Babcock, 1987; Sklar, 1986). Although women frequently had to claim that they simply sought to practice like their husbands and fathers, dissatisfaction with the status quo had inspired many.

A comparison of this brief narrative with that of women in the medical profession demonstrates that contemporary status hierarchies cannot explain historical resistance to women. Although women encountered resistance from particular male physicians, they generally fared better in medicine than law. As recently as 1971 women constituted 7 percent of American physicians but only 3 percent of lawyers (Harris, 1978). Much of this advantage can be attributed to the distinctive ideology and culture that women invoked in demanding entrance to the medical profession. Women argued that they would make particularly suitable physicians because of their natural maternal and nurturing capacities. In nineteenth-century America, more women entered the medical profession than any other (except teaching). The ideology of women's "separate sphere" and "moral superiority," which initially ousted them from health care, particularly midwifery, eventually led to a feminist-inspired preventative health reform movement emphasizing good sanitation.

The earliest female physicians in the United States, most notably Elizabeth Blackwell (the first formally trained and registered female physician in the world), supplemented their American medical educations with study in France and England, where there was great interest in more "scientific" medical research. Indeed, after founding a women's hospital and medical school in New York in 1868, Elizabeth Blackwell returned to practice and teach in England (Morantz-Sanchez, 1985; Forster, 1984). Blackwell and her contemporaries took a moralistic view of women in the medical profession, consistent with the cult of motherhood and domesticity. They virtually preached about health and sanitary conditions and believed women could make their greatest contributions caring for women (gynecology) and children (pediatrics). Although there were only two single-sex American law schools (Portia Law School in Boston and Washington College of Law in the District of Columbia), which were absorbed by New England Law School and American University to become coeducational institutions before World War II (Chester, 1985), women founded several colleges of medicine, one of which remained single-sex until 1970 (Women's Medical College of Philadelphia) (Harris, 1978; Morantz-Sanchez, 1985). Although the result was many more women physicians than lawyers, this strategy introduced other tensions into female medical practice. As Pasteur and Koch made progress in bacteriology, women physicians divided on the issue of "science" versus "sympathy" (Morantz-Sanchez, 1985: 188). Such battles were fought in terms of hospital mortality rates, and a cottage industry of medical historical scholarship continues to debate whether the lower incidence of puerperal fever in the women's hospitals was due to differences in drug dosages, length of stay, sanitary conditions, or the avoidance of forceps and other interventionist methods (Morantz-Sanchez, 1985: 225–231; Harris, 1978: 89–90). The eventual consequence of divisions within female medical schools was coeducation. Johns Hopkins opened with almost half a million dollars raised by M. Carey Thomas, the feminist President of Bryn Mawr College, who insisted that women be admitted. But these schools soon established quotas, limiting the number of women to 5 percent of enrollment between 1925 and 1945 (Harris, 1978: 117).

Similar claims about women's "special" talents were urged in Weimar Germany as reasons for creating women's police units in Cologne, Frankfurt, and Hamburg in order to control venereal disease and prostitution. Josephine Erkens, their founder, sought to expand their functions beyond social work, arguing that women should be present at all stages of arrest and interrogation. As *police*women, they resembled men in their work habits; but as police*women* they stressed their social work training and accepted protection from male officers. This experiment in integrating social work techniques with policing was terminated in the early 1930s by a scandal involving two policewomen who committed suicide in Hamburg (Fairchild, 1987). In the United States and elsewhere debate continues to rage over women's role in this archetypical male profession (S. Walker, 1980; Bittner, 1974).

The female-dominated professions, such as teaching, provide another framework for analyzing women's participation in the professional workforce. Here the claim that women had "special" skills combined with structural factors to make some professions "female" (Brand, 1978; L. Epstein, 1975). In the United States, for example, school teaching started as part-time work for men, when bad weather kept them from the fields. As the demand for education rose women were hired because they would accept lower salaries and such work was deemed appropriate training for future wives and mothers. There also is evidence that more women were drawn into the profession as it became centralized and bureaucratized, requiring a greater number of subordinates to support an administrative hierarchy that remained largely male (Strober & Lanford, 1986). At some point during the midnineteenth century, teaching "tipped" from a male to a female profession, with decreases in salary and prestige. This was rationalized by the argument that women were better with smaller children, while men had to be paid more for disciplining the older, more difficult students. Clerical work went through a similar transformation in the early twentieth century, particularly with the advent of the typewriter (Davies, 1975, 1982), and some have argued that the new computer professions are beginning to show signs of gender segregation as the industry undergoes structural changes and "tipping" begins to occur (Reskin & Hartmann, 1986: 31; Nieva & Gutek, 1981; Beller & Han, 1984). In female-dominated professions such as librarianship (Schiller, 1979) and social work, women may be found in only the subordinate jobs, while men continue to hold administrative and supervisory positions. Women dominate the upper reaches in only a relatively few professions, such as nursing. Such "semi-professions" (Etizoni, 1969) have an uncertain status in the eyes of both participants and the larger society (Spangler, 1986).

As women come to represent half of all new lawyers in some countries, the historical and sociological ramifications of "tipping" become evident. Although it is highly unlikely that women will dominate law (given its strong connection to public life and political power in most countries), occupational segregation within the profession ensures that some subfields or subprofessions may become more "feminized" than others.

WOMEN'S PARTICIPATION IN THE LEGAL PROFESSION

In every known society, the male's need for achievement can be recognized. Men may cook, or weave, or dress dolls or hunt hummingbirds, but if such activities are appropriate occupations of men, then the whole society, men and women alike, votes them as important. When the same occupations are performed by women, they are regarded as less important. In a great number of human societies men's sureness of their sex role is tied up with their right, or ability, to practice some activity that women are not allowed to practice. (Mead, 1975: 159–160)

The participation of women in the legal profession is remarkably uniform in the western industrialized nations (with a few notable exceptions). Since the 1970s women have entered in dramatic numbers, often accounting for all the growth in student enrollments and the profession. Because the profession has been growing, women generally have not displaced men or disturbed the male-dominated power structure. However, recent data demonstrate that the entrance of women has slowed the growth of the number of men (Curran, 1986).

Underemployment among lawyers also has increased. Women are disproportionately represented among those unemployed, employed part-time, and underemployed (Liefland, 1986). Women tend to earn less money than men in equivalent jobs. Perhaps most significantly, women and men are differently distributed across spheres of legal activity. Women are almost always found at the bottom of the professional hierarchy. Gender does not operate alone, however; occupational segregation is even greater when we add the variable of race (Sokoloff, 1987; Higginbotham, 1987) and marital status (Chambers, 1987; Swan, 1983).

WOMEN IN LEGAL EDUCATION

Women began entering law faculties in large numbers in the late 1960s and early 1970s (Neave, chap. 4, above). The reasons differ from country to country: in the United States the Vietnam war and its accompanying social reform and protest movements and the loss of draft deferments by male students, everywhere in Europe the expansion of universities, in Germany the decrease in teaching jobs (Blankenburg & Schultz, 1988). However, most nations felt the effects of the international women's movement (L. Gordon, 1976), postwar prosperity, and increased state subsidization of higher education (now declining in some countries, such as Great Britain) (Neave, chap. 4, above; Fossum, 1980). While the proportion of women climbed rapidly in most countries, it has leveled off at 30 to 40 percent (although women constitute more than half of all law students in France, Norway, and Yugoslavia) (Abel, chap. 3, above).

In the United States women were barred from many law schools until well into the twentieth century; Washington and Lee in Virginia was the last to admit them, in 1972. Women gained entry most easily in state universities in the West and Midwest and encountered maximum difficulty in the elite Ivy League schools of the Eastern establishment (Morello, 1986). In some cases they had to bring lawsuits; in others they mobilized the influence of sympathetic fathers and husbands. One of the greatest embarrassments to American legal education is the association of some of its leading figures with sex discrimination. Clarence Darrow thought that women were too kind to be good lawyers; Harlan Fiske Stone barred women from Columbia Law School for several years; Roscoe Pound and Erwin Griswold did the same at Harvard until Dean Griswold begrudgingly admitted them in 1950 in "small numbers" (Morello, 1986).

Until the 1960s, women represented about 3 percent of American law students. By 1970 the percentage took its first leap forward to a little over 8 percent and then climbed steadily through the decade, stabilizing at about 40 percent in the mid-1980s (although some schools had enrollments of more than half women, such as Rutgers and Northeastern) (C. Epstein, 1981; Curran et al., 1985; Abel, 1986, 1988a). This rapid growth of women in legal education in the United States can be explained in part by the increasing number of available seats; throughout the 1960s and 1970s new law schools opened and others expanded enrollments. Since the mid-1980s national enrollments have decreased, some schools have closed (e.g., Antioch), and legal educators have begun to worry about shrinking enrollments and declining student quality. As expansion slowed, the number of male applicants to American law schools has actually decreased (0.1 percent a year since the 1970s), while female enrollment has increased at an average annual rate of 41.4 percent (Abel, chap. 3, above).

Similar patterns are found in other countries. In England and Wales, the number of male university law graduates increased at an average annual rate of 5.4 percent between 1967 and 1978, but the number of female graduates increased at 31.2 percent (rates at polytechnics were similar) (Abel, 1988b). In Canada the number of male students doubled between 1962/63 and 1980/81, while the number of female students increased twenty-four times. Women now represent approximately 35 to 40 percent of new entrants in virtually all provinces (Arthurs et al., 1988). There seems to be a higher proportion of women lawyers in French than in English Canada, which would parallel developments in Europe (Abel, chap. 3, above). These differences may be explained by the varying status of the profession across cultures (Silver, 1974).

In Continental Europe, where law is an undergraduate degree, women represented 37 percent of German law students, 54 percent of French, 35 percent of Belgian, and 54 percent of Norwegian, as of 1983.

In Brazil, where law represents a liberal education for the elite, women were about 25 percent of law graduates in 1980. Although women never were barred from law practice in New Zealand, they were only 9 percent of law students in 1981. Two years later they were 35 percent of law graduates at one university and were expected to be half of all lawyers with less than seven years of experience by 1990 (Murray, 1988).

In India and Japan women continue to represent a small fraction of law students (Abel, chap. 3, above; Gandhi, 1988; Rokumoto, 1988). In Japan this is attributed to the persistence of traditional beliefs that men should be breadwinners and women should perform domestic chores at home. Although coeducation has been the official policy since the late 1940s, women frequently are educated in single-sex schools. Although 95.5 percent of girls entered high school in 1984, compared to 92.8 percent of boys, only 12.6 percent of women attended four-year universities and colleges, compared to 36.4 percent of men. Furthermore, more than a third of postsecondary women students attended single-sex institutions, and the percentage of women in the older, prestigious coeducational universities remains very low. Increased sexual equality can be attributed to international pressures, most notably the United Nations Convention on the Elimination of All Forms of Discrimination of 1979, to which Japan was a signatory, and to Japan's desire to be seen as a "progressive" nation. These pressures come from the government and not from activist women's organizations. The small women's liberation movement of the early 1970s is dormant if not dead, and women professionals are satirized in the media as wanting to be men and as "ego-centrist elitists" (Kamiya, 1986a).

These figures tell us only about women's entry into university law courses. There are wide national variations in the type of education and the likelihood that entrants will actually practice law. Italy and Brazil, for example, display high attrition rates during law study because entry is easy, but students must incur high opportunity costs in delaying earning capacity for as long as seven years, unassisted by government support. University law study is even less closely related to law practice than it is in the common law countries (Stevens, 1983), and practical legal education actually occurs in costly "crammer" courses, often established by private entities (and offering low-paid employment for law graduates). If legal education generally has become more available to women, entry into the profession remains controlled at later stages by alternative mechanisms. In Brazil, for example, women are 24.6 percent of law graduates but only 20.9 percent of legal professionals. These decisions are more particularistic, on the basis of factors such as personal affinity, and generally less visible.

Many students in Europe and South America study law part-time while working at some other job. This extended period, lasting as long as seven to ten years, frequently is interrupted by other employment opportunities, financial pressures, and changes in family structure (marriage and children).

The fact that female enrollment has stabilized at an almost uniform rate of 35 to 40 percent is difficult to explain. Is there some worldwide conspiracy to keep the profession predominately male, or have we collectively reached the "peak" of women's interest in the legal profession?

The increase of women in legal education in many countries has occurred at the expense of the working class (Neave, chap. 4, above). Despite democratization of the university, law students, including women, remain solidly middle- or upper-class in most countries (Abel, chap. 3, above). This presents a dilemma for feminist political activists, who want to align women with other groups excluded on the basis of race and class. However, in most Western industrialized nations feminism has represented a white middle-class movement (Hull et al., 1982; Bunch & Myron, 1974; Davis, 1981; Joseph & Lewis, 1981; Fox-Genovese, 1987). In the United States in recent years there has been a decrease in the number of ethnic minority students throughout higher education and particularly in legal education and admission to the bar.

WOMEN IN THE LEGAL PROFESSION: OVERVIEW

It will take another generation for the entry of women to have its full impact on the practicing legal professions of most countries. Although women constituted 34 percent of new entrants to the American profession in 1983, they still represented only 12 percent of lawyers. It is important to try to uncover the places and rates of female attrition, failure, or discouragement. There are many anecdotes about women leaving large law firms before the partnership decision because they fear negative decisions, but there is little systematic research (Liefland, 1986; Loden, 1986). One study of the Harvard Law School class of 1974 reported that many women opted off partnership ladder (Abramson & Franklin, 1986). Women still do not represent more than about 4 percent of partners in major law firms, though this is changing about one percent a year (C. Epstein, 1981; Fenning, 1984). It is said that women do not like the demands of the "greedy institutions," which require up to 2,300 billable hours a year, and they find the work inconsistent with childbearing plans (*Stanford Law Review*, 1982). If women graduate from law school at about age twenty-four and take about seven years to "make" partner, they must work hardest during the optimal years for bearing children (Harvard Woman's Law Association, 1985). Women also face greater discrimination at the higher levels of professional achievement and in discretionary employment decisions (Bartholet, 1982;

Fenning, 1984). A recent study of UCLA law students demonstrates that women may be preferred to men for summer law firm clerkships (especially if the interviewer is male) but still are less likely to be hired permanently (Png et al., 1988). This is consistent with national data demonstrating that women are now disproportionately likely to be large firm associates but remain underrepresented at the higher levels (Curran, 1986). Finally, many argue that it is simply too early to expect high rates of participation at the top levels of the profession, given career trajectories that require up to ten years before partnership. Thus, while rates of entry to legal education are quite high, rates of admission to the bar and actual participation in the profession are lower in most countries (Abel, chap. 3, above).

In the United States, the number of women admitted to the bar climbed dramatically throughout the 1970s, although the number of men admitted peaked in 1973. In Canada, women represent 35 to 40 percent of new entrants to the bar. In England and Wales 20 percent of those called to the Bar are women (although they constitute about 34 percent of law students); and in Scotland in 1982 they represented 36 percent of new advocates (and 40 percent of law students) (Paterson, 1988). Many countries report that women perform better than men in law school but still have greater difficulty finding jobs. In Norway, where 54 percent of law students now are women, a much smaller number actually enter the profession, partly because law study does not necessarily lead to practice but may serve as a general liberal arts education (Johnsen, 1988).

The British case illustrates the discrimination that appears during apprenticeship. Although comparable numbers of men and women law students receive honors, women have greater difficulty in obtaining pupillages and tenancies (only 40 to 45 percent of women obtain the latter, compared to 60 to 70 percent of men) and then finding clients (over half of the women surveyed reported problems) (Abel, 1988b).

Although women have been legally entitled to practice since 1919, the Sex Discrimination Act of 1975 does not apply to the Bar because barristers are not "employees." The Equal Opportunities Commission recommended to the 1979 Royal Commission on Legal Services that both branches of the profession register as "training agencies" under the Act in order to provide further opportunities for women, set aside seats on the governing bodies, and offer maternity leaves and other flexible working arrangements. There is little evidence that these things have been done (Royal Commission, 1979).

The United States Supreme Court recently held that partnership status, although not itself "employment," was a "condition or term of employment" under the civil rights laws, which a major law firm may have violated in denying partnership to a woman (Hishon v. King & Spaulding, 1984; cf. Hopkins v. Price Waterhouse, 1985).

Women in Great Britain report discrimination not only from male barristers but also from clerks and clients (Podmore & Spencer, 1982). As recently as 1967, two-thirds of London chambers had no women; in 1976 one-third still had no women. Many scholarships at the Inns of Court have been denied to women. In 1975, 17 percent of those called to the Bar were women but only 12 percent of those who commenced practice. In 1979, 50 percent of men called to the Bar had started practice but only 33 percent of women. Of those who began practice, 47 percent of the women had left within ten years of call compared to 13 percent of the men. Women barristers attributed these differences to the difficulty of obtaining a tenancy, whereas men said that women stopped working because they wanted to have children (Royal Commission, 1979). Apprenticeships may not constitute the same barrier for solicitors, but the attrition rate is quite high. In 1974 2,296 women were on the rolls, but only 1,299 women took out practicing certificates. A higher percentage of women law students than men express interest in becoming solicitors, a reflection of the greater discrimination in the barrister's apprenticeship (Abel, 1988b).

Thus, while the enrollment of women in meritocratic university education has expanded, the actual participation of women in law practice is increasing at a generally slower but widely varying pace because of resistance by the male-dominated profession. While some of the barriers express blatant or subtle discrimination, others are socially constructed impediments that are presented as external choices by women. As long as partnership decisions are timed to coincide with the years of childbearing, women may be unable to succeed in large numbers. Even when some American firms permit maternity leaves or allow part-time work, women who avail themselves of such "innovations" find they are considered less committed as lawyers (Abramson & Franklin, 1986; Fenning, 1985; Stanford Law Review, 1982). Thus, women are perceived as "opting out" without any thought whether the work structure contains impediments that preordain the outcome. Such "neutral" rules or constructs have a "disparate impact" on women. Both men and women law students still expect women to bear the principal burdens of childrearing, which are inconsistent with conventional work structures (Stanford Law Review, 1982).

Outside the Western industrialized world different patterns emerge. The number of women in the legal profession in Ghana is relatively high (over 8 percent as early as 1974) compared with many Western countries at that time. One analyst has attributed this to the strong and independent economic role of women in traditional Ghanaian culture, although women do not fare well in obtaining access to education if they must compete with brothers. In an ironic reversal of the patterns discussed above, women who graduate from law school may actually have an easier time obtaining initial jobs, precisely because they are expected to leave shortly after having children and thus do not represent as great a commitment for a law office. Although a large proportion of women lawyers do not marry, household help is much more available than in the West. Women still spend more time with their families than do men and consequently are more likely to be found in the less demanding public sector jobs, with lower pay and prestige (Houghton, 1981).

In the Soviet Union women are well represented in the legal profession (as well as in medicine). In 1975 they were more than half of those employed in the legal system: about 40 percent of lawyers, over one-third of judges, and about one-tenth of those in leading positions in courts and ministries of justice. As in other countries, however, the majority of women work at the lower levels, as notaries, investigators, and assessors (Matveev, 1977/78). The proportion of women in the legal professions is higher in socialist countries partly because those administrative jobs are less prestigious than the commercial work and litigation performed by lawyers in capitalist nations.

The proportion of women in the legal profession is smallest in Japan and India. In 1981 women represented 2.7 percent of the Indian bar. Even upper-caste women in the Punjab encounter structural barriers and are expected to interrupt their careers to bear and raise children (Sethi, 1987). In Japan women represent about 10 percent of those who pass the extremely difficult bar examination. Fewer than ten women are prosecutors, and only about fifty are judges, most at the lower levels (district and family court) (Kamiya, 1986b). These data suggest that traditional gender roles remain very strong in Asian cultures.

Although relatively large numbers of women work in the judicial system in Morocco, they suffer "humiliation" at home and have failed to act collectively to challenge a legal regime in which "polygamy, repudiation and unequal inheritance are daily practice," for fear of the repercussions at home. Women are largely excluded from the important spheres of politics and religion. Those who work at all are encouraged to remain in the "social-cultural" sectors of their professions—the arts, education, medicine, and some segments of the civil service (Mernissi, 1986).

OCCUPATIONAL SEGREGATION OF WOMEN IN THE LEGAL PROFESSION

The most significant finding of this comparative study is that women everywhere are concentrated in the lowest echelons of the profession, although these differ from country to country. There appears to be a push–pull effect: women are "pulled" into work for which they are thought to possess special talent (such as domestic relations) and "pushed" (or more likely kept) out of high-status work (such as private commercial matters in capitalist regimes). Gender segmentation of the work force is amplified by the fact that some occupations, particularly those in the public sector in Europe, have done much more to accommodate the burdens of child-bearing and childrearing.

Public Versus Private Sector and Litigation Versus Transactional Lawyering

In Germany, women prefer public sector jobs because the civil service, particularly the judiciary, permits part-time work and allows maternity leave for many years with guaranteed reentry to the same job. Women currently represent 28 percent of judges in practice training and 30 percent of all probationary judges (those with less than three years' experience). Unfortunately, these jobs are becoming less available as the economy slows. Since women experience difficulty in obtaining jobs in private corporations many are becoming advocates. In 1983 they represented 36 percent of advocates (Blankenburg & Schultz, 1988).

In Belgium, by contrast, where judges are less numerous and even more prestigious, women are less well represented. They constituted 14.5 percent of the judiciary in 1982, and only 3.5 percent at the highest level, but 20 percent of the bar. Women made up less than 5 percent of law graduates employed in banking and other commercial spheres but 23.4 percent of law teachers and 35.6 percent of advocates. They represented only 3.5 percent of notaries—a highly prestigious and remunerative office in Belgium—but 80 percent in the Soviet Union, where the functions are more bureaucratic and ministerial. Women represented 35 percent of law students but 50 percent of law graduates seeking work, which suggests higher levels of unemployment. Fifty percent of all Belgian women attorneys work in Brussels, perhaps because lifestyle is more anonymous in the city (Huyse, 1988). In contrast, French women lawyers are over-represented in suburban practices serving working-class populations and underrepresented in prestigious commercial Paris practices (Boigeol, 1988).

In Norway women are underrepresented in litigation partly because the role is viewed in Norway as requiring "aggressive defiance" and contacts with trade, both of which women are thought to lack (Johnsen, 1988). They are overrepresented in the lower ranks of the central government. Women in private practice handle two-thirds of all personal relations clients, while men handle three-fourths of all matters involving property (twice as many men as women reported having consulted a lawyer: 27 vs. 13 percent).

In Brazil women are 46 percent of all legal aid attorneys, who earn the lowest salaries, and 20 percent of public prosecutors. Because poverty makes the courts inaccessible to most people, police chiefs (who are law graduates) settle many disputes. Women constitute only 6 percent of police chiefs (Falcão, 1988).

In the common law countries the patterns are strikingly uniform. Women are underrepresented at the highest levels of private practice; and although they are overrepresented in public sector jobs, they are concentrated at the lower levels. Few women have been lawyers long enough to have climbed the ladder to a senior partnership or high court judgeship. In the United States, 21 percent of women but only 12 percent of men are in government positions (Curran et al., 1985; Vogt, 1986; Chambers, 1987). Women in the private sector are overrepresented in large firms (as junior associates) and in solo or very small practices and underrepresented in medium-sized firms. This may reflect their perception that large firms are more bureaucratic, adhering to universalistic standards, and small firms offer close personal relationships, whereas medium-sized firms permit the greatest scope for discrimination. In 1984 women were 15 percent of all law firm associates but only 2 percent of partners (Curran et al., 1985). This latter figure is changing yearly; a study of Los Angeles firms with over 100 lawyers revealed that 3 percent of partners were women in 1983 but 4 percent in 1984 (Fenning, 1984). Still, given the rapid increase in the number of women entering the profession in the 1970s, these partnership rates seem quite low. A recent study of the Harvard Law School class of 1974 revealed that, although women were more likely than men to begin working at large elite law firms, ten years later 23 percent of those women were partners, compared to 51 percent of the men. Over half of the 49 women who initially entered large firms had left within ten years (Abramson & Franklin, 1986).

In England few women are heads of chambers, Queen's Counsel, or judges. Women barristers are concentrated in the least favored specialties—criminal law, domestic relations, and general civil practice—and rarely found in the more remunerative fields of tax, commercial law, and chancery practice. In Scotland, only 2 out of 148 principals in the leading law firms were women (Paterson, 1988).

Women are also overrepresented outside the professional category. In the United States women account for almost all the paralegals—paraprofessionals who perform routine legal tasks and "assist" lawyers. In Japan women make up 67 to 78 percent of law clerks (Rokumoto, 1988).

Recent research confirms the relative stability of these patterns in the United States. A study of University of Michigan Law School graduates who entered the profession in the late 1970s demonstrates that five years after graduation 70 percent of men worked in private practice compared to 44 percent of women; 37 percent of women, compared to 21 percent of men, were in government service, legal aid, or offices of corporate counsel; 15 percent of women compared to 9 percent of men were in teaching; and 4 percent of women but no men described themselves as "full-time parents" (Chambers, 1987). A study of law school graduates from seven North-eastern law schools revealed that women were twice as likely as men to be in government positions eleven years out of law school and much less likely to be employed in law firms of all sizes. Women were greatly over-represented in legal aid and law-related work and greatly underrepresented in large firms and non-legal business positions (Vogt, 1986).

Although the Chambers study is limited to a single elite American law school, it does suggest some reasons for these differences. More men than women recall beginning law school with an intent to enter private practice; after five years of private practice, more women than men decide to leave. Men and women explain that pressures of work and family tend to push women out of private practice in both large and small firm settings. (This can be contrasted with the Stanford study, which revealed that women were much more likely than men to be conscious of family and work conflicts.) The national data, by contrast, reveal that women are found in very small firms specializing in "women's areas," like domestic relations work, where they may have more control over their work lives (Curran, 1986). Women's political values may explain some of the differences: women were more likely than men to describe themselves as liberals, and political orientation was the most powerful variable in explaining who chose government service and legal aid. Within each graduating class, smaller proportions of women than men obtained partnerships. Thus, there is support for the claim that women may be suffering discrimination in partnership decisions (Fenning & Schnegg, 1983). Preliminary data from the classes of 1982–1986 indicate that the proportion of women entering private practice has increased, so that at least at one elite school gender differences in choice of work setting may be narrowing.

Work and Life Cycle

In a study analyzing aggregate 1980 U.S. census data, Halliday et al. (1987) found that women lawyers were more likely than men to be employees in bureaucratic settings, where they worked fewer hours and were paid less. Women lawyers exhibited greater changes in the number of hours worked at different stages of their life cycle. One reason may be that more women attorneys than men were divorced with children and had no other source of support, either social or financial.

A recent proposal by the Working Party on Women's Careers of the Law Society in London has suggested that the profession must take responsibility for women's childrearing responsibilities by providing reduced fees for practicing certificates, refresher courses for those returning to work, tax relief for childrearing expenses, institutionalization of part-time work for solictors, and maternity leave, pay, and security clauses in partnership agreements (Working Party on Women's Careers, 1988).

Race

Occupational segregation is even stronger when race is combined with gender. Some have argued that black women have actually done "better" than white women. Sokoloff (1987) focuses on percent change, which draws attention to the small base from which black and other minority women began. Cynthia Epstein (1973) proposes a more qualitative argument that minority women have been able to take advantage of a "double negative" and that black women have done better as professionals, when compared to black men, than their white sisters have when compared to white men. She attributes this to the black woman's recognition that she may not be able to depend on male income and that, because she is black, she will not be considered a "woman" in the workplace (unless employers wish to take credit for hiring a member of two underrepresented categories).

Much of this analysis has been discredited in recent years. Given the broad definitions of "professional" job classifications in American census categories, the numbers of black women may appear to be greatly improving when many of the "professional" job classifications actually are "technical" or "assistance" jobs (such as paralegals) or female-dominated professions (teaching and social work) (Sokoloff, 1987). More detailed analysis of where minority women are located in specific professions, such as law, reveals even greater occupational segregation. Black women are more likely to work in the public sector (as a result of civil rights victories), the criminal justice system (disproportionately in public defender jobs), and small firms in large cities, serving mainly black populations (Higginbotham, 1987). This "ghettoization" within both specific jobs and geographic locations may parallel the American immigrant experience, particularly that of Catholics and Jews in large cities. But white male immigrant entry to the profession has been characterized by firms serving local communities (Heinz & Laumann, 1982), some with great success (the "Jewish" firms of midtown Manhattan), or by eventual integration into mainstream law firms (Auerbach, 1976). There is less evidence of such "success" among minority women, whose "communities" may be less affluent.

The Judiciary

Even when women attain prestigious jobs, their access routes may be different. A study of recruitment to the American judiciary reveals that women (both white and minority) were more likely than men to have attended Ivy League law schools and to have excelled academically and less likely to have been active in local politics or to have achieved judicial office by election (rather than appointment). Also, women (and minorities) were less likely to have come from private practice (especially as litigators) and more likely to come from academia, other judgeships, and other public offices (Slotnick, 1984).

Women in Legislatures

Recruitment to the legislature also appears to be different for women. While 44 percent of the men in the U.S. House of Representatives and 66 percent of the men in the Senate are lawyers, only one woman representative is a lawyer. Most women legislators have backgrounds in social work, served on school boards, or "inherited" their jobs from deceased husbands. Many of the most prominent women attorneys in American public life have been married to prominent male attorneys: U.S. Supreme Court Justice Sandra Day O'Connor; U.S. Court of Appeals Judges Shirley Hufstedler, Patricia Wald, and Ruth Bader Ginzberg; and Cabinet members Elizabeth Dole and Carla Hills. Although this should not detract from their own notable achievements, it does raise questions about access to power and the role of supportive spouses (and parallels the experience of many of the pioneer women lawyers in the nineteenth century) (Fossum, 1987).

Bar Associations

Most common law countries also report low representation of women in the governance of bar associations, whether compulsory or voluntary. Women are rarely to be found in the Councils of the Law Societies in Scotland, England, or New Zealand. Similarly, women are virtually absent from the House of Delegates to the American Bar Association and are just beginning to occupy leadership positions in state and local bar associations (Fenning, 1987). This, of course, is attributable to the fact that such positions are filled from the elite commercial sectors of the bar, where women remain underrepresented. In some countries women have formed their own bar associations in recent years. There is some evidence that women's bar associations improve women's status in the profession by serving as both a source of female candidates for public office and a powerful lobbying agent (Fenning, 1987). However, some feel that separate bar associations only exacerbate occupational segregation and distract women from becoming active in the male-dominated bar associations.

Substantive Law Reform

Many assert that women's bar associations are necessary for articulation of women's substantive law reform concerns. In Canada, for example, the Women's Law Association is a general membership organization, but the Women and Law group has a more explicitly feminist political agenda, focusing on the role of women in the profession and the impact of law on women (Arthurs et al., 1988; Harvey, 1970). In a recent California Supreme Court case involving the legal treatment of a professional degree at the time of marital dissolution, two women lawyers groups differed over appropriate political strategy. The Women Lawyers Association of Los Angeles argued on behalf of the wife's interest in having the degree considered community property (and thus shared), while the California Women Lawyers' Association identified with their professional class by seeking to have the degree treated as separate property (thus protecting women's new professional status and income investment) (Menkel-Meadow, 1985).

Similar conflicts faced American women lawyer groups in litigation over pregnancy disability leave. The issue was whether pregnancy was to be treated like any other disability, assimilating women to a male standard in a claim for equality (the federal approach), or whether to acknowledge actual physical differences requiring accommodation in the workplace in order to equalize opportunities (the state law) (Williams, 1984; Littleton & McCloud, 1986). The U.S. Supreme Court decided that states could go "beyond" federal formal equality in granting some "additional" protection for pregnant workers but were not required to do so (*California Federal Savings v. Guerra*, 1987; *Wimberly v. Labor & Industrial Relations Commission*, 1987; Littleton, 1987).

These differences in philosophy and approach can already be seen in the personal stories of women lawyers that demonstrate the variations in class and gender identifications (Couric, 1983; Smith, 1984; Abramson & Franklin, 1986; Morello, 1986; Warsaw, 1987).

WOMEN LAWYERS' INCOME

The extent of occupational segregation is confirmed by the available data on women lawyers' incomes. In Ontario, Canada, women may have little difficulty entering elite law firms, but five years after law school all women earned Can$2,946 less per year than men (Adam & Lahey, 1981). More recent Canadian studies confirm that women earn less than men with comparable experience, in large part because they practice less remunerative subjects (family law) and work fewer hours (Hagan, 1987; Hagan et al., 1988). Yet, as earnings at the Canadian bar have decreased in recent years, women have suffered slightly less than men (in part because their starting point was lower) (Stager & Foot, 1988a, 1988b). In New Zealand, only 2 percent of women earn over NZ$50,000 (compared to 25 percent of men), and 7 percent of women but no men earn under NZ$7,000 (Murray, 1988). In a poorer nation, Brazil, only 5 percent of men but 15 percent of women earn less than three times the minimum wage, and 21 percent of men but only 5 percent of women earned twenty times the minimum wage (Falcão, 1988). In England female barristers earned about half what male barristers earned with the same experience and type of practice (Royal Commission, 1979; Abel, 1988b; Pearson & Sachs, 1980).

Several American studies demonstrate that women continue to earn considerably less than men in comparable jobs. A 1982 study of Minnesota lawyers revealed that the median income for women lawyers was $27,960, compared to $43,690 for men. Disparities persist within age cohorts: among those who graduated between 1975 and 1981, women earned $26,810, compared to $33,410 for men (Silas, 1984).

The study of University of Michigan law graduates attributed income disparities within age cohorts ($48,000 versus $40,000) to the fact that women worked disporportionately in lower-paying fields (Chambers, 1987). The 1980 U.S. census data suggest that women are more likely to interrupt careers and to work for fewer hours. Women are more likely to be working in public sector jobs that do not require as many "billable" hours; and women's work hours drop when children are born (but increase dramatically when women become single mothers). Nevertheless, within all age cohorts women's mean hourly wage is less than men's and women's total income is considerably less than men's, the greatest differential occurring at the "peak" professional years of forty-five to fifty-five (Halliday et al., 1987).

Among those who had graduated from seven Northeastern law schools eleven years earlier, women earned less than men in every size of law firm and in nonlegal business positions. Women and men earned similar salaries only in legal services and "law related" occupations, such as teaching (Vogt, 1986).

EXPLANATIONS: THEORIES OF OCCUPATIONAL SEGREGATION

The composite picture that consistently emerges from these data despite difficulties of comparison, is that women legal professionals, while more numerous, continue to face occupational segregation, low status, and lower income. The segregation of the sexes in the workplace has been well documented across all types of work—unskilled, skilled, and professional—not only in the Western world but also in socialist and third world nations (Blaxall & Reagan, 1976; Reskin, 1984; Reskin & Hartmann, 1986; Bose & Spitze, 1987). Widely differing theories have been offered to explain these patterns, ranging from historical to psychosocial and economic, from patriarchal oppression to women's preferences (Rhode, 1988). With respect to the legal workforce, some have argued that the very recent entry of women into the legal profession explains much occupational segregation, which will soon fade away (Chambers, 1987). That has not happened elsewhere, however; gender configurations in the workplace are remarkably durable. As a profession such as teaching or clerical work begins to change gender composition it often "tips" and becomes the work of the other sex; or subfields within a profession remain sharply segregated, even when the "profession" broadly defined seems to become integrated (as in banks and the computer industry) (Nieva & Gutek, 1981).

Occupational segregation is measured by an index that represents the "minimum proportion of persons of either sex who would have to change to an occupation in which their sex is underrepresented in order for the occupational distributions of the two groups to be identical" (Reskin & Hartmann, 1986: 18). The index is 0 where there is complete integration and 100 where there is complete segregation. Indices of segregation are computed within occupational groupings, industries, and firms. Several researchers using census data for more than ten occupational categories found that race segregation fell dramatically between 1940 and 1981 in the United States (from 43 to 23 among men and from 62 to 17 among women), while gender segregation has decreased much less (from 46 to 41 among whites and from 58 to 39 among minority races) (Treiman & Terrell, 1975a, 1975b; Reskin & Hartmann, 1986). One researcher, using a limited number of occupational categories, computed national indices of occupational sex segregation, which ranged from a low of 27 for Japan to a high of 60 for Sweden, with the United States falling toward the high end with 47 (Roos, 1985). Men are more likely than women to work in sex segregated occupations: in 1980, 71 percent of all American men were employed in jobs that were at least 80 percent male, while only 48 percent of women were employed in jobs that were 80 percent female (Reskin & Hartmann, 1986). A recent California study demonstrates that segregation may be strongest within firms; women and men shared no job titles in 201 of the 393 firms studied, and 30 firms employed no women at all (Bielby & Baron, 1984). This is consistent with data showing that a small minority of law firms and chambers have hired virtually no women or made no women partners (Fenning, 1985; Royal Commission, 1979; Pearson & Sachs, 1980).

"Preferences"

It has been long claimed that occupational segregation is the product of individual preferences. Historically, this argument reflects the pride with which nineteenth-century women in the Western world claimed "moral superiority in their separate sphere" (Bernard, 1976). Women were said to choose occupations that were extensions of their nurturing familial roles: teaching, medicine, and social work. More recently, some psychologists and sociologists have claimed that little girls assert preferences for "female" work and that these are consistent with cultural stereotypes about appropriate sex roles and "innate" sexual differences in aggressiveness, endurance, capacity for abstract thinking, and emotionalism. However, the extensive research on gender differences has failed to demonstrate strong consistent differences in psychological or performance measures (Maccoby & Jacklin, 1974).

Socialization

Other have argued that any "preferences" are the result of socialization, not innate characteristics. They have demonstrated how early in life sex role education begins and how quickly it serves to differentiate sexual expectations about performance (Treiman & Hartmann, 1981). Occupational aspirations may become more sex-typed with age, education, and media exposure and continue well into adulthood (Marini & Brinton, 1984). Tracking, single-sex vocational training, and teacher expectations all have been related to expressed occupational preference (Reskin & Hartmann, 1986).

Human Capital Theory

Human capital theory suggests that women do not invest in the extensive training required for professional "careers" when they expect to hold temporary and interrupted "jobs" (Becker, 1974). Although this "explanation" is contradicted by the large number of women who have "invested" in legal education, law firms still invoke it, particularly the assumptions about women's commitment to work, in making partnership decisions and justifying the lower salaries paid to women.

Institutional Opportunity Structures

Opportunity structures in particular jobs and industries obviously are affected by formal barriers, such as the legal prohibitions against practicing a trade or profession. But perhaps just as important are the economic changes that occur during wartime mobilization or revolution. During both world wars women engaged in factory labor traditionally considered male work (Kessler-Harris, 1982; Milkman, 1982). Similarly, the shortage of labor in the Soviet Union allowed many women to take traditionally male jobs (Lapidus, 1976). Yet, such "horizontal" moves often are not accompanied by "vertical" moves within a profession, as demonstrated by the data on lawyers. Much significance has been attached to the role of women physicians in the Soviet Union, but men still dominate the supervisory positions (Lapidus, 1976), just as they dominate the higher levels of the legal profession in every country.

Employers may engage in "statistical discrimination" (Arrow, 1972) by attributing to each individual the stereotypes about the group, for instance, that all women will leave work at some time so that it is unprofitable to train them. It has been suggested that some women lawyers are assigned less desirable and less lucrative clients because firms assume that they will not be available over the long term; for similar reasons they may be retained as "permanent associates" rather than promoted to partnership (LaMothe, 1987). Structured socialization patterns, such as male clubs, may further deny women access to clients and "conventional" advancement information.

The structure of the profession is changing radically, just when women have entered and are approaching more "powerful" positions (Carter & Carter, 1981). In the United States (and other countries) there has been a growing trend toward bureaucratization, salaried employment, and larger work units (Schwartz, 1980). Although Chambers (1987) notes that women lawyers are more likely to hold supervisory positions in the public sector, the proportion of law firm partners who are women is not expanding as fast as the representation of women in those law firms (Curran, 1986; Vogt, 1986; Fenning, 1985). Women are disproportionately represented in a new class of legal professionals—"contract associates" (Kingson, 1988). Consequently, they are not in a position to influence structural change at the "top" levels of the profession (Halliday et al., 1987).[3] Changes in international commercial practice are having similar effects throughout the world. As large law firms open branch offices in all the major European and Pacific Rim cities the day of the multinational law firm has arrived. Cultural differences may reinforce structural barriers as Japanese businessmen encounter American female lawyers. In a legal culture where billable hours increase almost 100 a year (the "average" at a major Los Angeles law firm is said to be 2,300 hours per year) and competition intensifies for good lawyers and good clients, the demands of work increase sex segregation. This parallels the heightened professionalization of medicine, which has muted the effects of women's entrance into that profession (Morantz-Sanchez, 1985).

Gender segregation may be strengthened by other barriers, such as exclusions from informal work networks ("mentoring" in the popular literature) (Collins, 1983), male language and "shop" talk, and sexual harassment (MacKinnon, 1979). Some experimental research indicates that men prefer to hire men when selecting from among equally qualified male and female candidates (Fidell, 1970).

Exclusionary Patriarchy

Psychological and political theories explain occupational segregation as expressing men's desire to escape from women at the workplace—either to avoid powerful "mothers" or distracting "sex objects" or simply to bond with other males (Tiger, 1969; Bernard, 1981). A Marxist-feminist approach maintains that patriarchy advantages men economically by separating women as a class, paying them less, and preventing them from organizing, thereby fostering male-dominated hierarchical work structures (Hartmann, 1976). Thus, protective labor legislation, initially advocated by women, could be supported by union men as a means of excluding women from jobs by making them more expensive employees (Babcock et al., 1975).

An understanding of occupational segregation is complicated by different levels of analysis (individual choices vs. institutional structures) and paradigms (e.g., economic and socialization theories). It should not be surprising, therefore, that available quantitative and qualitative data do not sustain a single theory. Indeed, in a recent American lawsuit challenging discriminatory employment practices in the retail industry (*EEOC v. Sears Roebuck & Co.*, 1987), feminist labor historians appeared on both sides, one arguing historical female preferences for certain low-paying jobs while the other challenged the assumption that only men wanted "aggressive" high commission sales jobs, which underlay recruitment practices (Milkman, 1986).

IMPACT OF THE "FEMINIZATION" OF THE LEGAL PROFESSION ON THE PROFESSION, THE LAW, AND WOMEN

For if you agree to these terms then you can join the professions and yet remain uncontaminated by them; you can rid them of their possessiveness, their jealousy, their pugnacity, their greed. You can use them to have a mind of your own and a will of your own. And you can use that mind and will to abolish the inhumanity, the beastliness, the horror, the folly of war. Take this

guinea then and use it, not to burn the house down, but to makes its windows
blaze. (Woolf, 1938: 83)

The feminization of the legal profession is clearly well under way, if by
that we mean increasing the number of women. The more interesting
question, however, is whether women will have a different perspective to
offer the practice of law or the development of substantive doctrine. Such
questions implicate important issues in feminist theory. If women demand
equality with men on the basis that they are the same, then more women
in the profession should have no greater significance than more blue-eyed
lawyers. However, some feminists believe that equal participation does
not necessarily require "sameness," particularly conformity to a male
model. Although the male-dominated profession presently appears to be
"winning"—requiring women to adapt to its norms (C. Epstein, 1981)—it
is imperative to explore the possibilities of reversing that trend.

The argument that women may transform the profession by entering it
is dangerous and problematic because claims regarding difference can be
distorted into assertions about inabilities or stereotypic devaluing of what
is labeled "female" (MacKinnon, 1983; MacKinnon et al., 1985). Nevertheless, I have advanced this argument for several reasons (Menkel-Meadow,
1983, 1985, 1987, 1988). First, there is evidence that some women are
criticizing traditional lawyer roles, expressing dissatisfaction, and advancing
ideas for alternatives in both practice and doctrine. Second, a growing
body of feminist theory suggests that *socially constructed* (not *biological*)
differences explain gender correlates of behavior, attitude, and aspiration.
Third, there is a strong historical tradition of women's distinctive contribution to other professions (such as medicine, architecture, and social work)
as well as law. My view, simply stated, is not that all women will innovate
but that a larger, perhaps critical, mass of women will have a greater voice
in changing the practice of law (Schneider, 1986).

To elaborate this argument I will briefly review feminist theory, report
on "gender differences" already found in the legal profession, recount
some of the contributions by women to other professions, and speculate
about how women may transform the legal profession.

FEMINIST THEORY[4]

One central dilemma of feminist theory is the role of gender differences
in both explanatory models and reform projects. In contrast to nineteenth-
century claims about women's separate sphere or special contribution, the
second wave of feminism in the United States and Great Britain was based
on opportunities to demonstrate "sameness" or "equivalence" to men,

particularly in the legal sphere. In the United States this was manifested in a series of Supreme Court cases holding that women could not be excluded from certain male spheres, such as executing a will (*Reed v. Reed*, 1971) or serving on a jury (*Taylor v. Louisiana*, 1974). Many countries also enacted statutes formally prohibiting sex discrimination.

However, courts and legislatures also tolerated difference on the basis of either biology (pregnancy; see *Geduldig v. Aiello* [1974]) or the need to compensate for previous discrimination (tax benefits; see *Kahn v. Shevin* [1974]). As part of the national debate on the Equal Rights Amendment, feminists and antifeminists discussed the disadvantages that might befall women from being declared "equal" to (and, therefore, the same as) men. As feminist historians, literary critics, social scientists, and natural scientists conducted "equity" research, they uncovered examples of "great" women who had been overlooked by sexist constructions of knowledge (Harding, 1986; Donovan, 1985; Showalter, 1977, 1986). The resurrection of "great" women, however, also caused feminist scholars to question whether conventional measures of achievement were based on male models (S. Gordon, 1983), which privileged certain behaviors. This led, in turn, to "social" or "cultural" feminism—the celebration of women's accomplishments in traditionally female spheres. Legal theorists, by analogy, questioned why women's particular needs could not be "accommodated" or "accepted" within legal standards (Littleton, 1981, 1987). They argued for the deconstruction of the male norm of equality.

Another group of feminist theorists have argued that the gender differences extolled or condemned are reifications produced by an epistemology based on dichotomies and hierarchies in which the male always wins (MacKinnon, 1982, 1983, 1987; Frug, 1987). They insist that the power to define gender and regulate it should be our focus. One feminist scholar has urged that analysis should focus not on comparisons of men and women lawyers but on "discrete social practices involving topics of concern to women but containing the potential for an angle of inquiry that would disrupt conventional ideas which polarize women and men ... such as lawyer attitudes toward dress or childcare or serial monogamy in both marriage and law firm attachments" (Frug, 1987). Social and political analysis can clarify the role of gender without contributing to false polarization by creating and then studying reified categories (C. Epstein, 1987). Polarized categories make gender seem symmetrical when it is actually asymmetrical (MacKinnon, 1987; Harding, 1986) and when socially constructed gender may be more continuous (Littleton [1987]; on the third sex of berdache, see Mead [1967], and Kessler & McKenna [1978]).

French feminists (who differ among themselves) have taken a more "essentialist" position, arguing from a biological and psychoanalytic viewpoint that our language, knowledge, and self-conceptions have been "phallocentric" and must be corrected or "decentered" by women (Marks & de Courtivron, 1981; Eisenstein & Jardine, 1985; Moi, 1986). While the principal manifestation of this work has been in the literary criticism of Julia Kristeva (1987), Luce Irigaray (1977), and Hélène Cixious (1976), adaptations from French feminism and deconstructive criticism are finding their way into legal interpretation (Minow, 1987) and epistemological critiques of science and social science (Harding, 1986; E. Keller, 1984; Bleier, 1984). These feminist theorists argue that dualistic systems are man's creation and fail to take sufficient account of the relationship between scientist and subject. Difference here is viewed as a consequence of the political nature of the *relationship* between the genders.

"Difference" theory also emphasizes variation within genders. In recent years strong voices of nonwhite and non-middle-class women have been raised to assert that women's "stories" are not uniform (Hooks, 1981; Davis, 1981; Moraga & Anzaldua, 1981). This is of particular relevance to professional women, many of whom are enabled to seek and achieve traditional goals only through the assistance, and sometimes the exploitation, of nonwhite domestic and support workers (Miner & Longino, 1987).

Thus, feminist theory poses crucial questions:

1. Are there observable gender differences?
2. If so, are they constructed by research categories, social and cultural conditioning, or irreducible biological or psychological forces?
3. In addressing these questions should we use positivistic science (for example, conventional stratification theory as a measure of "success") or our own experience (participant observation, feminist consciousness raising groups, "war stories" told at women's bar association meetings)? Can we refrain from overgeneralizing? What is our self-interest in seeing differences and similarities?
4. Have we taken full account of the variation in historical, cultural, and material contexts?
5. What are the effects of the differences we perceive? Where are women located? What are they doing? Are there traces of oppositional culture, innovation, and knowledge, whether produced by oppression and exclusion, socially constructed, or even biological?

PERCEPTIONS OF DIFFERENCES: THE DATA

"Satisfaction" Studies

In a recent survey conducted by the American Bar Association, three-quarters of the women lawyers questioned said that women's entry would have "major" consequences for the profession. Only 40 percent of the men attorneys agreed, but 45 percent said that it would have "mostly favorable" consequences if there were any at all (Winter, 1983; *American Bar Association Journal*, 1983: 1388). Most men described the major consequences as broader access to the legal profession for clients. Women lawyers were more likely to anticipate "new perspectives on legal issues" and the "improvement of standards and ethics."

Both a subsequent ABA poll (Hirsh, 1985) and a follow-up study by the American Bar Foundation (ABF) (Nelson, 1987) also disclosed gender differences in career satisfaction. While rates of dissatisfaction varied from 16 to 40 percent, women were more dissatisfied than men. Nearly one-third of the women but only 16 percent of the men in the ABF study said they were "somewhat dissatisfied" with their work. The proportion of women who planned to change their jobs within the next few years was three times that of men (28.5 percent vs. 9.4 percent). When asked for their three most important reasons for becoming lawyers, 48.2 percent of the women but only 34.8 percent of the men mentioned social service, whereas 77.5 percent of the men but only 52.6 percent of women indicated financial opportunity as the main reason for entering the legal profession. Financial rewards were an important factor in job satisfaction for 38.4 percent of women compared to 55.9 percent of men. Women were also more likely to see "intellectual challenge" as an important reason for becoming lawyers (90.7 percent vs. 77.3 percent). Some of the gender differences in satisfaction diminished when controls for age and type of law work were introduced (Nelson, 1987). Thus, women's dissatisfaction may reflect their perception that they have been *relegated to* particular jobs and tasks. As age and experience permit them to "climb" the occupational ladders, dissatisfaction may decrease. Indeed, David Chambers's study of Michigan graduates revealed virtually no gender difference in satisfaction even though men and women earned different salaries in different jobs. The women in Chambers's study may be "happier" than other women lawyers because their position as graduates of an elite school increases their opportunities. Or, they may simply have lower expectations than men. Although there are fewer women partners, the women in government positions seem to rise fairly quickly to supervisory positions, which may enhance their job satisfaction.

Further explication and study of "satisfaction" may be necessary. A common pattern in such studies is that women are more likely than men to mention the relationship of family life to work life in evaluating a job (Ashburn, 1977; Quade, 1986). A 1982 survey revealed that both men and women law students continued to expect women to perform primary childrearing duties and that women, but not men, attributed weight to an employer's policie● on maternity and childrearing leave in choosing a job (*Stanford Law Review*, 1982). Thus, men are able to father children with little regard to work demands, which may help to explain why they are more satisfied with current work structures. Women who continue to express traditional "women's values" of connection and caring for children will find the currently constructed workplace less satisfactory (Hochschild, 1975; Frug, 1979; Finley, 1986). Yet, women who have struggled to achieve some "success" within the legal profession may be reluctant to express dissatisfaction even though they are juggling many tasks (at home and at work) and experiencing a great deal of stress. Chambers's study indicates that women lawyers who are married and have children are more satisfied than single and childless women, although they report difficulties in "having it all" and managing family and work life.

Holmes (1987) has suggested that, in order to consider themselves happy, women may need different rewards from men: a belief in the moral value of their work; connectedness in the workplace; and continual feedback, evaluation, and affiliation. This is consistent with some work in social psychology, which has demonstrated that men are "vertically" ambitious, seeking promotion up the hierarchical ladder, whereas women are "horizontally" ambitious, seeking to explore a variety of interests simultaneously—work, family, and friends (Klein, 1946; Theodore, 1971; Ashburn, 1977). Thus, while studies have demonstrated gender differences in "satisfaction," the focus on this conventional sociological or "yuppified" measure may conceal more than it reveals. We should also ask what people regard as meaningful work, what motivates them to continue working or quit, whether their expectations are fulfilled, and what are the relationships between attitudinal measures of "success" or "satisfaction" and "objective" measures of income, job location and type, work structures, family integration, and status as an employer or employee (Spangler, 1986).

Gender Difference and Work

A large literature in social psychology and the sociology of work begins to answer these questions (Feulner, 1979; Miller et al., 1979). In one of the most comprehensive studies of gender differences to date, Maccoby and Jacklin (1974) found only four: girls have greater verbal ability, while boys tend to have greater visual-spatial and mathematical abilities and higher levels of aggression. They found no difference in achievement motivation, risk-taking, task persistence, or other skills. Some have argued that even these few differences are produced by early socialization. Others have questioned whether aggression and the desire for domination are functional or necessary in particular jobs. Jessie Bernard (1964) found that women scientists gave noncompetitive "fascination with a problem" as the main reason for their productivity, while men were more likely to mention competitive pressures to "publish or perish." It is extremely difficult to disentangle causes: do men express distinctive motivations because of socialized expectations about financial responsibility?

Early research suggests that women and men may prefer different areas of work, reflecting classic stereotypes. Academic women prefer teaching and student service to research and administrative and committee work (Eckert & Stecklein, 1971; Centra, 1974). Also, women law students were more likely to prefer legal aid and government "service" work to private practice (Jacobs, 1972). Women supervisors and managers are said to adopt a more permissive, personal, informal, and expressive work style (Fogarty et al., 1971; Hennig & Jardim, 1977). Women physicians are more caring and sensitive to patients' needs (Menninger, 1973; Los Angeles Times, 1986). A burgeoning literature, including popular best sellers, has begun to document the differences in women's managerial styles, arguing that the influx of women into top business management could lead to more "androgynous" combinations of rational and instrumental leadership ("alpha") with caring, nurturing, and interpersonal skills ("beta") (Sargent, 1981; Nickles & Ashcraft, 1982).

Attempts to synthesize the literature on women's work styles must bridge different levels of analysis. Social psychologists tend to study what Rosabeth Kanter (1976) has called "temperament": personality and character factors that can be both individual and the product of gendered socialization. Reading such research through the lens of competing feminist visions can lead to the conclusion that either "equalized" socialization will eliminate or reduce such temperamental differences or aggregated differences will "temper" the workplace, producing alternative ways of doing business. Sociologists focus on such social structural variables as organization. Here competing feminist theories predict that either role definitions will become less rigid, changing both individuals and workplaces, or rigid roles in both the family and the workplace will frustrate change (Kanter, 1977; Hochschild, 1975; Ferguson, 1985).

The dilemma is the familiar one of trying to predict the sources and directions of social change. Present organizational structures seem inhospitable to women, particularly those who want or accept childrearing responsibilities. Only collective action can bring about change. Women's bar associations have been extremely effective at raising so-called women's issues and placing them on the agendas of national and local bar associations, as well as individual law firms (Fenning, 1987). Of equal interest, however, is a little studied source of change—senior partners or upper-level managers who are fathers of female lawyers. Although socialized in a "prefeminist mentality" that demanded total commitment to "greedy institutions" and believed that wives belonged at home, the father of daughters may be a surprising source of innovation. Like the intermarriages that facilitated immigrant entrance into elite law firms, this may be a powerful, if covert, stimulus for micro-level change, while preserving class privilege.

Rosabeth Kanter (1977) found that organizational expectations constrain "token" personnel who differ from the white male norms in large enterprises, preventing them from expressing their own values or culture until they reach a "critical mass" of at least 20 percent of the workforce. In the law school environment, Spangler, Gordon, and Pipkin (1978) found that women law students performed better academically and participated more in class discussions when they constituted a larger proportion of the student population. Rebne (1987) found that women academics produced more scholarship in departments containing other women (the critical mass was 18 to 30 percent).

If Halliday, Aschaffenberg, and Granfors (1987) are correct in concluding that women are clustered in work environments most resistant to change (at the lower levels of centralized bureaucracies), then the interaction between individual innovation, occupational segregation, and gender differences becomes very complex. How might women affect the practice and functioning of law, if they could? In the final section of this chapter I offer some speculative and frankly utopian thoughts about how developments in feminist theory, organizational and occupational sociology, and changes within the legal profession might combine to produce innovation rather than the continued segregation and assimilation of women.

PORTIA IN A DIFFERENT VOICE?

Some of the women who express dissatisfaction with the legal profession had different visions of what it would mean to practice law. One critic, for example, left litigation because she saw it as a "male" sport or war, directed toward the single goal of winning at all costs, rather than trying to solve the problem (Fox, 1978). In addition, there is some evidence that women are leaving the profession in greater numbers than men and disproportionately abandoning certain sectors, such as private firms (*Los Angeles Times*, 1986).

I argue below that women, particularly feminists, may have a different perspective toward the practice of law. This controversial argument is vulnerable to several objections. First, it is based on recent feminist scholarship that itself has been subject to criticism. Second, women historically have made a more distinctive contribution in other professions than in law, where they tended to use conventional equality arguments to gain entry. Third, the argument assumes that a critical mass of women, located in places where change is possible, will share these views. Finally, whatever fragmentary, anecdotal evidence may suggest that women lawyers have a distinctive contribution to make, there are also some contrary data.

"Affiliational Feminism"

Some recent feminist scholarship suggests women may ask different questions about the world because of their experiences of growing up in an affiliational relationship. Thus, Carol Gilligan (1982), Nell Noddings (1984), Nancy Chodorow (1978), and others suggest that because women (unlike men) do not need to separate from their mothers in order to grow up, they see the world in terms of relationship and caring rather than independence and abstractions. Others have suggested that this experience produces different ways of knowing (Belenky et al., 1986). Virginia Held (1985) and Annette Baier (1985, 1986) have proposed that in trying to understand what holds the world together we employ metaphors of the family and trust instead of the social contract and market. Susan Okin (1979, 1987) has argued that children may learn about justice within the family long before they acquire any conception of justice in the larger society. Regardless of whether women are mothers, therefore, they share the experience of being connected to others, now called "relational" or "affiliational" feminism.

In her studies of how children make moral decisions, Carol Gilligan (1982) found that girls emphasize relationship and responsibility to others, whereas boys stress universalistic, abstract notions of justice and rules. Prior theorists of moral development had studied only males (Kohlberg, 1981; Piaget, 1965; Erikson, 1950).

Gilligan asked her subjects whether Heinz should steal a drug to help save his wife's life when he cannot pay what the druggist is asking. Jake, an eleven-year-old boy, answered that the drug should be stolen because life is worth more than property. Amy, by contrast, asked whether the druggist and Heinz had tried to work something else out so that Heinz could have the drug and the pharmacist could be paid. Amy tried to address the needs of both the parties and satisfy them without having to declare a "winner." This approach to legal problem-solving—involving the parties directly and avoiding all-or-nothing results—may suggest other ways to structure the legal system. Women may be more inclined to look at nonlitigational forms of dispute resolution (Menkel-Meadow, 1985). There already is some evidence that women are overrepresented in the newer professions associated with mediation (Pipkin & Rifkin, 1984; Rifkin & Harrington, 1987; Rifkin, 1984).

Similarly, Gilligan's work suggests that women's ethical concerns might challenge an adversary system that demands total commitment to one's client. One of Gilligan's subjects, a lawyer, said that she would have preferred to give the court a document that opposing counsel had failed to use; this would have defeated her client's case but achieved the "just" result.

Gilligan's work has been criticized on the grounds that her sample was

too small and unrepresentative in terms of class and race, and her interpretations of the data have been challenged (Tronto, 1987; Broughton,
1983; Nails, 1983; Kerber et al., 1986; J. Walker, 1983). Ironically, some
have argued that minorities and oppressed classes share an ethic of care
engendered by survival strategies (Tronto, 1987), while others have asserted that class and race oppression serve to level gender differences,
making male and female "moralities" more similar among the oppressed
and both more different from mainstream "white" strategies (Stack et al.,
1986). On the basis of her ongoing research with inner-city minority
women, Gilligan has tentatively asserted that they resemble (white?) men
more than white women in their expression of individualism and abstract
universal principles (Gilligan et al., 1985, 1986).

Carol Gilligan's responses to these criticisms suggest that the twentieth-
century parallel to nineteenth-century "separate spheres" arguments may
be relevant to the issue of women in the legal profession in several ways
(Gilligan et al., 1985, 1986). First, such research questions the dominant
male paradigms of knowledge, psychological development, and the practice of law. To see that some have been historically excluded is to acknowledge that our systems of knowledge and practice are partial. Second, once
the "dominant" paradigm is challenged (an ethic of "justice" by an ethic of
"care") further challenges will be easier. Gender is one potential crack in
the professional hierarchy; race and class are others. Even if all women do
not subscribe to this "ethic" of care, some will seek a more mediational
and contextually specific form of justice, and some men also will find
this attractive. Third, the dispute regarding reified gender differences may
distract from substantive issues. Gilligan, Baier, Held, Okin, and others
who seek to develop previously unheard "women's" themes in political
philosophy, moral psychology, and the sociology of work (Feldberg &
Glenn, 1979) are arguing for serious consideration of other values. When
is an ethic of care appropriate in a legal system (Flanagan & Jackson, 1987;
Karst, 1984)? How is the concept of trust relevant to lawyer—client relations? How should the organization and responsibilities of the family be
related to public life, not just in the daily struggles to accommodate both
but also in the way values in one domain affect those in the other (Olsen,
1983)?

The Adversary System

If women are more likely to express care and concern for the other, then
they might practice law differently. Confrontational adversarial processes
might give way to more mediational forms of dispute resolution (Rifkin &
Harrington, 1987). Thus, Gilligan's Amy might ask Heinz and the druggist

to resolve their own dispute rather than looking to her as a neutral third party. She might encourage them to explore alternatives beyond binary solutions (an installment contract?). She might suggest that Heinz's wife be consulted. (It is her life, after all!)

Even within the context of traditional adversary lawyering some women litigators have argued for a different style of trial advocacy, such as conversations with fact-finders rather than persuasive intimidation (University of Southern California, 1983). This concept of the relationship between the lawyer and fact-finder is based on trust and mutual respect rather than drama. Some women have sought to broaden the criteria of relevance, in order to permit what feminist theorists call "contextualism and particularity" rather than the application of abstract legal principles to a few facts (Gilligan, 1982).

Work Organization and Oppositional Values

Work structures are one of the most significant influences on the practice of law. Early studies of feminist law firms in the United States found them to be more egalitarian and to involve more participatory decision-making (C. Epstein, 1981), characteristics thought to derive in part from the feminist methodology of the leaderless consciousness-raising group. Work was shared between lawyers and other staff, and sometimes income was evenly distributed. The emphasis on experiential sources of knowledge also has led to efforts to demystify professionalism, as in women's self-help groups that encourage pro se representation in divorce. Such developments parallel the activities of nineteenth-century women physicians, who emphasized public health and preventive care and education over surgery, drugs, and more interventionist forms of medical care (Lorber, 1985; Morantz-Sanchez, 1985).

Women have expressed and experienced a greater fluidity between work and family life, raising issues of childcare not only so that they can work but also to humanize the workplace (Hochschild, 1975). There is a danger of viewing men's work as job or career focused and women's work as an issue of family management (Feldberg & Glenn, 1979). Because women bear children, they are biologically compelled to reconcile personal lives and professional work. While most countries have passed social legislation that permits women (and sometimes men) to take temporary leaves of absence, many have not (Hewlitt, 1986). Issues such as maternity leave, reentry, seniority, and assessments for partnership thus become the province of women (Fenning, 1985). Some hope that women's connection to both the family and work may alter the lifestyles of all legal professionals, offering a healthier balance between the "greedy institutions" of work and the rest of life. In a recent study of employed lawyers in the United States, Eve Spangler (1986) concluded that male and female attorneys generally did not talk differently about their work, but only women seemed concerned about accommodating career and family (Spangler, 1986). Although some view this as a mere issue of working conditions or "fringe benefits," which may readily be resolved as more employees are affected, others view it as an opportunity for women's concern with care and family to create an "oppositional culture" within the workplace (Kessler-Harris, 1986; Westwood, 1985). The feminist project refuses to see these as "women's issues," insisting rather on involving both genders in production and reproduction (Finley, 1986; Olsen, 1983).

Because some women seek to infuse the workplace with familial and communitarian values, combining collaboration, self-disclosure, and social interaction with task-oriented demands (see Blumberg, quoted in Menkel-Meadow [1985]), women professionals may transform lawyer-client relations, at least in those circumstances where empathy and altruism facilitate deeper understanding of client needs (Menkel-Meadow, 1985; Eisenberg & Lennon, 1983; Hoffman, 1977), thereby reducing client domination (Rosenthal, 1974).

Leadership

In those rare circumstances where women have risen to leadership positions within the profession (judges, senior if not yet managing partners, cabinet secretaries, and law school deans), the question remains whether they will lead and manage differently—in more nurturing, communicative styles, building consensus rather than wielding power. This debate also flourishes in the corporate world (*Wall Street Journal*, 1986; Harlan & Weiss, 1981) and in medicine and education (Astin & Leland, 1986).

Early studies of women judges have failed to uncover any real differences in judging, except that women were more likely than men to sentence female offenders to prison (Gruhl et al., 1981). Cook (1979) also found that male and female judges respond differently to legal issues involving sex roles (such as custody). Scholars have speculated that women may be more likely to take account of a wider variety of "contextual factors" in making a decision, tempering justice with mercy (Menkel-Meadow, 1985).

Substantive Law Reform

In many nations the entry of women into the profession coincided with law reform on issues affecting women, such as civil rights, discrimination, abortion, divorce, pregnancy benefits, and marital property (Marcus, 1987; Fineman, 1983, 1987). Yet, women do not always seek liberal social reforms. In Germany, for example, recent women entrants to the legal profession seem to be politically more conservative than their male counterparts (Blankenburg & Schultz, 1988). American data also reveal that male and female prelaw college students are preoccupied with individual success and financial security, resembling each other more than those of their sex who are attracted to other fields of study (A. Astin, 1984; Komarovsky, 1985). However, the increasing number of women in the profession seems to have changed some of our juridical concepts: equality has been replaced by equity in some contexts (comparable worth in North America, equal value in Europe) and individualistic rights by more collective or group-based rights (in health care and reproductive freedom).

The Dangers of "Difference"

While exploring the creative possibilities of gender differences, we should not overlook the dangers of insisting on such "differences." Do women avoid litigation because they fear conflict? If so, can they be effective lawyers? Does solicitude or concern for the other side diminish loyalty to or zeal for one's own client? Are the stereotypic feminine qualities of empathy and altruism possible in the practice of law as currently constituted? As it can be imagined in a different society? Can women mobilize the stereotypes that devalue them ("women are good with people") to allow them to perform the functions from which they have been barred (such as client relations in large law firms)? Should projects to equalize legal rights be pursued only by women? Does even the suggestion of gender differences reinforce occupational segregation by either encouraging overt discrimination or inadvertently lending credence to "women's preferences"? Women in the corporate sector are allocated to particular jobs (personnel) and service industries (retail clothing, banking, and insurance) on the basis of stereotypes, while status and power lie elsewhere (in marketing and manufacturing) (*Wall Street Journal*, 1986).

Do Women Make a Difference in Other Professions?

Many early women lawyers were active in the suffrage movement in the United States and England and in the American temperance movement (Morello, 1986). In both movements women claimed moral superiority, arguing that their values would make a difference in the polity and morality of their nations. Most women lawyers were activists in political movements, however, not in their professional roles. In order to enter the bar, they emphasized their similarity to men. By the turn of the century some women lawyers had begun to champion legal issues of particular interest to women, such as domestic relations, occupational health and safety, and labor regulation (Babcock et al., 1975), but even here we see divisions that have contemporary parallels. The movement to improve working conditions in the United States was pursued not just through union organization but also by women activists in the National Consumers League, who sought to regulate the hours and wages of women and children. Some of these women also opposed the Equal Rights Amendment when it first was advocated in the early twentieth century, fearing that it would bar the "special" legislation needed to protect women laborers (Sklar, 1986). These arguments, which divided women lawyers, resemble contemporary arguments about the legal treatment of pregnancy in the United States (Williams, 1982; Kay, 1985, 1987; Wolgast, 1980; Finley, 1986).

Medicine.   Although women who entered other male-dominated professions also experienced ideological and professional divisions, the tradition of a distinctive "women's voice" may be stronger in professions where the entry of women originally was based on their claim of distinctive expertise, rooted in the "separate spheres" ideology. Several recent studies have described women physicians' support for preventive health care, public health, and more nurturing physician-patient relations as a direct outgrowth of women's roles in the family (Morantz-Sanchez, 1985; Lorber, 1984, 1985; Abram, 1985; Ward, 1986). In the early twentieth century, when the American Medical Association defeated the Sheppard-Towner Bill (which would have established maternal and child health centers, utilizing women physicians and lay medical personnel) and imposed formal quotas on the number of women attending medical school, their enrollment began to decline, and increasing numbers of women turned to predominantly female occupations—social work, nursing, and teaching—where they could continue their commitment to health education and preventive medicine (Rothman, 1978; Ward, 1986). Although women represented only 3 percent of American dentists in 1982 (Nissen et al., 1986), elsewhere they constitute a significant proportion (at least 50 percent in Greece, 80 percent in the Soviet Union, 33.3 percent in Norway, France, Sweden, and Denmark) (Talbot, 1960), perhaps because dentistry is considered work with children, which requires nurturant qualities.

Architecture.   In architecture, which was even less hospitable than law, women began by focusing on domestic space. Many women who could not gain admission to architecture schools learned their trade through apprenticeship. As a result of the efforts of Susan B. Anthony, women designed the Women's Building at the 1893 American exhibition in Chicago. It was praised as "feminine" for its "delicacy and elegance" and displayed economic, social, and artistic contributions of women throughout the world (Keller, 1981; Torre, 1977). In the early twentieth century women began to design schools, low-income housing, hospitals, and buildings for social service organizations and women's clubs—all considered appropriate "women's work" but not highly remunerative.

However, early women architects, unlike lawyers, established several all-women architectural firms and collaborated in several social reform projects. An architectural school for women was established in 1917 in Cambridge, Massachusetts. Dolores Hayden (1981, 1984) has documented the important role of women architects and designers in American communitarian and utopian projects. These "material feminists" designed "kitchenless houses" in which food, laundry, and other domestic tasks would be centralized while living units remained individual, thereby freeing women from domestic work so that they could participate in other parts of the feminist equality project. Contemporary feminist architects have criticized the large inhuman dimensions of much public space, urging that buildings and cities be redesigned to meet the needs of women, children, and other disempowered groups (Torre, 1977; Hayden, 1984).

Business Management. Many studies of business management conclude that although there is widespread occupational segregation, both vertical (intrafirm hierarchy) and horizontal (across industries and fields), men and women are similar in management style and effectiveness (Harlan & Weiss, 1981), although some popular writers claim that women will manage differently if they ever get to the "top" (Lenz & Myerhoff, 1985).

Science. Perhaps most resistant to claims that women may alter the structure and work of the professions is science, where methodological "objectivity" is widely thought to preclude much "feminization" (Haas & Perrucci, 1984). Yet, even here important theoretical work by feminist scientists and philosophers of science has asked whether methodological "objectivity" and the choice of questions asked might reflect distinctively male perspectives (Harding, 1986; Bleier, 1984; E. Keller, 1984; Haraway, 1978). For example, feminist scientists have challenged the dichotomous thinking that characterizes many scientific models and the primacy of the cell over the whole organism in biology.

"Women's" Professions: Teaching, Nursing, Social Work, and Librarianship. Here, again, women's qualities of nurturing, care, empathy, and service are said to be particularly well suited to such people-centered professions. Indeed, one significant issue raised by women's entry into male-dominated professions is who will teach, nurse, and do social work as women leave in

large numbers for better paying positions in law and business (Shanker, 1986). Where will we find the women to teach nonsexist classes, correct sexist library cataloguing, and mediate the impersonal medical and social bureaucracies?

Social Structure of the Professions

Whether women will structure and practice law differently remains unanswerable. As a result of widespread occupational segregation, women still occupy lower positions in the power hierarchy and particular fields and jobs on the horizontal axis. The evidence from other professions suggests that women will assimilate to male modes of practice. Chambers's study (1987) demonstrates that the gap may be narrowing between women and men in private practice. But studies of women in large firms (Fenning, 1984; *Law Letters*, 1984) and in management (Harlan & Weiss, 1981) suggest that, although they occupy entry-level positions, they have not made much progress vertically, even if we control for experience. And sexist behavior by senior male profesionals does not appear to decline with increased numbers of women professionals (Harlan & Weiss, 1981; *Hishon v. King & Spaulding*, 1984; *Hopkins v. Price Waterhouse*, 1985). Perhaps the degree of innovation will vary with the structure of the profession. To the extent that law and business are characterized by competitive cultures and large hierarchical organizations, it may be more difficult even for "critical masses" of women to alter the basic structures and cultural norms (Miner & Longino, 1987). In medicine, by contrast, where the cultural norm is to heal rather than win, there may be better opportunity for change. Yet, there, too, the delivery of care is increasingly bureaucratized, and women are more likely to be salaried employees than independent practitioners (Custer & Dimon, 1987). The unit of work may also be significant. In architecture and law, small work groups can develop egalitarian norms and engage in oppositional practices.

If the special contribution of women reflects the fact that they are excluded and dominated, it may disappear when parity is achieved (Wasserstrom, 1977). If it has other origins and persists, then we might hope that the different contributions of women and men to the practice of law would be equally valued.

If feminism's purpose is to advance humanism, then the feminization of the legal profession should help to redeem it from the flaws of domination (both by and of clients) (Rosenthal, 1974; Heinz & Laumann, 1982), unnecessary and harmful contentiousness, and alienating segmentation and stratification in the workplace. If it does not, then women will find themselves transformed by the male professional world—working long hours, estranged from their families, and perhaps exploiting another class of women to perform traditional female roles (housework and childrearing).

Finally, does the nature of law itself tell us anything about the contributions women might make? Do legal ideals of equality shape women lawyers' conceptions of their roles in ways that diverge from the service ideal prevalent in medicine and other professions? Will the contribution of women differ in common law and civil law countries? Do highly bureaucratic legal systems permit less innovation than individualistic, litigation-oriented systems? Do political regimes (socialist versus capitalist) or religious beliefs (such as Islam or Confucianism) affect the influence of women?

CONCLUSION: OF FEARS AND HOPES

This chapter has viewed the entry of women into the legal profession from several perspectives. It is easiest to adopt the dominant sociological discourse, describing demographic data concerning the number and location of women. From this perspective the most striking pattern is widespread occupational segregation. Women are located at the lower levels of the hierarchy, however prestige is defined in a particular country. They are overrepresented in particular fields, practice structures, and sometimes geographic locations. This occupational segregation is the result of complex forces that push or keep women out of particular jobs and locations and simultaneously pull them into others that are more compatible with family responsibilities, less attractive to men, or preferred by women because of their work structure, style, or substantive content. Indeed, the one factor that may be said to unify women as an analytic category is their common experience of exclusion and domination.

There are several ways to understand the significance of women's entry into the profession. Liberal feminists and equality theorists will be content as long as women are allowed to compete with men on a level playing field. Different socialization and job opportunities at the individual, organizational, and societal levels may be important in guaranteeing equal access. Whether women collectively will make particular contributions to the practice of law and the reform of substantive doctrine implicates complex issues of feminist theory. Simply because women share the experience of exclusion does not ensure that they will exhibit distinctive perspectives when they enter the profession, especially given variations in class, race, and ethnic origin. Feminist theorists who have universalized gender now are accused of mirroring patriarchical domination by reifying gender categories. In addition, social structural factors might prevent women from making a distinctive contribution even if they spoke with one voice. Occupational segregation might render them too powerless to transform the profession. The competitive and adversarial culture of the profession and increasing centralization and bureaucratization might produce individual assimilation rather than structural change.

To the extent that the nexus of work and family remain predominantly women's concerns, women may offer an oppositional critique of the profession. As our analysis of other professions demonstrates, a strong minority voice, and sometimes an explicitly separatist stance, can offer alternative models of legal practice and substantive doctrine. The diversity of feminist voices might actually increase the likelihood that one will prevail. All women do not share a feminist political ideology, if "a" feminist ideology can even be identified among so many different visions. To the extent that the feminist project seeks to humanize the profession and reform the law, men also will participate.

For me, gender remains a powerful analytic category not merely because it seems to explain significant behavior but because I agree with Virginia Woolf (1938) and Simone de Beauvoir (1952) that the position of women as "other" provides a starting point for critique, an outsider's view that makes us ask why things are this way. Is the practice of law modeled after medieval male games—why must one side "win" in litigation? Why do "greedy institutions" demand that we spend more time with work colleagues than with loved ones? Must work be hierarchically organized? Would women measure "success" or "fulfillment" by different criteria? Whether a feminist critique of the legal profession will emerge and transform the profession or social structural obstacles will silence feminist concerns and force assimilation is a question that must be answered empirically and theoretically. I fear that professional constraints are strong. I hope that the "feminization" of the profession will allow women to become lawyers without adopting the undesirable traits of "possessiveness, jealousy, pugnacity and greed" (Woolf, 1938), which participation in the professions seems to engender.

NOTES

I am grateful for the assistance, comments, encouragement, and support of Susan Gillig, Robert Meadow, Deborah Rhode, Anita Schiller, and David Trubek and the superb research assistance of Michelle Sherman and Laurie Taylor.

1. For example, Margaret Rossiter (1986) has persuasively argued that women serving as science bibliographers contributed to the transmission of science and should be recognized.

2. Unfortunately for comparative analysis, most of the historical material on which this review is based derives from Anglo-American sources (cf. Abel, 1982).

3. I have placed all traditional measures of stratification and professional hierarchy in quotation marks. This enables me to report the data within conven-

tional sociological categories but also to make the feminist theoretical observation that professional "success" need not be measured exclusively in these terms. See the discussion below on the impact of the "feminization" of the profession on the profession, the law, and women.

4. Most of the theory presented in this section is derived from Anglo-American and French feminism. One English writer recently has criticized the emphasis on work equality in American feminism, contrasting it with concern for the family in western Europe (Hewlitt, 1986; Hacker, 1986). My own view is that gains in one area (work achievement) have been won at the expense of the other. For example, while many socialist nations proudly proclaim women's participation in the work-force, there has not been much reduction in the work done by women in the home (Lapidus, 1976).

REFERENCES

CASES

Bradwell v. Illinois, 16 Wall. 130 (1873).
In re Bradwell, 55 Ill. 535 (1870).
California Federal Savings v. Guerra, 107 S. Ct. 683 (1987).
EEOC v. Sears Roebuck & Co., 581 F.2d 941 (D.C.Cir. 1987).
Geduldig v. Aiello, 417 U.S. 484 (1974).
Hishon v. King & Spaulding, 467 U.S. 69 (1984).
Hopkins v. Price Waterhouse, 618 F. Supp. 1109 (D.D.C. 1985).
Kahn v. Shevin, 416 U.S. 351 (1974).
Reed v. Reed, 404 U.S. 71 (1971).
Taylor v. Louisiana, 419 U.S. 522 (1974).
Wimberly v. Labor & Industrial Relations Commission, 107 S. Ct. 821 (1987).

BOOKS AND ARTICLES

Abel. Richard L. 1982. "The Underdevelopment of Legal Professions: Review Article on Third World Lawyers," 1982 *American Bar Foundation Research Journal* 871.

———. 1986. "Lawyers," in Leon Lipson and Stanton Wheeler, eds., *Law and the Social Sciences*. New York: Russell Sage Foundation.

———. 1988a. "United States: The Contradictions of Professionalism," in Richard L. Abel and Philip S. C. Lewis, eds., *Lawyers in Society*, vol. 1: *The Common Law World*. Berkeley, Los Angeles, London: University of California Press.

———. 1988b. *The Legal Profession in England and Wales*. Oxford: Basil Blackwell.

Abram, Ruth, ed. 1985. *"Send Us A Lady Physician": Women Doctors in America 1835–1920*. New York: Norton.

Abramson, Jill, and Barbara Franklin. 1986. *Where They Are Now: The Story of the Women of Harvard Law*. New York: Doubleday.

Adam, Barry, and Kathleen Lahey. 1981. "Professional Opportunities: A Survey of the Ontario Legal Profession," 59 *Canadian Bar Review* 674.

American Bar Association Journal. 1983. "Women in the Law," 69 *American Bar Association Journal* 1333–1588. (Special issue).

———. 1988. "Women in Law: The Glass Ceiling," 74 *American Bar Association Journal* 49 (June).

Antler, Joyce. 1977. *The Educated Woman and Professionalization: The Struggle for a New Feminine Identity, 1890–1920*. Ann Arbor, Mich.: University Microfilms.

Arrow, Kenneth. 1972. "Models of Job Discrimination," in Anthony H. Pascal, ed., *Racial Discrimination in Economic Life*. Lexington, Mass.: D. C. Heath.

Arthurs, Harry W., Richard Weisman, and Frederick H. Zemans. 1988. "Canadian Lawyers: A Peculiar Professionalism," in Richard L. Abel and Philip S. C. Lewis, eds., *Lawyers in Society*, vol. 1: *The Common Law World*. Berkeley, Los Angeles, London: University of California Press.

Ashburn, Elizabeth. 1977. *Motivation, Personality and Work-Related Characteristics of Women in Male-Dominated Professions*. Washington, D.C.: National Association for Women Deans, Administrators and Counselors.

Astin, Alexander. 1984. "Prelaw Students—A National Profile," 34 *Journal Of Legal Education* 73.

Astin, Helen, and Carol Leland. 1986. "On Behalf of Women: Issues and Accomplishments from A Leadership Perspective." (Draft paper for UCLA Higher Education Research Institute.)

Auerbach, Jerold S. 1976. *Unequal Justice: Lawyers and Social Change in Modern America*. New York: Oxford University Press.

Babcock, Barbara Allen. 1987. "Reconstructing the Person: The Case of Clara Shortridge Foltz." Presented to the conference on Women in the Legal Profession, Madison, Wisc., August.

———. 1988. "Clara Shortridge Foltz: 'First Woman,'" 30 *Arizona Law Review* 673.

Babcock, Barbara Allen, Ann E. Freedman, Eleanor Holmes Norton, and Susan Deller Ross. 1975. *Sex Discrimination and the Law*. Boston: Little, Brown & Co.

Baier, Annette. 1985. "What Do Women Want In A Moral Theory?" 19 *Nous* 53.

———. 1986. "Trust and Antitrust," 96 *Ethics* 231.

Bartholet, Elizabeth. 1982. "Application of Title VII to Jobs in High Places," 95 *Harvard Law Review* 945.

Becker, Gary. 1974. "A Theory of Marriage," in Theodore Schultz, ed., *Economics of the Family, Marriage, Children and Human Capital*. Chicago: University of Chicago Press.

Belenky, Mary Field, Blythe McVicker Clinchy, Nancy Rule Goldberger, and Jill Mattuck Tarule. 1986. *Women's Ways of Knowing: The Development of Self, Voice and Mind*. New York: Basic Books.

Beller, Andrea, and Kee-ok Han. 1984. "Occupational Sex Segregation: Prospects for the 1980's," in Barbara Reskin, ed., *Sex Segregation in the Workplace.* Washington, D.C.: National Academy Press.

Bernard, Jessie Shirlie. 1964. *Academic Women.* University Park: Pennsylvania State University Press.

———. 1976. "Historical and Structural Barriers to Occupational Desegregation," in Martha Blaxall and Barbara Reagan, eds., *Women and the Workplace: The Implications of Occupational Segregation.* Chicago: University of Chicago Press.

———. 1981. *The Female World.* New York: Free Press.

Bielby, William, and James Baron. 1984. "A Woman's Place Is with Other Women: Sex Segregation within Organizations," in Barbara Reskin, ed., *Sex Segregation in the Workplace.* Washington, D.C.: National Academy Press.

Bittner, Egon. 1974. "Florence Nightingale in Pursuit of Willie Sutton: A Theory of the Police," in Herbert Jacob, ed., *The Potential for Reform of Criminal Justice.* Beverly Hills, Calif.: Sage.

Blankenburg, Erhard, and Ulrike Schultz. 1988. "German Advocates: A Highly Regulated Profession," in Richard L. Abel and Philip S. C. Lewis, eds., *Lawyers in Society,* vol. 2: *The Civil Law World.* Berkeley, Los Angeles, London: University of California Press.

Blaxall, Martha, and Barbara Reagan. 1976. *Women and the Workplace: The Implications of Occupational Segregation.* Chicago: University of Chicago Press.

Bleier, Ruth. 1984. *Science and Gender.* New York: Pergamon Press.

Boigeol, Anne. 1988. "The French Bar: The Difficulties of Unifying A Divided Profession," in Richard L. Abel and Philip S. C. Lewis, eds. *Lawyers in Society:* vol. 2: *The Civil Law World.* Berkeley, Los Angeles, London: University of California Press.

Bose, Christine, and Glenna Spitze, eds. 1987. *Ingredients for Women's Employment Policy.* Albany, N.Y.: State University of New York Press.

Brand, Barbara Elizabeth. 1978. *The Influence of Higher Education on Sex Typing in Three Professions 1870–1920: Librarianship, Social Work and Public Health.* Ann Arbor, Mich.: University Microfilms.

Broughton, John. 1983. "Women's Rationality and Men's Virtues: A Critique of Gender Dualism in Gilligan's Theory of Moral Development," 50 *Social Research* 597.

Bunch, Charlotte, and Nancy Myron. 1974. *Class and Feminism: A Collection of Essays From the Furies.* Baltimore, Md.: Diana Press.

Carter, Michael, and Susan Carter. 1981. "Women's Recent Progress in the Professions or, Women Get A Ticket to Ride After The Gravy Train Has Left the Station," 7 *Feminist Studies* 476.

Centra, John A. 1974. *Women, Men and the Doctorate—A Report.* Princeton, N.J.: Educational Testing Service.

Chambers, David. 1987. "Tough Enough: The Work and Family Experiences of Recent Women Graduates of the University of Michigan Law School." Presented to the conference on Women in the Legal Profession, Madison, Wisc., August.

Chester, Ronald. 1985. *Unequal Access: Women Lawyers in A Changing America.* South Hadley, Mass.: Bergin & Garvey.

Chodorow, Nancy. 1978. *The Reproduction of Mothering: Psychoanalysis and the Sociology of Gender.* Berkeley, Los Angeles, London: University of California Press.

Chused, Richard. H. 1983. "Married Women's Property Law: 1800–1850," 71 *Georgetown Law Journal* 1359.

Cixous, Hélène. 1976. "The Laugh of the Medusa," 1 *Signs* 875.

Collins, Nancy W. 1983. *Professional Women and Their Mentors.* Englewood Cliffs, N.J.: Prentice Hall.

Cook, Beverly. 1979. "Sentencing Behavior of Federal Judges—Draft Cases," 42 *University of Cincinnati Law Review* 597.

Cott, Nancy F. 1977. *The Bonds of Womanhood: Women's Sphere in New England, 1780–1835.* New Haven, Conn.: Yale University Press.

Couric, Emily. 1983. *Women Lawyers: Perspectives on Success.* San Diego, Calif.: Harcourt, Brace & Jovanovich.

Curran, Barbara. 1986. "American Lawyers in the 1980s: A Profession in Transition," 20 *Law & Society Review* 19.

Curran, Barbara, Katherine J. Rosich, Clara N. Carson, and Mark C. Puccetti. 1985. *The Lawyer Statistical Report: A Statistical Profile of the U.S. Legal Profession.* Chicago: American Bar Foundation.

Custer, William, and Diane Dimon. 1987. *Gender and the Choice of Physicians' Employment Status.* Los Angeles: UCLA Institute for Social Science (Research Working Papers in the Social Sciences, No. 3[3]).

Davies, Margery W. 1975. "Women's Place is at the Typewriter: The Feminization of the Clerical Labor Force," in Richard C. Edwards, Michael Reich, and David M. Gordon, eds., *Labor Market Segmentation.* Lexington, Mass.: D.C. Heath.

———. 1982. *Woman's Place is at the Typewriter: Office Work and Office Workers, 1870–1930.* Philadelphia: Temple University Press.

Davis, Angela. 1981. *Women, Race and Class.* New York: Random House.

de Beauvoir, Simone. 1952. *The Second Sex* (transl. and ed. H. M. Parshley). New York: Knopf.

Donovan, Josephine. 1985. *Feminist Theory: The Intellectual Traditions of American Feminism.* New York: Ungar.

DuBois, Ellen, Mary Dunlap, Carol Gilligan, Catherine MacKinnon, and Carrie Menkel-Meadow. 1985. "Feminist Discourse, Moral Values and the Law—A Conversation," 34 *Buffalo Law Review* 11.

Eckert, Ruth E., and John E. Stecklein. 1971. "Academic Women," in Althena Theodore, ed., *The Professional Woman.* Cambridge, Mass.: Schenkman.

Eisenberg, Nancy, and Randy Lennon. 1983. "Sex Differences in Empathy and Related Capacities," 94 *Psychological Bulletin* 100.

Eisenstein, Hester, and Alice Jardine, eds. 1985. *The Future of Difference.* New Brunswick, N.J.: Rutgers University Press.

Epstein, Cynthia Fuchs. 1970*a*. "Encountering the Male Establishment: Sex Status Limits on Women's Careers in the Professions," 75 *American Journal of Sociology* 965.

———. 1970*b*. *Women's Place: Options and Limits in Professional Careers*. Berkeley, Los Angles, London: University of California Press.

———. 1973. "Positive Effects of the Multiple Negative: Explaining the Success of Black Professional Women," 78 *American Journal of Sociology* 912.

———. 1981. *Women in Law*. New York: Basic Books.

———. 1987. "Deceptive Distinctions: Old Biases in New Frameworks." Presented to the conference on Women in the Legal Profession, Madison, Wisc., August.

———. 1988. *Deceptive Distinctions: Sex, Gender and the Social Order*. New Haven, Conn.: Yale University Press.

Epstein, Laurily Keir, ed. 1975. *Women in the Professions*. Lexington, Mass.: D. C. Heath.

Erikson, Erik. 1950. *Childhood and Society*. New York: Norton.

Etzioni, Amitai, ed. 1969. *The Semi-Professions and Their Organization: Teachers, Nurses, Social Workers*. New York: Free Press.

Fairchild, Erika. 1987. "Women Police in Weimar: Professionalism, Politics and Innovation in Police Organizations," 21 *Law & Society Review* 375.

Falcão, Joaquim. 1988. "Lawyers in Brazil," in Richard L. Abel and Philip S. C. Lewis, eds., *Lawyers in Society*, vol. 2: *The Civil World*. Berkeley, Los Angeles, London: University of California Press.

Feldberg, Roslyn, and Evelyn Glenn. 1979. "Male and Female: Job Versus Gender Models in the Sociology of Work," 26 *Social Problems* 524.

Fenning, Lisa Hill. 1984. "Los Angeles Perspective on Hishon: The Slowly Eroding Partnership Barrier," in *Women in Law Firms: Planning for the Future*. Chicago: American Bar Association Press.

———. 1985. "Parenting and the Big Firm Career." Speech delivered to the National Association for Law Placement, August 22.

———. 1987. "Report from the Front: Progress in the Battle Against Gender Bias in the Legal Profession." Presented to the conference on Women in the Legal Profession, Madison, Wisc., August.

Fenning, Lisa Hill, and Patricia M. Schnegg. 1983. "The Status of Women in L.A.'s Biggest Firms," 6 *Los Angeles Lawyers* 27 (November).

Ferguson, Kathy E. 1985. *The Feminist Case Against Bureaucracy*. Philadelphia: Temple University Press.

Feulner, Patricia. 1979. *Women in the Professions: A Social-Psychological Study*. Palo Alto, Calif.: R & E Research Associates.

Fidell, Linda S. 1970. "Empirical Verification of Sex Discrimination in Hiring Practices in Psychology," 25 *American Psychologist* 1094.

Fineman, Martha. 1983. "Implementing Equality: Ideology, Contradiction and Social Change: A Study of Rhetoric and Results in the Regulation of the Consequences of Divorce," 1983 *Wisconsin Law Review* 789.

————. 1987. "Dominant Discourse, Professional Language and Legal Change: Altering Rules Under the Rubric of Altering Process," 101 *Harvard Law Review* 727.

Finley, Lucinda. 1986. "Transcending Equality Theory: A Way Out of the Maternity and the Workplace Debate," 86 *Columbia Law Review* 1118.

Flanagan, Owen, and Kathryn Jackson. 1987. "Justice, Care and Gender: The Kohlberg-Gilligan Debate Revisited," 97 *Ethics* 622.

Fogarty, Michael Patrick, Rhona Rapoport, and Robert N. Rapoport. 1971. *Sex, Career and Family*. Beverly Hills, Calif.: Sage.

Forster, Margaret. 1984. *Significant Sisters: The Grassroots of Active Feminism*. New York: Oxford University Press.

Fossum, Donna. 1980. "Women Law Professors," 1980 *American Bar Foundation Research Journal* 903.

————. 1987. "Some Thoughts on Women in the Legal Profession." Presented to the conference on Women in the Legal Profession, Madison, Wisc., August.

Fox, Priscilla. 1978. "Good-bye to Game-playing," *Juris Doctor* 37 (January).

Fox-Genovese, Elizabeth. 1987. "Women's Rights, Affirmative Action and the Myth of Individualism," 54 *George Washington Law Review* 338.

Freidson, Eliot. 1986. *Professional Powers: A Study of the Institutionalization of Formal Knowledge*. Chicago: University of Chicago Press.

Frug, Mary Joe. 1979. "Securing Job Equality for Women: Labor Market Hostility to Working Mothers," 59 *Boston University Law Review* 55.

————. 1987. "The Role of Difference Models in the Study of Women in Law." Presented to the conference on Women in the Legal Profession, Madison, Wisc., August.

Gandhi, J. S. 1988. "Past and Present: A Sociological Portrait of the Indian Legal Profession," in Richard L. Abel and Philip S. C. Lewis, eds., *Lawyers in Society*, vol. 1: *The Common World*. Berkeley, Los Angeles, London: University of California Press.

Gilligan, Carol. 1982. *In A Different Voice: Psychological Theory and Women's Development*. Cambridge, Mass.: Harvard University Press.

Gilligan, Carol, Mary Dunlop, Ellen DuBois, Catherine MacKinnon, and Carrie Menkel-Meadow. 1985. "Feminist Discourse, Moral Values and the Law—A Conversation," 34 *Buffalo Law Review* 11.

Gilligan, Carol, Linda K. Kerber, Catherine Greene, Eleanor Maccoby, Zella Luria, and Carol B. Stack. 1986. "Viewpoint: On *In a Different Voice*: An Interdisciplinary Forum," 11 *Signs* 304.

Glazer, Penina Migdal, and Miriam Slater. 1987. *Unequal Colleagues: The Entrance of Women Into the Professions, 1890–1940*. New Brunswick, N.J.: Rutgers University Press.

Gordon, Linda. 1976. *Women's Body, Women's Right: A History of Birth Control in America*. New York: Grossman.

Gordon, S. 1983. "The New Corporate Feminism," *The Nation* 1 (February 5).

Graham, Patricia. 1978. "Expansion and Exclusion: A History of Women in American Higher Education," 3 *Signs* 759.

Gruhl, John, Cassia Spohn, and Susan Welch. 1981. "Women as Policymakers: The Case of Trial Judges," 25 *American Journal of Political Science* 308.

Haas, Violet, and Carolyn Perrucci, eds. 1984. *Women in Scientific and Engineering Professions*. Ann Arbor: University of Michigan Press.

Hacker, Andrew. 1986. "Women at Work," 33 *New York Review of Books* 26.

Hagan, John 1987. "Gender, Income Inequality and the Structural Transformation of the Legal Profession." Presented to the conference on Women in the Legal Profession, Madison, Wisc., August.

Hagan, John, Marie Huxter, and Patricia Parker. 1988. "Class Structure and Legal Practice: Inequality and Mobility Among Toronto Lawyers," 22 *Law & Society Review* 9.

Halliday, Terence. 1986. "Six Score Years and Ten: Demographic Transitions in the American Legal Profession, 1850–1980," 20 *Law & Society Review* 53.

Halliday, Terence, Karen Aschaffenberg, and Mark Granfors. 1987. "Gender, Time and Structure in the American Legal Profession: Data From the 1980 U.S. Census." Data presented to the conference on Women in the Legal Profession Madison, Wisc., August.

Haraway, Donna. 1978. "Animal Sociology and A National Economy of the Body Politic: Part II: The Past is the Contested Zone: Human Nature and Theories of Production and Reproduction in Primate Behavior Studies," 1 *Signs* 1.

Harding, Sandra G. 1986. *The Science Question in Feminism*. Ithaca, N.Y.: Cornell University Press.

Harlan, Anne, and Carol Weiss. 1981. *Moving Up: Women in Managerial Careers*. Wellesley, Mass.: Wellesley College Center for Research on Women (Working Paper No. 86).

Harris, Barbara. 1978. *Beyond Her Sphere: Women and the Professions in American History*. Westport, Conn.: Greenwood Press.

Hartmann, Heidi. 1976. "Capitalism, Patriarchy and Job Segregation by Sex," 1 *Signs* 137.

Harvard Women's Law Association. 1985. *Employment Survey Directory: A Survey of Work and Family Policies in Private and Non-Profit Legal Organizations*. Cambridge, Mass.: Harvard Law School Placement Office.

Harvey, Cameron. 1970. "Women in Law in Canada," 4 *Manitoba Law Review* 9.

Hayden, Dolores. 1981. *The Grand Domestic Revolution: A History of Feminist Designs for American Homes, Neighborhoods and Cities*. Cambridge, Mass.: MIT Press.

———. 1984. *Redesigning the American Dream: The Future of Housing, Work and Family Life*. New York: Norton.

Heinz, John P., and Edward O. Laumann. 1982. *Chicago Lawyers: The Social Structure of the Bar*. Chicago: American Bar Foundation; New York: Russell Sage.

Held, Virginia. 1985. "Feminism and Epistemology: Recent Work on the Connection Between Gender and Knowledge," 14 *Philosophy and Public Affairs* 296.

Hennig, Margaret, and Anne Jardim. 1977. *The Managerial Woman*. New York: Pocket Books.

Hewlitt, Sylvia. 1986. *A Lesser Life: The Myth of Women's Liberation in America*. New York: William Morrow.

Higginbotham, Elizabeth. 1987. "Employment for Black Professional Women in the Twentieth Century," in Christine Bose and Glenna Spitze, eds., *Ingredients for Women's Employment Policy*. Albany: State University of New York Press.

Hirsh, Ronald. L. 1985. "Are You on Target?" 12 *Barrister* 17.

Hochschild, Arlie. 1975. "Inside the Clockwork of Male Careers," in Florence Howe, ed., *Women and the Power to Change*. Berkeley, Calif.: Carnegie Commission on Higher Education.

Hoffman, Martin L. 1977. "Sex Differences in Empathy and Related Behaviors," 84 *Psychological Bulletin* 712.

Holmes, Deborah. 1987. "Structural Causes of Dissatisfaction Among Large-Firm Attorneys: A Feminist Perspective." Presented to the conference on Women in the Legal Profession, Madison, Wisc., August.

Hooks, Bell. 1981. *Ain't I a Woman? Black Women and Feminism*. Boston: South End Press.

Houghton, Beverly H. 1981. "Women Lawyers in Ghana," in C. J. Dias, R. Luckham, D. O. Lynch, and J. C. N. Paul, eds., *Lawyers in the Third World: Comparative and Developmental Perspectives*. Uppsala: Scandinavian Institute of African Studies; New York: International Center for Law in Development.

Hull, Gloria, Patricia Bell Scott, and Barbara Smith. 1982. *All the Women are White. All the Blacks are Men, But Some of Us Are Brave: Black Women's Studies*. Old Westbury, N.Y.: Feminist Press.

Hummer, Patricia. 1979. *The Decade of Illusive Promise: Professional Women in the United States, 1920–1930*. Ann Arbor: University of Michigan Press.

Huyse, Luc. 1988. "Legal Experts in Belgium," in Richard L. Abel and Philip S. C. Lewis, eds., *Lawyers in Society*, vol. 2: *The Civil Law World*. Berkeley, Los Angeles, London: University of California Press.

Irigaray, Luce. 1977. *The Sex Which Is Not One*. Ithaca, N.Y.: Cornell University Press.

Jacobs, Alice. 1972. "Women in Law School: Structural Constraint and Personal Choice in the Formation of Professional Identity," 24 *Journal of Legal Education* 462.

Johnsen, Jon T. 1988. "The Professionalization of Legal Counseling in Norway," in Richard L. Abel and Philip S. C. Lewis, eds., *Lawyers in Society:* vol. 2: *The Civil Law World*. Berkeley, Los Angeles, London: University of California Press.

Joseph, Gloria, and Jill Lewis. 1981. *Common Differences: Conflicts in Black and White Feminist Perspectives*. Garden City, N.Y.: Anchor Press.

Kamiya, M. 1986a. "Japanese Women: The Legal Status and the Reality" (unpublished manuscript).

———. 1986b. "Female Judges and Lawyers in Japan" (unpublished manuscript).

Kanter, Rosabeth Moss. 1976. "Presentation VI," in Martha Blaxall and Barbara Reagan, eds., *Women in the Workplace: The Implications of Occupational Segregation*. Chicago: University of Chicago Press.

———. 1977. *Men and Women of the Corporation*. New York: Basic Books.

———. 1978. "Reflections on Women and the Legal Profession: A Sociological Perspective," 1 *Harvard Women's Law Journal* 1.

Karst, Kenneth. 1984. "Women's Constitution," 1984 *Duke Law Journal* 447.

Kay, Herma Hill. 1985. "Models of Equality," 1985 *Illinois Law Review* 39.

———. 1987. "Equality and Difference: A Perspective on No-Fault Divorce and Its Aftermath," 56 *University of Cincinnati Law Review* 1.

Keller, Evelyn Fox. 1984. *Reflections on Gender and Science*. New Haven, Conn.: Yale University Press.

Keller, Suzanne, ed. 1981. *Building for Women*. New York: D. C. Heath.

Kerber, Linda K., Catherine Greene, Eleanor Maccoby, Zella Luria, Carol B. Stack, and Carol Gilligan. 1986. "Viewpoint: On *In a Different Voice:* An Interdisciplinary Forum," 11 *Signs* 304.

Kessler-Harris, Alice. 1982. *Out to Work*. New York: Oxford University Press.

———. 1986. "Home Away From Home," 3 *Women's Review of Books* 13 (April).

Kessler, Suzanne, and Wendy McKenna. 1978. *Gender: An Ethnomethodological Approach*. Chicago: University of Chicago Press.

Kingson, Jennifer. 1988. "Women in the Law Say Path Is Limited by Mommy Track," *New York Times*, p. 1 (August 8).

Klein, Viola. 1946. *The Feminine Character: History of an Ideology*. London: Routledge & Kegan Paul.

Kohlberg, Lawrence. 1981. *The Philosophy of Moral Development*. San Francisco: Harper & Row.

Komarovsky, Mirra. 1985. *Women in College: Shaping New Feminine Identities*. New York: Basic Books.

Kristeva, Julia. 1987. *The Kristeva Reader* (Toril Moi, ed.). New York: Columbia University Press.

LaMothe, Louise. 1987. "For Women Lawyers, It's Still an Uphill Climb," *California Lawyer* (September).

Lapidus, Gail. 1976. "Occupational Segregation and Public Policy: A Comparative Analysis of American and Soviet Patterns," in Martha Blaxall and Barbara Reagan, eds., *Women and the Workplace*. Chicago: University of Chicago Press.

Larson, Magali Sarfatti. 1977. *The Rise of Professionalism: A Sociological Analysis*. Berkeley: University of California Press.

Law Letters, Inc. 1984. *The Woman Lawyer in the Firm: Expectation and Fulfillment*. Chicago: Law Letters, Inc.

Leach, William. 1980. *True Love and Perfect Union: The Feminist Reform of Sex and Society*. New York: Basic Books.

Lenz, Elinor, and Barbara Myerhoff. 1985. *The Feminization of America: How Women's Values Are Changing Our Public and Private Lives*. Los Angeles: Tarcher, Inc.

Lewis, Philip S. C. 1986. "A Comparative Perspective on Legal Professions in the 1980s," 20 *Law & Society Review* 79.

Liefland, Linda. 1986. "Career Patterns of Male and Female Lawyers," 35 *Buffalo Law Review* 601.

Littleton, Christine. 1981. "Toward A Redefinition of Sexual Equality," 95 *Harvard Law Review* 487.

———. 1987. "Reconstructing Sexual Equality," 75 *California Law Review* 1067.

Littleton, Christine, and Sheryl McCloud. 1986. Brief of Coalition for Reproductive Equality in the Workplace, *California Federal Savings & Loan v. Guerra*.

Loden, Marilyn. 1986. "A Machismo That Drives Women Out," *New York Times*, p. 2F (February 9).

Lorber, Judith. 1984. *Women Physicians: Careers, Status and Power*. New York, London: Tavistock.

———. 1985. "More Women Physicians: Will It Mean More Humane Health Care?" 16 *Social Policy* 50.

Los Angeles Times. 1986. "Justice and Gender," *Los Angeles Times* (September 10).

Maccoby, Eleanor Emmons, and Carol Nagy Jacklin. 1974. *The Psychology of Sex Differences*. Stanford, Calif.: Stanford University Press.

MacKinnon, Catherine. 1979. *Sexual Harassment in the Workplace*. New Haven, Conn.: Yale University Press.

———. 1982. "Feminism, Marxism, Method and the State: An Agenda for Theory," 7 *Signs* 515.

———. 1983. "Feminism, Marxism, Method and the State: Toward Feminist Jurisprudence," 8 *Signs* 635.

———. 1987. "Women Lawyers—on Exceptions," in *Feminism Unmodified*. Cambridge, Mass.: Harvard University Press.

MacKinnon, Catherine, Mary Dunlap, Ellen DuBois, Carol Gilligan, and Carrie Menkel-Meadow. 1985. "Feminist Discourse, Moral Values and the Law—A Conversation," 34 *Buffalo Law Review* 11.

Marcus, Isabel. 1987. "Reflections on the Significance of the Sex-Gender System: Divorce Reform in New York," 42 *University of Miami Law Review* 55.

Marini, Margaret, and Mary Brinton. 1984. "Sex Typing in Occupational Socialization," in Barbara Reskin, ed., *Sex Segregation in the Workplace*. Washington, D.C.: National Academy Press.

Marks, Elaine, and Isabelle de Courtivron. 1981. *New French Feminisms*. New York: Schocken Books.

Matveev, P. 1977/78. "Female Lawyers—Statistical Data," 16 *Soviet Law and Government* 87.

Mead, Margaret. 1967. *Male and Female: A Study of the Sexes in A Changing World*. New York: William Morrow (first published in 1949).

Menkel-Meadow, Carrie. 1983. "Women in Law?" 1983 *American Bar Foundation Research Journal* 189.

———. 1985. "Portia In A Different Voice: Speculations on a Women's Lawyering Process," 1 *Berkeley Women's Law Journal* 39.

————. 1987. "Excluded Voices: New Voices in the Legal Profession Making New Voices in the Law," 42 *University of Miami Law Review* 701.

————. 1988. "Feminist Legal Theory, Critical Legal Studies and Legal Education or the 'Fem-Crits' Go to Law School," 38 *Journal of Legal Education* 61.

Menkel-Meadow, Carrie, Mary Dunlop, Ellen DuBois, Carol Gilligan, and Catherine MacKinnon. 1985. "Feminist Discourse, Moral Values and the Law—A Conversation," 34 *Buffalo Law Review* 11.

Menninger, Karl. 1973. "The Psychological Advantages of the Women Physician," 37 *Bulletin of the Menninger Clinic* 333.

Mernissi, Fatima. 1987. "Professional Women in the Arab World: The Example of Morocco," 7 *Feminist Issues* 47.

Milkman, Ruth. 1982. "Organizing the Sexual Division of Labor: Historical Perspectives on Women's Work and the American Labor Movement," 49 *Socialist Review* 95.

————. 1986. "Women's History and the Sears Case," 12 *Feminist Studies* 375.

Miller, Joanne, Carmi Schooler, Melvin L. Kohn, and Karen A. Miller. 1979. "Women and Work: The Psychological Effects of Occupational Conditions," 85 *American Journal of Sociology* 66.

Miner, Valerie, and Helen Longino, eds. 1987. *Competition: The Feminist Taboo?* New York: Feminist Press.

Minow, Martha. 1987. "Law Turning Outward," 73 *Telos* 79.

Moi, Toril. 1986. *Sexual/Textual Politics.* London: Methuen.

Moraga, Cherrie, and Gloria Anzaldua. 1981. *This Bridge Called My Back: Writings By Radical Women of Color.* Watertown, Mass.: Persephone Press.

Morantz-Sanchez, Regina Markell. 1985. *Sympathy and Science: Women Physicians in American Medicine.* New York: Oxford University Press.

Morello, Karen Berger. 1986. *The Invisible Bar: The Women Lawyer in America, 1638 to the Present.* New York: Random House.

Murray, Georgina. 1988. "New Zealand Lawyers: From Colonial GPs to the Servants of Capital," in Richard L. Abel and Philip S. C. Lewis, eds. *Lawyers in Society,* vol. 1: *The Common Law World.* Berkeley, Los Angeles, London: University of California Press.

Nails, Debra. 1983. "Social-Scientific Sexism: Gilligan's Mismeasure of Man," 50 *Social Research* 643.

Nelson, Robert. 1987. "Preliminary Results from A National Survey on Lawyer Job Satisfaction." Presented to the conference on Women in the Legal Profession, Madison, Wisc., August.

Nickles, Elizabeth, and Laura Ashcraft. 1982. *The Coming Matriarchy: How Women Will Gain the Balance of Power.* New York: Berkley.

Nieva, Veronica, and Barbara Gutek. 1981. *Women and Work: A Psychological Perspective.* New York: Praeger.

Nissen, Linda, Dushanka V. Kleinman, and Ardell A. Wilson. 1986. "Practice Characteristics of Women Dentists," 113 *Journal of American Dental Association* 883.

Noddings, Nell. 1984. *Caring: A Feminine Approach to Ethics and Moral Education.* Berkeley, Los Angeles, London: University of California Press.

Okin, Susan M. 1979. *Women in Western Political Thought.* Princeton, N.J.: Princeton University Press.

———. 1987. "Justice and Gender," 16 *Philosophy and Public Affairs* 42.

Olsen, Frances. 1983. "The Family and the Market: A Study in Ideology and Legal Reform," 96 *Harvard Law Review* 1497.

———. 1986a. "The Sex of Law" (unpublished manuscript).

———. 1986b. "From False Paternalism to False Equality: Judicial Assaults on Ferminist Community, Illinois 1869–1895," 84 *Michigan Law Review* 1518.

Paterson, Alan A. 1988. "The Legal Profession in Scotland—An Endangered Species or A Problem Case for Market Theory?" in Richard L. Abel and Philip S. C. Lewis, eds., *Lawyers in Society*, vol. 1: *The Common Law World.* Berkeley, Los Angeles, London: University of California Press.

Pearson, Rose, and Albie Sachs. 1980. "Barristers and Gentlemen: A Critical Look at Sexism in the Legal Profession," 43 *Modern Law Review* 400.

Piaget, Jean. 1965. *The Moral Judgment of the Child.* New York: Free Press.

Pipkin, Ronald, and Janet Rifkin. 1984. "The Social Organization of Alternative Dispute Resolution: Implications for the Professionalization of Mediation," 9 *Justice System Journal* 204.

Podmore, David, and Anne Spencer. 1982. "Women Lawyers in England: The Experience of Inequality," 9 *Work & Occupations* 337.

Png, Ivan, David Eaves, and Mark Ramseyer. 1988. "Sex, Race and Grades: Emprical Evidence of Discrimination in Law-Firm Interviews," 38 *Journal of Legal Education.*

Quade, Vicki. 1986. "Myths vs. Ms.: Why Women Leave the Law," *Barrister* 28 (Winter).

Rebne, David. 1987. *Disciplinary Differences in Research Performance by Female Academicians: The Effect of the Proportion of Women.* Los Angeles: UCLA Institute for Social Science Research (Working Papers in the Social Sciences).

Reskin, Barbara, ed. 1984. *Sex Segregation in the Workplace: Trends, Explanations, Remedies.* Washington, D.C.: National Academy Press.

Reskin, Barbara, and Heidi Hartmann, eds. 1986. *Women's Work, Men's Work: Sex Segregation on the Job.* Washington, D.C.: National Academy Press.

Rhode, Deborah. 1988. "Perspectives on Professional Women," 40 *Stanford Law Review* 1163.

———. n.d. *Justice and Gender.* Cambridge, Mass.: Harvard University Press (forthcoming).

Rifkin, Janet. 1984. "Mediation From a Feminist Perspective: Promise and Problems," 2 *Law & Inequality* 21.

Rifkin, Janet, and Christine Harrington. 1987. "The Gender Organization of Mediation: Implications for Women in the Legal Profession." Presented at the conference on Women in the Legal Profession, Madison, Wisc., August.

Rokumoto, Kahei. 1988. "The Present State of Japanese Practicing Attorneys: On the Way to Full Professionalization?" in Richard L. Abel and Philip S. C. Lewis, eds., *Lawyers in Society*, vol. 2: *The Civil Law World*. Berkeley, Los Angeles, London: University of California Press.

Roos, Patricia. 1985. *Gender and Work: A Comparative Analysis of Industrial Societies*. Albany, N.Y.: State University of New York Press.

Rosenberg, Rosalind. 1982. *Beyond Separate Spheres: Intellectual Roots of Modern Feminism*. New Haven, Conn.: Yale University Press.

Rosenthal, Douglas. 1974. *Lawyer and Client: Who's In Charge?* New York: Russell Sage.

Rossiter, Margaret. 1986. "Women and the History of Scientific Communication," 21 *Journal of Library History* 39.

Rothman, Sheila. 1978. *Woman's Proper Place: A History of Changing Ideals and Practices, 1870 to the Present*. New York: Basic Books.

Royal Commission on Legal Services. 1979. *Final Report* (2 vols.). London: Her Majesty's Stationery Office (Cmnd. 7648).

Sargent, Alice G. 1981. *The Androgynous Manager*. New York: Amacom.

Schiller, Anita. 1979. "Women in Librarianship," in K. Weibel and K. Heim, eds., *The Role of Women in Librarianship 1876–1976: The Entry, Advancement and Struggle for Equalization in One Profession*. Phoenix, Ariz.: Oryx Press.

Schneider, Elizabeth. 1986. "The Dialectic of Rights and Politics: Perspectives From the Women's Rights Movement," 61 *New York University Law Review* 589.

Schwartz, Murray. 1980. "The Reorganization of the Legal Profession," 58 *Texas Law Review* 1269.

Schwartz, M., S. Brandt, and P. Milrod. 1985. "The Battles of Clara Shortridge Foltz," 1985 *California Defender* 7.

Sethi, R. 1987. "Women Lawyers: A Study of Professionalization." Presented to Working Group for Comparative Study of Legal Professions of the Research Committee on Sociology of Law of the International Sociological Association, New Delhi, August.

Shanker, Albert. 1986. "Teaching Losing in Career Competition," *Los Angeles Times* (March).

Sherry, Suzanna. 1986. "Civic Virtue and the Feminine Voice in Constitutional Adjudication," 72 *Virginia Law Review* 543.

Showalter, Elaine. 1977. *A Literature of Their Own: British Women Novelists From Bronte to Lessing*. Princeton, N.J.: Princeton University Press.

———. ed. 1986. *The New Feminist Criticism: Essays on Women, Literature, Theory*. New York: Pantheon Books.

Silas, Faye. 1984. "Women Lawyers," 70 *American Bar Association Journal* 33 (Sept.).

Silver, Catherine Bodard. 1974. "Salon, Foyer, Bureau: Women and the Professions in France," in Mary Hartman and Lois Banner, eds., *Clio's Consciousness Raised: New Perspectives on the History of Women*. New York: Harper and Row.

Sklar, Kathryn Kish. 1973. *Catherine E. Beecher: A Study in American Domesticity*. New Haven, Conn.: Yale University Press.

———. 1986. "Florence Kelley and the Politics of Women's Reform." Presented to UCLA Women, Culture and Society seminar, October.

Slotnick, Elliot. 1984. "The Paths to the Federal Bench: Gender, Race and Judicial Recruitment Variation," 67 *Judicature* 370.

Smith, Betsy Covington. 1984. *Breakthrough: Women in the Law*. New York: Walker & Co.

Sokoloff, Natalie. 1987. "The Increase of Black and White Women in the Professions: A Contradictory Process," in Christine Bose and Glenna Spitze, eds., *Ingredients for Women's Employment Policy*. Albany, N.Y.: State University of New York Press.

Spangler, Eve. 1986. *Lawyers For Hire: Salaried Professionals at Work*. New Haven, Conn.: Yale University Press.

Spangler, Eve, Marsha Gordon, and Ronald Pipkin. 1978. "Token Women: An Empirical Test of Kanter's Hypothesis," 84 *American Journal of Sociology* 160.

Stacey, Judith, and Barrie Thorne. 1985. "The Missing Feminist Revolution in Sociology," 32 *Social Problems* 301.

Stack, Carol, Linda K. Kerber, Catherine Greene, Eleanor Maccoby, Zella Luria, and Carol Gilligan. 1986. "Viewpoint: On *In A Different Voice*: An Interdisciplinary Forum," 11 *Signs* 304.

Stager, David A. A., and David K. Foot. 1988a. "Changes in Lawyers' Earnings: The Impact of Differentiation and Growth in the Canadian Legal Profession," 13 *Law and Social Inquiry* 71.

———. 1988b. *Lawyers' Earnings Under Market Differentiation and Rapid Supply Expansion, 1970–1980*. Toronto: Department of Economics, University of Toronto (Working Paper No. 8704).

Stanford Law Review. 1982. "Project: Law Firms and Lawyers with Children: An Empirical Analysis of Family/Work Conflict," 34 *Stanford Law Review* 1263.

Stevens, Robert. 1983. *Law School: Legal Education in America from the 1850's to the 1980's*. Chapel Hill: University of North Carolina Press.

Strober, Myra H. 1976. "Toward Dimorphics: A Summary Statement to the Conference on Occupational Segregation," in Martha Blaxall and Barbara Reagan, eds., *Women and the Workplace: The Implications of Occupational Segregation*. Chicago: University of Chicago Press.

Strober, Myra, and David Tyack. 1980. "Why Do Women Teach and Men Manage? A Report on Research on Schools," 5 *Signs* 494.

Strober, Myra, and Audri Gordon Lanford. 1986. "The Feminization of Public School Teaching: Cross-Sectional Analysis 1850–1880," 11 *Signs* 212.

Swan, G. S. 1983. "Gender Discrimination in Employment of Attorneys: Feminists Sharpen the Issues," 8 *Journal of the Legal Profession* 139.

Talbot, Nell Snow. 1960. "Why Not More Women Dentists?" 60 *Journal of American Dental Association* 114.

Theodore, Athena, ed. 1971. *The Professional Woman.* Cambridge, Mass.: Schenkman.

Tiger, Lionel. 1969. *Men in Groups.* New York: Random House.

Torre, Susana, ed. 1977. *Women in American Architecture: A Historic and Contemporary Perspective.* New York: Whitney Library of Design.

Treiman, Donald, and Kenneth Terrell. 1975a. "Sex and the Process of Status Attainment: A Comparison of Working Men and Women," 40 *American Sociological Review* 174.

———. 1975b. "Women, Work and Wages—Trends in the Female Occupational Structure Since 1940," in Kenneth C. Land and Seymore Spilerman, eds., *Social Indicator Models.* New York: Russell Sage.

Treiman, Donald, and Heidi Hartmann, eds. 1981. *Women, Work and Wages: Equal Pay for Jobs of Equal Value.* Washington, D.C.: National Academy Press.

Tronto, Joan. 1987. "Beyond Gender Difference in a Theory of Care," 12 *Signs* 644.

University of Southern California. 1983. Conference on Women in the Legal Workforce (March 9).

Vogt, Leona. 1986. *From Law School to Career: Where Do Graduates Go and What Do They Do? A Career Paths Study of Seven Northeastern Area Law Schools.* Cambridge, Mass.: Harvard Law School Program on the Legal Profession.

Walker, James. 1983. "In A Diffident Voice: Cryptoseparatist Analysis of Female Moral Development," 50 *Social Research* 665.

Walker, Samuel. 1980. *Popular Justice: A History of American Criminal Justice.* New York: Oxford University Press.

Wall Street Journal. 1986. *The Corporate Woman: A Special Report. Wall Street Journal* (March 24).

Ward, P. 1986. "Stubborn Women, Stubborn Sexism," 4 *Women's Review of Books* 21.

Warsaw, Janine N., ed. 1987. *Women Trial Lawyers: How They Succeed in Practice and in the Courtroom.* Englewood Cliffs, N.J.: Prentice-Hall.

Wasserstrom, Richard. 1977. "Racism, Sexism and Preferential Treatment: An Approach to the Topic," 24 *UCLA Law Review* 581.

Weisberg, D. Kelly. 1977. "Barred From the Bar: Women and Legal Education in the United States, 1870–1890," 28 *Journal of Legal Education* 485.

———. ed. 1982. *Women and the Law* (2 vols.). Cambridge, Mass.: Schenkman.

Westwood, Sallie. 1985. *All Day, Every Day: Factory and Family in the Making of Women's Lives.* Urbana, Ill.: University of Illinois Press.

Williams, Wendy. 1982. "The Equality Crisis: Some Reflections on Culture, Courts and Feminism," 7 *Women's Rights Law Reporter* 175.

———. 1984. "Equality's Riddle: Pregnancy and the Equal Treatment/Special Treatment Debate," 13 *New York University Review of Law and Social Change* 325.

Winter, Bill. 1983. "Survey: Women Lawyers Work Harder, Are Paid Less, but They're Happy," 69 *American Bar Association Journal* 1384.

Wishik, Heather. 1985. "To Question Everything: An Inquiry Into Feminist Jurisprudence," 1 *Berkeley Women's Law Journal* 64.

Wolgast, Elizabeth. 1980. *Equality and the Rights of Women.* Ithaca, N.Y.: Cornell University Press.

Woolf, Virginia. 1938. *Three Guineas.* New York: Harcourt, Brace and World.

Working Party on Women's Careers. 1988. *Equal in the Law.* London: Law Society.

8

Putting Law Back into the Sociology of Lawyers

RICHARD L. ABEL AND PHILIP S. C. LEWIS

Although the Working Group for Comparative Study of Legal Professions did not explicitly adopt a common theoretical framework when it began this project, the national reports in volumes 1 and 2 focus mostly on issues regarding the history and sociology of occupations (of which professions are a subcategory). We knew, of course, that these did not exhaust the range of interesting questions. However, we felt that they formed a necessary foundation for further inquiry. Consequently, we concentrated on such questions as the number of lawyers, their backgrounds and education, barriers to entry and limitations on practice, functional subdivisions and social stratification, career paths, structures of practice, and collective organization and governance. We still need to know more about these subjects, both in the twenty countries we have studied and even more in others, particularly in the socialist and third worlds.

In the present volume, however, some of our authors have shifted their gaze from lawyers as an occupational category to what lawyers *do*, that is, to the sociology of law. They have considered the consequences for the legal profession of the fact that women have been entering in almost equal numbers with men for more than a decade, the possibility that lawyers may be members of a "new class" that will play a decisive role in the future direction of the economy and polity, the relationship between lawyers and the state (as this varies across nations, through revolutionary ruptures, and in the emerging corporatist configurations), and what it means for lawyers to represent.

In this concluding chapter we want to frame a number of questions about lawyers that remain unanswered—often unasked—in the hope of suggesting fruitful paths for further research, and we want to encourage the reorientation initiated by our contributors. Instead of tracing the ways in which lawyers resemble other professionals (indeed, all other workers), we want to emphasize what makes them distinctive by putting law back into the sociology of lawyers. We do not offer a fully developed theory or even a comprehensive research agenda. Rather, we will concentrate on three areas we believe should be central: what lawyers know; what they do; and how they relate to the society, polity, and economy. Although we discuss these topics separately, they obviously are closely interrelated: knowledge with activity; social structure, state formation, and economy with each other; and all three with what lawyers know and do.

LAWYERS IN THE ECONOMY, SOCIETY, AND POLITY

COMPARISONS ACROSS SOCIETIES

Although some sociologists of law have explored the relationship between the emergence of legal specialists and social, economic, and political structures, usually from an evolutionary perspective (Hoebel, 1954; Nagel, 1962; Schwartz & Miller, 1964; Black, 1976, 1984; Unger, 1976; Newman, 1983; Abel, 1984; Griffiths, 1984), hardly anyone has extended this inquiry to compare the wide variety of ways in which precapitalist, capitalist, and socialist economies use law and lawyers. (Nonet and Selznick [1978] and more recently Teubner [1988] have explored varieties of law under advanced capitalism.) Indeed, the only effort with which we are familiar is Robin Luckham's magisterial but unfortunately neglected overview (1981a). His analysis is far too rich and global to be summarized here; the most we can do is sketch some of the connections he suggests and indicate how they might be studied. In doing so, we want to stress the reflexive relationship between law and lawyers on one hand and other social, political, and economic institutions on the other hand: the former shape the latter at the same time they are shaped by them. It also is important to avoid conflating law and lawyers: some legal systems dispense with representatives altogether or use those without legal training, and lawyers perform tasks that bear little connection to law.

Economies differ greatly in the use they make of law and lawyers. Those in which the productive units are relatively unspecialized and self-sufficient use little law: isolated bands of hunter-gatherers might be an extreme example (Marshall, 1960). As units specialize and trade increases, law becomes more important. Stable trading relationships among a limited number of partners have much less call for law than do transitory exchanges between numerous anonymous traders (Macaulay, 1963; *Wisconsin Law Review*, 1985). Law becomes even more important for mediating trade when the parties lack a common culture—as has been happening recently with the expansion of international markets for raw materials, commodities, labor, and capital. The common culture of lawyers may make a vital contribution here (even if they belong to different national professions). Economies that are more dispersed (containing many small producers and consumers) need more law to mediate interaction than do economies that are highly concentrated. In the latter, the few major actors can reach informal understandings with each other, while their economic power allows them to impose their will on smaller actors. Yet, as economic units grow larger, more internally differentiated, and more hierarchical, they may need more law for purposes of internal governance, especially if there is a separation of ownership and control.

The sectoral composition of the economy also may be relevant, at least in defining which property relations will be governed by law, if not the quantity of law and lawyers. We can trace the shifting emphasis among land, mineral rights, patents for commodities and manufacturing processes, copyrights, rights to pollute or to be free from pollution, rights to control markets or to enter and compete freely, and contractual rights. It seems plausible that law becomes more significant to the extent that property rights are established by private agreements rather than fixed by tradition or clearly demarcated by physical boundaries. Thus, the postindustrial economy characterized by a rapidly expanding service sector may increase the demand for legal services. Similarly, the relationship between labor and capital may affect the role of law: control over labor sometimes is secured by political influence, brute force, or economic necessity; it is difficult to control capital except through legal forms. Finally, the nature and extent of state involvement in the economy is extremely important. Notwithstanding the claims of laissez-faire ideologues, law is essential to construct and operate even the "free" market. And notwithstanding the promises of Marxist theoreticians (Pashukanis, 1980), no socialist regime has been able to replace law entirely by administration. Nevertheless, it may be the mixed economies characteristic of most contemporary societies that have the greatest need for law: to regulate economic interaction among "private" actors, redistribute resources, and legitimate the economic activities of the state (while also exposing them to private challenge).

If economies vary in their need for law and lawyers, how do lawyers shape those economies? First, they consume surplus. Although this evokes bitter complaints (suggesting that clients often view lawyers' efforts as superfluous makework) and undoubtedly hurts individuals, all the evidence suggests that the cost of lawyers and litigation is an insignificant proportion of the total surplus. Even in the United States—generally described as the most overlawyered and litigious country in the world—legal services represent less than one percent of the gross national product—a tenth of the proportion spent on medical care. Second, lawyers claim to create the predictability necessary to permit the exchange of commodities, labor, and capital. Although this is an essential element in the legitimation offered by most legal professions, it is empirically undemonstrated. There are other ways for economic actors to increase predictability: reciprocity (which scholars from Mead and Malinowski to Macaulay have shown is far more important than state sanctions), political influence (obtained from reciprocal favors or material help), bribery, or physical force. For all their other faults, command economies, which use many fewer lawyers, are at least as predictable as free markets. Moreover, it is unclear whether lawyers enhance certainty and predictability or rather aggravate uncertainty and unpredictability. Even if they foster the former, there are many ways of doing so, as Max Weber found in trying to resolve the "England problem" (how a system lacking the formal rationality of civil law could be the locus of the most advanced capitalist economy of the nineteenth century) (Sugarman, 1986; Ewing, 1987). Finally, lawyers seem to accelerate the concentration of economic resources (whether land, capital, labor, or intangible property) by amplifying existing economic power. At the same time, they allow economic upstarts to challenge entrenched interests, as the industrial, commercial, and financial bourgeoisie displaced the landed aristocrats. Also, they redistribute and disperse wealth horizontally when they engage in intraclass disputes over property (especially inheritance) and in competition for markets or corporate control.

Polities also differ in the extent to which they make use of law and lawyers. One of the most common distinctions is respect for the "rule of law" (the Rechtsstaat). Autocrats who govern by fiat, often supported by military power, have much less need for law and lawyers, whom they deliberately suppress. Yet, even they need subordinates to control large populations and often rely on those with legal training, who, in turn, may sympathize when citizens couch their claims in legal form. There are other surrogates for law besides force; ideology, both religious and secular, is one of the most powerful. This is particularly visible at the early stages of postrevolutionary regimes, whether Moslem or Marxist. Yet, the experiences of the Soviet Union, Cuba, and China all demonstrate that revolutionary fervor soon yields to routine governance, in which legality appears to play an increasing role. The size of the state, the heterogeneity of its population (including its class composition), and the pace of change all are relevant: very small, stable, homogeneous societies may be able to govern themselves through consensus and tradition. An intentional community like the Israeli kibbutz represents a limiting case (see the exchange between Schwartz [1954, 1976] and Shapiro [1976, 1985]). Larger, more heterogeneous societies may diminish their reliance on law through decentralization and forms of indirect rule. At the opposite extreme lie the federal state and the colonial regime, which seek to elicit obedience from people who owe no loyalty beyond what can be inspired by legality. Robinson and Scaglion (1987) have sought to demonstrate the connection between the rise of class opposition and the emergence of specialized police forces. We can generalize the relationship between state and economy, mentioned above: the more the state seeks to regulate civil society—social relations and cultural beliefs as well as economic production and exchange—the more need it will have of law.

Even in large heterogeneous societies experiencing rapid change, law is not the only mechanism of governance. A high degree of consensus on means and ends (or at least acquiescence in the face of overwhelming force) may permit the state to engage directly in administration rather than having to rely on law; examples might include postrevolutionary societies and third world countries intent on rapid development (Ghai, 1976). If there is no consensus on ends but enough agreement on how to reach them to avoid civil war, then politics may be the central arena—elections to and lobbying within national and local legislatures and executives as well as extraparliamentary activities (demonstrations, squats, occupations); much of western Europe illustrates this category. If there is consensus about ends or an inability to discuss them because the culture does not permit it or the political institutions are paralyzed, then legal institutions and processes become central arenas and lawyers essential actors; the United States is the preeminent example.

How do lawyers, in turn, shape polities? We really do not know the answer to this question. Does it make a difference whether civil servants or elected politicians are university graduates in literature, political theory, economics, or law? There is some justification for the cynical view that the qualification serves more to justify privilege than to confer competence. In Gilbert and Sullivan's "H.M.S. Pinafore," The Rt. Hon. Sir Joseph Porter, K.C.B., expatiates at length on how his career as an attorney qualified him to become First Lord of the Admiralty and concludes with the advice: "Stick close to your desk and never go to sea/And you all may be rulers of the Queen's Navee." Yet, legal training may imbue graduates with fidelity to legality. An Israeli Attorney General insisted on investigating murders by the Shin Bet, to the point where he was dismissed by the Prime Minister; a U.S. Attorney General refused to discharge the special prosecutor investigating the Watergate scandal and was fired by the President. How much of this behavior can be attributed to the office—which is supposed to embody legality—and how much to the background or training of its occupant? There is some evidence that professional identity strengthens the "independence" of the judiciary and its willingness to defy or at least obstruct grossly illegal acts by the more political branches. South African judges have blocked the destruction of African rural and urban settlements and temporarily stayed the execution of death sentences; Argentine judges have pursued inquiries into military atrocities in the "dirty war." Finally, individual private practitioners (although rarely more than a tiny minority) and bar associations sometimes challenge the state in the name of law (Luckham, 1981b).

Social structural variables (in addition to those that are primarily economic and political) also may affect the role of law and lawyers. Here the principal issue is the size and composition of the social unit and the nature and strength of the nonlegal "glue" holding it together. The process called "modernization" generally is seen as a progressive dissolution of collectivities based on kinship, locality, language, ethnicity, gender, and age, within which most social interaction previously occurred. Authority inside those collectivities was traditional or charismatic rather than legal. As those collectivities lost that authority and their members increasingly interacted with outsiders, state law became essential to mediate conflict and to govern. Yet we know that many of these traditional bonds (particularly within the family) never succumbed to the individualistic assault of capitalism, others have revived in recent years (such as race, ethnicity, religion, and gender), and new ones have emerged (class, especially within the workplace, age cohorts, and ideological groupings). Although state law may not directly rule these dyads or collectivities, it shapes (and is shaped by) informal or unofficial legality within them (Galanter, 1981; Macaulay, 1987a).

The role of law and lawyers in shaping social structure again is historically and culturally specific. There can be no doubt that individuals mobilized law in their assault on collectivities. Nuclear families challenged the authority of villages, landlords, and lineages over land. Individuals insisted on both choosing spouses and terminating marriages by themselves. Individual producers of goods and services resisted the control of the guild. Religious dissenters attacked the authority of the church. Yet, it is equally true that law helped to create some of the most powerful collectivities in the modern world, notably the joint stock corporation and its subsequent elaborations.

Finally, cultural variables obviously influence the use of law and lawyers (just as they do medicine and physicians; see Payer [1988]). Where appropriate behavior is strongly constrained by tradition (rather than structured by economic forces or directed by the state), lawyers may be irrelevant. In some precapitalist societies, for instance, only certain economic exchanges are conceivable, entitlement to property is clearly defined by group membership, inheritance follows invariant patterns, injuries mandate fixed payments, and kinship rules determine who may marry, rights to children, and property prestations (Gluckman, 1965). Where appropriate behavior is prescribed by religion as interpreted by a priestly hierarchy, its members perform many of the roles we attribute to lawyers (although their authority over economic life is limited, except perhaps within Islam). Culture also structures social inequality: which advantages are valued, which are legitimate. Where honor rather than property ownership is the principal source of status, lawyers play little role (Abel, 1979). Honor is created and enhanced by a person's own deeds: adherence to norms, rhetorical competence, physical strength, and courage. (Yet, there are contemporary instances where lawyers mediate conflicts over honor, such as defamation cases by prominent figures, or perhaps disputes between divorcing couples.) Similarly, where status is affiliational (as it frequently is for women), lawyers are irrelevant. Even in advanced capitalist societies, the strong value placed on preserving social relationships (including dominance and subordination) may discourage resort to law—Japan is the most frequently cited example, (Kawashima, 1963; Haley, 1978; Wagatsuma & Rosett, 1986; Miyazawa, 1987).

Law is related in complex ways to beliefs about inequality and equality. In the past, tradition and religion (sometimes, but not invariably, reinforced by law) have offered powerful justifications for inequalities of class, gender, age, ethnicity, and race. Law (and lawyers) have provided a means of challenging inequality in the modern era. Yet, law and lawyers also constitute a powerful legitimation for those inequalities that persist, which then are attributed to choice, effort, natural endowments, or the costliness of change. Nor do all contemporary lawyers attack ascribed inequalities in the name of universalistic laws: Basque notaries strictly maintain traditional inheritance patterns against French laws that would supersede them (Nicholson, 1987).

It hardly needs argument today that law and lawyers create culture as well as being its creatures (Macaulay, 1987b; Merry, 1986). Many contemporary Western societies appear to be highly legalistic. Few would dispute the continued force of de Tocqueville's observation, more than a century and a half ago, that sooner or later every important issue in American life is transformed into a legal question—although some would characterize the United States as extreme, if not aberrational. The explanation for this hegemony of legalism is less clear. Is it the number of lawyers or the dissolution of other belief systems? Or is it the inevitable consequence of ethical and cultural relativism? And how enduring is the hegemony of legal culture? There is some evidence that the discourse of economics is displacing that of law, making economists the new philosopher kings.

COMPARISONS WITHIN SOCIETIES

Thus far we have focused on the larger social environment and tried to understand the varying role of law and lawyers. Now we want to invert that analysis, starting with concrete variations in that role in order to arrive at testable generalizations about their meaning. Whereas our comparisons previously ranged across the entire gamut of societies, here we will be concerned primarily with differences within advanced capitalism, even within a single society. Our analytic strategy is to construct pairs of events that are otherwise similar and consider why one member of the pair appears to be more thoroughly legalized than the other, that is, more subject to legal rules and thus more likely to involve lawyers. Because we draw on our experience as common lawyers, it will be essential to test our generalizations in other legal systems.

In a number of very different contexts, the termination of a relationship is thoroughly legalized although its formation was not: death and birth, divorce and marriage, termination of parental rights (for child abuse or neglect) and becoming a biological parent, contract breach and contract formation, firing and hiring of an employee, eviction of a tenant and the leasing of real property, dissolution and formation of a collectivity (partnership, corporation), entry into a country and deportation (or even voluntary departure, as in the Soviet Union). We can think of several reasons for this. A complex series of expectations have accreted around the relationship, which require readjustment (this also might explain why more elaborate rituals and religious beliefs surround death than birth). Many of these expectations concern property, and lawyers are quintessentially the priests of property. The formation of a relationship is perceived as a consensual act; we typically explain and justify such action as an expression of economic, psychological, or political choice. The termination of a relationship, by contrast, commonly expresses or creates conflict and represents the exercise of power. If the conflict is sufficiently serious, the state may seek to regulate it. If the power relationships are sufficiently unequal, the state may seek to equalize them or to legitimate the outcome.

Some of the exceptions to these empirical generalizations offer further support for the underlying theory. When one or both parties anticipate future conflict, formation of the relationship may also be legalized, as in complex business contracts. A country concerned about immigration, like the United States, may bureaucratize the process of obtaining a visa but summarily expel those who overstay their term, denying them most due process rights. Also, the formation of a relationship may be subject to legal control where we lack confidence that "choice" will produce a desirable result: adoption is a long-standing example, surrogate motherhood a more recent one. At the other end of the continuum, consensual termination of a relationship is not legalized: voluntarily quitting an apartment or leaving a country, performance or mutual recission of a contract, agreements dissolving partnerships, even divorce by consent (the most common form of marital dissolution in Japan). The presence or absence of property can be equally decisive. Lawyers are not involved following the deaths of most people (who have no estates), the evictions of most tenants, or the firing of most employees. Where large amounts of property are invested in a relationship at the outset, la\ -yers are more likely to be involved in its formation: births and marriages among the very wealthy are examples (for they often are accompanied by the creation of trust funds or property settlements); or one can compare leases of commercial and residential property, or the creation of large corporations and small partnerships. Changes in the amount and kind of property can transform routine legal procedures into customized individual transactions. This has happened to divorce in California as a result of the incredible inflation of housing prices (which have made the family home a valuable asset) and increasing attention to the division of intangible property (such as academic degrees, professional qualifications, and pension rights). Property even can create a legal relationship where none previously existed, as in the recognition of a cohabitant's right to share in the couple's property when the relationship is dissolved.

We can see the importance of property in other contexts by contrasting situations where value is aggregated, capitalized, or congealed, with those where it is dispersed, fragmented, or individualized. Most individuals never control a large amount of value at any one time because their only source of value is their own labor power, which must be exerted continuously throughout a lifetime of work, producing daily increments, which are quickly consumed. Yet, sometimes an individual's labor power is tragically extinguished (or seriously diminished) through personal injury. In such cases the victim seeks restitution for the loss. American tort law (and similar bodies of law in most Western legal systems) offers compensation, a significant element of which is the capitalized value of the labor power the victim would have expended during the rest of a working life. (In precapitalist societies, compensation obviously is not proportioned to labor value.) Where this value is large, lawyers often represent both victim and alleged tortfeasor in the dispute over the amount of the loss and who should bear it. Again the exception proves the rule: where the victim is entitled to periodic payments rather than a lump sum, lawyer involvement is both less common and less energetic (workers' compensation in the United States and similar income replacement schemes elsewhere). The capitalization of value also explains the greater involvement of lawyers in transferring ownership of land than in forming month-to-month tenancies, or in drafting long-term employment contracts than in hiring hourly workers. It is not just labor power that can be aggregated—so can life itself. The response to personal injuries is so highly legalized in the United States partly because victims can recover "general damages" for the transformation of their lives: pain, loss of certain pleasures, disfigurement, injury to relationships, or even "lost years" for those whose life expectancy is shortened. For similar reasons (and far more universally) criminal prosecutions are thoroughly legalized. Even before the state began to provide poor defendants with defense counsel (after World War II), many indigent accused found ways to buy representation when they were facing long prison sentences. For similar reasons, those confronting deportation (or incarceration in a country where they could not practice their calling or religion) will borrow or call on the resources of relatives in order to secure legal representation. Value can be aggregated not only over time but also across individuals, when one actor possesses the ability to injure multiple victims through a single act, as in pollution, mass disasters, or abuses of concentrated economic power. The state may subject such behavior to legal regulation (through environmental or antitrust laws), and class actions may involve lawyers in representing individuals, each of whose stake in the matter is relatively small (Yeazell, 1987).

Property and the capitalization of value are intimately related to the legalization of behavior and the involvement of lawyers for two principal reasons. First, they increase the importance of the transaction to the participants to the point where it becomes worthwhile for them to invest in professional services. This, in brief, is why "repeat players" are strategically placed to take advantage of law, both prospectively (by drafting favorable "agreements," such as apartment leases or disclaimers of liability in contracts for the sale of goods or services) and retrospectively (making or resisting claims or negotiating settlements) (Galanter, 1974). Second, the capitalization of value often allows the object of controversy itself to become the source of the lawyer's fee, as in the sale of the family home on divorce, damages for personal injury or breach of contract, controversies regarding the ownership of property (real estate, patents and copyright, control of a corporation), or settlement of an estate. This is a prerequisite for lawyer involvement because, as our two earlier volumes have shown, lawyers everywhere have succeeded in inflating the cost of their services by restricting supply. Thus, the correlation between the involvement of lawyers and the capitalization of value (especially into a "res" whose liquidation can pay the lawyers' fees) is grounded in the self-interest of lawyers, whereas the correlation with the relationship between the parties (and more generally with the society, polity, and economy) stresses the functions of lawyers for the larger environment.

WHAT DO LAWYERS DO FOR THEIR CLIENTS?

We are interested in discovering *when* behavior is legalized and lawyers involved because we believe it makes a difference. There are many ways we could begin thinking about those differences. First, lawyers may augment or diminish inequalities between adversaries, either because only one side is represented or because it is represented more effectively than the other. To explore this we should examine pairs of potential adversaries. Second, lawyers often operate in settings that are not strictly adversarial; and even within contentious situations they perform a wide variety of functions. Here we want to analyze precisely what lawyers do for their clients. Third, the lawyer—client relationship is fraught with possibilities for tension, divergent objectives, and misunderstandings. We offer some speculations about the inconsistent expectations lawyers and clients may hold about each other. Finally, we must recognize that, despite the legal profession's official monopoly, many other actors do or could perform similar functions. We pose some questions about the difference it might make that a *lawyer* is doing so. In each of these inquiries we are limiting ourselves to what lawyers do for *clients*: lawyers also pursue their own goals (what Larson [1977] has called the "professional project" of market control and collective status enhancement) as well as engaging in altruistic, public interest behavior (Halliday, 1987).

LAWYERS AND THE BALANCE OF ADVANTAGE

Not everything lawyers do affects the balance of advantage in society. Much of their work is purely facilitative, neither responding to nor anticipating conflict: transferring residential land (in common law countries), forming corporations, drafting wills, creating trusts, filing adoptions, performing truly uncontested divorces. Indeed, such work may seem so minimally "legal" that nonlawyers challenge the professional monopoly, often successfully. Even in these situations, however, differential access to lawyers may amplify existing advantages: minimizing tax liability, permitting profitable investments, and avoiding the social stigma and uncertainties of unlegalized relationships.

In many other situations, the presence and quality of legal representation may have more momentous consequences (Marvell, 1978; Partridge & Bermant, 1978; Wheeler et al., 1987). The following is a preliminary list of adversarial pairs, which needs to be amplified and refined (particularly to eliminate ethnocentric common law biases): prosecutor and criminal defendant; spouses contesting custody, visitation, property, or support following a divorce; claimants to the same property (title to land, tenancy, inheritance, patent or copyright infringement, creditors of a bankrupt debtor); tortfeasor and victim; parties to a contract (commercial, consumer, loan); regulator and regulated (including tax collector and taxpayer, jailor and prisoner, state and citizens seeking to limit state power); state and benefits claimant; shareholders seeking corporate control; enterprises struggling over competitive advantage under antitrust laws; employer and employee (individually over job security or discrimination, collectively over the terms of the employment relationship); polluter and polluted; discriminator and victim of discrimination. It would seem fruitful to identify more such situations and study them cross-culturally to determine whether one side is represented or both are and, if the latter, the quality of representation on the two sides.

THE REPERTOIRE OF LAWYER FUNCTIONS

To reduce the significance of lawyers to amplifying or reducing inequality is to obscure the very wide range of functions they perform for their clients. A second research strategy, therefore, would map those functions and seek to understand why lawyers perform more of them for some clients and in some legal systems than others. This approach clearly owes much to the functionalism of the American legal realists and their successors (Llewellyn, 1960, 1962; Twining, 1973; Hurst, 1950). Within the large and growing literature on the legal profession, however, there are very few studies of what lawyers actually do (clinical teaching materials would be a useful source, although they are prescriptive rather than systematically empirical). Furthermore, the sensitivity of the subject has encouraged researchers to study "down"—concentrating on lawyers serving relatively low status clients: individuals undergoing divorce, legal aid recipients, personal injury victims, criminal accused, and dissatisfied consumers (e.g., O'Gorman [1963], Sarat & Felstiner [1986], Griffiths [1986], Cain [1979], Landon [1982, 1985], Carlin [1962], Rosenthal [1974], Hosticka [1979], Katz [1982], Macaulay [1979]; on the difficulty of studying what lawyers do, see Danet et al. [1980]). Although there are numerous accounts of dramatic trials, particularly personal injuries, almost all are written by or about the victims and their lawyers, not about the corporate tortfeasors and theirs (Ino, 1975; Upham, 1976; Teff & Munro, 1976; Erikson, 1976; Stern, 1977; Insight Team, 1979; Levine, 1982; Brodeur, 1985; Mintz, 1986; Schuck, 1986; Wallace, 1986; Riley, 1987; Ball, 1985; Kurzman, 1988). Very few have studied what lawyers do for the medium-sized and large commercial enterprises that provide most of their business (but see Nelson [1988], Galanter [1983], Spangler [1986], Kagan & Rosen [1985], Rosen [1986, n.d.], Flood [1986], McBarnet [1984], Mann [1985], Zion [1988]; on the behavior of government lawyers, see Eisenstein [1978]). The following enumeration inevitably is biased by the fact that we know more (if still very little) about lawyers representing individuals than about those serving companies and the state.

1. Lawyers provide knowledge about law so that clients can plan future behavior, know what to expect as a result of past conduct, and seek to change the law. Sometimes lawyers educate clients about how much of the law they can break without being caught or seriously punished because the government or a private adversary lacks the knowledge, skills or resources to enforce the law (Mann, 1985). Lawyers also misinform clients and conceal information from them, both out of ignorance and intentionally (because the lawyer has conflicting obligations to another or fears to reveal past misconduct).

2. Lawyers provide clients with knowledge about and contacts with influential people. Some of the people lawyers know are regular adversaries (such as prosecutors for defense counsel), to whom lawyers can talk and with whom they can negotiate in ways that clients themselves cannot (Mann, 1985: 77). As Jerome Carlin summarized the views of Chicago sole practitioners in the late 1950s: "the practice of law ... is more 'who you know than what you know,' ... it's all politics and connections" (1962: 194–195). Muckraking books about Washington lawyers urge the same conclusion (Goulden, 1972; Green, 1975). Lawyers tell clients who has the power to do what and open the doors to such people. There is considerable debate, however, as to whether lawyers themselves enjoy influence over governmental decisionmakers or merely are conduits through which clients exercise their own influence (Laumann et al., 1985; Salisbury et al., 1986; Nelson et al., 1987, 1988).

3. Lawyers speak for their clients, using rhetorical skills and technical knowledge to address adversaries, negotiating partners, judges, legislators, and administrators. Of course, they present legal arguments; however, although this is the core of legal education and of the image lawyers present to the public, it is not the only way they represent their clients. Lawyers say things that clients cannot because they lack the eloquence or courage or are too honest or emotionally involved. A white-collar criminal defense attorney who knew that this client had given high-level government employees valuable stock options asserted to the investigating U.S. Attorney: "We have examined books, daily accounts, the cash flow and find no indication whatsoever of expenditures that were not appropriate" (Mann, 1985: 82). Lawyers tell clients what they can and cannot say in view of the evidence that is likely to be available to an adversary or a decision-maker. Some clients cannot speak at all: women and slaves often were legally disabled; prisoners are physically disabled; collectivities may not have an agreed spokesperson; children may be too immature. In speaking for clients, lawyers endow them with the benefits (and detriments) of their own professional reputations and social standing. For the same reason, lawyers may refuse to represent some clients (those who commit heinous crimes or are politically anathema) or say certain things on their behalf. They may even seek to control the client's behavior so as not to be

compromised, in order to preserve a reputation for "reasonableness" (Katz, 1982). In some situations, lawyers may conceal the fact that they are ventriloquists, secretly scripting their client's communications and behavior (Flood, 1986: 26–27; Mann, 1985: 132). Lawyers also restrain clients from talking, when clients wish to be overly revealing (out of an emotional need to confess or in the hope that an adversary will reciprocate) but lawyers believe that "stonewalling" is a more effective strategy. Here (and in many other contexts) the lawyer not only represents the client to adversaries and legal officials but also represents the latter to the client. Lawyers do this, despite the strong professional ideology of fidelity to the client, for several reasons: their need to retain the goodwill of legal officials or adversaries (with whom lawyers may have ongoing relations)—plea-bargaining being the best documented example (*Law & Society Review*, 1979), the desire for future business from an adversary, or personal or ideological sympathy with the adversary (which may reflect their similar backgrounds). For instance, Stewart Macaulay (1979) reports that Wisconsin lawyers often are impatient with consumer complaints because the lawyers appear to accept the American faith in the market and to blame the consumers for unwise purchases. Indeed, lawyers sometimes explicitly embrace the role of mediator between opposing parties, for instance, in divorce.

4. Lawyers can engage in therapy, offering a sympathetic ear (perhaps even catharsis) to clients who want to express anger, fear, anxiety, or sorrow. (Similarly, lawyers are called on to offer business advice, often because the strong ethic of confidentiality makes them the only trusted outsiders to whom a corporate official can speak.) Lawyers can affirm or challenge those feelings. They can redirect them—away from an adversary and toward the legal system, for instance. This can change the goals and strategies that client and lawyer pursue. Lawyers also may refuse to perform this role, defining legal issues narrowly and suggesting that the client see a trained therapist.

5. Much of the work of lawyers consists merely in performing formulaic acts and utterances in order to produce legal results that are virtually automatic, as we mentioned in the previous section. Examples might include simple tax returns, insurance claims, guilty pleas, incorporation, name changes, adoptions, uncontested divorces, residential land transactions, and probate of small estates. A subset of these noncontentious activities demands greater creativity: eliciting a client's real wishes in order to embody them in a contract; and constructing the legal framework of a collectivity (partnership, corporation, trade union, voluntary association, cooperative).

6. Lawyers construct narratives (Lopez, 1984). They collect stories from clients, adversaries, officials, and other witnesses; examine records; study material evidence; and put together a story (or set of alternative stories)

about "what happened" or what the decisionmaker can be made to believe has happened (Genn, 1987: chap. 4). Sometimes lawyers have to work hard to elicit information from reluctant, suspicious, or confused clients; at other times they have to be just as diligent to remain ignorant of uncomfortable or inculpatory facts (Mann, 1985: 103—111). They tell clients what kinds of evidence are necessary to substantiate their accounts and those of their adversaries, so that clients can collect and preserve the former and conveniently lose, forget, or bury the latter (Flood, 1986: 40; Mann, 1985: chaps. 3—4). Lawyers suggest to clients what would be helpful or damaging testimony from witnesses—especially those over whom clients have influence. The process of questioning and recording simultaneously shapes what others believe and remember. Of course, lawyers are not the only ones who perform this role: insurance claims adjusters and shop stewards do so in personal injuries (Ross, 1970); police, in criminal investigations; and social workers, in welfare cases.

7. Lawyers transform their clients' objectives and strategies by telling clients what they can obtain from the legal system (Felstiner et al. [1980/81]; cf. Mather & Yngvesson [1980/81]). To use a Freudian metaphor, they are collective superegos, bringing a reality principle to bear on client ids. American criminal lawyers, for instance, may demand a preliminary hearing not to learn the prosecution's case (which they already know) but to persuade an accused that he has no choice but to plead guilty (Flemming, 1986). (A recent Dutch study, however, suggests that lawyers are consistently overconfident; see Malsch [1988].) In divorce cases, for instance, lawyers translate raw client emotion, such as the desire for revenge, into entitlements to a property settlement and support (Sarat & Felstiner, 1986). Sometimes this translation also reflects the lawyers' own beliefs about the appropriate legal response. John Griffiths (1986) reports that Dutch lawyers discourage noncustodial parents from seeking weekly visitation because they believe that it produces too much conflict. Lawyers' strategic decisions also are influenced by the amount in controversy and the client's own resources: they seek only as much "justice" as the client can afford. Stewart Macaulay (1979) describes the ways in which Wisconsin lawyers "cool out" dissatisfied consumers. Lawyers simultaneously explain to clients why they must accept less than they want, attributing this to the rigidity of legal rules, the arbitrariness of judges, or the malevolence of adversaries (both clients and lawyers). In the process, they persuade clients to accept what the law offers. Jack Katz (1982) offers vivid accounts of the ways in which legal aid lawyers allow legal "solutions" (or their absence) to define client problems. If clients refuse to accept "reality," lawyers may place the blame for failure on the clients themselves. Although laypeople perceive the law as incredibly complex—a perception lawyers encourage (Sarat & Felstiner, 1986)—the translation of lived experience into legal

language often is a process of simplification, just as a medical diagnosis invariably simplifies a patient's narrative of aches and pains. In both instances, the available legal or medical remedies come to shape the nature of the client's or patient's complaint—driving some to seek political solutions or nonprofessional healers.

8. There is considerable controversy, although relatively little information, concerning the extent to which lawyers intensify or moderate legal conflict or encourage clients to comply with or evade the law. It is essential to trace variation along these two crucial dimensions in different legal systems, across subject matters, and as it is influenced by the characteristics of lawyers and clients and the relationships between them. For instance, Sarat and Felstiner (1986) offer persuasive evidence that divorce lawyers moderate the adversariness of their clients, which is fueled by powerful emotions. Numerous accounts of the criminal justice system (beginning with Sudnow [1965] and Blumberg [1967]) depict defense lawyers persuading their clients to accept the state's offer and plead guilty (Matheny, 1979). Yet, it seems likely that lawyers may also intensify the conflict out of ideological commitment, the desire to play for long-term objectives (including rule changes), anger at a particular adversary (lawyer or client), eagerness for publicity, or simple greed (when the client can pay the costs). Similarly, lawyers may increase legal compliance: informing clients already inclined to be law-abiding about the content of or changes in the law; or urging compliance on reluctant clients because lawyers have an ideological commitment to the particular law or to obedience in general or an interest in preserving their professional reputations. However, much of what lawyers do is to show clients how to sail as close to the wind as possible, taking every advantage the law offers and offering nothing in return unless compelled. Certainly that is how popular guides to successful lawyering characterize the role. This does describe a good deal of tax planning, administrative law practice, negotiation, and litigation strategy. Such client partisanship may be simply a means of getting business (devising and marketing tax loopholes, for instance, or strategies for pursuing or resisting corporate takeovers; see Powell [1987]), or it, too, may be ideologically motivated (opposition to racial integration, for instance, or abortion, or even government regulation generally).

9. Lawyers may define problems narrowly or broadly. Most discussion of this choice has focused on those whose opposition to established power makes them appear more conspicuously "political": lawyers in legal aid offices or public interest law firms or those involved in political trials (Katz, 1982; Weisbrod et al., 1978; Handler et al., 1978; Barkan, 1985; Abel, 1985a, 1985b; Scheingold, 1988a, 1988b). However, it is important to recognize that private practitioners serving business clients actually have more leeway and greater resources in designing legal strategies. They can

coordinate the activities of discrete parties: members of a trade association or defendants in a white-collar criminal prosecution (Mann, 1985: 89–93). They can play for rules, fight cases that are economically unprofitable in order to discourage other claims, delay in order to force a settlement, and so forth. The ongoing litigation regarding the liability of tobacco companies to smokers who contract cancer and other diseases exemplifies this. When a jury returned the first verdict for a plaintiff in June 1988, a lawyer for the defendant Liggett Group responded: "The bottom line is to collect a $400,000 claim they [plaintiff's lawyers] spent more than $2 million. That can't be much incentive" (McGee, 1988). The lawyer for Phillip Morris, which controls 37 percent of the tobacco market, added: "The plaintiff bar is not likely to regard this verdict as encouraging because they got only 10 to 15 percent of their costs in prosecuting their suit" (Janson, 1988).

This list contains both overlaps and omissions and lacks a clear unified theoretical framework. Because it is written by common lawyers and informed by a literature that is predominantly American, it also is culturally biased. Furthermore, the interesting questions are *when* lawyers do *which* things for *which* clients. Given the paucity of research on what lawyers actually do for their clients, however, it may stimulate others to pursue these issues and offer a starting point for doing so.

HOW DOES THE LAWYER–CLIENT RELATIONSHIP SHAPE LAWYER BEHAVIOR?

What lawyers do for clients is influenced by the expectations that each group has about the other. Lawyers agonize endlessly about how they ought to behave: in their rules of professional conduct, in self-congratulatory and self-flagellating ceremonial speeches, and when deploring their poor public "image" and proposing ways to improve it. American legal scholars never tire of discussing how to balance the loyalties lawyers owe their clients against their countervailing obligations to the legal system and the larger society (for speculations about why this is a peculiarly American preoccupation, see Luban [1984]). We also have some survey research (and a few observational studies) on how clients think lawyers ought to behave (Curran, 1977; Steele & Nimmer, 1976; Rosenthal, 1974; Royal Commission, 1979, vol. 2: 223–237; Royal Commission, 1980, vol. 2: 64–70, 75–77). Clients appear to be most concerned that lawyers keep them informed, explain the situation thoroughly, and listen attentively to their questions. They also want loyalty but not necessarily the adversarial loyalty of the tactician who seizes every advantage and never makes a concession; rather, they want the therapeutic loyalty of the ally who unquestioningly accepts the client's sense of injury and injustice. Moreover, we know how frequently clients make formal complaints—to professional disciplinary bodies and by suing for lawyer malpractice—and the content of those grievances.

Lawyers' self-exhortations—in ethical codes, bar association journals, and annual conventions—presumably are intended primarily for public consumption, or at least as a means of collective self-deception or reassurance. For social scientists to confuse those prescriptions with actual behavior would display unpardonable naivete (Abel, 1981). Client expectations and desires are likely to be influential where clients exercise significant control over their lawyers. This is a function of: the relative wealth, status, and education of lawyers and clients; the duration of the relationship, especially when compared to the lawyer's relationships with adversaries, opposing counsel, and legal officials; the amount of business the client brings the lawyer, especially when compared to other clients of the lawyer and the firm; how easily the client could engage in self-representation or find another lawyer; whether the lawyer is an employee or independent practitioner; whether the client has proactively initiated contact with the legal system or is responding to the actions of another; and perhaps whether the use of law is facilitative or contentious.

Where these variables give lawyers power over clients, however, it makes more sense to consider lawyers' expectations about clients than either clients' expectations about lawyers or lawyers' public pronouncements. On the basis of the very little we know, it seems likely that the former are virtually the mirror image of the latter two. Although lawyers' expectations are not expressed in "rules of client behavior" or explicit lawyer grievances about clients, there are other sources of information: lawyer shoptalk (which is filled with "horror stories" about bad clients) and the ways in which lawyers consciously use their power to structure the relationship. Lawyers want clients to be passive. The best client is the absent client: physically distant (as when Washington lawyers lobby on behalf of clients referred by local counsel, or London solicitors litigate matters forwarded by provincial solicitors), socially distant (solicitors protect barristers from direct dealings with clients; house counsel may perform this role on the Continent and, increasingly, in the United States), or largely fictitious (some forms of public interest lawyering, especially class actions). Clients should accept the lawyer's judgments on what is feasible and how to achieve that goal. Lawyers want to control the construction of "what happened" for consumption by other audiences (adversaries, decision-makers), insisting that clients provide them with full accounts and complete records but retaining the skeptic's privilege of disbelief. (Sometimes lawyers prefer to preserve a strategic ignorance of what happened so that they are not implicated in client concealment and duplicity; see Mann [1985].) Although many lawyers send clients copies of ongoing correspondence and legal documents, their goal is less to keep clients informed than to protect themselves against recriminations and possible malpractice liability. It is the lawyer who constructs the narrative of "what's happening." Lawyers want respect—for themselves, if not for the legal system. Sarat and Felstiner (1986) describe lawyers seeking to enhance their own skills in the eyes of their clients by insisting on the arbitrariness and irrationality of most legal decisions, the unscrupulousness of opposing counsel, and the incompetence of judges. This contributes to the client's satisfaction with the lawyer (if it erodes public confidence in the legal system) and simultaneously constructs an excuse if the outcome is unsatisfactory. Both strategies seek to encourage clients to return and to refer others. Most of all, lawyers want clients to pay their bills. It is not being unduly cynical to interpret significant elements of lawyer behavior in this light: private criminal defense lawyers rely on the cooperation of judges and prosecutors to make a routine plea bargain appear to be a hard-won victory deserving a high fee; plaintiffs' personal injury lawyers may falsely report a low offer in order to return to the client with the "good news" that aggresive negotiation has persuaded the tortfeasor to raise it to an acceptable level—the real amount originally offered (Rosenthal, 1974: 110–112). In the course of a commercial lawsuit, one partner said to another: "Always give the client a bill when you've done something well for them" (Flood, 1986: 39).

LAWYERS AND FUNCTIONAL ALTERNATIVES

In considering whether lawyers tip the balance in adversarial relationships, what they actually do for clients, and how they and their clients perceive and structure the relationship, we have tacitly assumed that *lawyers* are acting for clients. However, others may be doing so: people with legal training who have not qualified to appear in court (German Syndici, French conseils juridiques and juristes d'entreprise, Japanese law graduates who do not pass the entrance examination for the Institute of Legal Training and Research, employed English barristers), people with other forms of expertise (accountants, architects in construction disputes, real estate brokers, bankers), and people with no special competence (employers, fellow workers, friends). Moreover, parties frequently take legal action on their own, without any advice or representation.

We can imagine various reasons why the identity of the representative might make a difference: technical knowledge, participation in networks, socialization in values, membership in a professional association, subordination to ethical rules and disciplinary procedures, the "independence" allegedly protected by fee-for-service arrangements, the structure of law firms, social or cultural background, and so on. One way to test it would be to reverse a strategy proposed earlier. Rather than taking a structural category (private law practice) as a constant and examining all the functions its members perform, we could hold the function constant and compare the way it is performed by various actors. In doing so, it is important not to give conceptual priority to lawyers: they are as much "functional alternatives" to other roles (whom they seek to supplant) as lay competitors are "functional alternatives" invading the lawyers' market. Some of the pairs could be found within a single legal system, but cross-national comparison would greatly increase the power of the analysis. The following are only a few examples of this line of inquiry.

1. Corporate middle managers often are legally trained. This is particularly true in Europe and Latin America, where law traditionally has been one of the most popular undergraduate degrees but few law graduates complete the additional professional studies, apprenticeship, and examination necessary to practice privately or enter the magistracy. It also is true in Japan, where many undergraduates study law but few take or pass the rigorous examination for the Institute of Legal Training and Research, which alone qualifies for private practice and the magistracy. In the United States, by contrast, most law graduates take and pass the bar examination and enter practice; only a few of the less than 10 percent who join offices of house counsel are likely to rise to upper management. We could compare the management styles of those with and without legal training and practice experience. This would be particularly challenging in light of the common allegation that American business, whose managers are less likely to be legally trained, is more legalistic. The comparison is very timely because those with legal training increasingly are being challenged—in Europe and Latin America as well as the United States—by technocrats trained in economics and business who, unlike many lawyers, are both numerate and computer literate.

2. A similar comparison could be made within the higher civil service. Once again, law graduates are prominently represented in Europe, Latin America, and Japan but considerably less common in the United States, whose civil service offers much lower material rewards and prestige (particularly compared to private practice). In the very highest policy-making positions, however, these proportions may be reversed. Private practitioners on leave of absence from large firms often hold cabinet posts in the United States; this seems quite uncommon elsewhere.

3. Many have commented on the fact that lawyers dominate political life at certain times and places. The United States is the preeminent example; elsewhere the proportion of lawyers in the executive and legislative branches appears to have shrunk in recent years. Yet researchers have been

unable to find significant differences between the behavior of those with and without legal training or practice experience. Thus, legal qualifications may be more relevant to questions of social mobility and recruitment to political careers than to those of political style.

4. In most countries, the judiciary is confined to those with formal legal qualifications. Yet it might be possible to make two kinds of comparisons within this role as well.

First, the judiciary is a lifetime career in civil law countries, but in common law countries it generally follows a successful career in private practice (less often as a prosecutor or legal academic). We could compare judges in terms of their previous legal experience, although it would be hard to hold other variables constant. Second, laypersons often perform roles similar to those of the lower levels of the judiciary, either as formally recognized lay magistrates (justices of the peace in England, for instance) or as functional equivalents (police chiefs in Brazil, labor arbitrators in the United States, and the host of alternatives fostered by the "alternative dispute resolution" movement). Here, both formal education and previous experience diverge and might influence styles of adjudication.

5. Thus far we have been suggesting comparisons of actors performing similar institutional roles. Another approach is to begin with particular legal problems, consider who handles them, and explore how their behavioral styles differ. In most instances, the lawyer performing the role is in private practice.

a. The transfer of title to land is an obvious example. In England one could compare solicitors (who long have enjoyed a monopoly), estate agents, chartered surveyors, building societies (i.e., mortgage lenders), and the new category of licensed conveyancer. In the United States, lawyers retain a monopoly in some states but have lost it to real estate and escrow agents in others. Similar comparisons could be made across Australian states. And, of course, notaries dominate the role in civil law countries. Finally, it might be useful to study the behavior of government employees in systems where land registration is well developed. The comparison might even be extended to anthropological accounts of preliterate societies in which elders preserve an oral history of land transactions, frequently celebrated by elaborate communal ritual. The transmission of property at death is another area where a multiplicity of private individuals and public employees play varied roles in different societies. Lawyers often compete with laypersons and scientists in filing patents and defending them against infringement (Van Zyl Smit, 1985).

b. Lawyers retain a monopoly over divorce in most countries. Comparisons between salaried legal aid lawyers and private practitioners—and, among the latter, between those paid by state funds and those paid by their clients—are feasible, however. In some American states and in Japan, couples often conduct their own divorces with little or no assistance from lawyers. Mediators, both lawyers and those without legal training, play an expanding role in divorce proceedings. Also, in countries where religion (both Catholicism and Islam) dominates family relations, clerics may play the central role.

c. A broad range of advisers and representatives may be involved in the legal response to personal injury. Lawyers dominate this field in the United States (although even there they are less prominent in workplace accidents). Insurance claims adjusters also play an important role. So do union officials, shop stewards, physicians, and police officers. In countries with highly developed compensation systems, such as New Zealand, civil servants and insurance company employees are the central actors. Even where private law continues to apply, large insurance companies may be able to mobilize data processing techniques to substitute clerks for fully qualified lawyers (Hartmann, 1988).

d. A last example—a frequent battlefield between professions—is tax advice, where lawyers compete not only with accountants but also with the relatively unskilled employees of national tax advice services. Furthermore, the taxing authority itself necessarily participates in giving advice. These comparisons could be generalized to advice on other subjects, such as immigration, consumer complaints, and landlord–tenant disputes.

6. A third strategy would limit comparison to those with the same formal legal credentials, focusing on contrasts within the group, according to four basic sets of variables:

a. Personal ascribed characteristics: gender, race, ethnicity, religion, class, and age. It has been suggested that women lawyers behave differently from men lawyers for a variety of reasons, including childhood socialization, continued disadvantage within the profession, divergent ambitions, and disproportionate housekeeping and childrearing obligations. Lawyers from minority ethnic, religious, or racial groups or working-class families may pursue different legal careers and display greater sensitivity to clients from similar backgrounds. Lawyer behavior may vary with age, either because of maturation or differences between entering cohorts.

b. Professional socialization. We could explore the effects of formal education by comparing the (dwindling number) of English or Australian lawyers without a law degree to those with one, solicitors without any university degree to those with one, and graduates of law schools at different levels of the status hierarchy (traditional Oxbridge versus more experimental faculties, or university versus polytechnic in England; elite, regional, local, and unaccredited in California). We could consider the consequences of different pedagogic techniques—lectures versus discussions, oral presentation versus writing, classroom versus clinic, doctrinal exegesis versus contextualization and social science—and of different kinds and lengths of apprenticeship. We could study the effects of experience: between English barristers and solicitors (who perform overlapping functions), or among American lawyers, who often move laterally across the roles of private practice (and between firms of different sizes), corporate counsel, civil servant, prosecutor, legal aid lawyer, academic, and judge during a single career.

c. The environment within which lawyers work. Much of the ideological preoccupation with lawyer "independence" presupposes that the structure of practice influences behavior. Such an assumption underlies the divided profession in England, limitations on rights of audience in civil law countries, and concern about the size and bureaucratization of productive units in the United States. These beliefs should be tested empirically by comparing the behavior of English barristers and solicitors, employed lawyers and those in private practice, lawyers employed by government and by private enterprise, lawyers paid by clients and by third parties (government, insurance), private practitioners in firms of various sizes and structures, lawyers in law firms and in multiservice firms (that advise on accounting, finance, and management as well as law), salaried lawyers in firms and profit-sharing partners, and similar pairs. It also would be interesting to know whether lawyers who represent only one category of adversary behave differently from those who represent both, comparing barristers who shift between criminal prosecution and defense briefs, for instance, with those who specialize in one side.

d. That amorphous concept "legal culture." Many observers have argued that lawyer behavior is influenced by notions of legality, rights, conflict, authority, and justice that are widely shared within a given culture but significantly different between cultures. We might be able to study this by looking at the ways in which lawyers in different cultures (regional, national, or subnational) defined and responded to similar problems, such as injuries (thalidomide, asbestos, Chernobyl), government regulation, multinational business transactions, and so on.

We do not mean to minimize the difficulty of making these comparisons: legal systems differ in many ways other than their personnel, and within a single legal system long-standing battles over turf have curtailed the number of markets in which lawyers and others perform similar functions. Nevertheless, the questions have great significance, both theoretical (are there distinctively legal behavioral styles) and practical (are the professional monopolies justified, what kinds of entry policies and training produce what results).

WHAT DO LAWYERS KNOW?

Having discussed what lawyers do for (or in relation to) their clients and whether it makes any difference that lawyers (rather than other specialists) perform these tasks, we can turn to lawyers' knowledge. Knowledge, or expertise, is treated by sociologists as a principal warrant of professional authority; however, its importance is not limited to academic observers. In social life a central reason for seeking help from members of one discipline rather than another is what they know. We distinguish occupations on that basis and in terms of the training and qualifications that are supposed to guarantee expertise. Qualifications and training, as Freidson (1986) shows, are also what allow occupations to claim monopolies over certain activities or titles, even though we may be skeptical as to whether such credentials deliver the expertise they promise. Furthermore, expertise is part of the self-image of many professions; this is particularly true of lawyers, who have seen themselves as a "learned" profession (although this self-conception varies across time and place). The previous section shows that any plausible description of what lawyers do must refer to their knowledge—of law, of influential people, and of technical procedures. The knowledge they use appears to influence the organization of practice. Indeed, increasing specialization confirms this. Finally, Bourdieu (1987: 828) suggests that the social space of the legal system—what he calls "judicial space"—is established by the division between those who do and do not have certain competences: "the technical mastery of a sophisticated body of knowledge that often runs contrary to the simple counsels of common sense."

These varying arguments show that we should be cautious about how we describe lawyers' knowledge. It is tempting to speak of lawyers using knowledge to deal with their clients' problems. However, this approach may make unwarranted assumptions, which we can best illustrate by contrasting two polar views of the world in which lawyers act.

According to one view, knowledge is about objects (statutes, decisions, rules, and practices), and professionals simply possess that knowledge (or are ignorant—as when they commit malpractice). Professionals make their knowledge available, and clients choose the appropriate professional for the specific problem. What is known is defined by membership in the profession.

From the opposite perspective, everything is process.[1] There are statutes and decisions (although not rules, which are more inflexible). But what lawyers know is a set of skills in using statutes and decisions to produce desired results, or how to devise mechanisms (for example, corporate forms) appropriate for given ends. These skills are not merely attributes of the profession, which predate any client contact; rather, particular professionals develop them in the service of, and in order to attract, particular clients (Dezalay, 1986, 1987). Skills are constructed in response to competition among members of a single profession and also between professions, as they assert that they can and should deal with certain kinds of situations. When lawyers advocate the values of legality, they simultaneously are insisting on their own involvement in certain kinds of problems—and this, indeed, may be one of their purposes, if often unconscious (on the ideology of legalism, see Arthurs [1985]). From this second perspective, the first may be no more than an ideology. Even if we cannot uncritically accept professionals' own definitions of "knowledge" and "problems," however, it does not follow that they know nothing or that no one benefits from their help (Illich et al., 1977).

It is not easy to disentangle expertise from the moral claims of professionalism: concern for the public interest or the client, altruism or disinterest. These warrants are clearly distinct as ideal types, although professions often present moral issues as though they permitted purely technical solutions (to which professionals alone are privy).[2] However, professional "knowledge" ranges from uncontrovertible expertise through matters about which professionals have more practical experience than laypersons to problems that are connected with professional work only indirectly, if at all. Whether the knowledge that professionals are mobilizing is relevant or reviewable is itself a moral rather than an empirical question.

Both the actions of individual professionals and the pronouncements of professional associations raise questions about the nature and source of their authority.[3] Halliday (1987) has described some of the problems confronting associations. When individual practitioners make decisions guided by experience (rather than dictated by rules), it often is difficult to distinguish knowledge and judgment from a willingness to assert or accept moral responsibility for the decision. These are the situations in which professionals, uncertain about both diagnosis and prescription, must exercise discretion: the decision as to whether to have an accused client testify, or the "informed, firsthand guess that the case is a possible, even if a statistically improbable, exception," or "individual situational judgment" (Freidson, 1986: 215–216).

Rueschemeyer's analysis (1964, 1973: 22 ff.) offers a valuable starting point. Because lawyers' knowledge concerns human actions and intentions, it is subject to deliberate change and reinterpretation. Because it concerns areas of social life about which there is moral disagreement, often severe, it is seen as representing particular interests rather than the public good.[4] Medical knowledge commands greater authority in part because medical practice rests on a body of scientific knowledge and in part because health is a universally accepted value about whose content there is substantial agreement.[5] To the extent that legal knowledge consists of skills such as negotiation or factual analysis, the gap in expertise between lawyers and clients may be quite small, and clients may come to see lawyers as unnecessary and even counterproductive (Macaulay, 1963). Such distinctions may also have the opposite effect. Spangler (1986: 184–185) points out that legal knowledge cannot be standardized because it is "cultural"; this indeterminacy may increase the professional's freedom from external control, whether exercised by an employer or a client.

Halliday (1985, 1987: chap. 2) has analyzed the authority of professions in terms of the epistemological bases of their knowledge and the institutional loci of their collective activity. Although he distinguishes between scientific and normative bases, he notes that they represent the ends of a continuum and tend to merge in ordinary practice.[6] They appear in pure form only when professions seek to justify their claim to authority (often in response to external challenges). Lawyers "point to the law finding of judges and the law making of legislatures," which Halliday characterizes as a normative activity. The more normative the epistemological core of professional knowledge, the more readily the profession will be able to exercise moral authority in the name of expertise (1987: 40). Its claim to authority will be greatest in its primary institutional locus—courts, in the case of the legal profession.

We do not deny that some lawyers and legal professions enjoy moral authority, even though it is difficult to exercise in modern, pluralistic, nondeferential societies. However, we are skeptical as to whether that authority rests on the grounds Halliday advances. Consider a counterhypothesis: because the legal profession operates in such an obviously normative domain, it will have to *restrain* its claims to moral authority to avoid appearing absurdly overweening. Just as the legal profession may limit its activities in order to preserve its autonomy, so it may acknowledge a more modest role for legal knowledge and judgment in order to protect itself from attack within those boundaries.[7] This may help to explain the plausible hypothesis (which merits further investigation) that practicing lawyers are positivists about the law (if often un-self-consciously) and generally deny that they are involved in a normative activity. They may wish to claim technical expertise but will be reluctant to make broader normative claims, although they may have difficulty distinguishing between positions they advocate on behalf of clients and their personal views about what the law is or ought to be.

Academic jurisprudence long has emphasized the leeway within adjudication for moral or political judgments, and some observers even have maintained that moral judgment is an integral part of adjudication. Similarly, sociologists studying legal activity (whether adjudication or daily law practice) may perceive the continued negotiation of reality that Dezalay posits. However, the nature of lawyers' authority is more likely to be structured by the interaction between their own understanding (or justification) of its basis and that of those who must acknowledge the authority. Although these understandings will vary between and within societies, we would expect lawyers and clients to treat law in most fields as relatively certain, adaptable only within narrow limits, and not subject to lawyer manipulation.[8] In some countries judges may believe they have some leeway in applying the law, but practitioners can do no more than seek change within boundaries that vary according to prevailing social attitudes and pressures and are influenced by the client's resources and time-horizon.[9]

Given all this, it is difficult to distinguish between the bases of authority that undergird science and law, as far as the experience of participants is concerned. If participants believe that there are limits on their authority, then those limits exist, and others who disregard them will be treated as deviant unless they produce arguments for change that fall within the accepted canons. Those who reject this account or criticize the arbitrariness of the system as a whole actually are denying that the profession possesses *any* authority, technical or moral.

Even so, two important differences still divide science and law. Lawyers produce new knowledge by changing the law, whereas scientists seek to discover new ways of understanding the natural world; and in each, authoritative interpretations are constituted by different social processes.

Let us begin by contrasting legal change and scientific discovery. These processes appear to be analogous, if very different, because each alters what is known. The law can change, especially through the partial diffusion of an innovation, without that change becoming widely known.[10] In science, by contrast, discovery implies that something has become known (or knowable) to all, and the rewards for priority strongly encourage diffusion. This difference is not accidental: the purpose of science is discovery; reputation is established not just by priority but also by validation through peer review. Most practicing lawyers, by contrast, rarely seek to change the law, although the interest of a particular client may be served by advancing new arguments or devising a novel legal instrument.[11]

Academic lawyers fall between these two extremes: their goal is to expand the discourse about law and, in doing so, to change it (on the tacit assumption that law is constructed through practice). However, they are sharply distinguished from scientists by the second difference between the two domains. In pure science, it is peers who evaluate whether an investigator deserves the success that confers "symbolic capital" (Bourdieu, 1976), which can be translated into position, command over resources, and possibly recognition of future achievements. Peers also validate the change in knowledge, according to generally accepted criteria. In law, change is both wrought and proclaimed by legislators, administrators, and judges. Credit for the innovation goes to official lawmakers, not the private lawyers who may have initiated the process, much less academic lawyers who provided the requisite intellectual framework.[12] Academic lawyers very occasionally validate the discovery of relevant facts by their peers; in the common law world the significant change is more likely to be a new conceptualization of the subject matter. If this is a new analysis of disputed legal provisions (as it usually is in the common law world), then judges have ultimate authority to validate or reject it. If it falls outside that area or if professors have more authority than judges (as they are said to have in civil law systems), there still may be no widely accepted criteria of validation.

Neither judges, practicing lawyers, nor legal academics have the same relationship to legal knowledge that successful scientists have to scientific knowledge. Does medicine offer a closer analogy? In light of Rueschemeyer's remarks, summarized earlier, this seems unlikely.[13] Some advances in medicine also are advances in science and are judged by the same criteria. Sometimes a novel treatment can be partially validated in a single case (as in some surgical procedures); and there are accepted protocols for testing the success of others.[14] The reputations of some physicians are based on their abilities to diagnose and treat individuals, which may correspond to the abilities of the trial lawyer. These do not increase formal or validated knowledge, but they are extremely important in practice. In some countries, the general public seems less aware of the reputations of individual lawyers than it used to be, although other lawyers still have strong opinions about their peers. Certainly law firms have reputations among business clients. High awards in personal injury cases or victories in well-publicized divorces attract new clients and may be associated with particular styles of advocacy. However, these legal strategies cannot be "tested" in the same way that scientific knowledge can be evaluated. Even when lawyers develop an institutional innovation, such as the "poison-pill" defense to hostile corporate takeovers (Powell, 1987), there is no peer system for assessing its efficacy. Although other lawyers may adopt it, courts will have the last word about its efficacy.[15]

In the long run, the structures and modes of validation have more influence on the social significance of different forms of professional knowledge than do their epistemological bases. The social context of legal knowledge might resemble that of science if those who created it also validated it; the German legal professoriate sometimes approaches this, as do academic international lawyers even in common law countries.[16] However, the legal profession generally is an exception to Freidson's (1986: 211) assertion that "unlike the crafts, professionals have been able to control technological innovation by having their own teacher-researchers to produce and legitimize new knowledge .... Their teacher-researchers control ... formal knowledge itself."[17]

Freidson (1986: 2) recently has elaborated a recurrent theme in the sociology of the professions, which associates their work and success with the relationship between their distinctive knowledge and both their daily practice and their exercise of influence: "it is necessary to understand how knowledge gets translated into action, which means understanding the human institutions that mediate between knowledge and power." Freidson is describing the institutionalization of formal knowledge in American society. Formalization is a process of theory formation or systematic reasoned explanation, the pervasive use of reason sustained, where possible, by measurement.[18]

Recent sociological writing on the professions strongly associates formal knowledge with the universities, where it is produced, taught, and validated; the prestige of higher learning is said to benefit professions. We question this association. In doing so, we continue to follow the lead of Freidson, who summarizes the basic thesis of his recent book in this fashion:

> the actual substance of the knowledge that is ultimately involved in influencing human activities is different from the formal knowledge that is asserted by academics and other authorities .... Down at the level of everyday human experience ... formal knowledge is transformed and modified by the activities of those participating in its use. (1986: xi)

Although we agree with much that Freidson says about firsthand experience and situational judgment and about the influence of the power, interest, and knowledge of clients on the selection of professional knowledge, we want to make problematic whether formal and practical knowledge are linked by the processes of transformation and modification. The practice of law mobilizes much knowledge that is neither situational judgment nor formal knowledge.

We consider the use of knowledge in legal practice at two levels. Some knowledge separates lawyers from laypersons, regardless of whether the lawyers know particular procedures, cases, or laws. Lawyers have a distinct way of thinking, which nonlawyers do not share. This point is made most strongly by Bourdieu (1987: 828 ff.), who interprets the restriction of the "judicial space" to those who know how to function within it as a means of separating it from the rest of social life in order to imbue its decisions with an aura of neutrality. Lawyers gain entry by their ability to distance themselves from ordinary common sense and ideas of fairness; they learn special techniques of reasoning and a "universalizing attitude" (ibid., 820). These and related skills are transmitted implicitly (ibid., 819 n. 25). Dezalay suggests that the emphasis on these skills, which can be learned at home or through apprenticeship, favors those raised in legal families, whereas anyone can learn rationalized or codified legal knowledge.[19]

Writers as different as Cain (1976) and Simpson (1973) also have emphasized that the coherence of legal practitioners owes more to convention than to knowledge of rules. In describing the shared understandings of common law judges before the emergence of formal rules of precedent, Simpson (1973) prefigures Bourdieu's remark (1987: 833) that the "predictability and calculability that Weber imputed to 'rational law' doubtless arise more than anything else from the consistency and homogeneity of the legal habitus."

At this more general level, what lawyers know is how to distance themselves from their clients and the world within which clients live, translating the latters' wishes into legal. language while purging their claims of emotion and particularity (Cain, 1979). These skills should not be confused with the formal knowledge they acquire in universities, even if in some countries the very formality of that knowledge enlarges the necessary social distance between the courts and the disputes they adjudicate.

In the remainder of this section we seek to specify the uses of knowledge in legal practice in order to determine whether it is a modified form of what is taught in universities, as Freidson suggests. We believe it is not—that practice has its own demands.[20] We draw exclusively on American, English, and French studies; in the spirit of the Working Group we seek to develop lines of inquiry that researchers can explore in other countries. Although there is some information about university teaching, we know little about the knowledge used in practice and even less about the relationship between the two. Finally, statements about the prestige or authority of a profession and its members and about the bases of that authority are inherently speculative.

Any comments on "formal" legal knowledge run the risk of undue attention to the American experience; but since our purpose is to trace the application of knowledge in legal practice, much of the literature is irrelevant. An obvious starting point would seem to be Weber's analysis of German legal thought, but he says little or nothing about the extent to which practitioners used the rationalized system he describes.[21] It would be fruitful to investigate the impact of academic scholarship on judicial decision-making, as in the English law of international trade or the widespread citation of law review articles by American judges. American lawyers who taught or wrote about poverty law starting in the 1960s presumably hoped to influence practice.[22] In these latter examples, however, academic lawyers were more likely to be analyzing particular issues than to be formalizing or rationalizing entire bodies of law, which is what interests Freidson.

We prefer to approach the topic more generally. The process of rationalization affects the totality of outcomes of the legal system, whereas practitioners are concerned with the interests of their clients.[23] These two perspectives may coincide by accident, but usually they will diverge and sometimes even conflict. If formalization begins with the immediate concerns of practitioners, academics who participate in the process may clash with colleagues more removed from practice,[24] especially in environments such as England, where academics only recently differentiated themselves from practitioners.[25] Dezalay (1986) describes the dilemma of labor lawyers who fear open identification with union interests.

Dezalay offers one view of the relations among practitioners, academics, and judges, which reveals how the process of formalization can shape the law without producing knowledge that is applied in practice. He sees academics and the higher judiciary engaged in a joint enterprise of purifying the law of social conflicts and ordinary language. By preserving their monopoly over legitimate interpretations, they can dismiss the unapproved innovations of practitioners as "so many marks of incompetence and error" (Dezalay, 1986: 101). By subordinating themselves to the legality thus produced, they can claim social neutrality and technical expertise (ibid., 102–103). Even this account does not fully support the sociological model described above, however, for rationalization is a *joint* activity of judges and academics rather than the sole domain of the latter. It also contrasts markedly with those (common law) countries where the judiciary alone validates the law and "purity" is not a legal virtue.

Dezalay believes that the creation of pure law as an autonomous sphere of knowledge enables the legal profession to distinguish its technical skills from those possessed by other functional specialists also engaged in symbolic mediation (just as Harry Arthurs [1985] saw lawyers in Victorian England promoting the ideology of legalism). From our Anglo-American viewpoint we argue, instead, that what legal professionals offer is "know-how" rather than formal knowledge. In support of this position we invoke not just the historical reliance of lawyers on apprenticeship as a mode of training but also their contemporary concern with competence and skills—what lawyers can *do* rather than what they *know*—and with pedagogical practices that can instill those skills.[26] A standard contemporary definition of competence renders legal knowledge only one of several elements (ALI-ABA, 1981: 56). Nor is "know-how" reducible to "knowledge-in-action," the skills of a tightrope walker, which do not consist "in rules or plans which we entertain in the mind prior to action" (Schon, 1983: 50–51).[27] Karpik (1985: 574) describes the way in which the domains of law form a solid and precise language for French avocats. Each delimits an ensemble of knowledge and know-how ("de savoirs et de savoir-faire") and is associated with particular courts and tribunals as well as clients: "habiletés, instances et clientèles [skills, jurisdictions, and clienteles]." These are not generalized skills but techniques developed and deployed in particular, recurrent contexts.

Recent research on lawyers' work in England and the United States coincides with the elaboration by Galanter and others of a framework for analyzing the civil litigation process.[28] They describe a world in which participants have clearly defined goals for whose attainment they use, or threaten to use, legal provisions and procedures. Participants seek and obtain endowments not only from legal rules but also from all the direct and indirect consequences of the legal system, including its institutional and processual characteristics. The effects are particularly diffuse in nego-tiations, where participants can compensate for weakness in one area by invoking strengths in another that may be legally unrelated. In the United States, for instance, defense counsel may seek to frustrate a criminal pro-secution or obtain a reduced sentence by demanding or threatening the disclosure of information the government fears may be harmful to national security.[29] The emergence of such strategies requires lawyers to mobilize a range of expertise that transcends the knowledge of legal rules and advocacy skills; a prosecutor may have to develop a new response to such threats.[30]

This research combines the methods of participant observation, inter-views, and questionnaires (Flood, 1986; Ingleby, 1988; Sarat & Felstiner, 1986; Griffiths, 1986; Genn, 1987; Mann, 1985; Erlanger et al., 1987). Mann characterizes the essence of the defense function in white-collar crime as information control and explores the numerous factors affecting the degree of control an attorney can exercise (1985: 231–240). He dis-cusses the extent to which evidence is exposed for government use, ambiguities in the definition of crime, uncertainty in sentencing practices, the relevance of client resources, agency precharge review, investigatory procedures, and the prosecutorial standard for indictment. Each of these creates endowments available to defense attorneys.

This enlarged picture of legal practice reveals numerous diverse oppor-tunities for creating innovative forms of legal expertise, and lawyers have taken full advantage.[31] First, there is the emergence of white-collar criminal defense as a specialty (Mann, 1985: 21 ff.). Such clients previously had been an insignificant component of a general trial practice; now lawyers are leaving the U.S. Attorney's office and joining or setting up small specialty firms or white-collar defense departments within larger firms. If older lawyers continue to believe that general trial experience is more useful than prosecutorial experience, younger lawyers who present them-selves as specialists are expressing "a real professional identity, although such statements are also something of an advertising strategy" (Mann, 1985: 24). Mann's invocation of the market reinforces Dezalay's reference to "la promotion d'un produit juridique, plus performant, mieux adapté aux besoins d'une clientèle potentielle [the promotion of a juridical product, more efficacious and better adapted to the needs of a potential clientele]" (1987: 5). It is no accident, according to Dezalay, that such innovations have been developed in tax and business law, where both the monetary amounts at stake and the client resources stimulate the imagination of jurists more effectively than they do in the fields of divorce or juvenile delinquency.[32]

The divergent views about the appropriate background for white-collar criminal defense lawyers conceal a number of debates about the value of different experiences and the benefits they confer. Those with experience as prosecutors emphasize the importance of knowing and being known by their former colleagues, although they are deliberately vague about the advantages that such knowledge confers.[33] More generally, Mann praises the high standard of practice in the U.S. Attorney's Office in the Southern District of New York (1985: 20). Those who assert the importance of general trial experience seek to project a very different image of both the work and the kind of person best qualified to perform it, which may correspond to an ideology of legal practice as well as to the material interests of those advancing this viewpoint.

Because Mann starts from the assumption that those charged with white-collar crimes are guilty of something, he sees the goal of the defense attorney as using both rights and ambiguities to control the information available to the prosecution. The problem of expertise, therefore, is not simply whether it is being used effectively on behalf of the client (the critique of many who accuse professionals of failing to meet their side of the "bargain") but also whether its use is consistent with the broader social interests underlying the criminal law. Mann deplores the "mistakes" and "incompetence" of defense counsel who unintentionally or negligently disclose inculpatory evidence about their clients (1985: 83). All the skills that Mann describes concern information control. Thus, when he speaks of the "refined" analytic skills an accountant brings to the review and presentation of financial records, this is simply another form of expertise needed by defense counsel (although lawyers may prefer to buy it from another profession rather than acquire it themselves). The purpose is to determine whether the client's records contain material that might arouse suspicion or demand explanation, thereby affecting the relationship between client, defense counsel, and prosecutor.

Sometimes the lawyer's knowledge is unsurprising and uncontroversial— for instance, that IRS review procedures exclude an agent who already has formed an opinion about the case (Mann, 1985: 190–191). Similarly, lawyers develop skill in portraying their clients as innocent—or at least in convincing prosecutors that they cannot prove the client is guilty (ibid., 192). Knowledge of government record-keeping practices and skill at using the Freedom of Information Act prompt more ambiguous strategies. Most lawyers would see nothing wrong with a colleague's attempt to obtain an IRS report acknowledging that it was customary for members of a particular industry not to report certain transactions and acquiescing in this practice; and they would approve the lawyer's use of the report to argue against prosecution for such nonreporting. Knowledge that the IRS was unable to verify tax returns against bank records of interest paid also is clearly helpful to clients; but few Americans may believe that that law schools ought to teach such things. Lawyers employ even more questionable skills in seeking to neutralize, overlook, or suppress information from the client about past—or, even worse, continuing—criminality (ibid., 113).

It is difficult to construct an account of these various kinds of knowledge, mistake, or incompetence that omits all reference to the values underlying the legal system and lawyers. Clearly knowledge and expertise cannot be understood without regard to purposes.[34] This is true not only about "knowing how" but also about "knowing that." Knowing the content of particular statutes and decisions, for instance, is socially irrelevant without knowing how to use them to formulate rules; and knowing those rules can only mean knowing how to apply them to particular facts and to plan actions on that basis.

Genn's (1987) work on the settlement process in personal injury cases in England describes the imbalance between the parties to litigation. She shows how the inevitable and desirable flexibility within tort law can create ambiguities or uncertainties that will be exploited by the party with greater resources and smaller stakes. Some of the plaintiff's disadvantage can be offset if the plaintiff's lawyer prepares with sufficient thoroughness to make credible the threat to go to trial, in order to maximize the defendant's settlement offer. The principal division among plaintiff's personal injury lawyers in England, therefore, is between those with extensive trial experience, some of whom adopt uncooperative and aggressive attitudes, and inexperienced litigators, who associate settlement with maintaining a "reasonable" and cooperative relationship with insurance company representatives.[35]

Here, again, the knowledge and skills are specific to the divergent goals of plaintiffs and defendants. Although both need to know changes in court procedure and recent decisions and settlements (particularly the amount of general damages), even this latter information is subject to construction. Insurance representatives try to get low awards reported and use their continuing relations with local solicitors (whom they retain in individual cases) to obtain access to such information; this behavior, in turn, becomes a useful piece of knowledge for those representing plaintiffs. Road accidents rarely involve complicated legal issues, and even the law of factory accidents can be learned quickly. Nevertheless, experience enhances the competence of litigators, encouraging them to reject inadequate settlement offers from insurance representatives, who readily identify ignorance and inexperience in an adversary (Genn, 1987: 131–133). The relevant skills involve preparation for trial, full investigation, and contacts with the right physicians (a variation on the theme that the important thing in law practice is "who you know, not what you know"). They also include the capacity to evaluate an adversary in face-to-face interaction in order to find out what the other side knows and to evaluate its bargaining position.

Genn quotes one solicitor who prefers to take a "reasonable" attitude as saying that, above some threshhold, "as long as the client is happy and is satisfied, then I think that probably is the correct measure of damages" (1987: 136). If one assumes that the lawyer's aim should be to maximize damages, then such a lawyer is incompetent. However, if the situation has been explained to the client, then such an approach may simply reflect the client's aversion to risk or stress. Some may feel that the lawyer is obligated to take responsibility away from the client and encourage continued litigation, but such a decision may be inconsistent with the lawyer's own personality and may also constitute unwarranted paternalism toward the client. This brief discussion again suggests that skill and competence can be evaluated only in terms of the purpose of a lawyer's services.[36]

While Genn and Mann are describing negotiations in the shadow of indictment or adjudication (Mnookin & Kornhauser, 1979; Erlanger et al., 1987), Flood (1986) observed commercial practice, where litigation is regarded as "on another plane" from negotiation. In one instance, legal advisers kept a low profile in order to preserve the informal relationship between their client and his employer; nevertheless, they drafted a letter for him, which was construed as a resignation, with fatal consequences for their client's continuing employment. Such mistakes indicate the complexity of the possibilities a lawyer must anticipate and may represent a mirror image of lawyerly skills. In another example the lawyer sought to obtain the best terms for a loan to his client by making a demand on the lender that could be relinquished in exchange for another, more important provision. Since this is a standard negotiating technique, we can see that some relevant skills are not peculiar to lawyers, even if lawyers employ them in situations where other forms of legal knowledge also are essential. Flood describes other skills in the realm of intraoffice behavior, which lead him to characterize lawyers' work as "not just the accomplishing of a set purpose for the client, but a political endeavor" (1986: 106).

Bosk (1987) emphasized the difference between public and private knowledge and urged us to consider what gets hidden. We might classify special techniques as private knowledge; the strategies for neutralizing inconvenient knowledge (described by Mann) and for maintaining one's intraoffice position (described by Flood) well illustrate the category of "hidden" knowledge. The latter are important because they reveal the lack of congruence between lawyers' public self-presentation and the realities of practice.[37]

A next step in studies of formal and applied knowledge would be to develop analytic tools analogous to the notions of diagnosis and prescription in medicine. These are folk as well as analytic concepts, and the absence of obvious equivalents in law is itself a matter of interest. At the same time, we should be cautious about using a catalog of lawyers' skills as a source of insight into the bases of their authority (individual or collective), since that authority depends on the degree to which others (including clients) perceive and value these skills and the ways in which they are transmuted into reputation among colleagues or within the wider community.[38] Just as the diffusion of knowledge among lawyers is a fruitful approach, so we urge research on the construction of lawyer reputations (Heinz & Laumann, 1982).[39]

CONCLUSION

The research agenda proposed above is extremely ambitious. The questions are broad; they call for comparisons across occupations, national boundaries, and historical periods; the theoretical and conceptual frameworks require further elaboration; and there are serious methodological obstacles to studying lawyers at work. Furthermore, many investigators undoubtedly will wish to continue pursuing the more traditional questions posed by the sociology of occupations. These are particularly timely because lawyers in many countries are encountering profound challenges to their professional hegemony—from other occupations, the revolution in information technology, large multidisciplinary service firms, and foreign competitors.

However, we believe that it is equally important to return to the questions that originally made the sociology of lawyers a central element of the sociology of law. If law is deeply implicated in politics (modes of governance and challenges to authority), economics (collective activity and exchange), society (interpersonal relationships), and culture (concepts of justice and attitudes toward conflict), then lawyers may play a central role in mediating this interaction. It is important to understand the different legal professions different societies produce and the ways those professions both sustain and change their societies. What, for instance, is the connection between the things a society values and where value is concentrated, on one hand, and the role of lawyers in acquiring and defending that value on the other hand? The balance of advantage—political, economic, social, and cultural—is a constant preoccupation of sociology of law, as of all social science. What do lawyers contribute to preserving or redressing inequality and hierarchy? Professional ideology, often formalized in ethical codes, prescribes how lawyers ought to behave. The roots of sociology of law lie in the recognition that formal law never is an adequate account of behavior, even that of legal officials. A vital inquiry thus becomes what lawyers actually do for their clients and employers (public and private), how this is shaped by lawyer–client and employment relationships, and what difference it makes that *lawyers* are doing these things. Another strand of sociology of law derives from jurisprudential concerns with the nature of legal reasoning. However, whereas philosophers typically address only a single element of professional thought processes—the polished final product embodied in appellate judicial decisions or legislative codes—sociologists must encompass the entire range of legal thought, the ways in which it is produced and validated, and relationships among the different forms as exhibited by law students, legal scholars and educators, private practitioners, laypersons, clients, and government officials (administrators, police, welfare officers), as well as judges and lawmakers. Sociologists also must examine the extent to which technical legal expertise confers moral and political authority, by contrasting it with other forms of knowledge—scientific, medical, economic, and religious.

By considering what distinguishes *law*yers from other professionals rather than the traits that *lawyers* share with other workers, we will advance the broader ambitions of the sociology of law.

NOTES

An earlier version of this chapter was presented to the Working Group for Comparative Study of Legal Professions at the annual conference of the Law and Society Association in Vail, Colorado in June 1988. We are grateful for the comments of Terence Halliday, Yves Dezalay, Elizabeth Mertz, and Michael Powell and others who attended that panel. Richard Abel wrote the first two sections; Philip Lewis wrote the third. Richard Abel wishes to thank the UCLA Law School Dean's Fund, which supported his work on this chapter.

1. What follows is a schematic account of important recent discussions by Dezalay (1986, 1987) and Arthurs (1985); we also have been stimulated by some quotations in Mann (1985: 142).

2. Physicians are notorious for expressing views on health-related matters that exceed their technical expertise. They may do so partly because they must live with the consequences of, say, rationing health care or failing to distribute clean needles to drug addicts. Even though they may not seek to exercise moral authority, the influence they wield remains a moral question.

3. A lawyer's authority may vary greatly with the context. Clients may consult particular lawyers because they view them as experts on litigation strategy; however, they may *not* regard them as experts when the issue is law reform, even in the same substantive area, perhaps because they believe that the lawyers are too closely associated with special interests.

4. The authority of knowledge may be more open to challenge the broader the social domain it affects. Preventive public health always has been more hotly contested than the treatment of particular patients. Law generally claims to influence a wider slice of social life than does medicine.

5. Hartmann (1988) points out that because law lacks scientifically founded systematics its partial sectors can often be mastered separately, which facilitates outside competition. This observation is important, but we cannot pursue it here.

6. In trying to respond to Halliday's arguments about the contrast between the scientific and normative bases of professional authority we have focused on scientists, physicians, and lawyers, excluding the clergy and the military. Perhaps we should have compared lawyers with accountants, tax advisors, and business consultants—occupations whose fields of expertise overlap with that of lawyers and who compete with lawyers. A satisfactory account would have to be grounded in the histories of each particular occupation, however, a task we cannot undertake at this stage.

7. Thus, the English Law Commission generally confined itself to the reform of "lawyers' law," whereas its Canadian counterpart undertook a far wider range of tasks.

Dezalay offers a fuller expression of this view:

ces nouveaux grands prêtres n'échappent pas plus que leurs prédécesseurs aux règles du jeu de tout champ symbolique qui imposent aux producteurs quels qu'ils soient—prêtres, juristes, experts, savants—de limiter leurs propres ambitions pour produire la croyance sans laquelle leur pouvoir s'effondre, d'autodiscipliner l'exercice de la pouvoir pour le faire accepter comme légitime par ceux aux dépens de qui il s'exerce [these new high priests who, no more than their predecessors, can escape from the rules of the game in all symbolic fields, which require the producers, whoever they are—priests, jurists, experts, scholars—to limit their own ambitions in order to inspire the belief without which their power collapses, to discipline the exercise of their power in order to ensure its legitimacy among those on whom its exercise depends]. (1987: 9; see also 1986: 91)

Both Church of England and American Catholic bishops recently have been criticized for expressing views on economic policy.

8. According to Sarat and Felstiner (1986), however, American divorce lawyers present the law to their clients as radically uncertain and arbitrary.

9. Even lawyers who emphasize the manipulability of law (e.g., an informant quoted by Mann [1985: 142]) acknowledged that there are limits on the likelihood of success, although these are not sufficient to deprive them of the normative freedom they seek.

10. Once decisions have been reported, they become known fairly quickly, especially in those countries where they are available electronically (although dissemination may be much slower in countries with less advanced technology). However, there is no systematic way to disseminate innovations in drafting even

after they gain legal acceptance. Powell (1987), however, describes the speedy diffusion of knowledge about the "poison pill" device to inhibit hostile takeovers; in this case the field was specialized enough to have a press of its own, and the device needed to be publicized in order to be effective.

11. A few lawyers specialize in changing the law: lobbyists, law reform commissioners, legislative drafters, public interest lawyers, and house counsel for trade associations and other collective interests.

12. In England, statutes previously were named after those who carried them through Parliament; that remains true in the United States and, to some extent, in France. Collegial decision-making reduces the degree to which the idiosyncracies of judges are known in civil law countries.

13. For the view that academic lawyers are to "practitioners of the art of law" what biologists are to physicians, see Duguit, cited in Dezalay (1986: 105 n. 7).

14. In medicine, publication may credit an innovation to a particular practitioner or group; it is very unusual for legal innovations to be similarly credited (even if English legal historians know who invented "trustees to preserve contingent remainders" in the seventeenth century).

15. Many tax-avoidance schemes sold in England in the late 1970s failed as a result of later court decisions. It would seem artificial to regard them as having passed an initial peer review but failing a later, more rigorous test, since there is no agreed testing method other than court approval. Cures for physical ailments do not need the validation of scientific testing if the patient believes they work, but taxes rarely can be avoided without satisfying a court.

16. Self-validation cannot guarantee success, but it may strengthen the successful (and its absence may weaken those who are failing). Might this be illustrated by the changing fortunes of fundamentalist and established religions?

17. This chapter emphasizes those elements in legal practice favoring the traditional view among common lawyers that everything a practitioner should know can be learned on the job and that university legal education is superfluous. Even now the English Bar examinations are being changed to emphasize practical needs. Young German Anwälte complain of the lack of practical training (Hommerich, 1988).

18. Freidson is referring to processes that start from particular experience and move toward formality; the historical claim of the professions, by contrast, is that they use their special knowledge to order particular experience. Freidson is describing the nature of formal knowledge, not its relation to professional work (although each may influence the other).

19. Dezalay's comments were made at the meetings of the Research Committee on Sociology of Law and the Law and Society Association in May and June 1988. The European Economic Community intends to allow legal professionals qualified in one country to practice in another once they have passed the latter's examination. This will certainly diminish the significance of the uncodified skills possessed by lawyers.

20. In a personal communication, Eliot Freidson has suggested that the more closely one views professional practice, the less connected to formal knowledge it appears. He cites Latour and Woolgar, who refer to the "craft practice" and "craftwork" of scientists (1979: 166, 257). For a similar contrast between formal and informal accounts of scientific research, see Gilbert and Mulkay (1984).

21. The use of economic theory by American judges may offer a contemporary parallel.

22. Activist lawyers may have chosen to become teachers for other reasons.

23. Even if a significant number of practitioners were motivated by self-interest or ideology, as sometimes is alleged, their objectives still are likely to be narrow compared to the ambitious goals of rationalization.

24. There also may be consequences for relative status: clinical legal education, by focusing on the poor, may seem less "academic" than courses on negotiation, whereas tax planning for the wealthy may enjoy the same status as a discussion of tax policy.

25. It may be relevant that civil procedure is still hardly a respectable subject in England.

26. The process view, which we mentioned earlier, emphasizes "knowing how" to argue about the law over "knowing that" the law has a specific content.

27. We owe this reference to John Flood, who has kindly allowed us to refer to his two unpublished papers on the rationality of lawyers.

28. The criminal process might also be described in similar terms, but no one has tried to do so. It is no accident that Mann (1985), who is discussing the criminal process, refers to none of the standard literature on the subject.

29. The American origins of this type of account, the newsworthiness of law in the United States, and the relative lack of professional inhibitions in litigation strategy suggest that the United States may be a special, and extreme, case. Yet, scholars in other countries have found this approach useful; furthermore, the tactical limitations that lawyers accept, and why they do so, seem to be important topics for comparative research.

30. "Prosecutor Who Knows How to Keep a Secret," New York Times, January 14, 1988.

31. Mann is able to describe white-collar criminal defense practice only because specialization produces recurrent and typical situations. His account is particularly valuable because it uncovers the orgins, method, and consequences of specialization.

32. Dezalay is speaking of particular innovations rather than subject matter specialization, but the association between expertise and market forces is the same (although he overlooks the innovation in salaried services for the poor). He regards the possibility of "homologation" (approval of a legal device) as more important than the resources of the clientele. Client resources are necessary, if not sufficient, however, for the strategies Mann describes (1985: 235–236); and since it is the attorney and his general skills that are being marketed, judicial approval

plays a lesser role. See, however, the reference to "Kovel" accountants (ibid., 62 ff.), who investigate on behalf of attorneys and whose work product was held privileged in *U.S. v. Kovel*, 296 F.2d 918 (2d Cir. 1961). Market control theories need to pay close attention to the difference between particular identifiable products, such as the poison-pill defense whose diffusion is traced by Powell (1987), and the generalized expertise of a defense attorney who may have to choose between strategies and techniques. While the former product is more "tangible"—to use a key, although unexplained, concept introduced by Larson (1977: 14), both receive much of their validation from practical success and none at all from systems of formal education.

33. Mann also refers to the advantages of being known to one's opponent as honest and trustworthy (1985: 77–79).

34. Williams (1983: 8) argues that the effectiveness of negotiation can be defined only if one considers the purposes and effects of the legal system as a whole and of the lawyers working within it.

35. In England, lawyers act regularly for trade union members and expect to be reimbursed by the union if the victim loses. Neither Genn (1987) nor Mann (1985) provides any evidence that lawyers compromise the interests of clients in order to maintain good relations with the adversaries with whom they deal (but see Rosenthal [1974] and Katz [1982]). Those whom Genn described as cooperative seemed to believe that they were advancing the interests of their clients, although such cooperation also reduced the time they had to spend on preparation. Genn did notice a tendency for solicitors not to apply for legal aid for eligible clients; legal aid is financially disadvantageous to the solicitor, although it usually improves the client's bargaining position. "Reasonableness" has a long and discreditable history in the context of legal aid for the poor (Katz, 1982). Macaulay (1979) has described it among Wisconsin consumer lawyers. Here, however, we are concerned with its relationship to experience and skill.

36. Garth (1983) suggests that pleas for greater competence actually amount to an attempt to encourage the expenditure of effort disproportionate to both the amount in dispute and any fee that could be obtained. More generally, all such value judgments can be seen as elements in intra- and interprofessional competition for the right to impose a view of appropriateness. Ingleby (1988) shows some of the ways in which solicitors perform the functions of mediators in divorce cases, even when the parties remain adversarial. His account is thoroughly contextualized, revealing how sensitive lawyers are to the impact of their actions on third parties, whether public authorities (in the areas of housing, welfare, and tax) or private lending institutions.

37. Dezalay has pointed out the tension between the absence of patent protection for legal innovations and the need for judicial homologation of their validity, which makes them publicly available. In the United States, some physicians have sought patents for innovative treatments.

38. Such outside judgments often are very general—for instance, that lawyers

know about claims for personal injury and are appropriate resources for this kind of problem. What lawyers are believed to know thus influences the problems that are presented to them as well as their individual or collective authority.

39. Have these mechanisms changed as professionals have grown less insistent (or less successful in persuading their audience) that they alone can judge each other? Has specialization allowed experience to serve as an indicator of ability? In this area, concentration on the American experience might be particularly misleading.

REFERENCES

Abel, Richard L. 1979. "The Rise of Capitalism and the Transformation of Disputing: From Confrontations over Honor to Competition for Property," 27 *UCLA Law Review* 223.

———. 1981. "Why Does the American Bar Association Promulgate Ethical Rules?" 59 *Texas Law Review* 639.

———. 1984. "Custom, Rules, Administration, Community," 28 *Journal of African Law* 6.

———. 1985*a*. "Law Without Politics: Legal Aid under Advanced Capitalism," 32 *UCLA Law Review* 474.

———, ed. 1985*b*. "Lawyers and the Power to Change," 7(1) *Law & Policy* (special issue).

American Law Institute–American Bar Association (ALI-ABA). 1981. *Enhancing the Competence of Lawyers: The Report on the Houston Conference.* Chicago: ALI-ABA Committee on Continuing Professional Education.

Arthurs, Harry W. 1985. *"Without the Law": Administrative Justice and Legal Pluralism in Nineteenth Century England.* Toronto: University of Toronto Press.

Ball, Howard. 1985. *Justice Downwind: America's Atomic Testing Program in the 1950s.* New York: Oxford University Press.

Barkan, Steven E. 1985. *Protesters on Trial: Criminal Justice in the Southern Civil Rights and Vietnam Antiwar Movements.* New Brunswick, N.J.: Rutgers University Press.

Black, Donald. 1976. *The Behavior of Law.* New York: Academic Press.

———. 1984. "Social Control as a Dependent Variable," in Donald Black, ed., *Toward a General Theory of Social Control,* vol. 1: *Fundamentals.* New York: Academic Press.

Blumberg, Abraham S. 1967. "The Practice of Law as a Confidence Game: Organizational Cooptation of a Profession," 1(2) *Law & Society Review* 15.

Bosk, Charles. 1987. Remarks delivered to the Working Group for Comparative Study of Legal Professions at the Annual Conference of the Law and Society Association, Washington, D.C., June.

Bourdieu, Pierre. 1976. "Le Champ Scientifique," 2 *Actes de la Recherche en Sciences Sociales* 88.

————. 1987. "The Force of Law: Toward a Sociology of the Juridical Field," 38 *Hastings Law Journal* 805.

Brodeur, Paul. 1985. *Outrageous Misconduct: The Asbestos Industry on Trial*. New York: Pantheon.

Cain, Maureen. 1976. "Necessarily Out of Touch: Thoughts on the social organisation of the Bar," in Pat Carlen, ed., *The Sociology of Law*. Keele: Sociological Review Monographs (No. 23).

————. 1979. "The General Practice Lawyer and the Client: Towards a Radical Conception," 7 *International Journal of the Sociology of Law* 331.

Carlin, Jerome E. 1962. *Lawyers on Their Own: A Study of Individual Practitioners in Chicago*. New Brunswick, N.J.: Rutgers University Press.

Curran, Barbara A. 1977. *The Legal Needs of the Public*. Chicago: American Bar Foundation.

Danet, Brenda, Kenneth B. Hoffman, and Nicole C. Kermish. 1980. "Obstacles to the Study of Lawyer–Client Interaction: The Biography of a Failure," 14 *Law & Society Review* 905.

Dezalay, Yves. 1986. "From Mediation to Pure Law: Practice and Scholarly Representation within the Legal Sphere," 14 *International Journal of the Sociology of Law* 89.

————. 1987. "La restructuration du champ des professionels et la restructuration des entreprises" (unpublished manuscript).

Eisenstein, James. 1978. *Counsel for the United States: U.S. Attorneys in the Political and Legal Systems*. Baltimore, Md.: Johns Hopkins University Press.

Erikson, Kai T. 1976. *Everything in Its Path: Destruction of Community in the Buffalo Creek Flood*. New York: Simon & Schuster.

Erlanger, Howard S., Elizabeth Chambliss, and Marygold S. Melli. 1987. "Participation and Flexibility in Informal Processes: Cautions from the Divorce Context," 21 *Law & Society Review* 585.

Ewing, Sally. 1987. "Formal Justice and the Spirit of Capitalism: Max Weber's Sociology of Law," 21 *Law & Society Review* 487.

Felstiner, William L. F., Richard L. Abel, and Austin Sarat. 1980/81. "The Emergence and Transformation of Disputes: Naming, Blaming, Claiming ...," 15 *Law & Society Review* 631.

Flemming, Roy B. 1986. "Elements of the Defense Attorney's Craft: An Adaptive Expectations Model of the Preliminary Hearing Decision," 8 *Law & Policy* 33.

Flood, John. 1986. "Counselors and Clients: The Art and Science of Lawyering." Presented to the International Conference on Exploring and Expanding the Content of Clinical Legal Education and Scholarship, Los Angeles.

Freidson, Eliot. 1986. *Professional Powers: A Study of the Institutionalization of Formal Knowledge*. Chicago: University of Chicago Press.

Galanter, Marc. 1974. "Why the 'Haves' Come Out Ahead: Speculations on the Limits of Legal Change," 9 *Law & Society Review* 95.

————. 1981. "Justice in Many Rooms: Courts, Private Ordering, and Indigenous Law," 19 *Journal of Legal Pluralism* 1.

————. 1983. "Mega-Law and Mega-Lawyering in the Contemporary United States," in Robert Dingwall and Philip Lewis, eds., *The Sociology of the Professions: Lawyers, Doctors and Others*. London: Macmillan.

Garth, Bryant G. 1983. "Rethinking the Profession's Approach to Collective Self-Improvement: Competence and the Consumer Perspective," 1983 *Wisconsin Law Review* 639.

Genn, Hazel. 1987. *Hard Bargaining: Out of Court Settlement in Personal Injury Actions*. Oxford: Clarendon Press.

Ghai, Yash P. 1976. "Notes Towards a Theory of Law and Ideology: Tanzanian Perspectives," 13 *African Law Studies* 31.

Gilbert, Geoffrey N., and Michael Mulkay. 1984. *Opening Pandora's Box: A Sociological Analysis of Scientists' Discourse*. Cambridge: Cambridge University Press.

Gluckman, Max. 1965. *The Ideas in Barotse Jurisprudence*. New Haven, Conn.: Yale University Press.

Goulden, Joseph C. 1972. *The Superlawyers: The Small and Powerful World of the Great Washington Law Firms*. New York: Weybright & Talley.

Green, Mark J. 1975. *The Other Government: The Unseen Power of Washington Lawyers*. New York: Grossman.

Griffiths, John. 1984. "The Division of Labor in Social Control," in Donald Black, ed., *Toward a General Theory of Social Control*, vol. 1: *Fundamentals*. New York: Academic Press.

————. 1986. "What Do Dutch Lawyers Actually Do in Divorce Cases?" 20 *Law & Society Review* 135.

Haley, John Owen. 1978. "The Myth of the Reluctant Litigant," 4 *Journal of Japanese Studies* 359.

Halliday, Terence C. 1985. "Knowledge Mandates: Collective Influence by Scientific, Normative and Syncretic Professions," 36 *British Journal of Sociology* 421.

————. 1987. *Beyond Monopoly: Lawyers, State Crises and Professional Empowerment*. Chicago: University of Chicago Press.

Handler, Joel F., Ellen Jane Hollingsworth, and Howard S. Erlanger. 1978. *Lawyers and the Pursuit of Legal Rights*. New York: Academic Press.

Hartmann, Michael. 1988. "Systemic Rationalization and Professional Work." Presented to the Annual Conference of the Law and Society Association, Vail, Colorado, June.

Heinz, John P., and Edward O. Laumann. 1982. *Chicago Lawyers: The Social Structure of the Bar*. Chicago: American Bar Foundation; New York: Russell Sage Foundation.

Hoebel, E. Adamson. 1954. *The Law of Primitive Man*. Cambridge, Mass.: Harvard University Press.

Hommerich, Christoph. 1988. "Die Anwaltschaft unter Expansionsdruck," 5/1988 *AnwBl* (Beilage).

Hosticka, Carl J. 1979. "We Don't Care About What Happened, We Only Care About What Is Going to Happen: Lawyer–Client Negotiations of Reality," 26 *Social Problems* 599.

Hurst, James Willard. 1950. *The Growth of American Law: The Law Makers*. Boston: Little, Brown.

Illich, Ivan, Irving Kenneth Zola, John McKnight, Jonathan Caplan, and Harley Shaiken. 1977. *Disabling Professions*. London: Marion Boyars.

Ingleby, Richard. 1988. "The Solicitor as Intermediary," in Robert Dingwall and John M. Eekelaar, eds., *Divorce Mediation and Legal Processes*. Oxford: Oxford University Press.

Ino, Masaru. 1975. "Diary of a Plaintiffs' Attorneys' Team in the Thalidomide Litigation," 8 *Law in Japan* 136.

Insight Team of the *Sunday Times of London*. 1979. *Suffer the Children: The Story of Thalidomide*. New York: Viking Press.

Janson, Donald. 1988. "Cigarette Maker Assessed Damages in Smoker's Death," *New York Times* (June 14), p. 1.

Kagan, Robert A., and Robert Eli Rosen. 1985. "On the Social Significance of Large Law Firm Practice," 37 *Stanford Law Review* 399.

Karpik, Lucien. 1985. "Avocat: Une Nouvelle Profession?" 26 *Revue française de sociologie* 571.

Katz, Jack. 1982. *Poor People's Lawyers in Transition*. New Brunswick, N.J.: Rutgers University Press.

Kawashima, Takeyoshi. 1963. "Dispute Resolution in Contemporary Japan," in Arthur von Mehren, ed., *Law in Japan*. Cambridge, Mass.: Harvard University Press.

Kurzman, Dan. 1988. *A Killing Wind: Inside Union Carbide and the Bhopal Disaster*. New York: McGraw-Hill.

Landon, Donald D. 1982. "Lawyers and Localities: The Interaction of Community Context and Professionalism," 1982 *American Bar Foundation Research Journal* 459.

———. 1985. "Clients, Colleagues, and Community: The Shaping of Zealous Advocacy," 1985 *American Bar Foundation Research Journal* 81.

Larson, Magali Sarfatti. 1977. *The Rise of Professionalism: A Sociological Analysis*. Berkeley, Los Angeles, London: University of California Press.

Latour, Bruno, and Steve Woolgar. 1979. *Laboratory Life: The Social Construction of Scientific Facts*. Beverly Hills, Calif.: Sage Publications.

Laumann, Edward O., and John P. Heinz, with Robert L. Nelson and Robert H. Salisbury. 1985. "Washington Lawyers and Others: The Structure of Washington Representation," 37 *Stanford Law Review* 465.

Law & Society Review. 1979. "Plea Bargaining," 13(2) *Law & Society Review* (Winter; special issue).

Levine, Adeline Gordon. 1982. *Love Canal: Science, Politics, and People*. Lexington, Mass.: Lexington Books.

Llewellyn, Karl. 1960. *The Common Law Tradition—Deciding Appeals*. Boston: Little, Brown.

———. 1962. *Jurisprudence: Realism in Theory and Practice*. Chicago: University of Chicago Press.

Lopez, Gerald P. 1984. "Lay Lawyering," 32 *UCLA Law Review* 1.

Luban, David. 1984. "The Sources of Legal Ethics: A German-American Comparison of Lawyers' Professional Duties," 48 *Rabels Zeitschrift* 245.

Luckham, Robin. 1981a. "The Political Economy of Legal Professions: Towards a Framework for Comparison," in C. J. Dias, R. Luckham, D. O. Lynch, and J. C. N. Paul, eds., *Lawyers in the Third World: Comparative and Developmental Perspectives*. Uppsala: Scandinavian Institute of African Studies; New York: International Center for Law in Development.

———. 1981b. "Imperialism, Law and Structural Dependence: The Ghana Legal Profession," in C. J. Dias, R. Luckham, D. O. Lynch, and J. C. N. Paul, eds., *Lawyers in the Third World: Comparative and Developmental Perspectives*. Uppsala: Scandinavian Institute of African Studies; New York: International Center for Law in Development.

Macaulay, Stewart. 1963. "Non-Contractual Relations in Business: A Preliminary Study," 28 *American Sociological Review* 55.

———. 1979. "Lawyers and Consumer Protection Law," 14 *Law & Society Review* 115.

———. 1987a. "Private Government," in Leon Lipson and Stanton Wheeler, eds., *Law and the Social Sciences*. New York: Russell Sage Foundation.

———. 1987b. "Images of Law in Everyday Life: The Lessons of School, Entertainment, and Spectator Sports," 21 *Law & Society Review* 185.

Malsch, Marijke. 1988. "Can Lawyers Predict the Outcome of Their Cases?" Presented at the Annual Conference of the Law and Society Association, Vail, Colorado, June.

Mann, Kenneth. 1985. *Defending White-Collar Crime: A Portrait of Attorneys at Work*. New Haven, Conn.: Yale University Press.

Marshall, Lorna. 1960. "!Kung Bushman Bands," 30 *Africa* 325.

Marvell, Thomas. 1978. *Appellate Courts and Lawyers: Information-Gathering in the Adversary System*. Westport, Conn.: Greenwood Press.

Matheny, Albert. 1979. "A Bibliography on Plea Bargaining," 13 *Law & Society Review* 661.

Mather, Lynn, and Barbara Yngvesson. 1980/81. "Language, Audience, and the Transformation of Disputes," 15 *Law & Society Review* 775.

McBarnet, Doreen. 184. "Law and Capital: The Role of Legal Form and Legal Actors," 12 *International Journal of the Sociology of Law* 231.

McGee, Kevin T. 1988. "Smoking Verdict: 'Suits rolling in,'" *USA Today* (June 14), p. 1.

Merry, Sally Engle. 1986. "Everyday Understandings of the Law in Working-Class America," 13 *American Ethnologist* 253.

Mintz, Morton. 1986. *At Any Cost: Corporate Greed, Women, and the Dalkon Shield*. New York: Pantheon.

Miyazawa, Setsuo. 1987. "Taking Kawashima Seriously: A Review of Japanese Research on Japanese Legal Consciousness and Disputing Behavior," 21 *Law & Society Review* 219.

Mnookin, Robert H., and Lewis Kornhauser. 1979. "Bargaining in the Shadow of the Law: The Case of Divorce," 88 *Yale Law Journal* 950.

Nagel, Stuart. 1962. "Culture Patterns and Judicial Systems," 16 *Vanderbilt Law Review* 147.

Nelson, Robert L. 1988. *Partners with Power: The Social Transformation of the Large Law Firm.* Berkeley, Los Angeles, London: University of California Press.

Nelson, Robert L., John P. Heinz, Edward O. Laumann, and Robert H. Salisbury, 1987. "Private Representation in Washington: Surveying the Structure of Influence," 1987 *American Bar Foundation Research Journal* 141.

Nelson, Robert L., and John P. Heinz, with Edward O. Laumann and Robert H. Salisbury. 1988. "Lawyers and the Structure of Influence in Washington," 22 *Law & Society Review* 237.

Newman, Katherine S. 1983. *Law and Economic Organization: A Comparative Study of Preindustrial Societies.* Cambridge: Cambridge University Press.

Nicholson, M. E. R. 1987. "The Basque Notary: An Intercultural Mediator," 15 *International Journal of the Sociology of Law* 85.

Nonet, Philippe, and Philip Selznick. 1978. *Law and Society in Transition: Toward Responsive Law.* New York: Harper & Row.

O'Gorman, Hubert. 1963. *Lawyers and Matrimonial Cases: A Study of Informal Pressures in Private Practice.* New York: Columbia University Press.

Partridge, A., and Gordon Bermant. 1978. *The Quality of Advocacy in the Federal Courts.* Washington, D.C.: Federal Judicial Center.

Pashukanis, E. B. 1980. *Selected Writings on Marxism and Law* (Piers Beirne and Robert Sharlet, eds.). London: Academic Press.

Payer, Lynn. 1988. *Medicine & Culture: Varieties of Treatment in the United States, England, West Germany, and France.* New York: Henry Holt & Co.

Powell, Michael J. 1987. "Professional Innovation: Corporate Lawyers and Private Lawmaking" (unpublished manuscript).

Riley, Tom. 1987. *The Price of a Life: One Woman's Death from Toxic Shock.* Bethesda, Md.: Adler & Adler.

Robinson, Cyril D., and Richard Scaglion. 1987. "The Origin and Evolution of the Police Function in Society: Notes Toward a Theory," 21 *Law & Society Review* 109.

Rosen, Robert Eli. 1986. "Professions and Institutions: Lawyers and Corporations." Presented to the Working Group for Comparative Study of Legal Professions, New Delhi, August 16.

———. n.d. "Serving the Corporate Client: The Problem of Problem-Setting" (unpublished manuscript).

Rosenthal, Douglas E. 1974. *Lawyer and Client: Who's In Charge?* New York: Russell Sage Foundation.

Ross, H. Laurence. 1970. *Settled Out of Court: The Social Process of Insurance Claims Adjustment.* Chicago: Aldine.

Royal Commission on Legal Services. 1979. *Final Report* (2 vols.). London: Her Majesty's Stationery Office (Cmnd. 7648).

Royal Commission on Legal Services in Scotland. 1980. *Report* (2 vols.). Edinburgh: Her Majesty's Stationery Office (Cmnd. 7846).

Rueschemeyer, Dietrich. 1964. "Doctors and Lawyers: A Comment on the Theory of the Professions," 1 *Canadian Review of Sociology and Anthropology* 17.

———. 1973. *Lawyers and Their Society: A Comparative Study of the Legal Profession in Germany and in the United States.* Cambridge, Mass.: Harvard University Press.

Salisbury, Robert H., with John P. Heinz, Edward O. Laumann, and Robert L. Nelson. 1986. "Who You Know versus What You Know: The Uses of Government Experience for Washington Lobbyists." Presented at the Annual Conference of the Midwest Political Science Association, Chicago, April.

Sarat, Austin, and William L. F. Felstiner. 1986. "Law and Stategy in the Divorce Lawyer's Office," 20 *Law & Society Review* 93.

Scheingold, Stuart A. 1988a. "Radical Lawyers and Socialist Ideals," 15 *Journal of Law and Society* 122.

———. 1988b. "The Social Organization of Radical Lawyers: The English Case." Presented to the Annual Conference of the Law and Society Association, Vail, Colorado, June.

Schon, Donald A. 1983. *The Reflective Practitioner: How Practitioners Think in Action.* London: Temple Smith.

Schuck, Peter H. 1986. *Agent Orange on Trial: Mass Toxic Disasters in the Courts.* Cambridge, Mass.: Harvard University Press.

Schwartz, Richard D. 1954. "Social Factors in the Development of Legal Control: A Case Study of Two Israeli Settlements," 63 *Yale Law Journal* 471.

———. 1976. "Law in the Kibbutz: A Response to Professor Shapiro," 10 *Law & Society Review* 439.

Schwartz, Richard D., and James C. Miller. 1964. "Legal Evolution and Societal Complexity," 70 *American Journal of Sociology* 159.

Shapiro, Allan E. 1976. "Law in the Kibbutz: A Reappraisal," 10 *Law & Society Review* 415.

———. 1985. "Law in the Kibbutz: The Search Continues." Paper presented to the Conference on Social Control and Justice: Inside or Outside the Law? (organized by the Research Committee on the Sociology of Deviance and Social Control of the International Sociological Association), Jerusalem, March/April.

Simpson, A. W. B. 1973. "The Common Law and Legal Theory," in A. W. B. Simpson, ed., *Oxford Essays in Jurisprudence* (2d series). Oxford: Clarendon Press.

Spangler, Eve. 1986. *Lawyers for Hire: Salaried Professionals at Work.* New Haven, Conn.: Yale University Press.

Steele, Eric H., and Raymond T. Nimmer. 1976. "Lawyers, Clients, and Professional Regulation," 1976 *American Bar Foundation Research Journal* 917.

Stern, Gerald M. 1977. *The Buffalo Creek Disaster.* New York: Vintage.

Sudnow, David. 1965. "Normal Crimes: Sociological Features of the Penal Code in a Public Defender's Office," 12 *Social Problems* 255.

Sugarman, David. 1986. *Weber, Modernity and "the Peculiarity of the English": On the Rationality and Irrationality of Law, State and Society in Modern Britain.* Madison, Wisc.: Institute for Legal Studies (Working Paper).

Teff, Harvey, and Colin Munro. 1976. *Thalidomide: The Legal Aftermath.* Westmead, England: Saxon House.

Teubner, Gunther. 1988. "Evolution of Autopoietic Law," in Gunther Teubner, ed., *Autopoietic Law: A New Approach to Law and Society.* Berlin: de Gruyter.

Twining, William. 1973. *Karl Llewellyn and the Realist Movement.* Norman, Okla.: University of Oklahoma Press.

Unger, Roberto Mangabeira. 1976. *Law in Modern Society: Toward a Criticism of Social Theory.* New York: Free Press.

Upham, Frank. 1976. "Litigation and Moral Consciousness in Japan: An Interpretative Analysis of Four Japanese Pollution Suits," 10 *Law & Society Review* 579.

Van Zyl Smit, Dirk. 1985. "'Professional' Patent Agents and the Development of the English Patent System," 13 *International Journal of the Sociology of Law* 79.

Wagatsuma, Hiroshi, and Arthur Rosett. 1986. "The Implications of Apology: Law and Culture in Japan and the United States," 20 *Law & Society Review* 461.

Wallace, Anthony F. C. 1986. *St. Clair: A Nineteenth-Century Coal Town's Experience With a Disaster-Prone Industry.* New York: Knopf.

Weisbrod, Burton A., in collaboration with Joel F. Handler and Neil K. Komesar, eds. 1978. *Public Interest Law: An Economic and Institutional Analysis.* Berkeley, Los Angeles, London: University of California Press.

Wheeler, Stanton, Bliss Cartwright, Robert A. Kagan, and Lawrence M. Friedman. 1987. "Do the 'Haves' Come Out Ahead? Winning and Losing in State Supreme Courts, 1870–1970," 21 *Law & Society Review* 403.

Williams, G. R. 1983. *Legal Negotiation and Settlement.* St. Paul, Minn.: West Publishing Co.

Wisconsin Law Review. 1985. "Symposium: Law, Private Governance and Continuing Relationships," 1985 *Wisconsin Law Review* 461–757.

Yeazell, Stephen C. 1987. *From Medieval Group Litigation to the Modern Class Action.* New Haven, Conn.: Yale University Press.

Zion, Sidney. 1988. *The Autobiography of Roy Cohn.* Secaucus, N.J.: Lyle Stuart.

Contributors

Richard L. Abel is professor of law at the University of California, Los Angeles. He has written about the legal profession, torts, dispute processes, and South Africa and has been editor of the *Law & Society Review* and *African Law Studies*. He edited *The Politics of Informal Justice* (2 volumes) (Academic Press, 1982) and the *Law & Society Reader* (New York University Press, 1995) and is the author of *The Legal Profession in England and Wales* (Basil Blackwell, 1988), *American Lawyers* (Oxford University Press, 1989), *Speech and Respect* (Sweet & Maxwell, 1994), and *Politics by Other Means: Law in the Struggle Against Apartheid, 1980–1994* (Routledge, 1995).

Erhard Blankenburg has been teaching sociology of law and criminology at the Vrije Universiteit Amsterdam since 1980. He received a master's degree from the University of Oregon and doctorates from Basel and Freiburg. After teaching sociology and sociology of law at Freiburg University (1965–70) he served as consultant with the Quickborn Team Hamburg (1970–72), senior research fellow at Prognos AG Basel (1972–74), and researcher at the Max Planck-Institut Freiburg (1974–75) and the Science Center Berlin (1975–80). He has published books on the police, prosecutors, civil courts, labor courts, legal aid, and sociology of law.

Luc Huyse is professor of sociology of law at the University of Leuven. He has written on politics in Belgium, deregulation, and the purge of quislings after World War II. He is currently studying the role of the judiciary in regime transitions.

Philip S. C. Lewis is an Emeritus Fellow of All Souls College, Oxford. He founded the Working Group for Comparative Study of Legal Professions and edited (with Robert Dingwall) *The Sociology of Professions: Lawyers,*

Doctors and Others (Macmillan, 1983). He has written about the legal profession and the sociology of law, is coauthor of *Social Needs and Legal Action* (Martin Robertson, 1973) and author of the eighth edition of *Gatley on Libel and Slander* (Sweet & Maxwell, 1981), and edited *Law and Technology in the Pacific Community* (Westview, 1994).

Carrie Menkel-Meadow is professor of law at the University of California, Los Angeles. She has written on the role of women in the legal profession and legal education, the delivery of legal services, and dispute resolution. She has edited *Lawyers and the Legal Profession* (Michie Co.) (with Murray L. Schwartz).

Rogelio Pérez Perdomo received a law degree and a doctorate from the Central University of Venezuela, a doctorate in philosophy of law from the University of Paris, and an LL.M. degree from Harvard University. He taught at the Central University of Venezuela from 1966 to 1988 and since then at the Instituto de Estudios Superiores de Administración. He has written on law and sociology of law and is the author of five books, including *El formalismo jurídico y sus funciones sociales en el siglo XIX venzolano* (Monte Avila, 1978), *Los abogados en Venezuela. Estudio de una élite intelectual y politica 1780–1980* (Monte Avila, 1981), and *Justícia y pobreza en Venezuela* (Monte Avila, 1986), and editor of two others, *Corrupción y control, una perspectiva comprada* (1991) and *Inseguridad personal, un asalto al tema* (1991). He was Scientific Director of the Oñati International Institute for the Sociology of Law in 1992–93.

Kahei Rokumoto studied law and political science at the University of Tokyo and sociology at the University of California, Berkeley. He is professor of sociology of law at the faculty of law, University of Tokyo, author of *The Sociology of Law* (in Japanese) (Yuhikaku, 1986), and editor of *Sociological Theories of Law* (Dartmouth, 1994).

Ulrike Schultz is Akademische Oberratin at Fern Universität in Hagen, Germany. She specializes in didactics and educational technology for teaching law through media and in schools. She has written about civil law and the legal profession and currently is working on the subject of women's rights and women in law.

Index

Abbott, Andrew, 10–11
Administrative scriveners, in Japan, 133
Advocates: in Belgian legal profession, 169, 179, 192; in German legal profession, 92–95, 103–104, 118; Jewish, 96, 116, 123 n.28
Allen, Sir George, 16–17
American Bar Association, 5; "Dignity in Advertising" awards, 7; Model Rules of Professional Conduct, 9
American Trial Lawyers Association, 7, 9
Anthony, Susan B., 260
Anwaltsblatt, 95
Apprenticeship, 17–18; in Belgium, 169, 180, 181–182
Arthurs, Harry, 311
Articled clerks, 68
Assistant solicitors, 68
Australia, legal profession, ix

Baier, Annette, 255
Barristers, in England: Bar Council, 73, 75; black barristers, 53–54; centralization of, 65; clerks, 69–70; clients served, 66; demand control, 61–62, 80; discrimination against women and ethnic minorities, 50–53, 71–72, 79; employment of, 57, 65, 79; entry control, 40–42,

45–47, 78, 79; entry rates, 45, 50–51; governance, 72–73, 74–75; legal aid practice, 61–62; market control, 55–56, 57–59, 78; number of by year, 83–89; proportion of with legal education, 45; pupillage, 46; relationship with solicitors, 64; Senate of the Inns of Court and the Bar, 75; size of chambers, 68–69; specialization, 66; stratification, 70–72; tenancy, 46–47; two-counsel rule, 57; two-thirds rule, 57
Belgium, legal profession: advocates, 169, 176, 179, 192; apprenticeship, 169, 180, 181–182; bar membership, 169; civil service lawyers, 170, 173, 178; class profile, 176; conservatism, 184; demand influences, 183–184; differentiation of, 168–169; distribution by practice settings, 193; employed lawyers, 170, 173; entry control, 177–181; Flemings in, 175; foreign advocates, 179; growth cycles, 170–172; heterogeneity, 185; house counsel, 179; judges, 170, 173, 192; law degree-holders, 186; law degree-holders by language group and gender, 191; law degree-holders by year, 187–190; law shops, 183–184; legal aid, 183–184; legal education, 170, 176–177, 196, 232;